SLAVISTISCHE DRUKKEN EN HERDRUKKEN

UITGEGEVEN DOOR

C. H. VAN SCHOONEVELD

HOOGLERAAR TE LEIDEN

XI

THE POLITICAL AND SOCIAL DOCTRINES

OF THE

UNITY OF CZECH BRETHREN

IN THE

FIFTEENTH AND EARLY SIXTEENTH

CENTURIES

BY

PETER BROCK
LONDON

MOUTON & CO · 1957 · 'S-GRAVENHAGE

SLAVISTIC PRINTINGS AND REPRINTINGS
EDITED BY
CORNELIS H. VAN SCHOONEVELD
LEIDEN UNIVERSITY
XI

PRINTED IN THE NETHERLANDS BY
MOUTON & CO., PRINTERS, THE HAGUE

To the Memory of my Mother

PREFACE

This study of the political and social doctrines of the Unity of Czech Brethren during the period of its early radicalism was originally submitted as a thesis for the degree of Doctor of Philosophy at the University of Oxford. It has since been revised for publication in book form.

I would like, in particular, to express my gratitude to Professor R. R. Betts for his constant advice and encouragement during the preparation of the original version; Professors J. M. Hussey, E. F. Jacob and S. Kot for their valuable suggestions and comments; and Professor W. Weintraub for his help in getting my work into print. To the British Treasury Committee for Studentships in Foreign Languages and Cultures I am much indebted for a grant, which enabled me to carry on my research for a period of over three years. Unfortunately it did not prove possible for me to visit Czechoslovakia personally; but I am grateful to the Czechoslovak Embassy in London and to the National Museum (Národní Museum) in Prague for providing me with microfilms of manuscript and other material from Prague libraries and archives. Finally, I wish to thank Mr. R. Gordon Wasson, Chairman, and the members of the American Committee for the Promotion of Advanced Slavic Cultural Studies for their generous grant towards publication, as well as the editor and publishers of 'Slavistic Printings and Reprintings' for their willingness to include this volume in their series.

London, November 1956   PETER BROCK

CONTENTS

ABBREVIATIONS

A. J. B.	—	Akta Jednoty Bratrské
Č. Č. M.	—	*Časopis Českého Musea*
Č. Č. H.	—	*Český Časopis Historický*

INTRODUCTION

THE HUSSITE CENTURY

The Czech Reformation preceded the German and Swiss Reformation by over a century. In the history of the Czech lands the hundred years and more that elapsed between the death of Hus at Constance in 1415 and the composition by Luther in 1517 of his ninety-five theses against the sale of papal indulgences may well be called the Hussite century. In the 1520s the spread of Lutheran doctrines and the accession of the Habsburg dynasty marked the end of an epoch in the country's history.

It was this period, too, that saw the active life of the rustic philosopher, Petr Chelčický, and the adoption of his radical political and social doctrines by the men who founded the Unity of Brethren. But, after less than a century, these doctrines had already been rejected by a later generation of Brethren. Within a hundred years of Hus's death they were on the way to being forgotten, kept alive only by a tiny and expiring group of obscure artisans. By the time Luther and Zwingli had appeared on the scene the Unity of Brethren had already made its peace with the existing social order, just as the larger and more conservative Hussite body, the official Utraquist church, had done very much earlier.

The Hussite century had been, indeed, a time of revolutionary upheavals and of profound changes in all spheres of life, religious and cultural, economic, social and political. In the fourteenth century Bohemia under Charles IV was the administrative centre of the Holy Roman Empire and the seat of the imperial court. Its university, founded in Prague in 1348, had made that city the intellectual centre of Central Europe. But both the deposition of Charles's successor, Václav, from the imperial throne in 1400 and the decree of Kutná Hora of 1409, which, by granting the Czechs a controlling majority in the administration of the university, led to the migration of its German scholars and the transformation of the university from a predominantly German into an almost entirely Czech institution, signified a shift in the international position of the Czech lands. This process of change culminated after 1415 in the revolution carried out by Hus's party, whose leaders came mainly from the ranks of former students of the University of Prague. The changes achieved in the religious, political and cultural spheres completely transformed the Czech lands and, for more than a century, marked them off from the rest of Europe.

The moral revolt which Hus and his followers raised against the abuses of the medieval church had sprung from the theological arguments of the Englishman Wyclif, as well as from a native source in the teachings of Hus's predecessors in the Czech reform movement. It was the chalice for the layman, communion in two kinds, approved by Hus shortly before his death at the stake, that became the standard under which every religious reformer in the Czech lands fought out the battle against Rome. This above all, combined as it was with the veneration of Hus's memory, united all wings of the Hussite movement and gave it its name of Utraquism.

In 1415 Hus had been supported by a powerful section of the Czech nobility and gentry as well as by the townsmen and university of Prague. Two years later the Hussite programme was first formulated that in 1420 was given definitive form in the Four Articles of Prague. These called for the free preaching of the Word of God, communion in two kinds, the confiscation of the secular possessions of monks and priests and for the punishment of public sin. But the same five years that saw the attempt to formulate the basic common principles of the movement were marked, too, by its break up into several conflicting groups differing both as to theology and social outlook.

On the extreme right were the conservative Utraquists under their leader, Jan of Příbram, whose disagreement with Rome extended to little beyond the demand for communion in two kinds. He and his followers rejected Wyclif's views on the sacraments and consistently sought recognition from Rome for their special standpoint. Occupying a central position between the two wings of the movement, and themselves probably the closest in spirit to Hus himself, there came next the party led first by Jakoubek of Stříbro and then, after his death in 1429, by Jan Rokycana. Their programme was represented in large measure by the Four Articles of Prague.

On the left were the Taborites sprung from the chiliast enthusiasts who, inspired by an immediate expectation of the second coming of Christ and the establishment of the Kingdom of God on earth, had gathered in the years immediately after Hus's death in the south-east districts of Bohemia, where they founded the town of Tábor from which they were to derive their name. Like Wyclif they rejected purgatory and maintained the doctrine of consubstantation; they simplified the church ritual and did away with clerical vestments as inconsistent with the practice of apostolic times; from among the seven Catholic sacraments they recognized only baptism and communion. In 1420 they took the epoch-making step of breaking with the tradition of apostolic succession by electing their own bishop, who acted indeed only as *primus inter pares*. In social matters they stood for a far-going radicalism, even after the disappearance in the early 1420s of the utopian communism of their first phase. Largely composed of peasants and lesser gentry, the Taborites had their equivalent in Prague in the party of the poorer townsmen led, until his execution in 1422, by the revolutionary Utraquist priest, Jan Želivský. On the extreme left came the so-called Adamites, a small group with rationalistic and even pantheistic tendencies, which regarded the communion as a purely commemorative act and completely denied the doctrine of the real presence. In 1421, however, they were savagely suppressed by the Taborite leader, Jan Žižka.

The appearance of divisions within the Hussite movement was accompanied by increasing danger of intervention from without. During 1418 King Václav, who partly under the influence of his wife Zofie had previously been favourably inclined towards the new movement, now began to take sterner measures against the Hussites. For this new policy his brother, the Emperor Sigismund, who had set himself up as the champion of the Church, was largely responsible. Václav's death in the summer of 1419, shortly after the riots which broke out in Prague under Želivský's leadership and in which the Catholic municipal council of the New Town were murdered, meant the opening of the succession question. The Hussites were only ready to recognize Sigismund as king if he would accept the Hussite programme. This he was clearly unprepared to do. In the spring of 1420, therefore, a crusade was proclaimed against the heretical Czechs; and in June Sigismund invaded the country with a large army and laid siege to Prague. He was successful in capturing the royal castle where he was crowned king in the Cathedral of St. Vít. The danger from without, however, succeeded in temporarily healing all the divisions among the Hussites. The Taborites under their leader, Jan Žižka, rallied to Prague's rescue; Sigismund was defeated at the battle of Vitkov Heights and compelled to withdraw. Returning in the autumn of the same year at the head of a new crusade he was once again defeated by Žižka at the battle of Vyšehrad. These two disasters, due largely to the military genius of Žižka, combined with the repulse of a second crusade in 1421, stiffened the Hussites' determination not to compromise on their faith and spelled the end of Sigismund's chances of acceptance as king by the Hussite majority in Bohemia for more than a decade. In the summer of 1421 the Bohemian diet meeting at Čáslav formally accepted the Four Articles of Prague and rejected Sigismund's claim to the throne.

With the disappearance of the danger of invasion from without, differences rapidly sprang up again among the Hussites. Negotiations had been opened with the Polish king, Władysław Jagiełło, who agreed to send his nephew, Zygmunt Korybutowicz, to take possession of the vacant throne. But Korybutowicz was only acknowledged as king by the more moderate Hussites. His obvious desire to reconcile Bohemia with Rome made him unpopular with the Taborites; and in 1427 he was finally forced to leave the country. Meanwhile, even within the Taborite camp unity had not been maintained. In 1423 Žižka had quarrelled on doctrinal matters with the Taborite priests and founded his own union of towns in east Bohemia. After his death in the following year his followers took on the name of the Orphans, remaining, however, in close alliance with the Taborites of south Bohemia.

Despite internal dissension during the 1420s, the Hussites were strong enough during this decade not merely to repel all attempts to bring them back into the Roman Church, but to carry their own creed by force into neighbouring lands. The expeditions into Germany and Poland made by an alliance of Taborites and Orphans under the leadership of Žižka's successor, Prokop Holý, and the propaganda which culminated in the Hussite manifestos of 1430 and 1431, carried the offensive beyond the boundaries of Czech-speaking territory. The defeat of attempted invasions of Bohemia in 1427 and again in 1431, when the crusaders were routed at the battle of Domažlice, showed clearly that the Hussites could not be crushed by force. At the same time, with the demoralization caused by continual warfare and the watering down of the original idealism by the increasing desire for the acquisition of wealth and plunder, the morale of the Hussites began to decline. While the successful repulsion of foreign intervention gave them sufficient strength to compel even the papal see to consider opening up negotiations with acknowledged heretics, by the early 1430s a considerable party among the Hussites themselves were now anxious to find some *modus vivendi* with Rome and the rest of Europe, which would not at the same time sacrifice their hard-won religious principles.

After Domažlice, therefore, negotiations were started between Hussite Bohemia and the Council of Basel, which had begun its sessions in 1431.

The Czechs were invited to the Council on an equal footing with the other delegates to argue their case before the assembled leaders of the church. In May of the following year emissaries of the Council and representatives of the Hussites met together at Cheb, agreeing there, by the so-called *Soud chebský*, to recognize as their 'judge' in matters in dispute the Scriptures and the practice of Christ and His apostles and of the primitive church, as well as the councils and fathers of the church in so far as they were based on these.

Though no compromise was reached during the visit of the Czech delegation to the Council of Basel in the early spring of 1433, the representatives sent by the Council soon after to negotiate direct with the Bohemian diet were successful in finding an agreed formula in the shape of the *Compactata*, which were signed in November of the same year. This proved in effect a triumph for conciliar diplomacy, since in practice little more of the original Hussite programme was granted than the exercise of communion in two kinds. The Taborites and Orphans now united to oppose the agreement as a betrayal of the principles of the Hussite movement and, as a result, the moderate Utraquist nobles joined with their Catholic fellow citizens to defeat the radicals at the battle of Lipany in May 1434. During the fighting the Taborite leader, Prokop Holý, fell with many other leading members of his party.

The Taborite defeat made it easier for the moderate Hussites to push forward further negotiations with the Council as well as with the Emperor Sigismund, who had never ceased to strive for the recovery of his hereditary kingdom. Though the Czechs were willing to abandon their claim that the cup for the layman should be made obligatory throughout Bohemia, they remained adamant in their demand that the new archbishop and his two subordinate bishops, who were to take charge of church affairs in the country, should be elected by the diet in conjunction with the Utraquist clergy. To this Sigismund finally consented; and, after the election in 1435 of Rokycana and his two coadjutors, he promised to do his utmost to obtain the church's confirmation of the elections. In July of the following year, therefore, a meeting took place at Jihlava between the Czechs, on one hand, and Sigismund and the delegates of the Council, on the other. The *Compactata*, as drawn up in 1433, were then formally recognized. The way was now open for Sigismund to return to Prague as King of Bohemia, recognized by both Roman Catholics and moderate Utraquists alike. With his entry into Prague in August 1436 the interregnum, which had lasted exactly seventeen years, was finally at an end.

Religious dissension and civil strife, however, were by no means ended by the settlement, which marked only the conclusion of the first stage in the Hussite revolution, in the struggle of Utraquist Bohemia against the Catholic world. The church had not in fact abandoned hope of bringing about the complete reconversion of the Hussites, nor in turn had the latter reconciled themselves to the legal existence of supporters of communion in one kind alongside the Utraquist majority. The Taborites continued in their negative attitude to even a temporary truce with the enemies of the chalice; while, on the other hand, outside Bohemia – in Moravia and in the other peripheral lands of the Bohemian Crown: the two Lusatias and Silesia – Catholicism still remained the dominant faith. Efforts to obtain the church's approval of Rokycana's election as archbishop were to prove unavailing.

With Sigismund's return to Prague, and the transference of the administration of the church in Bohemia to legates appointed by the Council, a period of reaction set in. In Prague only the conservative wing of the Hussite movement was granted a limited toleration. Rokycana, turned out of his Týn Church, fled to Hradec Králové in east Bohemia, where the Utraquists, under the leadership of a powerful nobleman, Hynce Ptáček of Pirkštejn, were extremely strong; and here he was to remain for the next eleven years.

The death of Sigismund in December 1437 once again reopened the question of the succession. Neither the claims of Albert of Austria, Sigismund's son-in-law, who died in October 1439, nor later those of the former's posthumous son, Ladislav, received general acknowledgement throughout Bohemia; and, although a general peace was established in 1440 between the supporters of Ladislav, mainly Catholics and conservative Utraquists, and the more radical Hussites under Hynce Ptáček, this second interregnum was to last until 1452.

The 1440s saw the consolidation in east Bohemia of the party led by Rokycana in the religious sphere and, after Hynce Ptáček's death in 1444, by a young Utraquist nobleman, George of Poděbrady, in political affairs. The Poděbrady Union of eastern counties, which the latter succeeded in building up, formed a base from which in 1448 he was able to set forth to regain Prague, where attempts to reintroduce old church practices had aroused much discontent. Rokycana, with whose party the conservative wing of the Hussite movement, led by Příbram, had by now merged, was once more reinstalled in his Týn Church as the acknowledged head of the Utraquist church, although all efforts to gain papal confirmation of his office were to fail.

After George of Poděbrady's entry into Prague only the Taborites still remained in open opposition. Their theological innovations, as well as their liturgical practices, had been condemned by the diet held at Prague in 1444, which had decided against them in their controversy with Rokycana's party, and ordered them to conform accordingly. In the summer of 1452, four years after his triumphal entry into Prague and virtual taking over of the reins of government in the land, Poděbrady was strong enough to force Tábor to surrender without a struggle. Several of the Taborite leaders, including their bishop, Mikuláš of Pelhřim, were put into prison, where they were kept until death. In the following year the town's defences were dismantled; and this marked the final defeat of the Taborites and the virtual suppression, in the name of religious orthodoxy and national unity, of the radical wing of the Hussite movement.

In 1451 negotiations had been opened up with Frederick of Austria, the boy Ladislav's guardian. Two years later Ladislav, who was at the time in the hands of the Austrian Estates, was brought to Prague where in October 1453 he was crowned king. Although, through Poděbrady's influence, he ascended the throne not by virtue of his hereditary right but through election by the Bohemian diet, the other provinces of the crown continued to support the young king's hereditary claims. Ladislav, however, agreed to recognize the *Compactata* and to seek papal confirmation for the archbishop-elect Rokycana. Poděbrady, too, carried on as governor of the realm in actual charge of the affairs of state during Ladislav's minority.

At this period both Poděbrady and Rokycana were anxious to effect a lasting reconciliation with Rome. With their belief in the validity of holy orders only if handed down as a result of apostolic succession, the Utraquists were faced with a difficult dilemma after the death in 1431 of the Archbishop of Prague, Konrád of Vechta, who had gone over to the Hussites. In order to be certain of a regular supply of priests they had either to become reconciled with Rome, even at the cost of unconditional submission, or to find some other church in the true line of the apostolic succession: a problem which proved insoluble and was to haunt their church throughout the greater part of its existence. An attempt in 1452 to establish contact with the Greek Orthodox Church was broken off prematurely by the fall of Constantinople in May of the following year. Poděbrady's subsequent efforts to effect a reconciliation with the Roman Church were likewise cut short by the death of the young king in November 1457. His brief reign had been marked by the increasingly menacing attitude taken up by the Catholic party towards the Utraquists, an attitude which helped to give a very radical colouring to Rokycana's public utterances of this period.

The throne once again left vacant by Ladislav's death was filled in March 1458 by the election of George of Poděbrady himself. Within a couple of years he had compelled recognition of his kingship throughout the lands of the Bohemian Crown; and his reputation at this time stood so high in Central Europe that plans were set on foot to make him King of the Romans and co-partner with the Emperor in the government of Germany. Though these schemes never actually materialized, they witness to the high esteem in which George was held by his fellow princes. However, in order to obtain his coronation by properly consecrated bishops, lent on this occasion by King Matthias Corvinus of Hungary, George had been forced to take a secret and somewhat ambiguously worded oath on the day before his coronation: an oath which could well be considered a renunciation of the *Compactata*, though not regarded as such by George himself. But neither compromise on this occasion, nor George's attempts to prove his abhorrence of heresy by the sterner measures taken in the early 1460s against the growing Unity of Brethren, founded about the time of his accession, were successful in persuading the papal see, occupied at that period by the humanist Pius II (Aeneas Sylvius), to accept the *Compactata*. Indeed, in 1462, the Pope went so far as to condemn communion in two kinds and to make his recognition of George's election as king conditional upon his renunciation of the *Compactata*. Three years later hostilities broke out between George and the discontented Catholic nobility, who had combined against him in the League of Zelená Hora. At the end of the following year, in December 1466, the Pope finally declared George an avowed heretic and deposed him from the throne, relieving his subjects of their duty of obedience. In the spring of 1468 King Matthias of Hungary, whose formerly friendly relations with George had gradually cooled over the years, now intervened in Bohemian affairs as executor of the papal sentence of deposition and protector of the Catholic rebel noblemen. These proceeded to elect Matthias king in place of George; as a result war ensued between the two kings, which was still undecided when in 1471 George died at the age of seventy-one.

The only Czech to occupy the Bohemian throne after the extinction of the Přemyslid dynasty in 1306, George went far to restore inside the lands of the Bohemian Crown the prestige of the monarchy, which had been lost during the long years of the interregnum, and to regain the position which Bohemia had occupied in the European community of nations before the outbreak of the Hussite wars. He once again established peace and order throughout the territory under his control and, though he lacked the burning sense of mission which inspired the first generation after Hus's death, he was able to secure the heritage of Utraquism against attacks from without and within.

He was succeeded on the throne by the fifteen year old Vladislav II, eldest son of the Polish King Kazimierz IV of the Jagiellonian dynasty. After Matthias's intervention George had wisely abandoned his earlier desire to obtain the throne for his own family. Though a devout Catholic, King Kazimierz had been ready to give George practical support against Matthias in return for a promise of the crown for his eldest son after George's death. The fact that a party of Magyar nobles opposed to Matthias had also offered the Hungarian crown to the Jagiellons proved a further important factor influencing Kazimierz's decision to come to George's aid.

The struggle for the Bohemian throne between Matthias and the Jagiellons did not end conclusively until 1478, when a compromise settlement was agreed to at the Peace of Olomouc. Moravia, Silesia, and the two Lusatias were retained by Matthias, while Vladislav was left with only Bohemia proper. The title of King of Bohemia was granted to both contestants. Though provision was made for the eventual reuniting of all the lands of the Bohemian Crown, there was now great danger that the peripheral lands would in actual fact become detached from the main centre of Czech culture in Bohemia. However, the death of Matthias in 1490 without a legitimate heir, and the election of Vladislav to the vacant Hungarian throne, removed the danger of disintegration.

Though Vladislav, like his predecessor, had promised at his accession to respect the *Compactata* and to strive to obtain papal recognition for the Utraquists' demands, after the conclusion of peace with Matthias in 1478 there was a marked increase in the activities of the Catholic party in Bohemia, and of the monastic orders in particular. The Catholic Upper Consistory in charge of the interests of the adherents of the old religion, which had been forced to flee from Prague to Plzeň in 1467, now returned to the capital. As a result of the rising tension between the supporters of communion in one kind and the protagonists of the chalice for the layman, serious rioting broke out in Prague in 1483. Fear of the renewal of civil war and foreign intervention led to the conclusion in 1485 of the famous Treaty of Kutná Hora, by which religious peace in the land was guaranteed for a period of thirty-two years, a period which was successively prolonged until the final suppression of Utraquism in 1627. By the Treaty the

Compactata were reconfirmed and full equality was to be maintained between Roman Catholics and Utraquists, who were both to continue to have the right to receive communion according to their own rite. Each party agreed to refrain from any attempt to persecute the other; and the number of churches in the possession of each was to remain as at the time of Vladislav's accession.

The remainder of Vladislav's long reign was marked by the absence of open religious strife, even though the growing Unity of Brethren was not covered by the provisions of the Treaty of Kutná Hora, and by the freedom of the country from entanglement in foreign war and from invasion from without. Vladislav's mild and somewhat ineffective character, while favourable to the maintenance of religious toleration, signified, on the other hand, a relaxation of the efforts made by George of Poděbrady to curb the increasing power of the nobility. The accession in 1516 of Vladislav's ten-year-old son, Ludvík, to his two kingdoms of Bohemia and Hungary, and the fact that for the former the boy king was an absentee for the greater part of his reign, strengthened even further the domination of the country by the nobility headed by the great magnates. But the rule of the Jagiellonian dynasty in Bohemia was abruptly ended in August 1526 by the defeat and death of the young King Ludvík at the battle of Mohács in an attempt to drive back the oncoming Turkish invasion.

The election of a Habsburg to the vacant throne in the same year and the gradual infiltration into the Czech lands during the 1520s of Lutheran ideas, which were supported within the official Utraquist chuch by the so-called neo-Utraquist party, brought the Hussite century to a conclusion. During this whole period neither the civil strife between moderate Utraquist and radical Taborite during the first half of the century, nor the secession from the main body, in the second, of some of the most spiritually alive to form a separate Unity of Brethren, nor even the spiritual deadness which gradually set in within the Utraquist church itself, was able to lessen the greatness of the religious inheritance left by the Hussite revolution.

In the political and cultural fields the permanent gains were less obvious. The republicanism of the Taborite wing had been suppressed; and the revolutionary political thought, which the upheavals of the time had generated, died away seemingly without an echo. The nation that had defied its anointed monarch and carried on its affairs for nearly two decades without a king was finally induced, under certain conditions, to accept him back again. Later, the native Bohemian Hussite king was succeeded by the foreign Catholic dynasties of Jagiełło and Habsburg.

Nevertheless, the independence and integrity of the Czech lands remained intact for almost the whole period until the disastrous battle of the White Mountain in 1620.

The Hussite revolution, too, gave a powerful impetus to the feeling of Czech nationality, if it did not actually initiate the national movement. This was shown above all in the cultural sphere. The use of Czech came to predominate in all branches of government, central and local: in the executive, the legislature and in judicial matters, as well as in the church and in private life. Through the efforts of the Taborites, and later of the Czech Brethren, with their desire to make the Bible accessible to their simple followers, the rudiments of education were extended to the masses of the population. Even hostile witnesses testified to the high level of literacy among both Taborites and Brethren. At the same time there arose a rich literature in the vernacular, which indeed had its origins in the previous century and even earlier. Numerous important theological and moralistic works, such as the writings of Hus himself or Chelčiký, popular songs, hymns and political satires, chronicles and histories, as well as works of pure literature in prose and verse, were now written in their authors' native Czech.

It was not only culture that was imbued with the national spirit. As a result of the Hussite revolution and the wars that followed, in Bohemia at least, the native Czech elements gained control in the towns through the expropriation of the largely German patriciate, which favoured Catholicism. The creation of a strong Czech burgher class was itself a powerful support for Czech culture and Czech national feeling as well as for the Hussite movement generally. The cities — the capital, Prague, and Tábor in south Bohemia in particular — influenced events to a remarkable degree, especially during the war years; and burghers were now admitted to the diet.

But not all was gain. The destruction of the war years, religious fanaticism in both camps, the breaking of cultural and economic ties with the rest of Europe, led to a narrowing of cultural interests, which expressed itself, for instance, in a decline in the intellectual level of the University of Prague. Towards the end of the fifteenth century, too, a tendency appeared — as in neighbouring Poland — for the nobility to try to exclude the towns, which ranked at the third estate in the Bohemian diet, from any important share in the work of government. In 1485, for instance, King Vladislav decreed that the burgesses might vote in the diets only on matters directly concerning their estate. The struggle between burgher and noble was to be a long one, but the seeds were already sown.

The results of the economic and social forces at work in the Hussite revolution were as usual less clearly visible, but in their final results certainly as far-reaching as in other spheres of life. The conditions in which the peasantry lived during the fourteenth century were certainly not worse than in the centuries succeeding the Hussite revolution. The many abuses which existed in practice, however, were denounced in forthright terms by a long series of moralists; and a cult of the simple man, the peasant, had grown up as a result of the writings and preaching of Hus's predecessors. An extensive literature existed in the period just before the Hussite revolution, inveighing against the oppression of the peasantry in all its forms and postulating the theoretical equality of all men in the sight of God. The peasantry in many places, and especially in South Bohemia where the conditions were particularly ripe for change, became the most enthusiastic supporters of the new religious movement.

They were joined by the lower strata of the town population, anxious to oust the German patriciate, and by many of the nobility – and even some of the magnates – eager to take the opportunity to seize the wealth of the Catholic Church, which at the beginning of the fifteenth century was in possession of at least a third of the total area of the country.

On the social side, indeed, despite the existence of many purely selfish motives, the Hussite movement at its best expressed the desire for a juster social order. Earlier radical political thinkers had usually been content to leave their radicalism in the realm of theory or to limit its application to those who consciously renounced the world. The Czechs put theory into practice. They broadened the medieval concept of freedom as a personal privilege to be acquired by rank or service or money into a universal moral principle, founded on the gospel Law of Love. They sought, however haltingly, to bring society into line with the teachings of the New Testament, as they understood them, and with their conception of the life of the early church. The social ideology of Štitný and Hus's other predecessors, of Hus himself, of the communistic chiliasts and the republican Taborites, of Chelčický and, later, of Rokycana in his more radical moments and the early Czech Brethren, reflected in varying degree the hopes and fears of the oppressed.

The Hussite revolution, however, failed to achieve a radical and lasting change in the existing structure of society. A shift in the centre of power was the sole outcome. The church lost the greater part of its secular possessions and its political power; and the nobles successfully extended their estates by swallowing up the church lands. The central authority, the power of the king, was weakened for over a century; and this accrued mainly to the advantage of the nobility and the magnates. Czechs had displaced Germans as the ruling element in the towns. The religious freedom of the official Utraquist church, which controlled the University of Prague and the educational system of the country, was to remain intact until the victory of the Counter-Reformation in the first half of the seventeenth century. A flourishing indigenous culture had grown up, though this naturally was enjoyed mainly by the educated classes. But the status of the peasantry, the class which had most to gain from the revolution, which supported it with most enthusiasm and sacrificed most on its behalf, deteriorated steadily during the course of the succeeding centuries.

The aftermath of the Hussite wars had left, on the one hand, vast wealth and power concentrated in the hands of the nobility and, on the other, a dearth of labour owing to the destruction of the war years. For the peasant this resulted in an increase in labour services, money dues, and the obligation for military service; the spread of pisciculture — the flooding of land by nobles and gentry in order to create fish ponds, a profitable source of income that called for little labour — was often at the same time detrimental to the peasants' interests. During the second half of the fifteenth century there was a gradual but steady loss of the peasants' personal liberty. Freedom of movement was restricted; every peasant was legally required to have a lord; and peasants were now allowed to leave their villages only with the permission of their lord, who obtained the right to reclaim those who had migrated to the town or another estate. It was made an offence, too, punishable by fine or imprisonment, to hide or in any way wittingly to help such a fugitive. The weakness of the central government also placed the administration of justice, so far as it affected the peasant, in the hands of the landowners, who in this way came to possess absolute power over their tenants. Thus, by the end of the century the peasants, together with all their family, had become *adscripti glebae*, serfs tied to the land they cultivated. Their unfree status was now enshrined in the great compilation of the laws of the land issued in 1500 under the name of the Land Ordnance (*Zřízení zemské*).

The worsening of the peasants' condition was, it is true, common not only to the Czech lands, but also to neighbouring countries like Poland and Hungary, which had been virtually untouched by the Hussite movement. Its causes, therefore, cannot be attributed solely to the results of this movement. Nevertheless, the long war years in particular proved a powerful stimulus to tendencies, which were already present in the social system. The bright hopes which the early Taborite chiliasts had entertained of a radical amelioration of the peasants' lot were to be entirely shattered by the course which events took over the next hundred years.

It is only, indeed, in the light of disappointed hopes for social betterment, of disillusionment after long years of sacrifice and struggle for an ideal which appeared to recede ever further as the years passed by, that the history of the political and social doctrines, first propounded by Petr Chelčický and then taken over by the Brethren of the early Unity, can be properly understood. These doctrines were, to a large extent, the outcome of their background, political, economic and social, as well as religious and cultural. In their turn they were themselves to help to mould the development of thought and the pattern of future events.

I

PETR CHELČICKÝ, FORERUNNER OF THE UNITY

The Czech nation has contributed several outstanding figures to European history. The achievements of Hus and Komenský, Žižka and George of Poděbrady, Palacký and Masaryk are well-known at least to all historians. The name of Petr Chelčický, however, the thinker whose chief work Tolstoy, for instance, has described as 'a most remarkable production of human thought, both from the profundity of its contents and the wonderful force and beauty of its popular language,'[1] has scarcely been heard of outside the frontiers of his native country. Chelčický, says Tolstoy, 'occupies within Christianity the same position as Christianity itself within the whole human community;'[2] and a great Slav scholar has claimed that 'if Chelčický had been born a German, a Frenchman or an Englishman he would undoubtedly have exercised an important influence on the history of law and social theory in Europe.'[3] For most historians his works are a closed book on account of the barrier of language. Since his rediscovery, however, a century ago by Palacký and Šafařík, after over three centuries of oblivion, Czechs of all schools of thought have at least agreed in assigning to Chelčický an outstanding role in the history and literature of their nation, and a growing number of foreign scholars have come too to realize his significance as a political thinker.[4]

[1] Tolstoy, *The Kingdom of God is Within You*, p. 26. It was Masaryk, struck by the similarity of their ideas, who first brought Chelčický to Tolstoy's attention. See A. Pawlow, 'L. N. Tolstoj und T. G. Masaryk,' *Wiener Slavistisches Jahrbuch*, 1955, pp. 66–70, 79, 80.
[2] Tolstoy, *Krug Chteniya*, III, p. 261.
[3] Jagić in his Intro. *Sochineniya Petra Khelchitskago*, p. XXV. Cf. Kamil Krofta, 'Bohemia in the Fifteenth Century,' *Cambridge Medieval History*, VIII, p. 87: 'His writings, indeed, are among the few medieval literary works which can even to-day captivate our interest.'
[4] Apart from Czech the only languages in which articles or books on Chelčický have appeared are German and Russian, though these are not indeed numerous. Free renderings of several of his works have also been published in these two languages. Further details are given in the bibliography. Nothing of any value has so far appeared in English.

Carrying the principles of the Hussite revolution to their logical conclusion, Chelčický at the same time provided the theoretical foundation on which was built up a new religious community, the Unity of Brethren (*Jednota bratrská*), which was in its turn to mark a fresh stage in the nation's political and religious development. The political and social doctrines of this body, therefore, cannot be understood without first considering the theories of their 'spiritual father,' Chelčický.[5]

I

Scarcely any information has come down to us about Chelčický's life or character. What little is known is usually open to doubt, consists largely of hypotheses more or less plausible. Precise dates are almost entirely absent; while it is quite impossible to gain any impression of his personality apart from the internal evidence of his own writings, which unfortunately contain comparatively few references to himself. Indeed, his works are almost the sole source of our knowledge of his life, since external documentary evidence does not exist. The originality and depth of his thought, the audacity of his theory and the obviously outstanding character of his intellect, make this ignorance the more tantalizing.

The date of Chelčický's birth – as of all the other events of his life – is, therefore, uncertain. He was probably born, however, about 1390 in the south Bohemian village of Chelčice near the small country town of Vodňany. He appears to have acquired his surname many years later from the founder of the Unity, Brother Řehoř.[6] The name though does not necessarily indicate the place of his birth, signifying only the spot where he spent most of his life. But the social conditions of the period make it probable that he was born and reared at least in the immediate neighbourhood.[7] Nothing is known for certain of his parents or family nor of his childhood and schooling: the sources give no indication whether he ever married. Even the social class to which he belonged and the calling he pursued during his life-time are matters of debate.

Some earlier hypotheses – for instance, that he was a cobbler, a tailor, a discharged soldier, a priest, or a Waldensian preacher – have been discarded. But he may have been a member of the squirearchy (*zeman*) or a yeoman (*svobodník*), independent of any feudal lord and owning his own land, or even an unfree peasant (*sedlák*). The supposition that he was a yeoman appears very possible. It would have given him the means to

[5] Palacký, *Dějiny národu českého*, V, p. 218.
[6] Šimek, 'O životě a díle Petra Chelčického,' *Sít' víry* (Modern Czech edition), p. 313.
[7] Vogl, *Peter Cheltschizki*, p. 13.

acquire some measure of education, sufficient leisure to pursue his literary activities, and an independence of attitude, which membership of the semi-serf peasantry would have made very difficult, at the same time allowing him to preserve that sympathy with his unfree fellow peasants and passionate advocacy of their rights which appear in all his writings. It may thus have been only later in life that he adopted the labourer's status as part of a programme of voluntary poverty.[8]

Since the last war, however, Professor Bartoš, the leading contemporary authority on the period, has put forward another theory: that of Chelčický's identity with a certain Petr Záhorka, a well-to-do squire from near-by Záhorčí, who was born about 1379–81. Záhorka's name disappears from the records after 1424; in Bartoš's view, because he was later known under the name of Chelčický. This theory, also, would explain the latter's education, astonishing at this time in a simple countryman, as well as his independent spirit and freedom from outside interference. Though Bartoš has expressed his belief in the validity of his theory, it must be stressed that it remains a hypothesis, even if an extremely plausible one; no positive proof of the identity of the two men has as yet been brought forward.[9] At any rate, Chelčický appears to have been for most of his life a working farmer, whatever his origins or his exact legal status.

It was not until 1419, four years after Hus's death, that Chelčický made his first appearance on the stage of history. Towards the end of this year, roused by the fanatical oratory of demagogic priest prophesying the overthrow of the existing social order and the imminent second coming of Christ in his glory, when only five holy cities – Klatov, Louny, Plzeň, Slane and Žatec – would be spared from the divine wrath, masses of peasants, especially from south Bohemia, crowded to the capital city of Prague. Among thousands of others came Chelčický, then quite unknown. At that time, indeed, he was almost certainly at one in most of his opinions with the masses of his fellow pilgrims, who had been flocking in thousands to participate in the religious ceremonies on Mount Tábor.[10]

[8] Chelčický, O trojím lidu, pp. 6, 7; Chaloupecký, 'Štitný a Chelčický,' Č. M. M., 1914, pp. 73–76; Urbánek, Věk Poděbradský, III, pp. 886–89; Krofta, Listy z náboženských dějin českých, pp. 205–06; Goll-Krofta, Chelčický a Jednota v XV století, pp. 4, 5; Vogl, op. cit., pp. 13–15.
[9] Bartoš, Jihočeský sborník historický, 1946, pp. 1–8; 1947, pp. 1–9. But cf. V. Chaloupecký, Č. Č. H., XLVIII/XLIX (1949), pp. 481–83.
[10] Goll-Krofta, op. cit., p. 6; Krofta, op. cit., p. 208; Yastrebov, 'Khelchitsky i Gus,' Novyy sbornik izd. uchenikami Lamanskago, p. 472; Ktož jsú boží bojovníci, pp. 37, 46, 66–69; Macek, Tábor v husitském revolučním hnutí, II, chap. II. Bartoš places Chelčický's arrival in Prague in the late spring of 1420. – J. S. H., 1947, p. 3.

For Chelčický was a true son of the south Bohemia which played such a significant role in the Hussite movement.

He may already have come to Prague as a convinced adherent of at least some of the tenets of the Waldensian heresy, which was widespread in that area.[11] The Waldenses date back to the second half of the twelfth century. They were founded by a wealthy Lyons merchant, Pierre Valdo (d. circa 1217), who in the mid-1170s, in a desire to return to the pure Christianity of the early church, had renounced his property and left his home to lead a life of poverty and asceticism. Soon a group of likeminded persons gathered around him; and they became known as the 'Poor Men of Lyons.' They attacked the abuses of the time, urged the virtues of poverty, and called upon their fellow citizens to model their lives on the example of the apostles. Because of their continued preaching without the permission of the ecclesiastical authorities, they early came into conflict with the church. In 1184, at the Council of Verona, Pope Lucius III put them under the ban of the church; and soon after Valdo and his 'Poor Men' were expelled from Lyons. The papal condemnation initiated a long period of intermittent, but often fierce, persecution lasting several centuries, which drove the Waldenses to break away from the Catholic church transforming them at the same time into an outlawed and heretical sect.

Meanwhile, however, the influence of Valdo and his followers had begun to spread outside the frontiers of the province, southwards into Spain and also into central and northern Europe. At the beginning of the 1180s a branch had been founded in north Italy as a result of fusion with a section of the Lombard *Humiliati*, a group within the Catholic church organized on ascetic and semi-monastic principles. Early in the thirteenth century, however, a split occurred between the more radical Lombard branch and the French Waldenses.

It had not, indeed, been Valdo's original intention to break away from the church, since the emphasis of his teaching was not on doctrine but on practice. He advocated, above all, a return to the primitive simplicity of the first Christians; the renunciation of property and the secular power being demanded for those accepted into full community. They were also forbidden to take oaths or to shed blood. Most of the sects' members, especially as persecution grew, were from the poorer classes, peasants and small craftsmen. In the course of time the Waldenses both in France and in Italy set up their own ecclesiastical hierarchy with the equivalent of

---

[11]   Goll-Krofta, *op. cit.*, p. 40; Hrubý, *České postilly*, pp. 61–65; Krofta, *op. cit.*, p. 206; Palacký, 'O stycích a poměru sekty Waldenské k někdejším sektám v Čechách, Č. Č. M., 1868, pp. 315, 316.

bishops, priests, and deacons, though some were ready to accept the Eucharist from 'good priests' of the Catholic church.

The Waldenses spread their doctrines, in particular, by means of lay preaching in the vernacular tongue. The missionaries who brought the sect's teaching eastwards into Germany and later into Poland, Hungary, and Bohemia belonged to the Lombard branch, which tended, possibly under Cathar influences, to make a more clear-cut break with the official church, regarding Rome as the seat of Antichrist and completely rejecting its services. By the fourteenth century the German Waldenses had become virtually independent of their fellow sectaries in Italy, though they continued in friendly relations with each other.[12] By this time, too, the existence of Waldenses in the Czech lands is authenticated. At first the sect was confined to the foreign immigrants, though later it won numerous adherents among the Czech population.

Throughout the fourteenth century the inquisition was active in its attempts to root out this heresy from Bohemia; and although our information is derived exclusively from the records of the sect's opponents and the exact nature of the heresy under examination is never completely clear, they leave no doubt of its comparative strength in the country. They show, too, that the main centre of its activities was in south Bohemia, in the area from which the Taborites sprang, the land of Chelčikcý's birth.[13]

The problem of Chelčický's relationship to the Waldenses is, indeed, only part of the larger question of the relationship of the Taborites and of the whole Hussite movement to this most important of the medieval sects. Though no mention of any connection is made by Chelčický in his writings, the similarity of his doctrines with Waldensian teachings, as will be seen in the second part of this chapter, is striking. But the Taborites too during their first period, circa 1415–19, had held similar views, which their sudden change during the momentous year of 1420 has tended to obscure.[14] Those earnest popular preachers who gathered together masses

---

[12] For the Waldenses generally, see the articles by W. F. Adeney, *Encyclopaedia of Religion and Ethics*, XII, pp. 663–68, and by H. Böhmer, *Realencycklopädie für protestantische Theologie und Kirche*, XX, pp. 799–834. There is, however, no comprehensive survey of the Waldenses during the Middle Ages, which is both scholarly and up-to-date. See also *Bibliografia Valdese*, ed. A. A. Hugon and G. Gonnet (Torre Pellice, 1953), esp. pp. 72–102.

[13] Harrison Thomson, 'Pre-Hussite Heresy in Bohemia,' *E. H. R.*, 1933, pp. 23–42; Holinka, *Sektářství v Čechách před revolucí husitskou, passim*; Chaloupecký, 'K dějinám Valdenských v Čechách před hnutím husitským,' *Č. Č. H.*, pp. 369–82; Goll-Krofta, *op. cit.*, pp. 277 ff.

[14] Cf. Preger's thesis in *Über das Verhältnis der Taboriten zu den Waldesiern des 14.*

of adherents among the peasants and small craftsmen of south Bohemia
during the four years after Hus's death likewise rejected all violence and
advocated a state of apostolic poverty with all things held in common, in
which every Christian man and woman was to be regarded as a beloved
brother or sister. Typically Waldensian doctrines, such as the rejection of
oaths and the death penalty and all other forms of violence, are to be
found among their articles of faith. But this first period of 'primitive
Taboritism (*vnikající Tábor*),' as Pekař has aptly called it, gave way
towards the end of 1419 to a powerful movement of mass hysteria, when
many of the more fanatical extremists among the priesthood proclaimed
the second coming of Christ, which was to occur between 10–14 February
1420. The inauguration of his kingdom, which was to last a thousand
years, was to be accompanied by the extirpation of the wicked and the
division of their goods among the righteous. Dues and labour services,
indeed all property rights, were to be abolished, and sovereignty was to
rest with the common people.

The failure to realize the chiliasts' prophesies by peaceful means, after a
few brief months of enthusiasm, and the menace of the approaching anti-
Hussite crusade commanded by the Emperor Sigismund with the support
of the rest of Christendom, led on to the third period in the evolution of
the Taborite movement, which marked a withdrawal from the social
radicalism of the chiliasts and their predecessors and a rejection of the
earlier non-violence. 'Nonne prius predicastis contra occisionem [protest-
ed the moderate Prague master, Jakoubek of Stříbro] et quomodo iam res
sit versa in oppositam qualitatem.'[15] The humble disciples of the peaceful
and communistic sectaries were now transformed into the armed 'warriors

---

Jahrhunderts, p. 111, that the Taborites especially as regards their social doctrines,
were 'die Fortsetzung der böhmischen Waldesier.', See Holinka *op. cit.*, pp. 152–65;
Martinů, *Die Waldesier und die husitische Reformation in Böhmen* pp. 90–120. Nejedlý,
Dějiny husitského zpěvu, II, pp. 609, 610, 826, 827, prints a very early Hussite song,
Poslúchajte, znamenajte, which vividly expresses the Waldensian gospel of passive
suffering, sentiments which are not usually found in later productions. However
Bartoš, *Husitství a cizina*, pp. 114, 121–23, denies that the Waldensians exercised any
significant influence on the beginnings of the Taborite movement. He maintains that
Waldensian social tenets, such as the rejection of the oath and the death penalty, as
well as a common disbelief in purgatory, came through Nicholas of Dresden, who
had reached such conclusions independently. See *ibid.*, pp. 136–38, 140, 142–46.

[15] Goll, *Quellen und Untersuchungen zur Geschichte der Böhmischen Brüder*, II, p. 60.
These remarks were addressed to the prominent Taborite priest, Jan of Jičín, author
of a non-extant treatise which his opponent, Jan of Příbram, described as 'tractatulus...
de bellis et effusione sanguinis et occisione omnium malorum in mundo, plenus
perfidia et mendositate et tyrannide a saeculo simili non audita' (quoted by Krofta,
'N. V. Jastrebova, Studie o Petru Chelčickem a jeho době,' *Č. Č. H.*, 1909, p. 67).

of God,' defending their religion by the sword, whose name – and especially that of their leader, Jan Žižka – was to be a terror to the rest of Catholic Europe for centuries to come. Under Žižka's leadership, and owing to the exigencies of war conditions, the minor gentry came to play an increasingly important role in the movement's direction until finally all traces of its social revolutionary beginnings had disappeared.[16] Among the many thousands who were attracted by this religious and social renaissance only Chelčický and the small group which he was to gather around him during the coming years were to remain faithful to the principles of those early 'Taborites before Tábor.'[17]

Little is known of Chelčický's stay in Prague. Since it is probable that he had no more than a smattering of Latin, the doors of the University would therefore have been closed to him.[18] He was able, however, to read many of the works of the leading theologians in translations made for him by his friends, and above all he was able to make use of one or other of the existing vernacular translations of the Bible into his native Czech.[19]

[16] Pekař, *Žižka a jeho doba*, I, pp. 14, 169–98; Krofta, *op. cit.*, pp. 118, 131, 170; Chaloupecký, *op. cit.*, pp. 376–79, 382; 'Vavřince z Březové kronika husitská,' *Fontes Rerum Bohemicarum*, V, pp. 400 ff., 454 ff; *Ktož jsú boží bojovníci*, pp. 36, 59–61, 66–69. (For Žižka, see especially Frederick G. Heymann, *John Žižka and the Hussite Revolution*, Princeton, N. J., 1955, which unfortunately was only available to me after completion of the present book.)

[17] Tábor, which gave its name to the movement, was founded in the first quarter of 1420 near the small south Bohemian town of Ústi. In *O boji duchovním*, pp. 27, 28, Chelčický expressed in strong terms his disagreement with 'our brothers,' the chiliast preachers of 1420, in whose doctrines, 'clothed in the prophets and the Old Testament,' he detected the devil's hand in spite of their advocacy of voluntary poverty. See also Hoch, 'Husité a Válka,' *Česká mysl*, 1907, pp. 200–04, 290.

[18] The anonymous introduction to his *Sít' víry* (ed. Smetánka, p. 2), which was written in 1521, says that he was 'unlearned in Latin,' and this tradition has usually been accepted by modern scholars as in line with the internal evidence contained in his writings. But cf. Bartoš's hypothesis mentioned above, *J. S. H.*, 1946, pp. 6, 7.

[19] Towards the end of the fourteenth century the whole Bible had been translated into Czech, though the work had not been carried through in any systematic way, since the different sections were completed by various people working independently of each other. During the early years of the next century – and especially with the growth of the reform movement – a large number of Czech Bibles were produced in revised form, though the destruction of the war years, as well as the constant use to which they were put, has meant that few copies have survived. The original inspiration for the task had been derived in part from Matěj of Janov's emphasis on the primacy of scripture; and Hus himself had a hand in later revision. See Jakubec, *Dějiny literatury české*, I, pp. 404–12, 374; Peschke, *Die Theologie der Böhmischen Brüder in ihrer Frühzeit*, I, p. 108. Among others, Jakoubek's chaplain at the Bethlehem Chapel, Martin of Volyně, translated or copied many manuscripts for Chelčický. – Hrejsa *Dějiny křest'anství v Československu*, II, p. 314.

A characteristic incident, however, occurred during this period: his two recorded interviews with the leading Utraquist theologian, Jakoubek of Stříbro (circa 1370–1429).[20] The first occurred in the spring of 1420 in Jakoubek's room at the Bethlehem Chapel at a time when, with the proclamation by Pope Martin V on 1 March of a crusade against Hussite Bohemia, the crusading armies were converging on Prague. The second interview took place after Žižka's victory at the battle of Vyšehrad (1 November 1420) had removed the menace, which had threatened not only Prague but the annihilation of the whole Hussite movement. These meetings testify to the contacts which Chelčicky had with the leading men of the day, as well as to the respect which he must have enjoyed among them.[21]

The subject of discussion on both occasions centred on the burning question whether a Christian was ever justified in resorting to force, whether his personal participation in war was consistent with following in Christ's footsteps. The problem, as will be seen later, was being widely discussed on all sides and from all angles, and the war situation had removed it from the sphere of pure theory into the field of current politics. What sanction have you in the Scriptures for warfare among Christians? – asked Chelčicky at the outset. Jakoubek was forced to admit that he had only the injunctions of 'the saints of old' for his interpretation. But he did not hesitate to accuse Chelčicky of heresy for his opposition to the war effort. Later, writes Chelčicky going on to describe their second meeting:

After many people had been killed on both sides, Jakoubek excused those who had done the killing, saying that [he] could not tax their consciences with such things, since otherwise the whole estate of knighthood (*stav rytířský*) would stand condemned... How your master would have flown out against anyone who dared eat pork on a Friday [adds Chelčicky with typically biting irony] and yet now he cannot make the shedding of men's blood a matter of conscience, this man whose own conscience has been filched from him by those saints of old.

Whatever our estimate of the practical value of such a point of view, the independence of mind of this young countryman standing out alone against the universally accepted opinion even on his own side, speaking up against the revered leader of the whole Hussite movement at this supreme moment of crisis, as well as his moral courage, must be acknowledged.[22]

[20] For Jakoubek, see Bartoš's essay in *Světci a kacíři*, pp. 82–105. For his conditional justification of Christian participation in warfare in his MS. tract *De bellis*, see Hoch, *op. cit.*, pp. 296, 297.

[21] Urbánek, *op. cit.*, pp. 898, 899.

[22] Chelčicky, 'Replika proti Rokycanovi,' *Listy filologické*, 1898, pp. 394, 395. But

Soon after the relief of Prague Chelčický left the capital to return to his native south Bohemia. This had been the only period which he is known to have spent away from the neighbourhood of his birth. He was by now at least thirty: a man whose outlook on life had already become formed. The influences shaping his opinions had already played their part in the creation of his social and religious philosophy. Above all there was the Bible, especially the New Testament, whose pages spoke directly to Chelčický as a clear revelation of the will of God to man. Fundamentally Chelčický remained a Taborite of the 'primitive' period, strongly imbued with the spirit of the Waldensian heresy. But other influences, too, of a more intellectual character left their mark on his writings: Hus and his predecessors in Bohemia and the Englishman, John Wyclif.

Chelčický's social teachings do not, indeed, appear so unexpected and novel if the social ideas which had developed in Bohemia over the previous fifty years – partly owing to outside influences – are taken into account.[23] A succession of writers and preachers had already established a tradition of moral protest against social injustice, of fellow-feeling for the oppressed, of exaltation of the humble and meek against the proud and rulers of the world. The cult of the little man, of the peasant (*dobrý náš sedláček*) was connected in the thought of Hus's predecessors with the attempt to renew the practice of Christian moral principles. They were primarily moral reformers, concerned with political questions only incidentally; and their political thinking is, therefore, neither systematic nor particularly profound.[24]

Konrad Waldhauser (c. 1326–1369), inveighing against those lords who oppressed their tenants, had proclaimed the moral superiority of the simple peasant. 'More deceit and disbelief arises from the towns than the village,' he wrote in words reminiscent of Chelčický's later advocacy of country life. Matěj of Janov (c. 1350–1394), like his master Milič of Kroměříž (d. 1374), carried on this tradition, adding a new note with his wholly negative attitude to the role of the state within a Christian society. He pointed to the early Christian church, with its community of goods and rule by love alone, as a model for his contemporaries to follow.[25]

these disagreements do not appear to have spoilt the friendly relationship between the two men.

[23]   Kulbakin, 'Petr Khelchitsky,' *Vestnik Evropy*, Nov. 1909, p. 51. Bartoš, *J. S. H.*, 1947, pp. 33–38, and Chaloupecký, *Selská otázka v husitství*, p. 41, among others, have stressed the influence of the native Bohemian religious reformers on Chelčický in contrast to the Waldensian element.

[24]   Betts, 'Some Political Ideas of the Early Czech Reformers,' *Slavonic and East European Review*, Dec. 1952, p. 20.

[25]   For Matěj's influence in forming Chelčický's views on the unchristian character of

Later Tomáš of Štitný (c. 1331–c. 1401), while adhering in principle to the medieval theory of class relationships, constantly reminded his fellow-noblemen that the only justification of their privileged position lay in their obligation to serve thereby the rest of the community. His maxim – 'the lord is made in order to serve the people (*Pán pro lid obecný jest ustaven*)' – was capable of revolutionary consequences.[26] Even the theologically and politically orthodox Jan of Jenštejn, Archbishop of Prague (1350–1400), took effective practical steps on his archiepiscopal estates against the grosser forms of social oppression, especially against the right of reversion (*odúmrt*) allowing the lord of the manor to claim the property of those among his peasants who might die without leaving an heir legally entitled to inherit, such as, for instance, a direct male descendant living on the holding.

On the eve of the Hussite revolution, therefore, a very extensive literature of protest against social abuses had sprung up, emphasizing at least the theoretical equality of man, remarkably modern in spirit in spite of its medieval framework. Hus, too, defended the peasants' rights and stressed – like Štitný – the obligations of lords towards their tenants, while at the same time eschewing any hint of incitement to rebellion. For Chelčický, however, it was Wyclif perhaps who proved the strongest direct influence, in spite of disagreement on many points, especially in the social field. He was later to write of Wyclif:

None of the first doctors did so zealously speak or write against the poison poured into the Holy Church, out of which the greatest Antichrist has been born with all the loathsomeness with which he has oppressed Jesus Christ and His Law. Wyclif has routed the hosts of Antichrist as well as those doctors who introduced cunning rules in the place of the Law of Christ. In this he pleases me above all others.[27]

Chelčický sometimes quotes from Wyclif under the somewhat ambiguous name of *Mistr Protiva*. He certainly knew at least three of his works from Czech translations: the *Dialogus* and *Trialogus* as well as his *De civili dominio*.[28] It was, indeed, from Wyclif's insistance on the Bible as the

the state, probably exercised indirectly through the medium of the latter's friends from among the radical Hussite priesthood, see Bartoš, 'Chelčický a Rokycana,' *Listy filologické*, 1922, pp. 119, 120, 127–30, and his *Husitství a cizina*, pp. 37, 157.

[26] For an interesting discussion of Štitný's influence on Chelčický, especially in his views on social questions, and of the numerous parallels in the life and writings of the two men, see Chaloupecký, 'Štitný a Chelčický,' *Č. M. M.*, 1914, pp. 73, 76–81. Of Hus's predecessors Štitný was the only one who wrote mainly in Czech.

[27] Chelčický, *op. cit.*, p. 264; Odložilík, *Wyclif and Bohemia*, pp. 49, 50; Betts, *op. cit.*, pp. 20–35.

[28] Hrubý, *op. cit.*, pp. 54–60; *Mistra Jakoubka ze Stříbra překlad Viklefova dialogu*

only fount of inspiration for real Christians and his call to a life modelled on the example of Christ and his apostles that Chelčický, like all his contemporaries in the Hussite movement, was to derive the motivation for his whole political and social superstructure.[29]

Most of Chelčický's ideas can, therefore, be found in the teachings of Hus and the earlier Bohemian reformers, of Wyclif or of the Waldenses and the early Taborites. But with his return home Chelčický was to devote himself to their elaboration, to drawing from them the consequences from which almost all his predecessors and contemporaries had shrunk.[30]

Chelčický's exact movements after leaving Prague are not easy to follow. He appears to have resided for a short time at Písek, a largish town not far from Tábor. Here he took part in a conference of Taborite theologians, defending his viewpoint on the incompatibility of war with Christianity against his former comrades.[31] But he was soon to settle in his native village of Chelčice, where he appears to have remained for the rest of his life, possibly making short journeys from time to time to nearby Vodňany or to the more distant Písek or even Tábor.[32] He began to

---

(ed. Milan Svoboda), pp. XXIII–XXXIV, XXXVIII. It was Krofta, 'Kněz Jan Protiva z Nové Vsi a Chelčického 'Mistr Protiva',' *Č. Č. M.*, 1900, esp. pp. 209–20, who first proved definitely that the passages cited by Chelčický as from *Mistr Protiva* were in fact taken from Wyclif's works and were not connected, as had previously been thought, with the contemporary priest, Protiva, at first an enthusiast for church reform and the first preacher at the Bethlehem Chapel, but later Hus's bitter opponent. Fr. Ryšánek, 'Mistr Protiva u Chelčického,' *Listy filologické*, 1915 (quoted in Jakubec, *op. cit.*, pp. 499, 500) was later able to explain why Chelčický used this seemingly opprobrious name for the master he so much revered despite disagreement on certain topics. It merely signified one who set himself against the corruption of the Christian church, the opponent (*protivník*) of Antichrist, a name devoid of any bad connotation. Chelčický probably returned from his visit to Prague with translations of the three works of Wyclif mentioned above, which may all have been made with at least Jakoubek's participation; but the Czech version of the *Dialogus* is the only major translation to survive. It is known, too, from Pope Martin V's bull of 1418 that Hus also translated Wyclif.

[29] For the similar standpoint of the early Taborites, see *Ktož jsú boží bojovníci*, pp. 38, 39, 63.

[30] Chaloupecký, *Selská otázka v husitství*, pp. 21–42; *O trojím lidu*, pp. 7, 8, 17–21; Jakubec, *op. cit.*, pp. 493, 494; Krofta, *Dějiny selského stavu*, pp. 88–93; Urbánek, *op. cit.*, pp. 890, 891.

[31] Krofta, *Listy*, p. 212; Holinka, *op. cit.*, pp. 100, 101; Urbánek, *op. cit.*, pp. 909, 910. Yastrebov, *Etyudy o Petre Khelchitskom i ego vremeni*, I, p. 118, considers that it may have been in the *convocatio* of 1422, the details of which are known, that Chelčický took part, though his exact words would seem to refer to an earlier unrecorded synod about 1420. For details of the discussions at the Taborite synods of 1422 and 1424 concerning the conditions of a just war, see Hoch, *op. cit.*, pp. 377–81.

[32] Bartoš, *J. S. H.*, 1946, p. 1, quotes a hypothesis of Sedláček, *Děje práchenského*

gather around him a group of disciples, though the genesis of these so-
called 'Chelčický Brethren' is obscure. It may have been the execution in
his absence of the village priest, Vojtěch, and the failure of the church
authorities to supply a successor owing to the general dearth of clergy,
which motivated his future activities. It is at least certain, however, that
he never attempted to break away from the official Utraquist church by
forming his own separate organization.

During these years he was to produce a series of books which, influential
during his own life-time, were to be of epoch-making significance for
Czech history, not least by the inspiration they gave for the foundation of
the Unity of Brethren. The range of his friendships during this period,
too, gives some hint of the respect which the village philosopher enjoyed
among the leading men of the Hussite movement. He had already come
into contact with Master Jan Hus himself during the latter's sojourn in
south Bohemia in 1413, probably attending his sermons given at Koží
Hradec. Later Jakoubek of Stříbro, Mikuláš of Pelhřim (Biskupec), Vacláv
Koranda the elder, and the Taborite left-wing leaders such as Martínek
Huska-Loquis, Peter Payne – the wandering Lollard scholar, who stayed
a year with him after his expulsion from Prague in 1437 – and Rokycana
himself were all, in spite of disagreement on important matters, to value
Chelčický's opinions highly enough to cultivate his acquaintance. Some
of them even visited him or recommended their friends to seek his advice
on weighty theological problems.[33]

The chronology of Chelčický's works has baffled the most assiduous
scholars. In no instance do we know the precise dates of their composition. In many cases expert opinion differs widely in its judgements, for
once again – as with the events of his life – the internal evidence of his
own writings is almost our only guide.[34] His first original work, however,
was probably written in the first half of 1421. O boji duchovním, the
spiritual fight against the powers of darkness which takes the place of
material warfare for the Christian, was in effect a pamphlet directed
against his Taborite friends, who had deserted their former standpoint of

---

kraje, 1926, p. 150, who otherwise found it inexplicable how Chelčický could have
survived the war years in an open village, that his permanent place of residence was
Vodňany. Perhaps he took refuge there in emergencies. Anyhow Bartoš, pp. 2, 7,
thinks Chelčický (alias Záhorka) had his own castle and that his views on the use of
force were at first merely of a theoretical nature.
[33] Bartoš, J. S. H., 1947, p. 3; Goll-Krofta, op. cit., p. 12; Urbánek, op. cit., pp.
900–06; Jagić, Intro. op. cit., p. VIII; Yastrebov, 'Khelchitsky i Gus,' pp. 471, 472.
[34] For a critical survey of the findings of previous scholarship on the subject, see
Cedlová, 'Náboženské názory Petra Chelčického a bratra Řehoře i jejich vzájemný
poměr,' Č. Č. M., 1932, pp. 63–78; Urbánek, op. cit., pp. 910 ff.

non-resistance to evil to take up the sword in defence of religion. It is significant for Chelčický's intellectual development that almost all the ideas which he was later to develop in greater detail appear here in embryo.[35] Even the short tract, *O církvi svaté*, which was probably written during the next few years, contains in a few thousand words the essence of his protest against the state as an unchristian institution.[36] His second major work, *O trojím lidu*, is usually assigned to 1424. It is written in the form of a reply to a Taborite priest, probably Markold of Zbraslavice, who was to fall at the battle of Lipany (1434), refuting the current medieval conception of the division of a Christian society into three estates.[37]

The predominance of social problems in Chelčický's thinking can be seen from the main themes of his first three works. But the religious basis of his philosophy is everywhere apparent; and, though as a layman he avoided entanglement in theological disputes, he could scarcely escape participation in the controversy which centred around the Eucharist. Denying the Catholic doctrine of transubstantiation to which both Hus and the Prague Masters still adhered, Chelčický accepted Wyclif's theory of remanence, and thus came to occupy a centre position among the conflicting views on this subject which existed within the Hussite movement. His disagreement with the prevailing opinion among the Taborite theologians, which appeared to him too radical in its total denial of the real presence in the sacraments, was to lead to his complete estrangement from the party from which he had originally issued, with those 'brother priests [as he calls them] with whom [he] had for long enjoyed friendship and unity on many matters of faith.'[38] Their disagreement on the right use of force was now matched by profound theological differences.

[35]   *O boji duchovním*, pp. IX–XII, XXIII, 27, 28; Pekař, *op. cit.*, p. 155. Urbánek, *op. cit.*, p. 910, links it up with the debates at Písek. See also Macek, *op. cit.*, II, pp. 170, 171, who dates the tract slightly earlier than Krofta.

[36]   Yastrebov, *Etyudy*, p. 151, who first established Chelčický's authorship, placed the date of its composition between *O boji duchovním* and *O trojím lidu*. On the other hand Holinka (*O trojím lidu*, pp. 105, 106, 109), who first published the tract in 1940, puts forward two possibilities: either that it forms part of a larger work of unknown date no longer extant or that it represents a very early literary work, probably written even before *O boji duchovním*. Without committing himself Holinka inclines towards the second hypothesis.

[37]   *O trojím lidu* (ed. Holinka), pp. 95, 104; Urbánek, *op. cit.*, p. 916; *O boji duchovním* (ed. Krofta), pp. XXIV, 142. Holinka thinks the tract was written soon after August 1424, while Urbánek and Krofta assign it to the following year. Bartoš, 'K počátkům Petra Chelčického,' *Č. Č. M.*, 1914, pp. 304–07, on the other hand, believes that it was addressed to Biskupec circa 1422–25.

[38]   Chelčický, *Replika proti Biskupcovi*, p. 426.

Sometime during the twenties the Taborite leader, Biskupec,[39] visiting Vodňany with another Taborite priest called Lukáš, summoned Chelčický to a meeting in order to sound his opinion on the eucharistic controversy. 'Sitting on the dyke by the fish-pond,' the Taborite bishop asked Chelčický what he thought of their doctrines on this subject. It appeared at the time as if they were both in agreement. Rather later a second equally amicable interview took place at Písek, and there may also have been other meetings. But it seems that Chelčický had not at first understood the full significance of the Taborite doctrine, for on obtaining some of their books he began to retract his previously favourable opinion. Biskupec appears to have considered that Chelčický obtained these under false pretences and an acrimonious correspondence, of which the first stages are no longer extant, led up to the composition of Chelčický's lengthy refutation of the Taborite position in his *Replika proti Biskupcovi*, in which he accuses the bishop of the dire heresy of the 'Picards.' Though no attempt was made to persecute him for his divergent views, the break with Tábor was now complete.[40]

Once again Chelčický disappears from view. He lived on some thirty more years in his little village. But scarcely any personal details have come down from this period. The first half, however, proved most fruitful in literary productions, and his two main works and a number of lesser ones are the results of this retirement from the world. The middle years of the thirties saw the composition of his lengthy *Postilla*. With Hus as his model, even taking whole passages from the master, Chelčický preserves his independence both as to form and content. While Hus and the other theologians of all parties wrote as scholastics, filling out their works with copious quotations from past and present church authorities, Chelčický relies mainly on the Bible and the weight of his own thought and argument, using a few church fathers and several of his most revered predecessors, such as Hus himself or Wyclif, to illustrate some of his points. The work contains a homily for each Sunday of the year, no attempt being made at systematic treatment of any theme, though almost all his social

[39]   For Biskupec, see Bartoš's essay in *Světci a kacíři*, pp. 175–96.
[40]   Chelčický, *op. cit.*, chap. II, p. 412; Bartoš, *Č. Č. M.* 1914, pp. 155–60; Goll-Krofta, *op. cit.*, pp. 13–17; Krofta, *Petr Chelčický*, pp. 26–29; Urbánek, *op. cit.*, pp. 920–31; Yastrebov, *op. cit.*, p. 194. Once again the dating of the controversy is uncertain. Goll, Jagić, and Urbánek place it in the first half of the 1420s, while Yastrebov dates its beginning to about 1428 and the actual composition of Chelčický's *Replika* to 1431/32. The second half of the 1420s would appear the most probable supposition. – The 'Picards' (sometimes known as Adamites or *Mikulášenci*), among other distinctive doctrines, held rationalistic views concerning the sacraments, denying altogether the real presence.

and political doctrines are touched on and often developed at some length.[41]

The thirties brought peace – at the price of the destruction of the military power of the Taborites and the *Compactata*, the attempt at compromise between the moderate Utraquists and Rome. Chelčický's attitude to political and social questions had remained unchanged through peace and war. Only the radicalism of his youth became somewhat softened in expression. The protest is more subdued; the virtue of resignation is more strongly emphasized. This may be seen from a comparison of the tone in which *O trojím lidu* is written with that of his masterpiece, *Síť' pravé víry*, which deals mainly with the same theme of the relationship of Christianity to the state.[42] *Síť' víry* is a product of the early forties.[43] The theme of the first and longer half of the book is an elaboration, a systematization, of his often repeated thesis that the association of church and state meant the fall of Christianity, that the state and all its works can have no place in a truly Christian community. His philosophical anarchism here reaches fullest expression. In the second part Chelčický surveys the various classes which represent the ruling elements of contemporary society: the nobility, the townsmen, the monks and friars and priests and learned theologians. All are found wanting when weighed in the scales of pure Christianity. For 'the net of true faith,' the Christian church and community, founded on the Word of Christ, is rent wide open by the two great whales – the Emperor or state power and the Pope – who have forced their way in; and thereby all the heathen customs of the pagan world have found acceptance among outwardly Christian nations. Taking the story of the miraculous draught of fishes (Luke, V, 1–11) as his text, Chelčický goes on to interpret it in his own way, to give it the 'spiritual' meaning so beloved of medieval thought. Within this loose framework he proceeds to erect one of the most powerful indictments of the state as an institution, as well as of the abuses of contemporary society, that has ever been penned.

Perhaps at the same time as he was writing *Síť' víry* Chelčický first

[41] Hrubý, *op. cit.*, pp. 48–66. Most authorities date this work within the years 1434–37. See Cedlová, *op. cit.*, pp. 69, 70; Bartoš, 'Chelčický a Rockycana,' *Listy filologické*, 1922, pp. 30–35; Krofta, *op. cit.*, pp. 29, 30; Goll, *Quellen und Untersuchungen*, II, p. 65; Urbánek, *op. cit.*, pp. 946–49, 953.

[42] Yastrebov, *op. cit.*, pp. 148, 149. For echoes of Štitný in *Síť' víry*, see Chaloupecký, 'Štitný a Chelčický,' *Č. M. M.*, 1914, pp. 79, 80.

[43] Earlier writers, e.g. Šafařík, Jireček, Schulz, erroneously assigned this work to the middle of the 1450s, while Bartoš's dating (*op. cit.*, pp. 122–24) in the late 1430s has not found general acceptance. Goll's assignment of it to the interregnum during the early forties, circa 1440–43, still holds (*op. cit.*, p. 66). See Cedlová, *op. cit.*, p. 72; Urbánek, *op. cit.*, p. 959.

came into into personal contact with the Hussite archbishop-elect, Jan Rokycana. In 1437 Rokycana had had to leave Prague owing to the increasing tide of reaction which set in with the return of King Sigismund to the capital, and had found refuge in the areas held by the Utraquist nobility. The personal meetings between the two men and an extended correspondence can probably be assigned to the eleven years of Rokycana's semi-exile.[44] In spite of their disagreements on such widely removed subjects as the functions of the state and the liturgy of the church, the relations between the two men remained friendly. Indeed Rokycana already had such a high opinion of Chelčicky's writings, at least of those dealing with theological questions, that in his *Tractatus de existentia corporis Christi in sacramento eucharistiae*, written in the early forties to refute Taborite eucharistic doctrines, he borrowed whole passages from the *Replika proti Biskupcovi*.[45] He was later, however, to be less pleased with the influence of Chelčicky's social and political doctrines on his own disciples. But it should be observed that Chelčicky always considered himself a loyal son of the Utraquist church, while Rokycana was able on occasion to play the radical when this did not conflict with the exigencies of practical politics. Only one fragment of their correspondence has survived in the form of Chelčicky's *Replika proti Rokycanovi*, which he appears neither to have completed nor dispatched. Anyhow their renewed contact in the fifties, when Rokycana was to show the respect in which he held Chelčicky's opinions by recommending his own disciples to him, shows that disagreement did not, as with Biskupec, lead to a complete rupture.[46]

During the last years of his life Chelčicky appears to have written no works of major importance.[47] But at an unspecified date in the fifties the founder of the Unity, Brother Řehoř, visited the ageing Chelčicky in his home on the advice of the former's uncle, Rokycana; and as a result

[44] Bartoš, *op. cit.*, pp. 35, 119, 120, 122, 126, 127, 135. Bartoš, indeed, claims that Chelčicky composed his *Replika proti Rokycanovi* at the same time, if not earlier, than his *Postilla*, that is, before any personal meeting. For Rokycana generally, see Bartoš's essay in *Světci a kacíři*, pp. 196–223 and Krofta, *Listy*, pp. 222–39.

[45] Yastrebov, *op. cit.*, pp. 243–58.

[46] Of Chelčicky's major works the *Replika proti Rokycanovi* is among the hardest to date. The opinions of the experts differ widely. Urbánek, *op. cit.*, pp. 938–46, 979, places it circa 1433/34, before the composition of his *Postilla*. Goll, *op. cit.*, pp. 67, 68, on the other hand, puts it as late as after Rokycana's return to Prague in 1448. Yastrebov, Müller, and Bartoš have also suggested the middle 1430s. It seems most probable that at least the contact between the two men began during Rokycana's absence from Prague. – Cedlová, *op. cit.*, pp. 72–74. See also Hrejsa, *op. cit.*, p. 311.

[47] For full bibliographical details concerning Chelčicky's minor works, see Jakubec, *op. cit.*, pp. 465–500; Urbánek, *op. cit.*, pp. 884 ff.

of these visits and of their reading of his works, the new religious community, the future *Jednota bratrská*, was to take over ready-made all Petr's political and social theories as well as most of his theological doctrines. Thus Chelčický, the philosopher in retirement, became one of the factors to influence the future course of events in the Czech lands.

The last years of his life, however, were clouded by disputes concerning the conditions under which the sacraments might be administered, which broke out with the Vilemov Brethren, one of a number of small groups similar to his own with whom Chelčický had long been in friendly contact. Rokycana, who was appealed to as arbitrator, decided virtually in Chelčický's favour; and the new relationship of the old man with the former's disciples perhaps helped to lighten his last years.[48] The exact date of Chelčický's death is not known. But it is very improbable that he lived to see the foundation in 1467 of their new church to be known in history as the Unity of Brethren; though he may still have been alive when the first step was taken with the settlement of the Brethren at Kunvald some ten years earlier.[49]

Chelčický's life, apart from the general meagreness of the biographical material which obstinately eludes all attempts at further clarification, presents two interesting problems. First, how was it that a layman, apparently with little formal education, who – even if it is uncertain if he actually sprang from peasant stock – was at least a working farmer for most of his life, should have evolved so startingly original a social philosophy and have expressed these ideas in a literary style which, despite a certain naivety and crudity of form, is rightly considered one of the glories of Czech literature? The answer lies indeed in these seemingly unfavourable circumstances. It was Chelčický's lack of book-learning that allowed him to free himself from the shackles of scholasticism and think through to new and daring solutions. It was his comparative ignorance of the theological systems of the past which enabled him to draw direct from the Bible unencumbered with the philosophical and other preconceptions of his contemporaries, and which endowed him with his courageous independence of thought. It was his humble status, whether

[48] Urbánek, *op. cit.*, pp. 905, 979; Hrejsa, *op. cit.*, III, p. 119.
[49] For estimated dates of his death, ranging from the later 1440s to the early 1460s, see Urbánek, *op. cit.*, pp. 978, 979. The late 1450s would seem the most likely supposition. But Bartoš, *J. S. H.*, 1946, p. 6, still considers circa 1450 as the most probable. The objection based on the difficulty of fitting in with this theory the contacts which are known to have existed between Chelčický and Brother Řehoř, can be countered by Bartoš's earlier assertion, 'Chelčický a Rokycana,' *Listy filologické*, 1922, pp. 130–33, 135, that these contacts took place before 1448. This, however, is strongly contested by Urbánek, *op. cit.*, pp. 980, 982.

inherited or voluntarily assumed, which gave him that insight into social questions which no theory could provide. It was, finally, his self-trained intellect which gave all his writings their wonderful freshness and directness of expression, their forthright honesty of thought, their almost modern outlook, despite the medieval framework, on so many of the most vital of our contemporary problems.[50]

But the second question is both more important and in some ways more difficult to answer. How was it, then, that Chelčický was able to produce over a period of some forty years work after work in which he proclaimed in no uncertain terms the total incompatability of the existing state system with the demands of religion, in which he preached a complete withdrawal from all contact with the state machine on the part of all true Christians, put forward in short opinions which in any age might be regarded as subversive of the political and social order? How can one explain in these circumstances Chelčický's untroubled existence in his south Bohemian village at a time when all over Europe persons expressing even the slightest variation from the accepted pattern of thought in matters both political and theological suffered savage persecution, provided they were not in possession of enough material strength to make the attempt unwise? The answer is twofold and lies both in the mental climate of his age and the geographical circumstances of his birth. In the fifteenth century all problems found expression primarily in theological terms. The religious element was uppermost in every sphere of life; and Chelčický himself followed the medieval practice of speaking of 'the church' when often in actual fact the whole Christian community in its social as well as its strictly religious relationships was meant. In such an age the political and social doctrines put forward, however radical, might escape that attention which similar views would attract in more modern times; and in theological matters Chelčický's opinions were more orthodox. At least they did not differ greatly from those held by many eminent Utraquist theologians; and in comparison with the majority of his Taborite neighbours he was almost reactionary. The crux of the matter lies in the fact that Chelčický lived in fifteenth-century Utraquist Bohemia and in those parts dominated by the armed might of Tábor. The contemporary treatment of the Waldenses in western Europe or of the Lollards in England is instructive. It is, therefore, one of the ironies of history that the greatest medieval exponent of the gospel of Christian

---

[50] Foustka, *Politické názory Petra Chelčického*, p. 6, points out that Chelčický, like the whole Hussite movement, belongs to the transitional period between the Middle Ages and modern times.

pacifism, of philosophical anarchism, owed his immunity from persecution, by the accident of birth and contrary to his own inclinations, to the
protecting presence of the terrible 'warriors of God' and the powerful
organization of the official Utraquist church, to the successful outcome of
a violent revolution. His disciples of the Unity, putting theory into
practice under different circumstances, were indeed to draw down on
their heads the fires of persecution, which might so easily have swept
away their master and all his works.[51]

II

The uncertainty which envelops the details of Chelčický's life is com-
pensated for, however, by the richness and abundance of his writings. All
his thoughts were clothed in a religious form. But it is not his theology,
however absorbing to the expert in that field, that provides the most
interesting material for the historian and gives him his value for the world
today. His genius lies rather in his original approach to those political
and social problems common to most civilized societies.

The source of Chelčický's whole philosophy lay in a return to the spirit
of primitive Christianity. He took over from Wyclif, as we have seen, his
conception of the Bible as containing all things needful for salvation; and
from Hus and his predecessors and the Waldenses, as well as from Wyclif
himself, he inherited the practical attempt to follow Christ's example in
everything. He made, however, a distinction – as, for instance, the
Waldenses had done earlier – between the Old Testament, 'material and
concerned with gross matters,' and the 'spiritual' New Testament; and it

---

[51] There is no mention in contemporary accounts of Chelčický's ever coming into
conflict with the authorities on account of his writings. Brother Lukáš, however, in a
frequently quoted passage from his *Odpis proti odtržencóm* (1924), fols. 28v, 29, relates
how Chelčický was summoned to the synod of clergy held at Kutná Hora in July 1443,
which was attended by Taborite priests as well as by conservative and moderate
Utraquists, in order to answer for his opinions, and how out of fear he wished to burn
all his books. Lukáš adds that he was often 'overlong angry and revengeful,' in this
way causing the death of a Taborite priest and bringing down persecution on other
Taborites. These stories, however, cannot be given credence. They were first reported
eighty years after the events described, by a professed opponent of Chelčický's doctrines,
and, according to Lukáš himself, were only hearsay. See Goll-Krofta, *op. cit.*, p. 210;
Goll, 'Petr Chelčický a jeho spisy,' *Vybrané spisy drobné*, II, p. 70; Vogl, *op. cit.*, p. 16.
The subversive nature of Chelčický's social doctrines was stressed in the sixteenth
century by the Jesuit Václav Sturm in his *Srovnání víry*, 1582 (quoted in Denis, *Fin de
l'Indépendence Bohême*, I, p. 230) and at the end of the nineteenth century by the
fanatically Catholic Antonín Lenz, who refers to him in his 'Soustava učení Petra
Chelčického na základě pramenů,' *Sborník historického kroužků*, as 'this mendacious
peasant.'

was only the latter which demanded unqualified obedience.[52] The example
of Christ and his apostles was to be the touchstone of all human conduct,
of all earlier and later teachings. 'For every doctrine [he writes] needs to
be tested by Christ's words and life, to see if it accords with His example
and teachings.' There is no need for any additional 'human laws (zákony
lidské),' he proclaimed with Matěj of Janov, 'since this law [i.e. of Christ]
is no less sufficient today than it was at the beginning.'[53] Chelčický,
however, did not entirely reject the authority of later church fathers,
provided they did not conflict with the gospels or preach anything not
found there.

I acknowledge [he writes] all the holy doctors, those of today too, so far
as they can point out to me through their learning the path of true understanding in those matters which God has shown me in His Law (zákon)...
and I follow them thankfully and regard them as right when they give real
understanding and enlightenment here or proclaim faithfully some hidden
truth.[54]

They were to act as additional confirmation of established truths, never to
alter or extend the already perfect revelation, a way of thinking to which
the Utraquists also gave expression in the famous Agreement of Cheb of
August 1432 and during the debates at the Council of Basel.[55]

The kernel of Christ's teaching, the secret of his power, lay, according
to Chelčický, in his law of love.[56] This was the rock on which the early
church had been built. Its whole existence for the first three centuries had
been one long attempt to regulate every activity, personal or public, in
accordance with this law. The idealized picture of the primitive church
which Chelčický draws – in line with earlier writers such as Wyclif or
Richard Fitzralph, Archbishop of Armagh (d. 1360), in his De pauperie
salvatoris – is, whatever may be its historical shortcomings, in effect a

---

[52]   Chelčický, 'Řeč základu zákonů lidských,' Menší spisy, I, pp. 75, 76; Peschke,
op. cit., p. 159; Holinka, Sektářství v Čechách, p. 178. Cf. Marsilius of Padua, writing
about a hundred years earlier in his Defensor pacis (1324): 'Non omnia, quae in Lege
seu Testamento Veteri Iudaico populo consulta vel custodiri praecepta fuerunt,
observare tenentur Christi fideles; quinimo quorundam est ipsis observatio interdicta,
ut quae ceremoniarum sub poena perditionis aeternae' (Dict. II, cap. IX, pt. 10),
quoted in Previté-Orton, 'Marsilius of Padua,' Proceedings of the British Academy,
1935, pp. 146, 171, 179. In opposition to the main stream of Hussite thought, Chelčický
thus returns to the Marsilian position on this point. It is, of course, extremely unlikely
that Chelčický was directly acquainted with Marsilius's writings. For the influence of
Marsilius on the Hussite movement, see Bartoš, Husitství a cizina, chap. V.
[53]   Sít' víry, pp. 15–17, 32, 345; 'Replika proti Rokycanovi,' p. 266.
[54]   'Replika,' p. 264.
[55]   Jacob, 'The Bohemians at the Council of Basel, 1433,' Prague Essays, pp. 106, 107.
[56]   Sít' víry, p. 63.

representation of the conditions which, in Chelčický's opinion, would exist if a truly Christian society were to replace the feudal order of his day, and not at all a retrograde conservatism with its face to the past. It is a political Utopia placed on a historic background. The early Brethren were to attempt, within the framework of the existing social order, to make of this Utopia a reality.

Constantine's acceptance of the persecuted religion had meant the fall of Christianity. This was a familiar theme among the medieval sectaries and, linked up with the legend of Constantine's Donation which allegedly gave the Pope temporal power in Italy, it provides an oft-repeated motif running through all Chelčický's writings. Wyclif had supported this interpretation: 'Silvester [he had written] peccavit donacionem acceptando,'[57] and the *Supplementum* to his *Trialogus*, which Chelčický certainly read in Czech translation, consists mainly of an attack on church endowment.[58] The Donation itself on which Rome based much of its case in its struggle with the imperial power was in fact an eighth-century forgery. Opponents of the church's temporal claims, however, believed that with the acceptance of worldly wealth and power on the part of the church its apostolic purity was corrupted: the poison was injected into God's Church, as the angel proclaimed according to legend. In the version which Chelčický used, Pierre Valdo was made a contemporary of Pope Sylvester, his companion in their hiding from persecution among the forests and caves, who, however, remained faithful to Christian principles after their betrayal by Sylvester. For Chelčický, the perfection of the church before the Donation was matched now by its total depravity henceforth.

The conception of historical evolution, of progress, was alien to his mental outlook. The pure faith was now kept alive only by the handful who remained with Valdo and their successors.[59]

What then was the root cause of this fall? How should contemporary

[57] Wyclif, *De Christo et suo adversario Antichristo*, p. 43. Cf. *De civili dominio*, II, p. 108.
[58] Wyclif, *Trialogus*, pp. 407–56.
[59] *Ibid.*, pp. 47, 48, 59, 61, 62; 'Replika,' pp. 393, 394, 455. Holinka in his Intro. to *O trojím lidu*, pp. 29, 30, considers that Chelčický inherited this particular form of the legend from the Waldenses, who in their turn, according to Böhmer, *op. cit.*, p. 826, took it over from the Cathars. See also Holinka, *Sektářství v Čechách*, pp. 17–19, 181, for the growth of this legend among the Waldenses. Bartoš, *J. S. H.*, 1947, pp. 35–37, on the other hand, thinks he picked it up from the stories on this theme which were circulating at the time in circles quite uninfluenced by the Waldenses. Not all the church's opponents, e.g. Wyclif, believed that the church's sudden and total corruption ensued on the Donation. The first person to discover that the latter was not authentic was the Italian humanist, Laurentius de Valla, in his *De falso credita et ementita Constantini donatione declamatio* (1440); and his findings became known in Bohemia

society be ordered if it was to accord with Christian principles? Chelčicky's answer was clear: the state organism must be totally rejected and Christ's Law of Love put into its place. Chelčicky was already writing in the middle of the twenties:

These two divisions, the temporal order of force and Christ's way of love, are far removed from each other. ...An action done because of the compulsion of authority is quite different from one done through love and from the good will arising out of the words of truth. Thus civil authority is as far removed from Christ's truth inscribed in His gospel as is Christian faith from the necessity of using such authority. Those in power are not led by faith nor does faith need them.... For the fullness of authority lies in the accumulation of wealth and vast gatherings of armed men, castles, and walled towns, while the fullness and completion of faith lies in God's wisdom and the strength of the Holy Spirit. Faith supported solely by spiritual power stands firm without the power of authority, which only brings fear and can only attain what it wishes under the threat of compulsion.[60]

The early church had been perfect in principle and in practice, and it had existed for over three hundred years without its members participating in temporal power. Christians of those times had held no offices, had in fact completely withdrawn from the official business of the state. With Constantine's acceptance of Christianity, however, 'the emperor with his pagan authority, his pagan offices and laws and statutes' had, like a monstrous whale caught up in a fisherman's net, torn a gaping rent in the fabric of the primitive faith. Instead of accepting wealth and power for himself, Chelčicky considers that Sylvester should have made Constantine renounce his temporal power before receiving him into the church, thus condemning in effect the foundations on which rested the twin pillars holding up contemporary feudal society: the church and the state. No real Christian then or in later ages, therefore, could hold any state office: princes and rulers on becoming convinced of the true faith must resign their authority. 'No one may stray from the way of Christ and follow the emperor with his sword, for this way is not changed just because Caesar has become a Christian.'[61]

All government would seem to be for Chelčicky, as for the modern anarchists, solely an instrument of oppression, of legalized robbery. The conception of a welfare state would have been wholly foreign to him.

---

towards the end of the fifteenth century. See Sokol's notes to Přeloučský, *Spis o původu Jednoty bratrské a o chudých lidech*, p. 113.
[60] *O trojím lidu*, p. 48.
[61] *Sít' víry*, pp. 21–35, 40, 56, 57, 69, 156, 163.

Domination and cruelty lay at the roots of the state organism, were inseparable parts of its make-up. 'Authority cannot exist without cruelty [he says]. If it ceases to be cruel, it will at once perish of itself, since none will fear it. ... Therefore, authority is far removed from love.' Warfare between Christians, too, is an inseparable concomitant of the participation of Christians in the state.[62]

Chelčický sweeps aside all attempts to justify such participation. Some urged that much benefit would accrue if Christians ruled for the purpose of reforming bad Christians or those outside the faith. The only way to convert such people, Chelčický replies sternly, is through 'the workings of the law of God,' which consists in loving God and one's neighbour. Such conversion must come as a result of free-will, never from compulsion. The only outcome of the use of force would be that the Christian ruler himself would inevitably fall into sin.[63] Others argued that prayers for those in authority, of which Chelčický approved following 1 Timothy, II, 1–3, implied a recognition of the place of the ruler in a Christian society. On the contrary, anwered Chelčický, the reason for such prayers is 'to gain the good will of heathen and cruel princes and soften their anger against us,' and to prevail upon God to prevent them from bringing much misery upon their peoples through war.[64] Chelčický gave an equally negative answer to those who urged, as for instance Tomáš of Štitný had done, that the existing social system could be purgued of its defects, that the state could be guided by love in its exercise of authority. Power could only be wielded, in Chelčický's opinion, 'by the worst of men who are without any faith or virtue, since it is by means of terrible punishments that the state compels evildoers to some measure of justice in outward matters.' Mercy and state authority were self-contradictory terms.[65]

A more powerful argument against his position, however, might be found in the words of St. Paul, Romans XIII, 1–7, which were, he admitted, the main authority quoted by 'Ceasar's priests' – as, like Wyclif, he called the clergy – to justify Christian participation in the state. In reply, Chelčický differentiated first between submission to pagan rulers in matters proper to them and the, for him, wholly untenable reading which would justify Christians becoming rulers themselves. He then went on to prove the absurdity of his opponents' arguments by a consideration of the historical circumstances in which St. Paul wrote these words, a member

[62] *O trojím lidu*, p. 44; *Sít' víry*, p. 56.
[63] *Sít' víry*, pp. 107–13.
[64] *Ibid.*, p. 212–15.
[65] *O trojím lidu*, pp. 45, 66, 102.

of an outcast sect living under the rule of the pagan Romans. St. Paul's call for submission was in part a protective measure to ward off from the little flock any suspicion that they were plotting against the state. But if persecution did come in spite of everything, Chelčický was quick to point out, then there was nothing for the Christian to do but to suffer without retaliation.[66]

For Chelčický's was the Tolstoyan gospel of non-resistance to evil, not the revolutionary's creed. Armed rebellion was never justified even under the greatest provocation, for though 'rulers sin by acting unjustly, [subjects] also commit a sin in seeking vengeance on such lords.'[67] He advocated for the Christian obedience to the civil authorities as a matter of conscience and not merely out of fear of the consequences of disobedience. At the same time as he condemned the whole existing social order he preached throughout his life its conditional justification. This seeming paradox, however, was a logical development of his first principles. Orthodox medieval political theorists had granted that the institution of the state was a result of sin: without the Fall civil government would lose its justification. Chelčický, too, was ready to assent to the existence of the state: but, slightly modifying the accepted view, he restricted its validity to the community of the non-Christians and the false Christians, 'the foolish people who neither know God nor are under his yoke.' If, however, the non-Christians and the false Christians all truly followed in Christ's footsteps it would wither away.[68] In the meantime the remnant, the true Christians, must hold to their principles. A pessimism as to the nature of man common to many medieval thinkers, and a belief in the approaching end of the world shared by many contemporaries, led Chelčický to disbelieve in the possibility of ever dispensing with the coercion necessary to save human society from the chaos, which would ensue if man's passions were given free sway. The lack of consistency, which a recent writer[69] has detected in the varying stringency with which Chelčický regarded Christian participation in government, may also partly be explained by the mellowing of his views with the passing of the years. Chelčický, indeed, represents – to borrow a phrase usually used in con-

---

[66]   *Ibid.*, pp. 53–55; *Sít' víry*, pp. 124–30, 202–05, 208, 209. Similarly Christ's attitude towards the centurion in Luke VII did not in Chelčický's opinion (*O trojím lidu*, pp. 60, 61) signify approval of his office.

[67]   *Sít' víry*, p. 145.

[68]   Foustka, *op. cit.*, p. 35, draws an interesting comparison between Chelčický's relativist views on the state and those propounded by Marx.

[69]   *Ibid.*, p. 27.

nection with the history of socialism – the stage of Utopian anarchism. His ideals were to be put into practice only by a minority.[70]

Obedience to the authorities, however, was to be strictly limited to 'the things which be Caesar's.' 'The saints [writes Chelčický of the true Christians] should be obedient to the higher powers, but with circumspection (*opatrně*), that is to say, in those things ... which are not contrary to God. They should, therefore, render the dues and services which rulers require of their subjects.'[71] But in cases where the authorities compel some wrong action, the Christian subject is bound to disobey, passively suffering the penalties for his disobedience. 'For a man opposing the state in such perverse wickedness commits no sin nor is he in fear of damnation, since we can find in the scriptures similar examples among righteous men.'[72]

Closely linked with Chelčický's rejection of civil authority was his demand for the complete separation of church and state. A revolutionary suggestion in the fifteenth century it was destined to gain increasing support in recent times, in contrast to his more radical social progamme. Throughout the Middle Ages, however, the right and duty of the civil authorities under certain conditions to intervene in church affairs was generally acknowledged. Wyclif had championed the obligation of the state to disendow the church, if need be by force, in view of its excessive wealth. The Hussites, especially, urged such intervention to control and oversee the private moral of the state's citizens;[73] and their outlook found

[70] *Sít' víry*, pp. 5, 128–30, 135, 140, 152–54, 166, 218–20; *O trojím lidu*, pp. 45, 56, 59, 60. I cannot agree with Vogl's assertion, *op. cit.*, pp. 214, 215, that Chelčický's condemnation of civil authority is of a similar nature to his advocacy of celibacy for Christians living without sin. Anyhow the early Brethren, attempting to put his teachings into practice, did not understand him in this way. Participation in the state was forbidden to all, while marriage understandably was permitted at least to all lay persons. Vogl, pp. 147, 148, is right, however, when he emphasizes the difference between Chelčický's ideal of a Christianity valid for all men and the medieval monastic conception of the flight from the world of the chosen few. Nevertheless, the ascetic element is marked in all Chelčický's writings.

[71] Chelčický, *Postilla*, I, p. 61.

[72] *Sít' víry*, pp. 147–49.

[73] Vogl, *op. cit.*, p. 43, cites passages from Hus's tract on simony, advocating the state's duty to depose a bad bishop and preaching submission to the state in purely church affairs. For a discussion of the Hussite attitude towards the relations between church and state, see Betts, *op. cit.*, pp. 21, 23, 25–31. Cf. also the far-reaching Erastianism of an earlier medieval radical, Marsilius of Padua, Previté-Orton, *op. cit.*, pp. 144, 159, 160. The fact that so outstanding a medievalist as Previté-Orton could, without any reference to Chelčický's contribution to medieval social radicalism, make the comment that Marsilius was 'the most radical of the theorists on Church and State in the Middle Ages,' shows the extent to which the Czech's writings have been neglected by the historians of Western Europe.

its clearest expression in the fourth of the famous Prague Articles (1420).[74] Likewise few contested, at least in theory, the rightness of the forcible conversion of heretics and unbelievers to the true faith.[75] In Chelčický, however, the whole idea of the use of force in spiritual matters was to find one of its sternest opponents.

Chelčický saw clearly that the power of the church of his day was inextricably bound up with the state. He was at one with the whole Hussite movement, which was indeed largely inspired by the writings of Wyclif, in its attack on the temporal wealth of the clergy and of the mendicant orders in particular, in its condemnation of the church lands, and of the secular dominion which went with possession, as inconsistent with following Christ's example: feelings which were to find expression in the third of the Prague Articles.[76] Chelčický, too, followed Hus very closely in his attacks on simony. But in his consideration of the relationship of church and state he was to go a step further. Priests, in his opinion, should only concern themselves with preaching the gospel, relying for their safety on the example of a pure life and never calling in the aid of the secular arm. The kind of compulsory virtue which the Prague Articles envisaged was worse than useless. Though in a 'pagan' state the ruler was justified in maintaining public order, Christians – and all the more priests – should never resort to force in such matters. 'Whoever is not sincerely brought to the Christian faith through preaching of the gospel, will never be brought by force [he says] just as no one will

---

[74] 'Quod omnia peccata mortalia et specialiter publica alieque deordinaciones legi dei contrarie in quolibet statu rite et racionabiliter per eos, ad quos spectat, prohibeantur et destruantur' (F. R. B., V, p. 394). This article on the punishment of public sin was defended at the Council of Basel (1433) by the Taborite bishop, Mikuláš of Pelhřím. Vavřinec of Březov in his Chronicle gives the text of the Articles as they were drawn up and sent 'ad exercitum' in 1420. There were a number of subsequent versions, arranged in varying order.

[75] Cf. the Waldensian position (quoted by Goll-Krofta, op. cit., p. 36): 'Dampnant et reprobant dominum apostolicum mittentem bellatores contra Sarracenos et crucem dantem vel predicantem contra quoscunque paganos.'

[76] 'Quod dominium seculare super diviciis et bonis temporalibus, quod contra preceptum Christi clerus occupat in preiudicium sui officii et dampnum brachii secularis, ab ipso auferatur et ipse clerus ad regulam evangelicam et vitam apostolicam, qua Christus vixit cum suis apostolis, reducatur' (F. R. B., V, p. 393). This point was defended at Basel by Peter Payne. For the standpoint of the early Taborites, see Ktož jsú boží bojovníci, pp. 40, 64. The whole of Wyclif's Dialogus, and much of his earlier De civili dominio are devoted to detailed attacks on the temporal possessions of the clergy, as well as on the very existence of the mendicant orders. Vigorous condemnation of these temporal possessions and of the civil authority enjoyed by the church and the worldliness of the monastic orders is to be found, too, in almost all Chelčický's works, see esp. Sít víry, pp. 247 ff., 277 ff.

ever learn the Czech language properly by means of the German.'[77] He compares elsewhere those who use 'the sword of the temporal power on drunkards and thieves and other sinners, wishing by this sword to conceive Christ's spirit,' to 'a company of priests gathered round an old woman demanding that she should give birth.'[78]

Chelčický's conditional approval of the maintenance of public order by the ruler, in whose own interest he shows such a policy to lie, has given rise to discussion as to how far elements of republicanism or of monarchism can be detected in his works. Historians have seen in him both a defender of monarchical institutions (e.g. Pekář, Urbánek and Vogl) and an embryo Cromwell (e.g. Lenz and Návratil).[79] The Taborite chiliasts had, indeed, preached 'that it is not proper to have kings even by election, for kingship should be handed over to the people.'[80] During much of Chelčický's lifetime Bohemia remained without a king; and at least the more radical Taborites certainly favoured this state of affairs. It seems quite clear, however, that Chelčický considered the kingly office a necessary evil for the 'pagan' world. 'Kingship is needed [he writes in his unpublished tract, *O Svatostech*] to subdue the populace so that everyone should be content with what they have and not reach after others' goods. ... And when as now [i.e. during the interregnum from 1439] order is absent, then the wicked will want to reign over the honest, and whoever had something will have nothing, and whoever did not work will now enjoy the fruits of others' labour.'[81]

But Chelčický is equally emphatic that no Christian could himself become king. He would, in the first place, be usurping a position which in a Christian community rightfully belongs to Christ alone, and ruling it according to entirely contrary principles of conduct. His very reason (*rozum*) should be against it. His conscience also would recoil from doing many things condemned by God, but inseparable from the exercise of kingly power. The Christian has the Law of Love inscribed in the gospels as his guide, and that is sufficient for all branches of life.[82] Urbánek, however, is right in pointing out that Chelčický's 'republicanism' is largely a theocratic ideal, which his doctrine of non-resistance to evil prevents him from any attempt to realize in the field of practical

---

[77] *O trojím lidu*, pp. 49, 97.
[78] 'Replika proti Rokycanovi,' p. 458. See also *Sít' víry*, pp. 165, 218; *Postilla*, II, pp. 108–10.
[79] Pekář, *op. cit.*, p. 188; Urbánek, *op. cit.*, p. 984; Vogl, *op. cit.*, pp. 27, 262.
[80] Krofta, *Listy*, p. 118. See also *Ktož jsú boží bojovníci*, pp. 60, 61.
[81] Quoted by Urbánek, *op. cit.*, p. 936.
[82] *Sít' víry*, pp. 90–95, 104, 156, 163.

politics.[83] It is in the private lives of the small Christian community within a wholly 'pagan' society, in their hearts, that Christ the King has replaced all earthly rulers.

There can be no doubt, however, of Chelčicky's unqualified condemnation of the whole judicial system as well as all the other branches of government, when measured by the precepts of the gospel. This obligation of all true Christians to boycott the organs of justice, to participate in them neither as litigants nor in any executive capacity, may indeed have been taken over from Waldensian doctrine.[84]

Among Christians [he writes] secular courts are a disgrace and a sin.[85]

God never set up [i.e. among them] magistrates (rychtáři) or aldermen (konšele), in order that the Holy Church should appear before them litigating about the goods of this world, nor did he appoint constables (biřici) and hangmen so that its members might hang one another or torture each other on the rack on account of temporal things. Such conduct should be left to the pagan and the worldly. ... For the Holy Church is spiritual and needs only spiritual officials for its edification.[86]

But, granting that Christians should completely ignore the judicial machine, on what principles should they settle any disputes which might arise within their own community? During the very first years of the early church, Chelčicky explained, the imperfection of many of the new converts from Judaism and paganism had led the apostles to ameliorate the stringency of the ban upon all forms of litigation, Matthew, V, 40. They permitted the establishment of courts within their own community, to prevent greater scandal from arising on account of those not yet ripe enough to accept the full Christian doctrine of voluntary suffering appealing in their disputes to the pagan courts (1 Cor. VI, 1–8). Here, as Foustka points out, Chelčicky ran into difficulties in his interpretation, owing to the attempts which had been made by St. Paul to reconcile the growing Christian community with the Roman state.[87] These were only temporary measures, Chelčicky claimed, and the fact that it was the most lowly (nejpotupnější) members of the community who were to act as arbitrators, showed in his opinion that the passage in question could not be taken to

[83] Urbánek, op. cit., pp. 984.
[84] Goll-Krofta, op. cit., p. 36.
[85] O trojím lidu, p. 47.
[86] O církvi svaté, pp. 82, 83. Chelčicky, p. 79, following Wyclif and Hus here, defines the Holy Church as consisting of 'the community of the elect (zbor vyvolených k spasení).' This definition covered, therefore, the relationship of the Christian to every sphere of life and had a much wider application than at present. Cf. Foustka, op. cit., pp. 35, 36.
[87] Foustka, op. cit., p. 10.

justify the contemporary judicial system. The proper method of dealing with shortcomings within the Christian community, the only one indeed consistent with the Law of Love, was quite different; while injury from outside must be suffered in a spirit of humility and love.

The Christian method was that of arbitration and of restitution for damage done, of punishment by exhortation and by rebuke. 'But if the guilty person cannot recompense his brother in any other way, he must humbly do penance [Chelčický went on] and with this his fault shall be forgiven him and a sincere reconciliation take place. In this manner evil shall be curbed, and love and peace shall reign among the brethren.' If all other sanctions failed and the erring brother continued in his evil ways, he was to be expelled from their company. 'No harm should be done him, such as killing him in his sins, but let him be cast out, thereby preserving our own purity.'[88] Such an attitude, applied to the whole community, was incompatible, of course, not only with any form of state organization but, as the Polish branch of the Unity of Brethren were to discover over a century later, when church membership became almost obligatory for the tenants settled on the estates of noblemen belonging to the Unity, it excluded, too, the very conception of an all-embracing state church.[89]

All forms then of punishment based on violence were wrong, and no Christian could apply them. While Chelčický was more sweeping in his condemnation than almost all his contemporaries, protest against the more brutal penal sanctions, especially the death penalty, was indeed widespread amongst the more radical sections of the Hussite movement, a current of opinion which has its parallel, for instance, in Russian history. Once again we are dealing here with a Waldensian tenet of long standing.[90] Advanced theologians like Peter Payne and Nicholas of Dresden, himself strongly impregnated with Waldensian teachings, and in his turn influencing the Taborites, condemned the use of the death penalty as did such popular leaders as Jan Želivský.[91] At the Council of Basel in 1433

[88] Sit' viry, pp. 21–31, 180.
[89] Müller, Geschichte der Böhmischen Brüder, III, pp. 68, 69: 'Diese polnischen Brüdergemeinden auf dem Lande trugen ... einen wesentlich anderen Charakter als die böhmischen und mährischen und waren auch viel weniger widerstandsfähig in Zeiten der Verfolgung oder wenn sie in den Besitz einer katolischen Herrschaft gelangten.'
[90] Goll-Krofta, ibid.; Holinka, Sektařství v Čechách, pp. 23, 163, 178, 182; Neumann, České sekty ve století XIV a XV, pp. 39, 55, 59, 75. Bartoš, J. S. H., 1947, p. 35, here as elsewhere denies the influence of Waldensian doctrine on Chelčický and the early Taborites.
[91] Müller, 'Magister Nikolaus von Dresden,' Zeitschrift für Brüdergeschichte, 1915, p. 102; Hresja, op. cit., II, pp. 51, 80, 92; Pekař, op. cit., pp. 13, 14, 127, 206, 122, 251. J. Sedlak, Hlidka, 1914, p. 625 (quoted by Pekař, p. 206), says of the sermons Nicholas preached in Prague in the summer of 1415 to an audience of priests and students:

Biskupec, during his defence of the punishment of public sin, also attacked
the use of the death penalty in no uncertain terms. Neither Old Testament practice on which his opponent largely based his arguments, nor
any other human law was to be the touchstone of Christian action in this
matter: 'sed lex specialiter evangelica et praxis ecclesie primitive in
punicione reorum est attendenda.' The reform of the criminal was to be
the aim of punishment. Judges were to act as fathers rather than as
tyrants. 'Fateor [he says in explanation] ex quo non possum restituere
vitam occiso, non gaudebo in talibus occisionibus nec faciliter ad mortem
alicuius consenciam.'[92] The more moderate Hussites, however, e.g. Hus
himself, his successor Jakoubek of Stříbro, and the conservative Príbram,
justified the use of capital punishment in certain cases, provided it was
carried out by the properly constituted authorities.[93] The severity of the
prevailing penal laws, when death or the amputation of limbs were
frequent for minor offences and theft was always punished by the death
penalty, was largely responsible for this widespread movement to reform
legal practice.[94] Reaction against the Inquisition's methods and against
the universal custom of executing convicted heretics was also a powerful
factor in the attack against capital punishment.[95]

The words of Christ, writes Chelčický, forbade the execution of the death
penalty on sinners, their murder in a state of sin without repentance,
thereby helping them along to hell on account of their crimes; and even
the Old Testament did not allow the Jews to punish theft with death. 'The
doctors and servants of the Holy Church [he writes] have said that we

---

'No one can reach the truth about the beginnings of the Taborite movement, Chelčický
and the Czech Brethren, without taking these sermons into consideration,' Nicholas
was burnt at Meissen in 1416. See also Bartoš, *Husitství a cizina*, pp. 125–53.

[92] *Orationes* (ed. Bartoš), pp. 5, 53, 54; *Sacrorum conciliorum nova et amplissima
collectio* (ed. Mansi), XXX, p. 357; Yastrebov, *op. cit.*, pp. 86–89. Both Biskupec's
speeches at the Council are reprinted in *Orationes*, while only his reply to his opponent,
Gilles Charlier, as well as the latter's two rejoinders are given in Mansi, XXIX, XXX.
For the Czechs' participation in the Council, see Jacob, *op. cit.*, pp. 81-123. Cf. the
Waldensian standpoint: 'sicut nos non posse vivificare, sic nec debere occidere' (quoted
in Neumann, *op. cit.*, p. 75), which is very similar to that of Biskupec. Only God has the
power to give and take life, likewise argues Chelčický in his 'Replika proti Rokycanovi', p.
392, and it is impossible, as some doctors have argued, to kill with love in one's heart.

[93] Hrejsa, *op. cit.*, II, pp. 90–92, 138, 203. A succession of articles on the subject
issued by both the Prague masters and the Taborite clergy in 1419, 1422, and 1424
expressly allowed capital punishment for incorrigible criminals.

[94] Chaloupecký, *op. cit.*, p. 17. For the Taborites' practical efforts in this direction,
see *Orationes*, p. 34. Cf. J. Huizinga, *The Waning of the Middle Ages* (London, 1955
edition), p. 23, where the late Middle Ages are described as 'the special period of
judicial cruelty.'

[95] Bartoš, *J. S. H.*, 1947, p. 35.

should never lose hope in any man so long as the patience of God may lead him to repentance.'[96] In other words, not punishment but the reform of the criminal was the proper aim of penal method. Like Nicholas of Dresden, Chelčický confirms his argument by reference to the parable of wheat and the tares. Capital punishment, above all, was totally incompatible with Christ's injunction to love one's enemies. 'The executioner who kills is as much a wrong-doer as the criminal who is killed.'[97] In addition, it was only sins against the material well-being of the state and not the more serious offences against the Law of Christ that were punished by the authorities.

But Chelčický held a testimony not merely against the death penalty for any kind of crime, but against all the cruel punishments of his day. Here he was more radical than the Taborites themselves, whose theoretical condemnation at their synods during the early twenties of the death penalty and other forms of physical punishments, as well as of killing in war, was hedged round with such numerous limitations that they largely deprived their protest of any practical effect.[98] The Orphan leader, Ulrich of Znojmo, speaking at the Council of Basel, for instance, claimed that in Hussite Bohemia a priest found sinning with a woman would be castrated, and the legal codes of all countries were for long to retain almost every variation of barbarity.[99] But Chelčický condemned as unchristian all 'cruel punishments . . . torture, blinding, cutting-off of hands, confiscation of estates, deportation from towns.' He should, therefore, be reckoned as one of the earliest and most uncompromising advocates of modern penal reform.[100]

---

[96] *Postilla*, II, p. 131; *Sit' víry*, pp. 31, 141.

[97] *Postilla*, I, pp. 181–83; Pekař, *op. cit.*, p. 206. Chelčický characteristically adds the rather strange argument that through the execution of criminals God is deprived of opportunities of testing the righteous through the former's evildoings.

[98] Yastrebov, *op. cit.*, pp. 67–72.

[99] Jacob, *op. cit.*, p. 107, quoting *Orationes*, p. 132.

[100] *Postilla*, II, pp. 131, 132. For Chelčický's answer to the arguments in defense of the death penalty put forward by Carlier at Basle, see *Sit' víry*, pp. 169–75, 181–87. Annenkov and Patera, 'O nově nalezeném rukopise spisů Petra Chelčického,' *Č. Č. M.*, 1882, p. 282, attribute to Chelčický a short MS. tract, formerly in the archiepiscopal library in Prague and now apparently lost. It is entitled *Pro krádež nenie hodné člověka na smrt vydati*, and deals specifically with the incommensurability of death as a penalty for theft in words which often bring Chelčický to mind. The use of the death penalty in such cases is regarded as inconsistent with the Law of God. The writer of the tract proposes, instead, that incorrigible thieves should be condemned to hard labour under penal conditions for as long as might be necessary for repairing the injury done. Even though, in view of its rather positive attitude to the role of the state and the administration of justice, the tract is probably not actually Chelčický's work, it is interesting as an example of contemporary opinion on the subject.

Though closely connected with his rejection of the whole administrative and judicial system, Chelčický's testimony against oaths, on the other hand, did not hold the key position that it was later to occupy in the arguments of his disciples of the Minor Party in the controversy within the Unity at the end of the century. The words of Christ, Matthew, V, 33–37, appeared to him, too, as a clear injunction not to swear under any circumstances. But, although this alone might have entailed abstention from participation in the state, Chelčický based his arguments, as has been seen, on far wider grounds. The denunciations of oathtaking scattered about his writings are all couched in very general terms, and this practice is rarely singled out for special condemnation. It is possible, however, that Chelčický devoted a separate work to the subject, which is now lost. The taking of oaths had indeed been denounced by the more radical sections of the Hussite movement, even by those far removed from Chelčický's anarchism, as well as by the Waldenses, Cathars and other medieval sects; and abstention from oaths was later to be a feature of many of the radical Reformation sects.[101]

If his objection to oaths found ready consent in Bohemia among many of his contemporaries, Chelčický's testimony against all wars, defensive as well as offensive, was shared by scarcely anyone outside the narrow circle of his Brethren. But this had not always been the case. We have already seen that at the very beginning of the Taborite movement many of its leaders had rejected all violence; though as early as 1417 the idea of reform had already become linked in the popular imagination with the use of force, so that it is difficult to say for certain whether chiliasm moved over from a non-violent into a violent phase or whether both elements had not existed within the movement from the beginning.[102] About this time, indeed, the question whether a Christian was ever justified in taking up arms was being warmly debated among all sections of the Hussite movement. Previously some mediaeval sects, above all the Waldenses,[103] had

[101] *Sít' víry*, p. 99; Müller, *Z. f. B.*, 1915, pp. 94–96; Preger, *op. cit.*, pp. 98, 99; Jagić, Intro., *op. cit.*, p. XXXIV; Jones, *Studies in Mystical Religion*, pp. 135, 142, 143, 211, 260, 366; Neumann, *op. cit.*, pp. 32, 46, 59; Yastrebov, 'Khelchitsky i Gus,' p. 488; Holinka, *op. cit.*, pp. 23, 163, 177, 181, 182. But Hus and the conservative Prague masters expressly allowed oaths. – Hrejsa, *op. cit.*, II, pp. 86, 91. According to Preger a certain watering-down of their testimony against oaths seems to have taken place among the Waldenses towards the end of the fourteenth century.
[102] Pekař, *op. cit.*, pp. 22, 23; Yastrebov, *Etyudy*, pp. 44, 45. The opponents of violence included at first even such later militants as Jan Želivský, Jan of Jičín, and Biskupec himself (Hrejsa, *op. cit.*, II, pp. 92, 141; Pekař, *op. cit.*, pp. 127, 251).
[103] Holinka, *op. cit.*, pp. 23, 67–72, 163. Holinka, however, cites the case of the German-speaking Waldensian peasants on the Rožmberk estates near Jindřichův Hradec in south Bohemia, who in 1340 rose in revolt against their lord as a result of

condemned all warfare, and it was they whom Nicholas of Dresden and the early Taborites had followed in this matter. Neither the Catholic church nor even the later Taborites allowed their priests to participate as combatants in battle.[104] Though this question, therefore, was not entirely new in the fifteenth century, it was, however, the threat of invasion in 1419-20 that gave it its vital importance.

Then two priests, Mikuláš and Václav, who were at that date carrying on a controversy as to the conditions of a just war, appealed to the two most eminent Prague masters, Jakoubek of Stříbro and Křist'an of Prachatice, to give their opinion in this matter. The masters returned an affirmative answer to their first question: 'an domini seculares tenentur gladio materiali defendere legis veritatem?' The priests' second query ran as follows: 'si domini seculares ad tantum sint desides, quod nolunt veritatem gladio accepto defendere, an communitates fideles subiecte possent et debeant eam gladio defendere materiali, adversantes videlicet corporaliter perimendo?' Here the masters hedged their assent round with the most stringent conditions. The right to wage wars, they said, belongs properly to the civil authorities: for the ordinary Christian the best way of resisting evil, the only course of action free from grave dangers, is that of patient suffering. A just war, they believed with Wyclif, needed three prior conditions: 'iusta vendicacio, licita autorisacio et recta intentio.' Only under the most extreme provocation were the people justified in themselves undertaking the defence of God's truth. Neither appellants nor arbitrators, therefore, denied that under certain circum-

---

their bad economic and social conditions. But it is not clear to what degree these sectaries were in fact imbued with Waldensian doctrines.

[104] Goll-Krofta, *op. cit.*, p. 36; Jones, *op. cit.*, pp. 135, 142, 162, 365, 397; Pekař, *op. cit.*, pp. 13, 14, 132–35; Yastrebov, p. 70. According to Preger, *op. cit.*, p. 101, the invasion of 1420 caused the Waldenses in and around Bohemia, like the Taborites, to throw over their objection to defensive wars. Opposition to warfare, at least in theory, may also have been one of the doctrines of the Adamites or 'Picards' who, with their leader Martin Houska-Loquis, represented the radical section of the Taborite movement. Closely akin to the free-thinking Brethren of the Free Spirit they are said by their opponents to have practised nudism and free love. After putting up a fierce resistance, which would seem to disprove any pacifist tendencies on their part, they were savagely suppressed by Žižka in 1421. See *F. R. B.*, V, pp. 517–20. On the other hand, Tůma Přeloučský, *op. cit.*, p. 47, writes of those who were burnt at Klokoty near Tábor in April 1421, that the reason for their persecution was 'because they spoke out against warfare.' Přeloučský was, however, writing some eighty years later, and the other evidence definitely indicates that they put up armed resistance, at least towards the end. Both Chelčický (*O boji duchovním*, pp. 8–10) and the early Brethren were careful to disassociate themselves from them on theological and moral issues. Macek, *op. cit.*, II, pp. 321–31, believes the Adamites were identical with the left-wing chiliasts within the Taborite camp; and this may explain why anti-war doctrines were ascribed to them, since they had shortly before been held by many of the chiliasts.

stances the people could take up arms without the intervention of the civil authorities, still less did they contest the possibility of a just war.[105]

But Chelčický remained firm in his opinion that participation in warfare was quite incompatible with the Christian way of life. We have seen him debating the point with Jakoubek of Stříbro during the most critical months of 1420 with the crusading armies at the gates of Prague. The sixteen years of war that were to follow, its material devastation and the accompanying moral deterioration, only confirmed him in his opinion.

For the sake of the future [he was to write] we should not pass over those things which we have now been suffering, and been eyewitnesses of, for over fifteen years, ... when for reasons of faith one side has risen up against the other in its wrath and savageness. ... What this side has proclaimed as truth, the other has condemned as error. ... The fire they have lit they have been unable to quench. Everywhere murder, rapine, and want have flourished and multitudes have perished. ... Every town in the land has girded itself to battle, has been enclosed with walls and surrounded with moats. ... Whoever would enter or leave the town is imprisoned and robbed and killed. ... On every side there is only want and fear, in the home and in the fields and in the forest and on the mountains. Nowhere can they hide one from another. In the towns and castles every man must be ready for battle. ... Nowhere may one find rest and peace. The labouring people is stripped of everything, downtrodden, oppressed, beaten, robbed, so that many are driven by want and hunger to leave their land. Some even must pay their dues to castle or town thrice over, even four times, now to one side, now to the other.[106] For otherwise

[105] Several other tracts on the same subject, written during the first months of war from standpoints ranging from fiery patriotism to a conditional justification of non-resistance, all grant the legitimacy of Christian participation in war under certain conditions. Chelčický, indeed, appears from his works to have been well acquainted with this early Hussite literature on the war issue. Lengthy extracts from five such documents, as well as the Masters' decision in full, are given in Goll, *Quellen und Untersuchungen*, II, pp. 47–60. See also Pekař, *op. cit.*, pp. 96–102; Yastrebov, *op. cit.*, pp. 55–67; Macek, *op. cit.*, II, pp. 162–70. Goll identifies the two priests, Mikuláš and Václav, as Biskupec and Koranda the elder and dates the decision in November 1419. Bartoš, *Č. Č. M.*, 1914, p. 307, however, puts it forward to January or February 1420, and sees in Václav not Koranda, but another priest called Věněk, founder of Tábor. See also Bartoš, *Husitství a cizina*, p. 156. For the strong influence of Wyclif's *De civili dominio* on the Prague Masters and later the Taborites in their formulation of the conditions of a just war, see Yastrebov, *op. cit.*, pp. 92–95.

[106] Cf. the words of the conservative Utraquist, Jan of Příbram, written in 1429, concerning the failure of the Hussite movement to realize the early hopes entertained by the peasantry of a betterment of their social position (quoted by Krofta, *Dějiny selského stavu*, p. 98): 'Those peasants who used quietly to pay one year's rent (*jeden úrok*) now have to pay such rents five or six times over, as well as other dues. Nor can they be left alone either at home or in the forests or in holes in the earth. Yea! Everything is plundered and ransacked and driven away.' For a discussion how far the material conditions and social status of the peasant deteriorated during the Hussite period, see

they would be driven from house and fields. And what is not taken from them by the castle in dues is eaten up by the armies ... that pray upon the land.

This striking passage brings out clearly the social background on which Chelčický composed his stirring denunciations of the scourge of war.[107] What then was the basis on which Chelčický's pacifism rested, as distinct from the emotional protest which the cruelties and destruction of the contemporary religious conflict aroused in him? War originated in his opinion with Antichrist. 'God cannot say: 'Thou shalt not kill,' since the Beast commands men to kill, hang, burn, execute, destroy villages and homes.'[108] The Old Testament, he agreed, permitted the Jews to fight their enemies; and warfare was also natural among pagans, ignorant of the Christian way of life. But even Maccabeus was for him 'that mighty murderer.' He pointed out, too, that the Jews indeed had been forbidden by God to fight among themselves, a higher standard of conduct than the one common among his contemporary fellow Christians with their constant internecine strife. With the coming of Christ, however, the new Law of Love forbade his disciples to take human life under any circumstances; and this was proved by the example of Christ himself, of his apostles and the early church. All men were now brothers. The Christian's weapons were spiritual, not material; and his aim was to redeem souls and not to destroy bodies and souls. For warfare would inevitably corrupt even the protagonists of a righteous cause. Wars waged by persons claiming to be Christians were more to be condemned even than unjust wars among Jews or pagans.[109] The fact that leading church authorities over the previous thousand years, as well as the most eminent of his contemporaries, had accepted the possibility of a just war carried no weight with Chelčický, when compared to the injunctions of Christ. 'If [St. Peter] himself should suddenly appear from Heaven [he writes] and begin to advocate the sword and to gather together an army in order to defend the truth and establish God's order (zákon boží vysvoboditi) by worldly might, even then I would not believe him.' In trying to convince Christians that warfare was some-

R. R. Betts, 'Social and Constitutional Development in the Hussite Period,' *Past and Present*, no. 7, pp. 50–54.

[107] Müller, 'Starý rukopis dvou spisů Petra Chelčického,' *Č. Č. H.*, 1907, pp. 166, 167, where he gives extracts from a fuller MS. version of the *Postilla*, which he discovered at Nuremberg. Cf. *Sít' víry*, p. 130. For the cruelties inflicted on the peasantry by both armies, see Yastrebov, *op. cit.*, pp. 76, 77.

[108] 'O šelmě a obraze jejím,' *Menší spisy*, I, pp. 40, 41, 64. Chelčický usually identified Antichrist or the Beast with the rulers of church and state.

[109] *O boji duchovním*, pp. 7, 8, 18, 128; *Sít' víry*, pp. 122, 196, 197; 'Řeč svatého Pavla o starém člověku,' *Menší spisy*, II, pp. 51, 52; 'Replika proti Rokycanovi,' p. 386.

times a necessity, he went on, church fathers like St. Augustine and even
Hus himself had drunk 'from the hand of the Great Harlot.' The minis-
tration of the sacraments by Taborite priests 'to murderers and robbers,'
as he calls the soldiers who had taken part in battle, filled him with
disgust.[110] He poured scorn on the blind and false followers of Christ,
who had perverted their master's teachings. He denounced with biting
irony the absurdity of prayers offered for victory. Such prayers, he says,
are 'a terrible blasphemy.'[111] The commandment 'Thou shalt not kill'
was absolute.

Chelčický did not hesitate to express his disagreement here with the
two men of recent times whom he most revered: Wyclif and Hus. The
doctor evangelicus was indeed, like the Prague Masters, an advocate of the
superiority of that spiritual warfare, which Chelčický had taken as the
subject of his first treatise. But his disapproval of all kinds of material
warfare was not an absolute prohibition. 'Sicut anima est dignior corpore
[he wrote] ita debet fidelis pugnam preponere anime et exclusa eius
sufficiencia per invasionem diaboli ad pugnam abstraccionis temporalium
inclinare, et supposito quod ista non sufficiat, tunc . . . hostes corporaliter
expugnare.' Though, this only applied to laymen: 'clerici autem debent
aliam viam securiorem eligere.'[112] Hus, too, in his *Výklad desatera božieho
přikázanie* permitted warfare 'in defence of faith and the truth (*pro obranu
viery a prawdy*),' while at the same time recommending the spiritual fight
with evil as the better way. Hus had been deceived, in Chelčický's view,
by the specious arguments of the doctors of the church, and the use of his
name in justification of recent wars was of great disservice to the cause of
truth. Once again Chelčický showed his remarkable independence of
judgement, his audacity in challenging the most revered authorities.[113]

The path of non-resistance to evil was the only one open to consistent
Christians. They were to conquer by meekness and suffering, and God

[110] 'Replika,' pp. 264, 392, 393, 466.
[111] *Síť' víry*, pp. 193–98, 215–17.
[112] Wyclif, *Sermones*, III, p. 97–105. It was probably, however, from *De civili
dominio* that Chelčický learnt of Wyclif's viewpoint on war. At least some of the
Lollards, according to the testimony of their clerical opponents, appear to have been
more absolute in their condemnation of both war and capital punishment than their
master. See also Hoch, *op. cit.*, pp. 138–40, 143, 338, 441. Hoch considers that
Chelčický's pacifism was largely derived from Wyclif's more moderate position.
[113] 'Replika proti Rokycanovi,' pp. 264, 392; Yastrebov, 'Khelchitsky i Gus,' pp.
485–88. See also Hoch, *op. cit.*, pp. 137, 138, 193, 194. It was not indeed until Wyclif's
protest against war became known in the Czech lands, that the question as to whether
warfare was consistent with Christianity was debated by Czech theologians and moralists.

would protect them even during the worst persecution. Anyhow, those who suffered for their faith in this life would get their reward in the next: while those who had stirred up strife and warfare would inevitably receive eternal damnation as their portion. In view of this, 'it would, therefore, be shameful to fight or to quarrel over material injustice, over worldly goods.'[114] But the contemporary church, 'unmindful of God's flock, false shepherds, have fled from Him in time of trial and have walled themselves in castles and towns, stirring up wars and shedding men's blood.' Over against all such false Christians, priests or laymen, unwilling to undergo persecution, Chelčický puts his ideal of the early church. 'Humble and lowly (*pěší*) people [he calls them] who, when kings and princes came against them, prayed to God, dispensing with shield and firearms (*pušky*).'[115] As indeed Tolstoy was later to realize, it is his doctrine of non-resistance, central to his whole philosophy, that determines Chelčický's significance in the history of political thought. It is his attitude on this question, too, that marks him off from all his contemporaries in the Hussite movement.[116]

During the long war years the peasantry, especially, were frequently conscripted against their will into one or other of the opposing armies. Chelčický bitterly complains of such practices. 'In time of war [he says] you make warriors (*rytíři*) of tanners and shoemakers and weavers, of anyone able to wield a club. ... For neither the king nor the princes nor the nobles nor the lesser gentry do the fighting themselves, but compel their peasants to do it for them.'[117] 'The people [he writes elsewhere] are herded together like sheep and driven to the slaughter.' They are forced by the combined authority of church and state to a course of action utterly contrary to the Christian gospel, Christian against Christian, brother against brother, men 'whose consciences otherwise might draw back from killing and robbing their fellows.' But 'they have neither sufficient understanding, nor charity enough, to realize that they should prefer to die at the hands of their lord than commit such evil acts.' Princes and prelates ought not be obeyed when they command evil things. Therefore, since participation in war was inconsistent with the gospel teachings, Christians should refuse military service; and, if all did this, 'whom would the rulers find to accompany them to the wars (*s kým by páni na vojnu jeli*)?' Although, as Chelčický admits, this would inevitably bring down

---

[114] *Sít' víry*, pp. 157, 200.
[115] *O trojím lidu*, p. 70; *Postilla*, I, p. 320.
[116] Kulbakin, *op. cit.*, pp. 66, 67; Peschke, *op. cit.*, p. 189.
[117] 'Replika,' p. 393.

persecution from the side of 'those paganized rulers,' nevertheless, 'according to the faith they must be more eager to be put to the sword than to commit such actions contrary to God's commandment.'[118]

A strongly-felt sentiment of internationalism was a natural corollary to Chelčický's pacifism. The Hussite revolution, both in its genesis and during the course of its history, was to some extent a nationalist reaction to the encroaching German element. Traces of national feeling, as Czech historians have been quick to point out, are not absent from Chelčický's writings. They are, however, rather implicit, half formed and never aggressive in expression. The Church for him was international. 'Everywhere, among all nations and languages [he writes] there have been people who have believed in the gospel as preached by the apostles.' For the Christian every human being in distress is a neighbour to be helped. 'If anyone, a Jew or a heathen or a heretic or an enemy, is ever in need, then according to our principles of love it is our duty to see that he does not die from hunger or cold or any other calamity.' Only for the false Christians did the boundaries of speech and nationality play any role in defining their attitude to their fellows.[119]

Chelčický was not only an opponent of national animosities. He was to direct his fiercest invective against contemporary social inequalities and the theories by which class divisions were justified. As we have seen, Hus and his predecessors had championed both in theory and practice the rights of the small craftsmen and peasants. They proclaimed the moral superiority of the simple countryman. But neither Hus's predecessors, nor any party within the Hussite movement, had consistently advocated a total revolution in social relationships: the abolition of serfdom (*poddanství*) and the establishment of an egalitarian society. The Taborite chiliasts in 1419-20 had, it is true, preached a complete reversal of the existing social order. But the disappointment of their hopes of Christ's second put an end to these communistic dreams after a few months; and by the autumn of 1420 the Taborites, under Žižka's leadership, had returning to the old social pattern.

While he did not share their apocalyptic delusions, Chelčický came very near to the chiliasts in his social ideals. He protested, above all, against the traditional arguments on which the existing inequalities were based, against the theory of 'the threefold people,' the three estates into which the Christian commonwealth was divided: the nobility, clergy, and commonalty. The first two estates, according to this conception, repre-

[118] *Sít' víry*, pp. 67, 150.
[119] *Ibid.*, p. 20; *Postilla*, II, p. 243, 250; Urbánek, *op. cit.*, p. 985.

sented the divine and the human elements in Christ's mystical body, which were united with the third element, the working people, destined to serve their material needs, by the bonds of Christian love as members together of Christ's Body. The lords temporal were to defend society by arms; the clergy's task was to follow the way of Christ in poverty and in prayer and to teach the laity; while the third estate were to carry the whole burden of supporting the other two estates by their manual labour. The Taborites, after rejecting the communism of their chiliastic period, had taken over this theory from Wyclif – as Yastrebov has shown clearly by comparing extracts from the Taborite Manifesto of 1431, addressed to the rest of Catholic Europe, with identical passages taken from Wyclif's *Dialogus*.[120] It was, therefore, to them that Chelčický addressed the refutation of this conception that he wrote in the middle twenties. But even before *O trojím lidu* he had outlined his opposition to current theory in *O církvi svaté*, just as he was to return to this theme in his later works.[121]

Chelčický saw in a society founded on class inequalities the antithesis of a Christian social order. It was as completely pagan as the violence on which its whole structure rested. Since he denied, as we have seen, the need for armed force in a Christian society, the only justification for the privileges of the nobility, whose task it was to protect the other two estates, lost thereby its validity. The granting of titles meant giving that homage to men which should be reserved for God alone. The superiority of these 'coroneted escutcheons (*erby korunované*),' as he scornfully calles members of the nobility, was based solely on robbery and violence. Their ancestors had obtained property and titles either through force of arms or by money. 'If they now had no money in addition to their birth, hunger would force them to drop their coats-of-arms and take to the

[120] Yastrebov, *Etyudy*, pp. 155, 156; *O trojím lidu*, pp. 99, 100. Wyclif's version ran as follows: 'Ecclesia autem militancium ... dicitur communiter tripartita, scilicet ecclesia clericorum qui debent esse propinquissimi ecclesie triumphanti et iuvare residuum ecclesie militantis, ut sequatur Christum propinquius. ... Secunda pars militantis ecclesie dicitur esse militum ita, quod sicut prima pars istius ecclesie dicitur instrumentum oratorum, ita secunda pars ecclesie dicitur corporalium defensorum. Tercia vero pars ecclesie dicitur wulgarium vel laboratorum. Et in harmonia ista trium parcium ad imitacionem trinitatis increate consistit sanitas corporis istius ecclesie militantis.' (from *De Christo et suo adversario Antichristo*, p. 33). Cf. *Dialogus*, pp. 2–5, which contain the passages actually cited by Chelčický from the Czech translation; Tomáš of Štitný, *Knižké šestero o obecných věcech křesťanských* (ed. K. J. Erben), 1852, IV, quoted in Helinka's edition of *O trojím lidu*, pp. 17–21. This theory of 'the three-fold people' was of course common in medieval times throughout Western Europe. Chaloupecký, 'Štitný a Chelčický,' *Č. M. M.*, 1914, p. 77, considers that Chelčický's attacks on this theory were directed more against Štitný's fuller exposition of it than against either Wyclif or the Taborites.

[121] *O církvi svaté*, pp. 82–85; *Sít' víry*, p. 43.

plough [he writes]. Wealth alone, therefore, sustains the honour of their
nobility and the fame of their birth. .... Lacking money, they would soon
sink back to the level of the peasantry and, as they scorn work, they would
often go hungry.' They were at present only able to live out their lives in
idleness and luxury because of the labour of their peasants. 'If this disappeared, their noble birth would decay miserably.' Chelčický's denoun-
ces their whole way of life: their refined luxuries, their class education,
their pride, their loose morals, their unwillingness to suffer wrong as
Christians should, their contempt for manual work, and their oppression
of the workers. Even their frequent ablutions were in his eyes an abomi-
nation, 'a burden to the servants.' The nobles were only a millstone round
the necks of the hardworking common people, 'useless drones' who only
corrupt others by the bad example of their lives.

Serfdom, that bastion of the feudal order, is for Chelčický a sin against
God and man. 'If your forefathers [he says, addressing the nobility and
gentry] bought human beings together with their hereditary rights to the
property, then they bought something that was not theirs to buy and sell.'
Christ has redeemed mankind with his blood: how, then, do so-called
Christians dare to traffic in human lives? All their legal documents will
not be of any avail on the Day of Judgement (*A nepomuož tu nic kaupení
ani zápisové ve desky vepsaní*). For there is no basis for social inequalities
in Christianity, where, 'when one member suffers, all the other members
suffer with him.' 'They are quite unable to show any passage from God's
scriptures [he writes] why, apart from their superior descent, they are any
different from other people.' They are indeed doubly accursed, he cries,
once through original sin and a second time by reason of their noble
birth.[122]

The privileges of the clergy, too, the close association between church
and state, originated with Antichrist. The task allotted the priesthood of
preaching the Christian gospel of love, forgiveness, and humility, to the
nobility, whose very existence depended on violence and inequality, and
to the commonalty, whose status in itself meant a denial of Christian
brotherhood, was an absurdity. 'It is as if someone were to forbid the
bakers to bake [he writes] and at the same time order the people to eat.'

Let priests work like other honest men 'and not become a burden on
the labouring community (*aby duchovní kněžie na obec robotný* [*ne*]
položili se).' They should set a good example of industry, should do
nothing to justify the taunt that they had chosen their calling from
material considerations, 'though worthy preachers [he concedes] should

[122] *Sit' víry*, pp. 114–16, 221–34; *O trojím lidu*, pp. 63–72; *Postilla*, I, pp. 197, 320.

not be disallowed from taking those things necessary.' As with Wyclif and the Hussites in general, monks and mendicant friars were especially singled out by Chelčický for attack. He accuses them of leading a luxurious life at the expense of the working people. 'Some are as strong as horses [he writes] ... and are more fit to work than aged peasants.' Tithes, too, should be abolished. The apostles had not considered themselves as a specially privileged class within society. Work was the hall-mark of every true member of the Christian community.[123]

Indeed, I trust God [writes Chelčický] that till my dying day I shall never assent to this doctrine concerning Christ's Body, which holds it right that these two arrogant estates [i.e. nobility and clergy] should exempt themselves [from hard work] and lay the whole burden on the common folk, should as it were ride upon them, and consider themselves superior within Christ's Body to the commonalty on whom they ride, these subject to them, not as one limb to another, but as beasts whom it is of little account to work to death.[124]

Chelčický was certainly ruthless in his analysis of the class basis of the society of his day. In the conflict which he revealed between feudal landlords and serf peasantry, he stood unhesitatingly with the latter. Chaloupecký has pointed out with some justification that the apostle of non-violence was not uninfluenced by the general atmosphere of social hatred generated by the reform movement; and that some may have misunderstood his message, conceiving it as one of revenge and violence against the ruling classes.[125] Apart from the acerbity of his language the element of revenge is not altogether absent: only it is postponed until the after-life. During his first sojourn on earth Christ was meek and loving, he writes, 'but at the end he will come in his might to destroy all the great and proud of this earth ... who have oppressed the poor and devoured the fruit of their labour and ruled with cruelty over them. Then will you see the Lord, the avenger of the poor. ... It will go hard in that time with the lords of the earth, who have ridden without mercy on the backs of the labouring poor, whom Christ has redeemed,' Such passages, indeed, are not far removed in tone from the voices of the chiliasts, the mouthpieces of the downtrodden proletariat of town and country.[126] But in this world

---

[123] *O trojím lidu*, pp. 57–59, 72–74; *O církvi svaté*, p. 84; *Síť víry*, pp. 247–67. The rule that priests should keep themselves by some form of manual work was put into practice by the Unity of Czech Brethren and later by the more radical Reformation sects.
[124] *O trojím lidu*, p. 71.
[125] Chaloupecký, *Selská otázka*, p. 45.
[126] *Postilla*, I, p. 20; II, pp. 82–94. See also the 'Articuli Valdensium' from the last decade of the fourteenth century, which show similar sentiments: 'Item dicunt ...

reform, according to Chelčický, could only come by the conversion of the powerful through the long-suffering patience of the oppressed.

The positive side of Chelčický's social doctrine was never so well developed as his critical analysis. He was a prophet crying in the wilderness rather than the patient reformer bent on a gradual transformation of society. Kautsky, for instance, has seen in Chelčický 'a communist in the primitive Christian sense.'[127] Though indeed he did not expressly condemn property in itself, apart from inordinate wealth or its improper use, the apostolic poverty of the first Christians remained Chelčický's ideal throughout. 'If man was not deceived by avarice [he asks] why should he need property (*zbožie*) or take any heed of worldly things?' His views on property, indeed, recall Wyclif's theory of *dominium*.[128] 'Whoever is not of God [writes the Czech] cannot truly enjoy or hold anything belonging to God, except as the man of violence unlawfully enjoys and holds what is not his own.' The whole earth belongs to God: therefore only those who were putting into practice the principle of Christian equality had a real claim to the use of enough to satisfy the bare necessities of existence. The path of voluntary poverty was the only way open to a true Christian, indeed the only rational course in view of the vanity of temporal things. His injunction to give alms to the poor would seem to show, however, that Chelčický did not advocate communism of goods – at least as an immediately practicable solution.[129]

Asceticism, otherworldliness, was a prominent feature of Chelčický's philosophy. This is particularly evident in his negative attitude to the refinements and amenities of urban civilization. He speaks here as the representative of a peasant culture, a protagonist in the long battle between town and country. Town life in his opinion is inseparable from violence and deceit. Cain founded the first city to protect himself from

---

cardinales, archiepiscopos, episcopos, imperatores, reges, duces, principes et omnes iudices, tam spirituales, quam seculares una cum presbyteris esse dampnandos' (quoted in Holinka, *Sektařství v Čechách*, p. 177).

[127] Kautsky, *Communism in Central Europe in the Time of the Reformation*, p. 79. Communistic tenets were certainly held by many medieval sectaries, especially the Waldenses, though the practice of apostolic poverty was probably confined only to their priesthood, see Keller, *Die böhmischen Brüder und ihre Vorläufer*, p. 31; Jones, *op. cit.*, pp. 144, 145, 200, 208, 319, 320, 249, 354, 365. Community of goods was preached, for instance, by Nicholas of Dresden and the Taborite chiliasts (Pekař, *op. cit.*, p. 14), and even among orthodox theologians property rights during the Middle Ages were never considered absolute (Vogl, *op. cit.*, p. 267).

[128] For the influence of this doctrine from the beginning of the fifteenth century on Hus and his contemporaries, see Betts, *Slavonic Review*, Dec. 1952, pp. 23, 31–35.

[129] *O boji duchovním*, pp. 73–80, 124; *Postilla*, I, pp. 169, 420; II, pp. 87, 88, 133, 270; *Síť víry*, pp. 73–76, 115; 'O šelmě a obraze jejím,' *Menší spisy*, I, pp. 54, 55.

the consequences of murdering his brother, and as a result the former simplicity of life was lost for ever. This myth, indeed, derives from a very strained interpretation of Genesis, IV, 17, not unknown among other medieval writers. Apeing the manners of the nobility, the townspeople in turn exercise a corrupting influence on the countryside. Few, coming into contact with their way of life, are strong enough to escape its snares. Surrounded by walls to protect their illgotten possessions, the burghers are unable, even if they wished, to follow in Christ's footsteps, nor will they suffer those who attempt to do so. Instead, they live in constant fear of losing their lives and goods. If the ruling elements ever became true Christians, 'they would fill in their moats and tear down their walls.' They would abandon their whole satanic way of life. But only the urban proletariat, those 'who own neither houses within the city nor land without,' were likely to favour such a policy.

In Chelčický's opinion, it was 'difficult to sell or buy without sin on account of excessive greed,' and for him a trader was 'one who has the mark of the Beast.' 'Every kind of trade and profit-making occupation connected with the town should be avoided in order not to harm one's soul.' Markets and fairs were equally immoral, as were the taverns and usurious practices always to be found in the towns. Only agriculture and certain crafts, necessary for even the simplest existence, were permissible. Chelčický condemned the use of weights and measures as well as boundary marks, likewise produced by Cain, the outward symbols of unchristian mistrust. His ideal seems to have been a loose association of independent and self-sufficient village republics founded on a barter economy.[130]

As with Matěj of Janov Chelčický's ideal, then, was 'the simple man.' University learning, the erudition of the schoolmen, filled him with loathing. Suspicion of higher studies had been strong among the Waldenses[131] and early Taborites;[132] and even Wyclif,[133] as well as Hus and his predecessors, while not condemning them as such, were highly critical of

---

[130] *Sít' víry*, pp. 98, 234–47; *O trojím lidu*, p. 74; *Menší spisy*, I, pp. 33, 41. According to Pekař, *op. cit.*, p. 187, add. note 2, the early Taborites also objected to trade and commerce, usury and taverns, and classed a number of other occupations as immoral; while, according to Chelčický himself, *Sít' víry*, p. 239, the legend about Cain is taken from Wyclif (cf. his *De civili dominio*, I, p. 152). A similar position as regards usury was taken up by many contemporary church authorities.

[131] 'Dampnant et reprobant omnia studia privilegiata ... Universitates scholarum Parisiensis, Pragensis, Viennensis et aliarum reputant inutiles et temporis perditionem' (Goll-Krofta, *op. cit.*, p. 36). See also Holinka, *Sektářství v Čechách*, pp. 118, 119, 178, 182.

[132] *Ktož jsú boží bojovníci*, pp. 38, 39, 61, 64.

[133] Wyclif, *Dialogus*, pp. 53–55.

the universities' failings and inconsistencies, their immersion in scholastic subtleties. On the other hand, by their emphasis on the Bible, by their use of the vernacular tongue, these reformers were a powerful factor in the spread of popular education.[134] Chelčický likewise, while inveighing against the university masters – *roty mistruo kolejských*, as he slightingly calls them – stresses the need for all to be able to read the scriptures for themselves, even though this may give rise to dangers in interpretation. 'It is not enough [he writes] ... that some learned person knows the Bible, a rector or prelate, if the simple man does not also know and understand it for himself.' Chelčický saw clearly that education was too often misued for the purpose of perpetuating class differences. The treatment meted out at Constance to Hus and Jerome of Prague had shown him that learning had become an instrument in the hands of the state, that truth had ceased to be its goal. He does not indeed condemn learning in itself, provided it teaches nothing contrary to the New Testament, no doctrine not to be found there. Even so, learning is not necessary to mankind's salvation, and judged by its fruits it is indeed evil. Simple faith is, therefore, to be prized above all the learning of the universities. 'If only they would cease to look down on the unlettered [thus he appeals to 'the wise'] and try out instead God's gospel, proclaiming it to the people, the simple would indeed bear no grudge against them' for their learning.[135]

The puritanism in art and culture, which was a marked feature among the Waldenses as well as among almost all sections of the Hussite movement, was also present in Chelčický.[136] All matters connected with the world were dangerous for the soul's salvation. Music and singing in church services, he argues, were wrong since they tended to distract the congregration from the real purpose of their attendance, the worship of God. Cultural refinements, worldly luxuries – 'lovely and delightful things, colours, fine costumes, beautiful dresses, scents, tasty dishes, out-of-the-way objects, soft raiment, fine rooms, physical beauty in man or woman' – were all snares set by the devil for the unwary; and Chelčický returns repeatedly to this theme. He saw, indeed, in the amenities of civilization, in art and culture, solely the privileges of the upper classes, who were only able to indulge their aesthetic tastes through the oppression of the masses. 'Even a great kingdom [he writes] cannot satisfy its king nor a great estate its lord on account of such display and bottomless

---

[134] Urbánek, *Jednota bratrská a vyšší vzdělání*, pp. 5–17.
[135] *O boji duchovním*, pp. 121–25; *Sít' víry*, pp. 228, 267–74.
[136] Pekař, *op. cit.*, pp. 8, 203. Cf. Rokycana's fulminations, as fiery in expression as Chelčický's, against all kinds of extravagance in matters of dress, Hrubý, *op. cit.*, pp. 144–46.

greed. Violence, therefore, must be applied to their own poor and the poor of other lords.' Social as well as moral considerations, the good of the whole, demanded the abolition of a culture based on violence, oppression and social inequality.[137]

At the outset of the Hussite movement the element of social protest had, indeed, been a powerful driving force. But the only classes to derive permanent gain from the long years of war were the nobles and gentry, who had ousted the church from political power and confiscated its lands for themselves, and the wealthier townsmen, who had taken over the privileged position of their former German rivals. After 1420, even among the Taborites, democratic and communistic tendencies began to disappear under pressure from the representatives of the minor gentry, whose leadership was essential for carrying on the war. The battle of Lipany (1434) merely marked the completion of this process of social reaction. War, therefore, had brought only misery to the peasants and urban proletariat, while at the same time the political and social aims with which they had set out were no nearer fulfilment. The peasants' legal status, in particular, deterioriated steadily throughout the century.[138]

Chelčický's teachings, with their negation of the state and all forms of violence, now began to find a ready hearing among the disappointed peasants and small craftsmen, deceived in their hopes of social betterment through war and state action.[139] The first step towards the establishment of a Unity of Brethren independent of church and state, taken in 1457-58 probably still during Chelčický's life-time, marked, therefore, the fusion of his theoretical protest with the increasing discontent of the masses with the results of the war to defend God's word. *Pravda vítězi*, the Hussite leaders had proudly proclaimed. But for the downtrodden in town and country, as for Chelčický himself, the Truth had not prevailed.

---

[137] *O boji duchovním*, p. 13; *Postilla*, I, p. 105; II, p. 85; 'Replika proti Rokycanovi,' pp. 269, 270; *Síť víry*, p. 232.

[138] Krofta, *Listy*, pp. 126–35; *Dějiny selského stavu*, pp. 97–103; Chaloupecký, *op. cit.*, pp. 55–60; Pekař, *op. cit.*, chap. XIV.

[139] Mágr, 'Piotr Chelczycki i Szymon Budny,' *Przegląd Zachodni*, 1951, pp. 390–95, accepting Bartoš's recent theories as proved, sees in Chelčický a representative of the interests of the minor gentry. But, as for instance Foustka, *op. cit.*, p. 69, has shown, Chelčický – whatever may actually have been his social origins – was in fact speaking on behalf of the peasantry among whom he lived, championing the rights of those who had remained in their villages and not been drawn into one or other of the opposing armies.

THE OLD BRETHREN

The origins of the Unity of Brethren reach back to the middle fifties of the fifteenth century. Founded during the winter of 1457-58, the Unity form-ally broke both with Rome and the official Utraquist church a decade later, in 1467, by instituting its own separate priesthood and dispens-ing with the usual channels of apostolic succession. Though the Unity, which concerned itself little with complicated theological problems, still maintained the seven church sacraments, and for long transubstantiation and the celibacy of its clergy as well, its action was a revolutionary one even in fifteenth-century Bohemia. Indeed, during the reign of King George of Poděbrady, in 1461 and again from 1468–71, the Unity was to meet on this account with severe persecution at the hands of the authorities.

But from the accession of King Vladislav II in 1471 until the beginning of the next century, the Brethren were to enjoy a period of comparative quiet and freedom from outside interference. This was due in large measure to the increasing power of the great nobles, who in some cases found it to their advantage to extend protection to the communities of industrious and frugal Brethren established on their estates. Vladislav II's reign, therefore, was a period of fairly steady growth in numbers and influence, when an efficient administrative organization was set up to govern the young church. At the top was the chief elder – or bishop, as he was to be known in the next century – with his council (*Úzká rada*) of lay and clerical advisers, who acted together as the executive organ of the Unity, responsible only to synods or general assemblies held at first at irregular intervals and composed of all the priests in charge of the local congregations and of the lay functionaries of the church. The end of the century was to mark an epoch in the history of the Unity: the renewal of persecution on the part of the state and, more important, the abandon-ment by the overwhelming majority of its members of the radical political and social doctrines, which give a specific character to what may be termed the period of the Old Brethren.

Half a century earlier, with the predominance won by George of Poděbrady in 1448 and his entry into Prague in the same year accompanied by the archbishop-elect, Jan Rokycana, the prospects for Utraquism had brightened. But the final destruction of Tábor in 1452 and the arrival in Bohemia of the young Catholic King, Ladislav, signified a new turn of events: many feared a return to the state of affairs which had existed in the years following Sigismund's assumption of the crown in 1436, since Poděbrady himself was now pursuing a conciliatory policy towards the papal court. These fears were shared, too, by Rokycana as the official head of the Utraquist church; and they soon led to an estrangement between him and Poděbrady.

The tone of Rokycana's sermons, which he was now able to give in his old church, the Týn church in Prague, became increasingly outspoken. He began to denounce abuses in church and state, to call for a return to the pattern of primitive Christianity, a theme in line with early Hussite thought. Here Matěj of Janov and Jakoubek of Stříbro provided his inspiration. He spoke out against excessive wealth, against the pride and ostentation of the rich, made possible only through the labours of the poor, against the oppression of the peasantry by their lords, who cloaked their avarice under a pretence of maintaining order, against usury, the taking of oaths, and the use of the death penalty for such crimes as theft. Any eagerness to shed blood, said Rokycana, was unbecoming in a Christian. The adoption by many Czechs of soldiering as a profession, the increasing number of men who became mercenaries, met with his sternest disapproval. Trade, industry, and commerce, too, were to be carried on only according to strictly defined rules; and the luxurious and sinful life of the richer burghers was condemned in the strongest terms. Indeed, in Rokycana's opinion, the simple country folk were more concerned to attain salvation than those who lived in towns, where the temptation to yield to sin was so much greater. In general, he tended to extol the virtues of the poor and oppressed over against the tyranny and moral corruption of the upper classes. Officials and judges were to act justly and not oppress the poor and the weak. Those who sought office to satisfy a lust for power or fame were no better than thieves or even murderers.

In spite of their radical colouring, however, Rokycana's sermons were essentially the product of a man, whose aim was 'to choose the middle way (*v mieru uchoditi*).'[1] It was only excesses that were condemned. For wealth might be put to good purpose. Civil government and the existing social system could be instruments of God's will if rightly administered.

[1] *Postilla Jana Rokycany*, II, p. 934.

Rokycana did not in fact condemn all war, every form of oath, the use of the death penalty for exceptionally grave crimes. For his belief that the only outcome of war was to 'fill the air with the cries of the poor, the earth with blood and hell with spirits,' and his reference to the parable of the wheat and the tares in connection with the death penalty, was not necessarily tantamount to an absolute prohibition of these two institutions. No more did he ever conceive of a social order in which class divisions did not exist. Almsgiving, the exercise of Christian charity by the rich, was to offset some of the grosser forms of social inequality, but – like Hus and most of his contemporaries and predecessors – he left the framework of feudal society untouched.[2]

Often, however, the followers whom such a leader easily gathers around him are not prepared to draw back from the logical consequences of their master's doctrine, from those conclusions which he himself expressly rejects. This, indeed, was to be the case with Rokycana.

His sermons were given probably over a period of more than a year, from April 1454 to July 1455. Rokycana's eloquence as a preacher, the simple and comprehensible language in which he spoke, free from learned theological formulae, attracted many listeners; and a group soon arose among those who regularly attended, which met from time to time to discuss the subjects raised in the course of their delivery. One of the group was designated to note down their contents. Few personal details about these individual 'hearers (*posluchače*)' have come down. Krasonický, a leading member of the Unity, was later to write that they were drawn both from simple men and also from the ranks of 'the learned, students and scholars,'[3] in fact from the intelligentsia of the capital.

We know the name of at least one priest who was a member of the group: Martin of Krčín, one of the earliest Brethren. But its acknowledged leader was Řehoř, Rokycana's nephew and the future founder of the Unity. A member of the minor gentry who worked as a tailor for his living, then aged about thirty, Řehoř had originally been a follower of the

---

[2] *Ibid.*, esp. I, pp. X–XIV, 7, 22–25, 92, 93, 100, 106, 272, 273, 336, 417, 426, 494–500, 522, 523, 746, 747, 794–96, 831, 832; II, pp. 73, 74, 134, 174–79, 188–92, 365, 550, 556, 714-18, 850-53; Hrubý, *České postilly*, pp. 129-49; Goll, 'Rokycanova Postilla, Č. Č. M.,' 1879, pp. 62, 63, 70, 201–06; Bartoš, 'Neznámá díla Jana Rokycany v musejních rukopisech,' Č. Č. M., 1919, pp. 12, 13. Rokycana's *Postilla*, which finally took on its present form in the early years of George of Poděbrady's reign, to some extent represents a toned-down version of his sermons of the middle fifties, which he may even have begun to preach as early as 1453. They have not, however, survived in their original form.

[3] Krasonický, 'O učených,' fol. 7v. Cf. Blahoslav, *O původu Jednoty bratrské a řádu v ní*, p. 36.

conservative Utraquist, Jan of Příbram, and had for a number of years been an inmate of the Hussite monastery *na Slovanech*, while remaining a layman throughout. He had apparently had little formal education, though he possessed some knowledge of Latin. But he was a man of remarkable energy with an outstanding gift for organization and for inspiring others with his own enthusiasm. He was in fact a born leader.

Řehoř and the other members of his group appear to have interpreted Rokycana's fiery words in a more radical spirit than the preacher himself had meant them; or, possibly, the latter in the heat of the moment expressed himself in more unqualified terms than he would normally have used, and his words were seized upon by his followers as confirmation of their own views. For instance, on the subject of oaths and war they read into them a total condemnation along Chelčický's lines, which it is evident was not the Master's intention. 'You used to brand as evil [the Brethren were to write to him in 1468] swearing or going to war in one's own person in order to kill others.'[4] Later, Rokycana himself was to deny explicitly the validity of that hostility to the state in all its manifestations, which the early Brethren were to adopt from Chelčický. The Christian position, he wrote, was 'not, as some maintain, that no one should be constrained and compelled. That is a lie. But rather, anyone who has accepted the faith may be constrained and forced to keep and preserve it aright as he promised on baptism.' It was the Christian duty of those in authority, the kings and princes, lords and squires, to enforce right living on the refractory.[5]

Nevertheless, the source of many of the Unity's later ideas in the political, social, and moral field can be traced back to the words that the earnest young men heard at this period from Rokycana's pulpit and to the inferences that they drew from them.

Not only had Rokycana implanted in his followers the seeds of the ideas from which the Unity was later to grow, he was also to be responsible for directing their attention to the man whose direct influence on the Unity, especially as regards its social and political doctrines, was to be even greater than his own. Petr Chelčický was then nearing the end of his life, and his contact with Brother Řehoř and Rokycana's 'hearers' is the

---

[4] *Akty Jednoty bratrské* (ed. Bidlo), I, Intro. p. 49, text pp. 53, 605; Goll-Krofta, *Chelčický a Jednota v XV století*, pp. 62–64, 68–72, 88–90; Hrejsa, *Dějiny křest'anství v Československu*, III, pp. 93–95, 109, 113, 125–27; Müller-Bartoš, *Dějiny Jednoty bratrské*, pp. 20-22, 27, 29; Tapié, *Une église tchèque au XVe siècle: L'Unité des Frères*, pp. 37–42; Urbánek, *Věk poděbradský*, III, pp. 726–29; Vlček, *Dějiny české literatury*, I, pp. 189–92. For Řehoř, see Bartoš's essay in *Světci a kacíři*, pp. 224–43.

[5] *Postilla Jana Rokycany*, II, p. 852.

last incident in it of which we have certain record. The Brethren were later to remind Rokycana that, during the period when he was giving his famous sermons, 'he had praised Petr Chelčický before us; then later [they add] we spoke with him and read his works.' The Chelčický Brethren lent them two of their master's books, one on Antichrist and later another on 'the temporal power (*moc světská*),' which has usually been identified as *O trojím lidu*. At that period however Rokycana's disciples were so much under his influence that they at once brought these books back to him for his opinion. 'We sent you the books we received from them [they wrote in 1468] and, if you had disapproved, it is very doubtful, indeed, if we should have accepted them (*a by ty byl nám zhyzdil, nevíme, bychom byli přijali*).'

It is indicative, too, of the radicalism of Rokycana's outlook at that time that apparently he did not feel called to say a word of criticism, even about Chelčický's views on civil government, with which he was certainly in basic disagreement. However, a reading of Chelčický's works soon began to raise doubts in the minds of Rokycana's disciples as to the consistency of the bold words, which they heard from their master's pulpit, and his actual position as the head of a state church, as one of the main bulwarks of the existing social order. 'From all this [they wrote of the effect which Chelčický's works had upon them] we saw that there was much evil in priests and people, so that we finally came to doubt even about you; whether you did not do in fact that which you held to be wrong.' Indeed, by putting his disciples into touch with Chelčický Rokycana had unwittingly laid the first brick in the edifice of a rival church.[6]

A feeling of spiritual unrest, a desire to discover similar religious communities free from the blemishes of the state religion, in particular the search for priests of pure life from whom the sacraments might be received without fear of their being tainted by the prevailing moral corruption: all these motives impelled Řehoř and others from his circle to make contact, not only with Chelčický and his Brethren, but also with other religious groups, with those small bands of seekers which had sprung up at that period within the Utraquist church. They were in close touch with Martin Lupáč, Rokycana's assistant bishop and a theologian of radical views. They visited the community which had been established in the former Benedictine monastery of Vilémov, but were later repelled by irregularities in its eucharistic practice, as well as by the fact that these Vilémov Brethren were accustomed 'to accept wealth, as well as dues, from the peasants

---

[6] Bidlo, *op. cit.*, p. 3, 13, 14, 606. See also Krasonický, *op. cit.*, fol. 8v.

and from their woods, not resting content with their tithes and free-will offerings.'[7]

It is difficult, indeed, to discover why Rokycana's 'hearers' did not use Chelčický's group as the nucleus for a new religious community. Possibly they did not consider Chelčice remote enough from the world, probably too the split which occurred soon after Chelčický's death, when the so-called Vitanovice Brethren broke away from the main group, suspected by them of a Taborite deviation in the doctrine of the Eucharist, may have been an important factor. Anyhow the decision, taken in the winter of 1457-58, to settle in the village of Kunvald in north-east Bohemia seems to have been connected with the fact that the priest of the neighbouring townlet of Žamberk was Michal, in whose person Rokycana's disciples had found their ideal priest. The archbishop, who approved of their desire to flee from the corruption of the cities to find refuge in the remote mountain valley, then intervened with George of Poděbrady to obtain his permission for them to settle on his estate of Litice, where Kunvald was situated. But it was Řehoř, who since at least 1456 had been traveling up and down the country, visiting especially often south Bohemia, who was responsible for the expansion of the group from a tiny circle, consisting mainly of intellectuals and restricted to the capital, into a movement which had adherents in many other districts. Apart from Kunvald and Prague itself, another centre of Brethren activity was Krčín, where one of Rokycana's 'hearers,' Martin, was priest; and elsewhere too, owing to Řehoř's journeyings, many individuals must already have been drawn into the movement.[8]

The settlement of the Brethren at Kunvald marks the virtual foundation of the Unity as an independent group, though it was nearly ten years before a formal separation from the Utraquist church actually took place. This new church was to represent a fusion of several social elements and of different religious groupings. Unfortunately, the records tell us little of the social strata from which the Unity drew its original membership. They speak only of 'certain educated persons and priests and certain

[7]   *Ibid.*, pp. 224, 225. Two priests of exemplary life, whose names occur in the earliest records, were Jan Opočna and Jakub of Divišov. They do not appear, however, to have possessed the gifts of religious leadership.

[8]   Goll-Krofta, *op. cit.*, pp. 64–68; Tapié, *op. cit.*, pp. 43, 45; Urbánek, *op. cit.*, pp. 645, 986–88; Bartoš, 'Z počátku Jednoty bratrské', *Č. Č. M.* 1921, pp. 203–06. Urbánek, p. 987, places the settlement at Kunvald in the period just after George's election to the throne, while Goll, p. 68, puts it between Vladislav's death (Nov. 1457) and George's election (March 1458). Bartoš identifies Jan, the leader of the Vitanovice Brethren, as Jan Táborský, while Goll considered him identical with Jan Kolář of Vitanovice (later known as Jan Chelčický). Both men were to become leading members of the Unity.

simple people.'[9] Of the three laymen to be chosen later, in 1467, as the
Unity's first priests, two came of peasant origin: Matěj, the first bishop,
and Eliáš Chřenovický. But there was from the beginning a sprinkling of
educated members, some even with university degrees: Prokop of Jindřichův Hradec and Augustin Halař of Chrudím, both bachelors of the
university, Jíra Pětikostelský, who retracted his views under torture in
1461, Veliký Vít, and Tůma Přeloučský, one of the three first priests.[10]
The leadership, then, came mainly from Rokycana's 'hearers,' priests and
laymen, while the bulk of the membership was drawn from the peasantry
and small craftsmen, the same elements which had previously formed the
rank and file of the Taborite movement.[11]

At the end of the fifties, through Řehoř's proselytizing efforts in south
Bohemia, a group with radical Taborite, even 'Picard,' antecedents fused
with the groups centred around the settlement at Kunvald. This Taborite
group was indeed to constitue, with the remnants of the Chelčicky
Brethren, the nucleus of the south Bohemian branch of the Unity. This
fact, which partly explains the strength of social radicalism among the
Brethren of that area, already the birthplace of the Czech revolutionary
movement, was to be of great importance during the schism which occurred
at the end of the century. The group had originated in the early fifties
from Kroměříž in Moravia, where a Utraquist priest, Štěpán, who advocated a literal carrying-out of the injunctions of apostolic poverty on
the part of the priesthood, had gathered a considerable following around
him. Driven out from Kroměříž by the bishop of Olomouc in 1456, he
and his followers wandered first to Meziřič. Here a split occurred when
those who held 'Picard' views on the eucharist, that is to say, who denied
the real presence in the communion bread and wine, broke away under a
cutler, Řehoř, and joined up with a wandering Taborite priest, Štěpánek.
Soon they were in turn expelled from Meziřič, on account of the denunciations of their former master, Štěpán (who however eventually ended
up himself as a member of the Unity), and pursued their wanderings amidst
continual persecution, finally settling at Klatov in south Bohemia. Here
Brother Řehoř found them about 1458-59 and brought them into the
rapidly expanding Unity. Klatov then became an important centre of

---

[9]   Bidlo, op. cit., p. 322.
[10] Krasonický, op. cit., fol. 9; Urbánek, op. cit., p. 988. See also Goll-Krofta, op. cit.,
pp. 241–45.
[11] Tapié, op. cit., pp. 119, 120. Cf. Denis, Fin de l'Indépendence Bohême, I., p. 318:
'Les disciples de Kheltchitsky [sic], les Frères, nous apparaissent ainsi comme les
continuateurs des Taborites, précisément parce qu'ils sont si different d'eux: c'est la
dernière et nécessaire phase de la maladie révolutionnaire: après les héros, les martyrs.'

Unity activities.[12] At the end of the fifties, largely through Brother Řehoř's influence, extremist Taborite and 'Picard' eucharistic doctrines were, however, dfinitely rejected, and henceforth those suspected of such antecedents had to go through a probationary period, being accepted into the Unity only after repentance.[13] Nevertheless, the former Klatov Brethren continued to act as a focal point for radical theological and social ideas within the Unity.

The sixties were a period of rapid expansion for the Unity, despite the persecution which broke out in 1461, the first of a long series in its history. The Brethren were temporarily driven from Kunvald, finding refuge, however, on the near-by estates of a sympathetic nobleman, Jan Rychnovský of Rychnov; and some of their leading members, including Řehoř himself and Michal of Žamberk, were imprisoned. Many members, too, had to hide in the forests and mountains. The measures taken, which were due to King George's desire to prove to the rest of Europe that Bohemia was not a hotbed of heresy, as well as to the fears aroused by the new religious community among Utraquist priests, were not enforced with sufficient vigour, however, to prevent the Unity from increasing in numbers and influence. They were enough, though, to show the Brethren that there was no room within the framework of the Utraquist church for a community such as theirs, bent upon bringing public life and private morals into complete conformity with the demands of the gospels. It had taken almost a decade to bring this fact home to them; but fears of losing, either through death or imprisonment, the services of the few 'good' priests of Roman ordination, whom they possessed, strengthened the feeling that a radical solution was necessary. Finally, therefore, at the Synod of Lhotka (near Rychnov) in 1467 they took the ultimate step of electing their own priesthood from among the ranks of the laity, thereby formally breaking not only with official Utraquism, but with the whole Catholic church.

The synod had been preceded by protacted, but ultimately unsuccessful, negotiations for fusion with the Waldenses. Indeed, the role played by the latter in the setting up of an independent priesthood in the Unity has been one of the most debated points in its history. 'Die Weihe der ersten Priester [writes Goll] is das schwierigste Problem der Brüdergeschichte.'[14]

[12] Urbánek, op. cit., pp. 636–41.
[13] Bidlo, op. cit., pp. 33, 550; Goll-Krofta, op. cit., pp. 83, 86, 93.
[14] The first volume of Goll, Quellen und Untersuchungen zur Geschichte der Böhmischen Brüder, was one of the earliest attempts to deal with this problem in detail, though, as Goll himself points out, it is as old as the Unity itself. The standard Unity histories – Müller-Bartoš, Hrejsa, and Tapié – give the results of later research on this subject.

But the direct influence which the Waldenses exercised on the political and social ideas of the Brethren is equally unclear, since fundamentally the same attitude was taken up in regard to such subjects as the state, war, and the death penalty, oaths, education, etc., by both Chelčický and the Waldenses. It is, therefore, almost impossible to disentangle one influence from the other. Chelčický's was probably the more conscious one. His writings obviously shaped the thoughts of those leading members of the Unity, who in turn framed the theoretical basis of its ideology. But the circulation of Waldensian influences among the masses of the population from whom the Unity drew most of its members prepared the ground for acceptance of such doctrines.[15]

Direct contact with the Waldenses probably began about 1461, after the Brethren's break with Rokycana. But, as with Chelčický, it may have been Rokycana himself who recommended the Brethren to seek out the Waldensian leaders. For he and his assistant, Martin Lupáč, were on friendly terms with their bishop, Stephen of Basel, who functioned just across the border in Austria. Martin of Krčin, writing to Rokycana in 1463, remarks on the latter's tolerant and friendly attitude towards the Waldenses, adding that, as for the Brethren, 'whenever we have held converse with them, we have not found them far removed from us, especially in matters of principle.'[16] This shows that negotiations between the two groups were already under way. The Brethren at this period were indeed looking far afield in their search to discover if a pure church, whose members still put into practice the teachings of the gospel, had survived anywhere from apostolic times. Their enquiries had ranged as far as Russia, Greece, and even India; and, though they were to continue to believe in the existence of true Christians among the various churches and among all nations, the failure of their hopes was, indeed, to be one of the main factors in their decision to establish their own independent organization.[17]

The reasons why – apart from its intrinsic importance – the problem has figured so prominently in Unity history are threefold. In the fifteenth, sixteenth, and seventeenth centuries, when Unity historiography was born, the Brethren were persecuted under the nomenclature of Waldenses: hence their anxiety to deny too close a connection with this sect. With the national revival in the nineteenth century Czech historians (e.g. Palacký, 'O stycích a poměru sekty Waldenské k někdejším sektám v Čechách,' Č. Č. M., 1868, pp. 316–17) were likewise keen to stress the native origins of the most prominent of the Czech reformation churches. Thirdly, the problem figures largely in the claims put forward until recently by the Moravian Church for the apostolic succession of their bishops through the Unity and the Waldenses.

[15] Goll, op. cit., I, p. 16.
[16] Bidlo, op. cit., p. 567.
[17] Ibid., pp. 34, 35, 193, 326–28.

Conversations with Stephen had at first progressed favourably. The Waldensian had agreed to all conditions laid down by the Brethren, and the stories the latter heard from Stephen concerning the apostolic succession, which supposedly existed in his church, led them later to seek confirmation for their orders from the Waldenses. But in the meantime Stephen himself had been seized by the authorities and burnt at Vienna in August 1467. Thereafter, negotiations for fusion took a turn for the worse, and Martin the German, who now represented the Waldenses after Stephen's death, under pressure from his friends among the Utraquist clergy, categorically refused the terms of the alliance previously agreed upon. Several Waldensian priests – and undoubtedly many of their followers in Bohemia – later joined the Unity and relations between the two churches continued to be friendly. But there was to be no formal union.[18]

What were the conditions put forward by the Unity as a *sine qua non* of a united church? These were, indeed, directly concerned with social practice. The Brethren found the Waldenses' priests had fallen off in their practice of apostolic poverty. They complain in their tract *Kterak se lidé mají míti k církvi římské*, written in 1471, several years after the negotiations had finally broken down, of the Waldensian priests' behaviour:

They take from their people and, neglecting the poor, amass much wealth. For it is indeed not only against the faith for a Christian priest to lay up treasure from earthly things, but even to inherit property from his parents. Rather should he distribute it as alms, not forgetting the poor in need, for otherwise – according to the writings of the apostles – he has abjured the apostolic faith and thereby excluded himself from grace.

The Waldensian unwillingness to accept the partial communism of the early Brethren, therefore, together with a disinclination to break entirely with official Utraquism, was responsible for the fact that no merger took place between the two groups.[19]

---

[18] Bartoš, *op. cit.*, *Č. Č. M.*, 1921, pp. 214–18; 'Valdenský biskup Štěpán z Basileje a jeho účast při ustavení Jednoty bratrské,' *Č. Č. M.*, 1916, pp. 273–77; Müller, 'Der Waldenserbischof Stephan und die Weihe der ersten Brüderpriester,' *Z. f. B.*, 1916, pp. 128–44. Stephen, who until recently was believed to have been the Waldensian bishop who consecrated Brother Michal in 1467/68, was a member of the radical branch founded by Friedrich Reiser (burnt at Strasburg in 1458) as an organization entirely independent from the official church. Stephen and Reiser's orders were derived from the Taborite bishop, Mikuláš of Pelhřím, and their followers were strongly under Taborite influences. For Reiser, see Jung-Schmidt, *Friedrich Reiser: Eine Ketzergeschichte aus dem fünfzehnten Jahrhundert.*

[19] Bidlo, *op. cit.*, p. 328. Cf. Blahoslav, *op. cit.*, p. 38. For rather similar criticisms

For during the middle sixties the Brethren's views had, indeed, crystall-
ized far enough for them to be able to issue a clear statement on the
relationship which should exist between the various grades within the
Unity. This embryo constitution dates back to 1464 and was promulated
at a synod in that year held somewhere in the mountains near Rychnov.[20]

According to the decree issued by the synod, members of the Unity –
at that time apparently called the 'Brethren of Christ's Gospel' (Bratři
zákona Kristova) – fell into three categories. In the first group came the
priests and teachers and those laymen who had voluntarily renounced all
worldly wealth. Then came the ordinary Brothers and Sisters, described as
'those who live from a handicraft or from the land.' These formed the
overwhelming majority of the membership. Finally there were 'the
penitent (kajíci),' probationers not yet admitted into full membership of
the Unity.[21] Complete fulfilment of the injunctions of apostolic Christianity was, however, demanded only of the first category, though a high
standard of social and moral behaviour was indeed expected of all
members.

Communism of goods, the renunciation of all private property, in line
with the practice of other medieval sects, was the mark of the highest
category, 'the perfect' – as they were also called, for instance, by the
Waldenses. Such an arrangement was believed to have been enforced in
the apostolic church: it was, therefore, obligatory for all those who
sincerely tried to put Christ's teachings into practice.

Priests and those who teach [thus ran the synodal decree] should give an
example to others in word and deed. ... Also in material concerns some
have come to a common decision to renounce such things, to hold nothing
of their own, neither private property nor money nor any other thing,
according to the example given by the first Christian leaders, about whom
it is written that they held all things in common, having nothing of their
own but sharing everything with those in need. For it is right and proper
that those who are called to Christ's service should be abstemious in their
eating and modest in their dress. ... They should, therefore, avoid all
superfluities, receiving sufficient for their proper needs – whether at
home or on a journey – from those who, having means, are allotted the

---

made in the second half of the sixteenth century by the Polish Arians of the Moravian
Anabaptists, see Kot, Ideologja politycznai spoleczna Braci Polskich, chap. IV.

[20] Most authorities follow the date given in Akta Jednoty Bratrské, V, fol. 261 v. But cf.
Tapié, op. cit., p. 49: 'sa date est ... douteuse, et je penche à croire qu'il s'agit d'un état
ultérieur de l'Unité.' At any rate the regulations contained there at least refer to the
Unity in the period before the schism in the nineties.

[21] For a detailed discussion of the relationship of the first Brethren to the earlier
medieval sectaries with their three categories of membership, see Keller, Die böhmischen
Brüder und ihre Vorläufer.

task of providing for their material support. Therefore, let them be without care, putting their trust in God. ... And whichever among them
possess wordly wealth, let them do with it as the gospels ordain: give to
the poor, and having shared their goods out among them, let them earn
their bread by the labour of their hands, for this is, indeed, good. ... If
after that anything still remains over, let them share it with their nearest.
But if, on the other hand, they are unable to supply their own material
wants, let them take from their brethren, who have indeed concurred in
this decree.

The decree included instructions for those who wished to renounce their
property, for those who felt a call to join 'the perfect' in their practice of
Christian communism. They were, in the first instance, to carry-out the
distribution themselves, 'giving to the poor, the needy, the sick as well as
to orphans and widows.' But if they themselves knew no needy and
deserving Brethren in their neighbourhood, they might entrust the job to
some Brother of good repute, provided he later gave an account of his
transactions. It was apparently only the needy among the Brethren – and
there must have been many such during the periods of persecution – who
were to be covered by such distributions: their charity does not seem to
have embraced the poor who did not belong to their church. In no case
was pressure to be put on a Brother to join 'the perfect': the latter's total
renunciation, it was stressed, was to be an entirely voluntary act. 'If
anyone wishes to keep anything for a good reason, and to give it into safe
keeping or to bequeath it to someone after death, all this may be done
according to proper testimony (*podle svědectví hodného*).' But the
ordinary Brethren, while permitted personal possessions which they could
pass on by will, were still obliged to assist those in need out of their own
property, as well as to offer hospitality to those Brethren travelling on
lawful business. This was the task especially of the heads of households.

If anyone sees that a Christian of like faith is in want, he should out of
love give him from his own estate according to need. Thus all believing
Christians should strive to fulfil the Law of Christ, carrying one another's
burdens. ... If anyone fails to care for fellow Christians who think
alike with him, then has he denied the faith and is lacking in love, and is
worse even than the heathen.

The category of laymen who had voluntarily adopted the rule of apostolic
poverty was to disappear soon after 1467. Only among the priesthood
were these precepts to continue in force, though even with them the passage
of time was to soften their former rigour, until the custom for priests to
earn a living by manual work became the only surviving remnant of the
Unity's earlier communism. Müller has pointed out that, by the aban-

donment of this tenet of voluntary poverty, the danger of a division growing up in the Unity, similar to that existing in the Catholic church, between those who practised a higher social morality and those for whom a lower sufficed, was averted. The regulation was originally enacted as a compromise between the demands of the minority, who believed community of goods was an essential part of true Christianity, and the more numerous section which was unwilling to go so far. Its abandonment reflected the shift in the social basis of the Unity's membership, which was to be such an important factor in causing the schism in the nineties.[22]

The settlement at Kunvald in 1457-58, the Unity constitution of 1464, the creation of a separate priesthood in 1467: these events marked the first stages in the establishment of the new church. The sixties had commenced with a period of persecution, which had lasted several years; and once more in 1468 a wave of renewed persecution started, which continued until Vladislav's accession in 1471. In both cases the measures directed against the Unity, which had even included the execution of a small number of Brethren and were in general aimed at suppressing public manifestations of the new sect, had been taken for reasons both of external and internal politics. Fear on the part of the Utraquists at the successive steps taken by the Brethren towards final separation, and King George's eagerness to show the rest of Christendom that Bohemia did not willingly suffer the growth of heresy, both played their part in bringing about these two periods of persecution. They led, too, to a break with Rokycana, who had failed to respond to the Brethren's pleas to put himself at the head of their movement. The Brethren, indeed, never quite gave up hope of winning Rokycana over, of bringing him to see the wisdom of following 'the narrow path.' Shortly before the latter's death, Řehoř addressed 'a seventh and last letter' to the master, a final appeal to him to see the light. Something of the warmth which had persisted between the two men despite their diverging ways, and of the esteem in which the Brethren continued to hold Rokycana for his superior judgement, comes out in this letter, mingled with their disappointment at what they considered his moral cowardice for not breaking with the world and throwing in his lot with those who believed they were now only putting into practice what he had himself formerly preached. They were ready, Řehoř writes, to follow him in everything once he had openly accepted their basic principles. But

---

[22] Müller-Bartoš, *op. cit.*, pp. 58–62; Müller, 'Die Gemeinde-Verfassung der Böhmischen Brüder in ihren Grundzügen,' *Monatshefte der Comenius-Gesellschaft*, 1896, pp. 142–48; *Dekrety Jednoty bratrské* (ed. Gindely), p. 57. Cf. Goll-Krofta, *op. cit.*, pp. 167–68. There are two versions of the decree in A. J. B., V, fols. 260–61v, 262v–63v.

it was already too late for any reconciliation of their two points of view. Rokycana remained for the Brethren the classic example of the apostate leader.[23] The impression gained from Unity historiography of Rokycana as the directing force behind the persecution has, however, little historical foundation. He appears to have done all in his power – short of abandoning his position as head of the Utraquist church and himself joining the Unity – to soften the severity of the blows dealt out to his former disciples.

In 1471, with the deaths of Rokycana and George of Poděbrady[24] and the accession to the Bohemian throne of Vladislav II, eldest son of King Kazimierz IV of Poland, a new era dawned for the Unity, which had survived successfully its first times of trial. A period of comparative calm, of freedom from persecution in spite of several abortive and short-lived attempts in the opposite direction, now ensued; and the religious peace which was to last indeed into the next century gave the Unity the opportunity to develop its influence and expand in numbers, until it had covered the whole of Bohemia and Moravia with a net-back of small congregations.[25] When its founder, Brother Řehoř, died in August 1474, worn out by the effort and strain of constant pastoral visitations among the scattered groups of Unity adherents, often in extremely dangerous circumstances which could result in imprisonment or even death, a period of quiet, but steady expansion had set in, only to be broken by the momentous schism which began at the outset of the nineties. On two occasions during this

---

[23] Bidlo, op. cit., II, pp. 1–4.

[24] It is interesting to note that, despite the king's continuous hostility to the Unity, his jester, Jan Paleček (or Palček), a man later famous in Czech literature for his witty sayings, appears to have been a Brother, possibly a secret adherent. Paleček, who was of gentry origin, was probably one of the Klatov Brethren, who joined the Unity at the end of the fifties. He was much loved by the king, who took his advice in many matters; and, if he really was a member or at least a secret sympathizer of the Unity, doubtless on occasion Paleček used his influence with his royal master in favour of the Brethren. He appears to have died before the king. There is no foundation for the theory of his identity with Jan Klenovský, which was current in the last century. See Herben, 'Klenovský – Paleček,' Sborník historický, 1883, pp. 43–51; Jakubec, Dějiny literatury české, I, pp. 611, 612; Hrejsa, op. cit., III, p. 205; Bidlo, op. cit., I, p. 118.

[25] According to Hrejsa, op. cit., IV, 38, 39, about 1479 the whole Unity numbered only between 1000–2000 members. Congregations (sbory) usually contained fewer than a hundred members, and there were a number of individual members scattered in groups too small to form a separate congregation of their own. Apart from Kunvald and Prague, the earliest known congregations, dating back to the sixties, were situated at Rychnov nad Kněžnou, Lenešice near Louny, Vinařice near Mladá Boleslav, Benatky, Německý Brod, Přerov in Moravia and at some unspecified spot in the Prácheň area. See also Hrejsa, 'Sborové Jednoty bratrské,' Reformační sborník, 1935, pp. 22, 23; Müller-Bartoš, op. cit., p. 149.

period, in 1473 and again in 1478, the Brethren were given the opportunity, through the instrumentality of their protectors among the magnates, of stating their case publicly in *colloquia* with the representatives of the Utraquist church, the Prague masters. The seventies and eighties of the fifteenth century represent the period of the Old Brethren, a patriarchal age when the Unity, already a completely separate religious entity, attempted to put into practice, within the framework of the existing social order, the pattern of life of the apostolic Christian communities as portrayed in the works of Petr Chelčický.

It was due almost entirely to Brother Řehoř that the Unity's theoretical doctrines as well as its practical organization took shape. Bidlo in particular has pointed out how the earlier view denying any originality to Řehoř as a writer is an exaggeration, even though he is usually dependent on Chelčický for his inspiration.[26] Řehoř was, indeed, responsible, either alone or in collaboration with such 'learned' Brethren as Prokop of Jindřich Hradec or Tůma Přeloučský, for almost all the works issued in name of the Old Brethren, a body of writings which, until the nineties, remained the foundation on which they based their conduct in every sphere of life. These oldest sources for the history of the Unity, which in addition contain almost all the information obtainable concerning their social and political doctrines, fall from the point of view of their contents into two categories. First, there are the apologetic writings, of which the Unity throughout its history was to continue to pour forth a steady stream, destined for such personages as Rokycana, King George, the Prague city council, and sometimes just 'for all people (*vsem vůbec*)'. The second group comprises those pieces which were intended for private circulation within the Unity alone and not for public consumption. Chronologically, on the other hand, they can be divided as a whole into three distinct categories: those pieces composed during the first and second persecutions respectively, and those written during the first few years of Vladislav II's reign with the object of inducing a more favourable attitude on the part of the new king. The style in which they are written is usually, indeed, remarkable for its freedom from lengthy citations from Latin authors, showing that, like Chelčický, Řehoř's education was based mainly on writings in Czech, of which the vernacular translation of the Bible took the central place. For a literal interpretation of the injunctions contained in the New Testament was to be the hallmark of the

[26] Bidlo, *op. cit.*, I, Intro., pp. 41, 108, 109. See also Cedlová, 'Náboženské názory Petra Chelčického a bratra Řehoře i jejich vzájemný poměr,' *Č. Č. M.*, 1932, pp. 317–22.

earlier Brethren's conduct, both within the Unity and in their relationship with society outside.[27]

How far had Řehoř and his assistants taken over intact from such writers as Chelčický the social and political doctrines which were to be a distinctive feature of this first period in the Unity's history; how far, on the other hand, can any original elements be detected in their social theory and practice? These questions can only be answered after a detailed examination of the doctrines as they appear in those writings of the early Brethren which have survived.

Chelčický had written for the small handful of his contemporaries who were prepared to frame their lives according to the model set out in the gospels, for Christ's 'flock, who, hearing His voice and believing on Him, are ready to follow in His footsteps, turning aside from the world for His sake and placing their hopes for their own welfare in Him alone.'[28] Through Řehoř's untiring activities this small circle which had gathered around Chelčický had been widened to embrace a multitude of small congregations, all living according to this same pattern and now numerous enough to form their own separate church. For them, as for Chelčický, the early church, living strictly according to the rule of life laid down by Christ himself and his apostles, was their ideal of a Christian society. They, too, were lacking in any conception of historical evolution. The history of the church in the centuries following Constantine's conversion was painted by them as a steady descent from the perfection which had existed within the Christian community until that date, a story of corruption mitigated only by the continued existence outside the official body of a small and savagely persecuted remnant of true Christians, whose spiritual heirs the Brethren felt themselves to be.[29]

[27] For a discussion of the dating of Řehoř's writings, see Cedlová, op. cit., pp. 78–82; Bidlo, op. cit., Intro., I, p. 146; II, p. 92. Reference to the detailed list of early Brethren writings given in the German edition of Müller, Geschichte der Böhmischen Brüder, I, pp. 585–91, shows that scarcely anything of importance was issued by the Unity during the sixteen years intervening between Řehoř's death and the beginning of the schism in 1490. This fact illustrates the paramount role played by Řehoř in framing the ideology of the Old Brethren, even though some of their later writings may have been lost.

[28] Chelčický, Síť' víry, p. 333.

[29] Bidlo, op. cit., I, p. 73. Cf. 'Interrogati quando desiit potestas et auctoritas romane ecclesie responderunt, se nescire, tamen usque ad tempora Silvestri pape et amplius credunt eam durasse, quousque in ea non fuerunt tanta peccata' ('Některé prameny k náboženským dějinám v 15. století,' Věstník kralovské české společnosti náuk, 1895, p. 6). In this article Goll reprints almost in full the report of the official examination (výslech) by Catholic priests of four leading Brethren – Michal, Jan Táborský, Prokop of Jindřichův Hradec, Tomáš of Lanškroun – held on 4/5 June 1480. The four Brethren had been intercepted at Kladsko by order of Henry Duke of Munsterberg on their way to visit the Waldensian communities in Brandenburg, which since 1458 had experienced

The broad outlines of their ideal community come out very clearly in a passage in the letter Řehoř addressed in their name to the Vice-Chamberlain (*podkomoří*) of the Kingdom of Bohemia in 1461. Their aim, he writes, was 'to live according to the scriptures alone (*samým čtením*), following the examples of Christ and His holy apostles in quietness, humility, and patience, loving one's enemies and doing good to them . . . and praying for them.'[30] They would always, so they believed, form a minority in this world plunged in unbelief and sin, a society of poor men and women of humble origin leading a frugal and laborious existence.[31] Reliance on the scriptures as the only fount of morality, public or private, an attitude which divided them off not only from the whole Catholic church but even from the majority of Utraquists, had been one of the conditions in the agreement for fusion with the Klatov Brethren in 1458–59. But the early Unity followed Chelčický in making a distinction between the New and Old Testaments. The Old Testament had preached physical warfare, the execution of sinners and other bloody punishments, in short the law of an eye for an eye, a tooth for a tooth. The Jews had been justified in following this law as they were then on a lower plane of development. But Christ had substituted for it his new Law of Love, which 'neither condemns to death . . . nor coerces anyone to fulfil its commandments, but rather with loving patience calls for repentance, leaving the impenitent to the last judgement.' It is only the false Christians – the Brethren write, with an eye perhaps to those of their number who had come across from the Taborites – who cannot distinguish between the two revelations; and here indeed they showed a remarkable historical sense, which was absent in their treatment of the development of the Christian church.[32]

The early Christians had lived as an outcast minority within a pagan empire, expecting at first the speedy return of Christ in his glory. The whole of the Unity's political philosophy was, indeed, shaped by parallel

severe persecution. These Waldenses – who had earlier been in contact with the Taborites – as a result of negotiations with Tomáš, himself of German origin, who alone had been able to proceed on his journey, soon after emigrated to Moravia, where they settled around Fulnek in the German-speaking frontier district. It was from these communities, formerly forming the main German language group within the Unity, that the founders of the Moravian Church in the early eighteenth century originated.

30   Bidlo, *op. cit.*, p. 545.
31   *Ibid.*, pp. 343, 527.
32   *Ibid.*, pp. 423–37, 453, 508; Müller-Bartoš, *op. cit.*, pp. 52, 53. Cf. 'Nullam probacionem nisi ex evangelio vel epistolis apostolorum in evangelio capiunt aut exemplis Christi vel apostolorum in evangelio et epistolis contentis; vetus testamentum, ubi eis placet, ubi non placet, quod sit imperfectum, dicunt, et figura, et quod perfeccio Christi et apostolorum est attendenda' (Goll, 'Některé prameny', p. 6).

conditions, permeated by similar notions. Theirs was a minority creed. For them the world was hopelessly corrupted. They pictured themselves as 'pilgrims and guests here on earth, afflicted by the world with many tribulations and dangers, because in their ideas [they] have separated themselves off from this world.' Sharing the widely-held view that the end of the world was then imminent, the Brethren's desire to preserve their small circle of believers intact in a morally fallen world soon to be destroyed was indeed, in Bidlo's opinion, one of the reasons prompting them to found an independent church. As with the early Christians the adoption by the Unity of its radical social and political doctrines – and their later abandonment – may have been influenced in part by such beliefs.[33]

These doctrines were, therefore, the logical outcome of the early Brethren's determination to order every aspect of their lives in accordance with the example of Christ and the apostles. 'If anyone would like to know how we conduct our affairs [they were writing at the end of the sixties] let them enquire how things stood in the early church.' Modelling themselves on the early Christians they were to be 'humble, retiring, temperate, magnanimous, long-suffering, loving, full of pity and kindness, meek, pure, modest, peaceable, desirous only of the right, compliant, willing, and ready for every good action.' Certainly a counsel of perfection, but one which throws an illuminating light on the early Unity's ideal of Christian virtue.

In their interpretation of the scriptures the writings of Chelčický, as we have seen, were their main guide. The early Brethren, including Řehoř himself, were practical men, who had neither the leisure nor the freedom from material cares and worries necessary for the composition of works elaborating their views from a theoretical standpoint, which Chelčický appears to have possessed. They were all at first either the victims or potential victims of prolonged periods of persecution. Most of them were, indeed, simple craftsmen and peasants, for whom theoretical speculation held no attractions. 'These teachers, Michal the priest and Řehoř the tailor [the masters of Prague University report with some astonishment] derive salvation most of all from a virtuous life.' For them the attempt to practice morality in everyday existence was more important than any

---

[33] Bidlo, *op. cit.*, pp. 10, 21, 191, 579; Tapié, *op. cit.*, p. 78. For the somewhat obscure story of how, during his first imprisonment in 1461, Brother Řehoř was tricked by a certain Jan Vocásek, a Utraquist priest, into admitting not only the right of the civil authorities to use force in religious matters, but the compatability of coercion in general with christianity, see Bidlo, *op. cit.*, p. 552; Müller-Bartoš, *op. cit.*, pp. 42, 43, 56.

abstract considerations about correct doctrine.[34] Although in fifteenth-century Bohemia no religious community could of course escape being involved in technical discussions of abstract theological problems, the bulk of early Brethren literature nevertheless has a decidedly utilitarian character and was written with a definite practical aim in view. It is natural, therefore, in the circumstances under which they lived, that among the political problems which loom largest in their writings is that of the relationship between church and state, the problem of religious toleration.

The interference of the civil authorities in matters of faith had, as we have seen, been condemned unconditionally by Chelčický, who stood however – even among the Hussites – almost alone in his attitude. The constant threat of persecution, which from the beginning hung over the Brethren's heads even when active measures were not being taken to suppress them, gave their demands for religious freedom a special urgency. As early as 1461, when the first attempt was made to destroy the infant church by force, Brother Řehoř had written an impassioned appeal for religious liberty from his prison at Teplice in an open letter addressed to King George's adviser, the moderate Utraquist, Vaňek Valečovský.

For God has given this sword to the kings of the earth [writes Řehoř] only in order that the world might be preserved according to His will, and to direct it against those who do evil against the common good. ... But when through priestly guile your sword is turned against people on account of their faith, it is acting against God's commandment, since ... no earthly ruler can put faith into people's hearts without their assent or force them to believe.

Even the Romans and Turks, he goes on, did not interfere in their subject's religion. 'Although you may burn a man, you will only increase thereby the numbers of the faithful.'[35]

Disagreement on this question of religious toleration was one of the causes of the Brethren's estrangement from Rokycana who, as head of the state church, was held responsible by them for the persecution of which they were the victims. This comes out in the following exchange, which took place between the Archbishop and Martin of Krčín during their disputation (hádka) in 1463:

Rokycana: If you became reconciled with us, you too would obtain the help [of the civil authorities]. They would defend you also, since they have been instituted in order to punish the wicked and help the good to prosper.

[34] Bidlo, op. cit., II, p. 125.
[35] Ibid., I, pp. 545, 548.

Martin: In that case the way of Christ would no longer be the narrow one
and his cross would have been in vain (*Nebyla by cesta kristova
úzká a kříž jeho byl by vyprázdněn*).

Five years later the Brethren were once more to call upon Rokycana to
take 'the narrow path,' to renounce the protection of the state for his
church as inconsistent with true Christianity. But their pleas were to be
without effect.[36]

For not only did the Brethren condemn the almost universally accepted
practice of the forcible conversion of heretics, but the aid of the temporal
arm was not to be invoked even in defence of the faith, to repel attacks
made by those who did not share their tolerant attitude. Řehoř writes:
'Not only are [the civil authorities] not entitled to use force in matters of
faith, but they should also refrain from defending the faith by the sword.
For Christ sent out his apostles into the world to preach the gospel without
the help of the civil power, of magistrates, of hangmen or of armies.'
Unlike the majority even of the radical Hussites, as Řehoř himself
remarks, true Christians – like sheep among wolves – were to suffer
martyrdom rather than to call in the 'pagan' authorities to their defence.
The final sanction for erring brethren, who remained impervious to
admonition and rebuke, was to be, as Chelčický had recommended,
expulsion from the Unity. Any recourse to the state in such matters was
firmly ruled out.[37]

The early Unity followed Chelčický not only in his advocacy of complete religious toleration and of the separation of church and state, ideas
which have found widespread acceptance in the modern world, they also
took over from him in its entirety the negative attitude towards the state
and the whole social order, which forms the most distinctive feature of
their social and political ideology. No members of the Unity might occupy
any position, however humble, in the administration of government, nor
might they become masters in a gild. This attitude resulted, indeed, in
part from their rejection of oaths. They were permitted neither to take
oaths themselves, nor to accept any office where they might have to
demand oaths of others. These considerations alone would have excluded

[36] *Ibid.*, pp. 462, 463, 471, 589. Krofta *Listy z náboženských dějin českých*, p. 238,
gives an able apology for Rokycana's attitude.
[37] Bidlo, *op. cit.*, pp. 514–19, 553. Cf. 'In ecclesia, ut asserunt, sua nullum iudicium
sanguinis permittunt dicentes fore contra ewangelium, nec leges nec canones advertunt,
nullam iurisdiccionem inter se faciunt, sed seniores fratres, si cause vel casus emerserint,
conveniunt et pie et fraternaliter componunt; quod si quis eorum est excessivus et
incorrigibilis, a congregacione sua tanguam anathematizatum et excommunicatum
excludunt, quod si se recognoscit et penitenciam petit, iterum eum ad ecclesiam reas-
sumunt' (Goll, *op. cit.*, p. 7).

all participation in the state, even had the Brethren not possessed further weighty arguments in favour of their standpoint. For, as with Chelčický, this refusal was not based simply on a literalist interpretation of the scriptural injunction against taking oaths, but flowed from their whole political philosophy. Civil authority with its coercive power was totally unchristian, the offspring of Antichrist. 'All those placed in offices according to rank and dignity [they write in 1469-70 in their tract *O rozdiele, kterej jest mezi bratřiemi, tak že jedni sou praví a druzí falešní*] are factions (*roty*), not subject to the Holy Spirit.' Like Chelčický, the early Unity considered that the task of governing a state could not be carried out without the infliction of cruelty. Naturally too, they, specifically rejected the theory of 'the threefold people,' which attempted to square the social order with the demands of Christianity. They equated the essence of government with 'fear, cruelty, beating, fighting, killing, reviling, violence, imprisonment, cutting-off of limbs, murder, and other physical torments.' True Christians therefore, in addition to non-co-operation in the machinery of government, were also obliged to boycott the courts of law, whatever the provocation.

A collision with the state could scarcely have been avoided if the Brethren were to attempt to put theory into practice. As early as 1463 Martin of Krčín, writing to Rokycana, reports that 'certain Brethren ... have been kept in prison many weeks because they prefered to bear much pain and suffering rather than swear as newly-elected alderman (*v konšelství přísahati*), thus breaking God's commandment.'[38] In later years, too, they were to endure fines and imprisonment for their refusal to co-operate with the state. Sometimes the right to reside in towns and villages was refused them because of their unwillingness to accept office. So long as the members of the Unity were drawn mainly from country people there was less occasion for conflict, since the executive and judicial powers of village officials were strictly limited. But with the extension of the Unity during the seventies and eighties among the small craftsmen of the towns the problem became increasingly urgent. Indeed, it is not clear how far even at the beginning all Unity members consistently refused to take up office. Brother Lukáš who, though no impartial witness, was at least closely connected with the Unity from the eighties

[38]   Bidlo, *op. cit.*, pp. 396, 464, 469, 506, 510, 534–43, 564. Bartoš, 'Neznámá díla Jana Rokycany v musejních rukopisech,' *Č. Č. M.*, 1919, p. 12, considers Rokycana's influence to have been a more powerful factor than Chelčický's in leading the Unity to reject oaths. Goll-Krofta, *op. cit.*, p. 309, on the other hand, attributes this to Waldensian influences. Bidlo believes that the Brethren began to collide with the state on this issue even before the outbreak of persecution in 1461.

onwards, asserts indeed that throughout the Unity's existence, even in Brother Řehoř's time, some members had become aldermen and magistrates. 'While regarding it as an evil [writes Lukáš, describing the situation at that time] many were yet forced to comply. Some took the oath, others were imprisoned and fined for their refusal but later gave in, coming to the Brethren on such occasions for counsel.' Evidently, then, there was no uniform practice in face of the demands of the state, though undoubtedly, wherever possible, members of the Unity attempted to remain true to their principles.[39]

A further source of potential conflict with the authorities lay in the fact that all participation in war, even of a defensive nature, as well as the infliction of any form of punishment involving an element of coercion, was also forbidden to a member of the Unity.[40] Řehoř, indeed, had taken over without change Chelčický's argument against war and all forms of violence. This comes out very clearly in the only attempt made by the early Brethren to deal systematically with this subject; their tract on the civil power and the power of the sword (*Psaní o moci světské neb o moci mečové*), written probably by Řehoř between the years 1468–71, is for the most part merely a transcription of Chelčický's *O trojím lidu*, in which even the latter's wording often remains unaltered. Indeed, no passages of importance from Chelčický's work are omitted, and the Brethren's new edition makes no original contribution to the theoretical groundwork. Their additions consist mainly of a number of observations relating to the probable results of the application of theory in the existing situation.

With the outbreak in 1467 of war against King Matthias Corvinus of Hungary and the king's decision to call out the militia (*veřejná hotovost*), many peasants and townsmen were called up for military service, an obligation of which they were normally free. This at once presented a serious danger for the Unity, since many Brethren coming from these classes were liable to be forced to serve in the army; and their testimony against war, therefore, would be likely to bring them into conflict with the law. Some brethren went into hiding, probably retiring into the forests and mountains as they had done during the first period of persecution. Some stood their ground and undoubtedly suffered severe penalties, while

---

[39] Müller-Bartoš, *op. cit.*, p. 156, quoting Lukáš in A. J. B., IV, fol. 28v.

[40] Objection to the death penalty, even if not unconditional, still continued among moderate Utraquists during the last few decades of the fifteenth century, as is shown by the strongly worded protest against capital punishment contained in the manuscript sermons of an unknown disciple of Rokycana, probably composed after his master's death; see Šimek, 'Ukázky kazatelské činnosti neznámého husitského kněze,' *Č. Č. M.*, 1933, pp. 200, 204.

others probably conformed with an uneasy conscience to the demands of
the state. Anyhow, as early as 1468, the Brethren report to Rokycana of
the tribulations they were having to endure on account of their non-
conformity. Explaining their objections to the demands of the authorities
in such matters as military service and the taking of oaths they write:
'We acknowledge our insufficiency, which arises from fear of bodily
suffering, beatings, imprisonment, etc., and that sometimes we have fled
or hidden, mainly out of fear of our own weakness, in order that we should
not be driven by force to do anything or utter anything against our
conscience and thereby against God.'[41] Their tract on war mentioned in
the preceeding paragraph, which dates from the same period, marked an
attempt to justify their stand before the bar of public opinion, to defend
their refusal to take part in the defence of the country and religion against
foreign invasion. It represents in fact a detailed apologia for their whole
attitude to the state as a political institution.

The contemporary custom of enrolling 'poor people, workers and
tenants,' the Brethren claim in a passage recalling Chelčický's earlier
protest, only dated back as far as Žižka's time, even though many people
imagined it had existed everywhere since time immemorial. But even
now in other lands, and formerly in Bohemia itself, 'ploughmen' were not
thus snatched away from their labours. Fighting was the business of the
nobility, who received temporal power with the dues and services of
labouring people in exchange, and of hired mercenaries. To-day, however, in Bohemia, 'whoever is capable of bearing arms is reckoned among
the warrior class (*kdož jedné muože braň nésti, vše rytířský lid*).' The
Brethren forsee that heavy punishment will fall upon those who oppress
the poor with such burdens as compulsory service in the armies, making
soldiers out of simple peasants and craftsmen. In their protest against the
conscription of these classes by the state, the Brethren were expressing the
grievances of those sections of the population for whom such military
measures were a heavy burden.[42]

Bohemia, at least, was successfully defended from invasion, and the
Brethren do not appear to have had their pacifist principles put to the test

[41]   Bidlo, *op. cit.*, p. 52.
[42]   *Ibid.*, Intro., pp. 119–23; Text, pp. 504–43. Following the date given in the MS.
of the Akta, historians (e.g. Palacký and Goll) formerly assigned the tract's
composition to 1485, tying up its origin with the beginnings of the schism in the Unity.
It was Bidlo who first established that it was written between 1468–71, probably by
Řehoř himself. I cannot, however, agree with Bidlo, *op. cit.*, Intro., p. 122, that any
member of the future Major Party would have been able to give his assent to the
theoretical principles expressed in it. The unconditional rejection of war and the state
which it contains, is a complete denial of the validity of the latter's standpoint.

during this period. Some years later a number of Brethren who, being forced to leave Moravia in 1481 as a result of measures taken against them by the Hungarian king, Matthias Corvinus, had settled in Moldavia, were, however, faced on more than one occasion with the threat of Turkish invasion. Michal Slanský, who as a young man had accompanied these Brethren into exile as their priest, twice reports that he had to flee before the Turkish armies. With Ladislav's accession to the Hungarian throne in 1490 the exiles were able to return to Moravia; and we possess no detailed information as to how they reacted to the Turkish invaders.[43]

However, a perusal of the Unity literature of the period leaves no doubt as to how the Brethren would have solved the problem in principle. The Christian way of facing evil was that of voluntary suffering without retaliation, of non-resistance to evil, of dissuading the wrongdoer from his evil ways without destroying his body or soul. 'True Christians [they write] must suffer every form of tribulation from the world even unto the loss of life and property, repaying good for evil.' Their reward was to be in heaven and not during their lifetime on earth. Their ideal was the practical application of the precepts of the Sermon on the Mount as much in social and international relations as between private individuals.[44]

The threat not only to national independence but to the very existence of the Hussite religion, which the Pope's proclamation of a crusade against heretic Bohemia represented, may well have caused some members of the Unity to reconsider the implications of their peace testimony. It may have been this danger of foreign invasion that induced Martin of Krčín, an early leader of the Unity and one of the first Utraquist priests to join the new organization, whose connection with Řehoř dated back to their association in the group of Rokycana's 'hearers,' to leave the young church which he had himself helped to found. The complete disappearance of Martin from the records after his arrest in 1463 has long puzzled historians in view of the prominent part he had played in it till then. The

[43] Müller-Bartoš, op. cit., p. 115. The Polish Arians about a century and a quarter later were faced with a similar problem by the Tartar invasions of Poland's eastern provinces. It is interesting to note that the synods, which they held in 1604 and 1605, advised the Brethren to flee from the threatened provinces and settle elsewhere, if they were unable to protect themselves without killing or wounding. See Kot, Ideologja polityczna i społeczna Braci Polskich, pp. 94, 95.

[44] Bidlo, op. cit., pp. 209, 282, 401, 546, 624. Cf. 'Dicunt . . . nec ex scripto nec exemplo Christi habetur, quod liceat aliquem interficere sive in bello justo, sive sentencia iudicis iusta. Et hoc dicunt, quod si Turci prosequerentur eos aut quicunque inimici, nollent se defendere, sed pocius mori in simplicitate sua, et ex hoc concludunt, quod neque pro iusticia aut pro fide liceat bellari, sed simpliciter mala pati, allegentes apostolum: 'Non vosmet ipsos defendentes.' Et Christum: 'Diligite inimicos' (Goll, op. cit., p. 6).

possibility of his having died before 1467 could not entirely explain the complete silence with which the Unity surrounded his name henceforth. Later Brethren tradition seems to have lost all recollection of him.

The discovery, however, by Bartoš in the National Museum in Prague of a hitherto unknown manuscript dating from about the beginning of 1470 has offered a possible explanation of the mystery. This manuscript, a call to repentance and inner rebirth, addressed 'to the Czechs and the whole Christian world,' is characterized by many features peculiar to Unity doctrine. It is likely, therefore, that it was composed by someone who had been closely associated with the Brethren. At the same time, in his attitude to war and violence, the author takes up a diametrically opposite standpoint from that of the early Brethren. He calls on the civil authorities to take forcible action against monks and secular priests. He calls on God for revenge against the enemies of the faith. He is filled with hatred of the Germans; calls them 'snakes and scorpions in the bosom of the Czechs'; and demands their expulsion from the kingdom. 'Let [the King] offer a hundred talents of silver or gold to whomsoever shall bring in a hundred German or Hungarian noses.' He taunts those priests who hung back from accompanying the armies in the field, which he would obviously have been glad to do himself. He accepts the division of a Christian society into classes, which had aroused both Chelčický and the early Brethren to vehement protest. Bartoš goes on to identify the author of this fiery pamphlet, recalling something of the militant social radicalism of the Taborites, with Martin of Krčín, whom long years of imprisonment and the subsequent period of war had led to abandon the Unity's opposition to war and violence. This would explain why Martin was passed over at the time of the establishment of the Unity's priesthood in 1467 and his complete disappearance from their records. If Bartoš's hypothesis is correct – and it has not been contested by later historians – we can see in Martin of Krčín the neglected forerunner of the Major Party (*Větší strana*) in the Unity.[45]

The early Unity's attitude to the state, therefore, had brought down severe persecution on the heads of its members. There had been defections from its ranks. Even more had its bold defiance in 1467 of the whole Christian world in formally establishing its own priesthood, as well as its theological unorthodoxy, made it suspect in the eyes of the authorities. Nevertheless, despite severe persecution, the Unity continued to thrive. The reasons for its continued growth must certainly be sought partly in external circumstances, in national and international politics. But the

[45] Bartoš, 'Kněz Martin zv. z Krčína,' *Č. Č. M.*, 1917, pp. 137–42, 280–86.

doctrines held by the Unity themselves contributed to this growth both in membership and influence, and helped it to find powerful protectors among the great magnates of Bohemia and Moravia, both Utraquist and Catholic, whose increasing power meant under the prevailing anarchic social conditions that the royal mandates against the Brethren remained a dead letter.

The Brethren repeatedly stressed that they were against any form of armed rebellion, that they were on principle good and submissive subjects and tenants. 'We wish [they write in a typical passage from the *Zpráva bratří kunwaldských*] from a loving spirit to be submissive, each in his own place and station, and to hearken to all those placed in authority, whether in spiritual or secular offices;' though they add the characteristic proviso: 'so long as nothing be done contrary to God and our own conscience.'[46] In the famous Decree of Rýchnov of 1464, too, they state that: 'In all just, proper and honest matters ... under whatsoever authority any of us may be placed, we are taught to obey and be subject in all humility as to taxes and labour services and to be loyal in all things and to pray to God for' such authorities.[47] Following Chelčický they allotted the civil power with all the paraphenalia of coercion and killing a place in the divine world order, conditionally justified its functioning for the purpose of establishing good order among the 'pagan.'[48] They were confident that, given a chance to put them before the authorities, their social and political doctrines would appear as harmless as they believed their theological ones were. They demand in 1470 'a peaceable hearing (*slyšení pokojné*)' for their views, social as well as theological, in order among other reasons that they may inform those responsible for government 'how we think about the ordering of the world by the power of the authority ordained by God, and how true Christians should be obedient.'[49] The public hearings which they obtained through the intervention of their powerful protectors in 1473 and 1475 appear, however, to have dealt exclusively with theological problems, which doubtless loomed largest in the minds of both parties.

They vigorously denied, too, any connection with the much feared Taborites and Adamites, with their subversive doctrines on the relationship of subjects to rulers. The acceptance into the Unity of a number of former members of these sects had given rise to apprehension on the part

[46] Akta Jednoty Bratrské, III, quoted in Palmov, *Cheshkie bratya v svoikh konfessiyakh*, I, part I, p. 135.
[47] A. J. B., V, fols, 261, 261 v.
[48] Bidlo, *op. cit.*, pp. 51, 94, 224, 263, 549.
[49] *Ibid.*, p. 288.

of the powers that be that the Brethren were planning armed rebellion. Such fears had been partly responsible for the two outbreaks of persecution during the sixties. In their opinion, the Brethren retort, the Taborites were, indeed, 'murderers,' 'legions of damnation,' whose willingness 'to further the faith by material warfare' was totally inconsistent with the way of Christ and his apostles. The Adamites or Picards, too, were often opprobriously termed by the Brethren 'the very worst people . . . who do not consider sin as sin,' partly because of their theological radicalism in propagating a purely commemorative view of the eucharist, their supposedly loose morals and their hypocrisy in not making an open break with the ruling church, but also partly because of their readiness to take part in war. The appropriateness for the Brethren of the name Picard, applied to the Unity by its enemies throughout its history, was always fiercely contested.

The peaceable attitude of the Brethren, in contrast to the revolutionary propensities of the Taborites, comes out clearly in the statement made in June 1461 before Rokycana by those Brethren arrested in Prague for supposedly conspiring to take arms to restore Taboritism. They assert:

Although it is suspected and spread abroad that we have banded together and gathered forces to overthrow this kingdom with bloodshed, yet it is not true. Such a course of action has never entered our minds; not only would we not seek such an outcome, but we would never sanction it even unto death. It is well-known to all those who have associated with us that our one aim has been to please God and be humbly obedient to our Elders.[50]

It is not surprising that many secular lords for whom the returns from their estates were of greater interest than nice theological differences, some of them even from practical considerations sincere advocates of religious toleration, welcomed the settlement of the Brethren on their estates as dutiful and obedient subjects, hard-working and frugal tenants. Just as later certain Reformation sects, mainly belonging to one of the branches of the Anabaptists, were to obtain from the ruler privileges exempting them from demands which they could not conscientiously fulfil, sometimes in exchange for the discharge of some economic task for which their frugality and diligence peculiarly suited them, so the Brethren by their way of life recommended themselves from the beginning to the attention of the magnates.[51] Among their earliest protectors were Jan

[50]   Ibid., pp. 398, 473, 586, 604.
[51]   Palacký, Dějiny národu českého, V., p. 157, even believed that by its inculcation of a submissive spirit the expansion of the Unity contributed indirectly to the deterioration of the peasants' status.

Rychnovský of Rychnov, the two brothers Ctibor and Jan Tovačovský, Jan Kostka of Postupice, and many other leading noblemen. In 1475, for instance, Vilém of Pernštejn freed all new settlers at his town of Přerov in Moravia from the obligations of military service and service in public offices, a move obviously made to attract the Brethren.[52]

As long as their protectors belonged to another religious community, however, the Unity could never feel quite certain of their lasting support. Changing political conditions, the succession of an heir unsympathetic to the Brethren, pressure from Utraquist or Catholic clergy, might entirely alter their previously privileged situation, might lead once more to the imposition of just those obligations which their original settlement had been designed to escape. The conversion of a noble landowner to the Unity might mean, therefore, not only reasonable security during his lifetime, but the education of his heir in the Brethren's faith.

What, then, was the attitude taken up by the Unity during this period to potential recruits from the nobility? Having ascertained the applicant's sincerity in wishing to join their church, what further demands did the Unity make on him? The nobility, those in authority, were indeed required to follow 'the narrow path' to the same extent as members from other classes.[53] The custom prevailing in the Unity at that time is well summarized in the report preserved of the examination of four leading Brethren at Kladzko in 1480. The section dealing with the acceptance of members of the nobility into the Unity runs as follows:

Quicunque dominus aut potens mundł eorum fraternitatem petit et unionem, super omnia primum oportet iurisdiccionem temporalem resignare ... ut iudicium sanguinis non admittat neque intersit. Similiter et castra. Cetera vero bona temporalia sicut agros et piscinas potest et debet retinere vel dimittere secundum consilium rectorum ecclesie. Aliqui ex eis tenent propria bona, aliqui resignant omnia.[54]

It was, therefore, not the Unity's communism which, as we have seen, was always voluntary and soon became confined to the priesthood, but their anarchism and pacifism, which made them demand in some cases that nobles should renounce their property. An owner of an estate was indeed

[52] Hrejsa, op. cit., IV, pp. 21, 30. Gindely, Geschichte der Böhmischen Brüder, I, p. 55, has thus characterized the motives of the Unity's powerful protectors: 'Es wandelte nun weder die adelichen Herren noch die Patricier der Städte die Lust an, auf alle Macht und Grösse, auf ihre kleinen Landesherrlichkeit Verzicht zu leisten; aber es flösste ihnen gleichwohl der gehorsame, übertänige, treue und arbeitsame Sinn der Brüder Achtung selbst wohlwollen ein.' In the existing conditions the patricians were naturally a less powerful factor in protecting the Unity than the landed nobility.
[53] Bidlo, op. cit., p. 210.
[54] Goll, op. cit., p. 7.

ipso facto an administrative official, a judge, and a military leader. He was inevitably involved in carrying out actions which were contrary to the Unity's principles. Not only would he have to commit wrong himself, but he would be obliged to force others to do so. Even so the exact situation is obscure. We know that there were members of at least the minor nobility within the Unity from the beginning, 'though not very many' even as late as 1470,[55] and also that at least two members with large estates were obliged to renounce them before being accepted into membership. One of these was probably a certain Methodius Strachota, a nobleman of whom it is related that 'on joining the Brethren he gave up his castle at Orlice [near Kyšperk, where his family had their seat] and lived in poverty as a nobleman's secretary' and later as a miller. He is described as 'a wise man, well versed in godly matters,' and seems to have enjoyed great respect among the Brethren, probably largely due to the sacrifices he had made for their cause; though scarcely anything is known for certain about this attractive figure. The other nobleman mentioned has sometimes been identified as Jan Kostka of Postupice, who joined the Unity probably in the early eighties. However, even from the report cited above, it would seem that noble members might retain at least part of their former possessions, though how in this case they avoided all connection with the machinery of government is not clear. Probably practical considerations led to an amelioration of the stringency of theory.[56]

During the period of the Old Brethren the Unity retained its agrarian character. It continued to be suspicious of urban life, despite the migration of an increasing number of Brethren into the towns and a vigorous propaganda among those already resident there, especially among the small craftsmen. The Unity's decrees, although they have come down to us in a form dating from a later period, show clearly that at this time the Brethren frowned upon most forms of commerce, trade, and industry, especially upon those connected with the production of luxuries and the satisfaction of man's carnal desires or associated in any way with usury and immoderate gain. The life of the countryman, comprising agriculture,

---

[55] Bidlo, *op. cit.*, p. 217.
[56] Goll-Krofta, *op. cit.*, pp. 57, 73, 174, 244. The story of Strachota comes from Krasonický's *O Učených*. Jan Kostka (d. circa 1486) was the brother and heir of Zdeněk (d. 1468), who had been responsible for savage reprisals against the Unity in that year. Müller-Bartoš, *op. cit.*, p. 155, disagrees with Goll that Jan Kostka was one of the two noblemen mentioned later by Brother Lukáš in his 'O obnovení,' fol. 95 (quoted in Goll-Krofta, *op. cit.*, p. 201) as having renounced their estates on joining the Unity, since Tůma Přeloučský in his 'Cedula panu Janovi Kostkovi,' A. J. B., III, expressly states that his sons obtained his estates only on his death.

fishing, and the crafts which supplied the modest needs of those engaged in these occupations, was the only safe calling for the true Christian. Here the Brethren were the heirs of a long line of thought, running through Chelčický and Hus back to the latter's predecessors in the second half of the fourteenth century. For Unity members, indeed, even the allowable forms of commerce and industry were hedged around with numerous restrictions and qualifications. In short, a federation of rural communities, a peasant 'stateless state' remained its ideal, a reflection of the predominantly peasant character of its membership.[57]

The asceticism so often associated with movements of this type, which we have already observed in Chelčický, is present too in the attitude of the Brethren to the cultural refinements usually produced only by an urban civilization. Fine clothes, rich food, sweet music, objects of beauty were only hinderances in following 'the narrow way.'[58] There is in their whole social philosophy something of the outlook of the downtrodden peasant excluded by his lack of education, his poverty, and his toilsome existance, from participating in the culture reserved for his masters alone. They inherited the hatred which such a class culture inspired in their master, Chelčický.

The Brethren, however, despite their antipathy to certain aspects of cultural life, made an important contribution to the spread of popular education in the Czech lands as, for instance, before them the Taborites with their similar views had also done.[59] While rejecting the learning of the universities as an instrument of class and religious oppression, the Brethren laid great emphasis on the spread of the rudiments of education among the simple peasants and craftsmen, who formed their rank and file. Many even of their leaders – Řehoř, Eliáš Chřenovický, Matěj, etc. – were entirely self-educated men. Everything needful for salvation was, it is true, to be found, as Chelčický had taught, within the covers of the Bible. But every believer should have easy access to this unique fount of wisdom, must master at least the art of reading, in order to be able to dispense with the mediacy of 'learned' priests and challenge securely the claims of the

---

[57] *Dekrety*, pp. 126–31.
[58] Bidlo, *op. cit.*, p. 427.
[59] Hrejsa, *op. cit.*, III, pp. 79, 80. The well-known account of the visit of the papal representative Aeneas Sylvius (the future Pope Pius II) to Tábor in July 1452, a few months before its final overthrow, which is quoted by Hrejsa, gives some interesting details as to the exceptionally high standard of education existing there among all sections of the population, despite their theoretical rejection of school learning. Even the women, reports the future Pope, have a sound knowledge of the Bible. Testimony to the high standard of education among the Taborites was also borne by the conservative Utraquist, Jan of Příbram.

state religion. The early Brethren became, therefore, pioneers in the field of primary education.

At first there were only two types of Brethren schools. Since during its early years the authorities precluded the Unity from openly establishing its own schools, and as religious scruples prevented the Brethren from sending their children to Utraquist or Catholic schools where they existed, the obligation of teaching the young fell upon the heads of each household. Possibly here and there a more enterprising brother may have gathered together under his care the children of his neighbours. The main onus of providing a basic education for the children of the Unity fell, therefore, upon simple peasants and artisans, the fathers of the families. Naturally such a system of education was extremely primitive and imperfect. It can seldom have advanced beyond the inculcation of reading and writing, with the Bible as the only text-book. Certainly some Brethren remained illiterate and more mastered alone the ability to read. Only in the priests' houses were the more advanced stages of education given to the brighter lads specially picked to enter the priesthood. But even here Latin was not taught, at least during the fifteenth century. The first report of the establishment of a proper school by the Unity dates back to 1482. But scarcely any details are known beyond the name of its founder, Master Havel of Žatec, and its location at Brandýs nad Orlicí. At the end of the century – 1498 in Moravia; 1500 at Mladý Boleslav in Bohemia – more schools were officially set up under the Unity's direction; and henceforth their educational system continuously expanded, wherever the patronage of some powerful landowner protected them from the envy and malice which the generally high standard of education among Unity members aroused in their Utraquist and Catholic rivals. The latter, indeed, did not hesitate to spread the most absurd rumours about the satanic origin of the ordinary Brethren's proficiency in letters.[60]

Though university men among the Brethren had played a prominent role from the very beginning, Řehoř himself had always shown a certain suspicion of learning, which impressed its mark on the early Unity and had caused the main emphasis to be laid on simple faith, free from the shackles of intellectualism. In view of the presence already within the Unity of a number of university bachelors and masters, Řehoř's death-bed adjuration to Bishop Matěj 'to beware of educated and learned persons who might corrupt the faith (*aby moudré a učené měli na péči, aby skrze*

[60] Bidlo, *op. cit.*, pp. 217, 409, 430–39; Ball, *Das Schulwesen der Böhmischen Brüder*, pp. 49–54, 80; Urbánek, *Jednota bratrská a vyšší vzdělání*, pp. 26–28; Winter, *Život a učení na partikularních školách v Čechách v XV. a XVI století*, pp. 62–64.

ně nepřišla skáza víry a lásky)', cannot be taken as a total rejection of all university education: it indicates, nevertheless, that once more the Brethren had followed Chelčický with his contempt for the superiority claimed by the erudite, by the academic world of his day. Afeter Řehoř's death, however, under the weak leadership of the 'unlearned' Bishop Matěj, the educated members of the Unity increased in significance and numbers, attracted by the genuine religious life which the young church displayed. The story of the part they were to play in the momentous changes which occurred within the Unity during the nineties will be told in the next chapter. But during the preceding decades, whatever internal strains may have existed beneath the surface, both learned and unlearned were outwardly at one in upholding the Unity's special testimonies in social and political matters.[61]

The Old Brethren, as this chapter has attempted to show, had followed Chelčický closely in his political and social theories. They owed something indeed to the radical Rokycana of the fifties as well as to the Waldensian sectaries. The general atmosphere of Hussite Bohemia, with all its cross-currents of native and foreign influences, also left its mark on the Unity in this as in other aspects of its doctrine. The leadership of Brother Řehoř was another important factor shaping the theory as well as the practice of the Unity; while the social origin of the bulk of the membership explains why he so easily found a large number of converts ready to accept and, if necessary, to endure persecution for their new creed. These peasants and artisans, whose fathers had provided the chiliastic preachers with their most enthusiastic audiences and the Taborite armies with their most determined fighters, had now become disillusioned by the trend events had taken with the destruction of the Taborite movement, the establishment in power of the moderate Utraquists, defenders of the old social order, and a progressive deterioration of their economic status. The direct source of the Unity's social and political ideology, which made such an appeal to these sections of the population in town and country, lies, however, in the writings of Petr Chelčický, in his

---

[61] Krasonický, *op. cit.*, fols. 11–13, 14, 16v, 17; Urbánek, *op. cit.*, pp. 22–25. See also Goll-Krofta, *op. cit.*, pp. 241–45. In addition to those mentioned earlier in this chapter as members of the Unity at its foundation, a number of other educated persons joined during the following decades, among whom Krasonický mentions the following: Jan Klenovský, Jan Táborský, Tůma the Scribe, Jan Turnovský, Ambrož Škutecský (later a bishop of the Unity), Ondřej (formerly abbot of the Utraquist monastery *na Slovanech*), Lukáš and his brother Jan Černý (famous as a doctor), Master Havel of Žatec, etc. Krasonický himself was a typical 'learned' member of the Unity of this second generation.

total rejection of the state following from an uncompromising acceptance of the example of Christ and the early church as the sole guide to the conductor of societies as well as of individuals.[62]

Palmov has remarked that the internal development of the Unity showed most independence of outside influence during the first period of its history before its contacts with the German Reformation.[63] But the importance of the Old Brethren in the history of political thought does not lie in the originality of any of their theories, but rather in the consistency with which they tried to put the ideas of their master into practice. What the village philosopher had expounded to the narrow circle of his disciples, the Unity was now attempting to live out in countless small communities under the disturbed conditions of life in fifteenth-century Bohemia and Moravia.

[62]   Cf. Denis, *op. cit.*, p. 302: 'Rokycana est le père involontaire et repentant de l'Unité, Grégoire en est l'organisateur, mais Kheltchitsky en est le théoricien.'
[63]   Palmov, *op. cit.*, p. 52.

III

THE GENESIS OF THE SCHISM

The years of freedom from outside interference, which the Unity enjoyed during the seventies and eighties of the fifteenth century, had resulted in a rapid expansion in membership.[1] Its influence now began to reach out to new classes of the community which had previously been untouched by its teachings. The typical Brother was still for the most part an obscure peasant sectary living in rustic seclusion from the affairs of the world. But the importance of the townsman, of the educated and even the titled member, was beginning to weigh more and more in the affairs of the Unity. This growth, therefore, though a sign of health and vitality, at the same time brought with it the seeds of disunity.

The roots of the schism which rent the Unity in the last decade of the century should be sought, therefore, in the changes which took place in the character of its membership during the two previous decades. The revolution in its political and social doctrines was a reflection of the underlying changes resulting from those new social elements which were slowly gaining predominance.

During the lifetime of Brother Řehoř the validity of the body of social doctrine taken over from Chelčický remained unquestioned. Řehoř's position as the founder of the Unity – its 'patron and patriarch,' as a later Unity chronicler, Vavřinec Orlík called him[2] – was sufficient to override any latent opposition, which might exist, to the rigid application of the Unity's social tenets. But, after his death in 1474, the leadership of the Unity was taken over by the well-meaning, but weak and vacillating Matěj, a man of simple piety, respected throughout the Unity, but no match against superior will-power or intellectual capacity; and among the

---

[1] Hostile accounts have tended to exaggerate the figures, which in any case were merely approximations. By the end of the century, however, it is probably that the Unity numbered well over 10,000 adherents, see Hrejsa, 'Sborové Jednoty bratrské,' *Reformační sborník*, V, pp. 23, 24.

[2] Fiedler, *Todtenbuch der Geistlichkeit der Böhmischen Brüder*, p. 219.

other leading Brethren who had been in the Unity since its foundation, there was none who was capable, or indeed willing, to come forward as the champion of the old ideas, when finally these were to be openly challenged. Michal, the first priest to join the Brethren, was of a like character to Matěj, devout, amiable, but lacking in resolution, a man who was always happy to give place to others in the affairs of the Unity. 'He did much in his time [Orlík wrote]. Faithful to God, he underwent much self-denial and many hardships during his life.'[3] His later career was to show, however, that he was in no way fitted to be leader of a losing cause. Matěj's two colleagues elected with him in 1467 as the first priests of the Unity – Tůma Přeloučský, who, busy at Přerov in Moravia, appears to have taken little active part at this time in the main stream of Unity life, and the shadowy Eliáš Chřenovický – were to join the opponents of the old doctrines, possibly from the very beginning of the controversy. Another influential Brother of the early years, Jan Chelčický, a member of the Inner Council (Úzká rada) and a former disciple of Petr Chelčický, who might have been expected to champion the old ideas, died in 1484.[4]

The strongest personalities in the Unity during the two decades following Řehoř's death were, indeed, to be found among those who were later to provide the leadership in the struggle to modify, and finally completely to transform, the Unity's attitude to society. There was, first, Jan Klenovský. A layman, probably springing from a wealthy Moravian family, he may even have joined the Unity at the time of its foundation; little, however, is known of his early career. Though without a university degree he was well-educated: 'a learned man [writes Orlík] full of wit,' which could be extremely biting at times.[5] It is clear from the letter (psaní) he addressed to King George's son, Prince Jindřich, in 1471 that at first he still shared fully the Unity's attitude to war and the civil authorities. Referring to St. Augustine Klenovský writes there with indignation: 'If you, too, had followed Christ's gospel as a servant does his master, you would not have admitted the sword and wars into the unity of the holy church. Though you may say that fighting and war should only be undertaken from necessity, not of one's own will, that is no excuse at all, for to St. Peter in his necessity it was said: 'Put up they sword into the sheath.''[6]

[3] Ibid., p. 220.
[4] Ibid., p. 219; Goll-Krofta, Chelčický a Jednota v XV. století, p. 80. Jan Chelčický does not appear to have been related by blood to his namesake Petr.
[5] Fiedler, op. cit., p. 220.
[6] Goll-Krofta, op. cit., pp. 232, 233; Müller, Geschichte der Böhmischen Brüder, I, p. 590.

Second only to Klenovský at this time in the counsels of the Unity came Jan Vilimek Táborský. These two men, says Krasonický, 'for a number of years held the leadership (přednost) of the Brethren.' He describes Táborský as 'a small, thin man, rather bent.'[7] Táborský, indeed, was a person of some education, who had once been Utraquist priest at Tábor after the suppression of its radicals in 1452. The exact date of his joining the Unity is unknown, but tradition puts this before 1467.[8] With the names of Klenovský and Táborský that of Prokop of Jindřichův Hradec was also later to be associated during the controversies of the nineties. Prokop was a university man, well acquainted with the works of the church fathers and later theologians, whose learning was to be second in the Unity only to the younger Lukáš. In 1467 he became bachelor of arts at the university in Prague. Orlík specially mentions 'his extremely penetrating wit.'[9] He, too, probably joined the Unity during Řehoř's life-time, though the first reliable mention of his name in connection with the Unity occurs only in 1478, when he was one of the three Brethren to take part in the discussions (hádání) held in that year with the Prague masters. Two years later both he and Táborský upheld the accepted Unity viewpoint on the state during the examination (výslech) of their opinions after they had been intercepted at Kladzko on their way to visit the Waldensians in Brandenburg.[10]

It was in the early eighties that two young university men, Lukáš of Prague and Vavřinec Krasonický, who were both to play a decisive part in the coming schism, were first drawn into the Unity. Unlike Klenovský, Táborský or Prokop, both men have left accounts of the circumstances in which they were led with such epochmaking consequences to join the Brethren.

Lukáš was born shortly before 1460 in Prague, where he spent his childhood and student years. In his youth he came under the spell, as did

---

[7]   Krasonický, 'O učených,' fols. 21v, 22 (quoted in Goll-Krofta, op. cit., p. 208).
[8]   Bartoš, 'Z počátku Jednoty bratrské,' Č. Č. M., 1921, pp. 203–206; Fiedler, op. cit., p. 219. Bartoš identifies Táborský with Jan Vitanovický, the leader of a group of Chelčický's disciples who still continued after their master's death to share his reluctance to break entirely with the official Utraquist church. But Jan, though he disagreed with Řehoř's acceptance of former Taborites and Adamites into the Unity, finally himself joined the Brethren after Chelčický's disciples had split up into several mutually conflicting groups. It is interesting to note the renewed conflict in the nineties between elements within the Unity of partly Adamite origin, led by Amos, and the party of Táborský and his friends.
[9]   Fiedler, op. cit., p. 222.
[10]   Jireček, Rukovět k dějinám literatury české, II, pp. 150–52; Goll-Krofta, op. cit., p. 159; Goll, 'Některé prameny k náboženským dějinám v 15. století,' Věstník královské české společnosti náuk, 1895, pp. 3–10. See Chap. II, p. 85, note 29.

Krasonický and the famous humanist, Viktorín Kornel of Všehrdy, of the fiery radical Utraquist preacher, Michal Polák, who died in prison in 1480. Lukáš evidently felt Polák's death keenly since, as he relates, it was the latter who first made him feel 'the burdensome hunger after truth.' As a result of Polák's sermons 'about corruption and about truth,' and through the intermediacy of a fellow student, Vojtěch, Lukáš was led on to discover the works of Petr Chelčický, 'which I sought to get to know with great diligence.' At first, however, they served only to increase his spiritual unrest. 'Of what use is such truth to me [he cried out] since I am ignorant as to where it is to be found, whether among any people with whom I could share it.' Ironically enough, therefore, it was the writings of this man, whose influence on the Unity he was later to do his utmost to erase, that had drawn Lukáš in the first place to seek out the Brethren.

About this time Lukáš belonged to a small circle of young university graduates and students who, discontented with official Utraquism, were seeking some more satisfying creed. Among its members it numbered, besides Lukáš himself, his brother Jan Černý, Krasonický, Viktorin Kornel, and Master Jakub Střibrský, who in 1497 was to became Koranda's successor as administrator of the Utraquist consistory; all these men, indeed, were later either to join the Unity or at least to become its warm friends and admirers.

The year 1481 brings the first definitely ascertainable date in Lukáš's career, for in this year he took his degree as bachelor of arts. He does not, however, appear to have been an outstandingly brilliant student; in religious matters, however, he was sensitive to the lack of spiritual depth in the Utraquist church of his time, in which the heritage of the early Hussites had become to a large extent merely a lifeless tradition. His considerable erudition, which increased with the years and was later to be such a bone of contention among the Brethren, was to be of undoubted service to the Brethren in many respects: 'Er ist der erste Mann der Unität gewesen [writes Gindely] der eine systematische Bildung genoss, eine hinreichende Kenntniss der alten Klassiker, der heiligen Schrift, der Kirchenväter und der mittelalterlichen Doktoren besass.'[11]

The same Vojtěch who had introduced him to Chelčický's writings now told him of the existence of the Unity, with which Lukáš had previously had no contact, and gave him its writings, too, to read. Indeed, the Unity had only a few isolated adherents at this time in the capital; so it was probably to Litomyšl, then a centre of Brethren activity, that Lukáš now

[11] Gindely, *Geschichte der Böhmischen Brüder*, I, p. 63.

went on a journey of discovery. The initiative, the desire to make this personal contact with a group of people who might prove to be those genuine followers of Christ whom young Lukáš was seeking, came rather from the latter than from Vojtěch, who had previously hung back from closer acquaintance with the Brethren – perhaps out of fear of the consequences, for the Unity was still only half-tolerated in the land. Lukáš, indeed, in the first place had had to ask Vojtěch three times before he overcame his friend's suspicion of his intentions. But once personally acquainted with the Brethren, Lukáš was to recognise in them 'the people near to truth,' the object of his spiritual quest.[12]

It is significant of the powerful influence which Chelčický exercised over enquiring minds of the younger generation during the half-century after his death, that once again it was his writings that brought yet another future leader of the Brethren into the Unity. Soon after 1482 Krasonický, a young Utraquist priest who had taken his bachelor's degree in 1479, came to work at the Bethlehem College in Prague. Here several friends, among them Viktorín Kornel, Jakub Stříbrský, and Lukáš himself, lent him the works of Chelčický and the early Brethren, giving him at the same time their views on the existing 'corruption (zavedení)' of the church and praising the way of life practised among the Brethren. Attracted by the picture they painted of the purity of life in the Unity Krasonický, too, made the journey to Litomyšl. 'Residing among them [he writes later of his first visit] I saw they were sincere and simple people ... and I liked them then as I do now.' In this way another young university graduate was led to join the despised and lowly Brethren.[13]

Not only did Lukáš win over Krasonický, who in turn brought in Master Havel, founder of the Unity's school system; but he also converted his elder brother, Jan Černý, later famous as a doctor. His college friend, Vojtěch, was also to join the Unity. Though many of the Unity's sympathizers among the Prague intellectuals never actually took the final step of breaking with Utraquism, while some like Stříbrský even reached the highest rank in the official church, and still others, like Viktorín Kornel, were later to turn against the Brethren, nevertheless the eighties

---

[12]   Lukáš, 'O obnovení,' fols. 54v–55v (quoted in Goll-Krofta, op. cit., pp. 159, 160); Molnár, 'Lukáš Pražský před svým vstupem do Jednoty bratrské,' Teologia evangelica, 1948, no. 1, pp. 21–32; Jireček, op. cit., I, p. 467. The exact date when Lukáš joined the Unity is not known. Goll puts it in the years immediately after 1481 and identifies Lukáš's first visit to the Brethren with his joining the Unity. But Molnár thinks he may have visited them first to get acquainted with their life before finally leaving Prague to throw in his lot with the Unity, and dates this first visit to 1481 or 1482.
[13]   'O učených,' fols. 13–14 (quoted in part in Goll-Krofta, op. cit., p. 161).

saw a definite movement on the part of the most spiritually awake among the university students and younger graduates towards the Unity of Brethren.

There is no evidence to show that those who joined did not at that time share to the full the prevailing views of the Unity on political and social matters.[14] But their education, their whole background of university and capital city, so different to that of the simple, unlettered country Brethren of Řehoř's day content to live out their lives in obscurity detached as far as possible from the world around them, made conflict at some future date almost inevitable. Wider horizons, the desire – free though it might be of personal ambition – to see the Unity extend its influence and to make a stronger impression on the affairs of the land, the personal ascendancy within the Unity that education brought in its train, were sooner or later likely to clash with the views of those who clung to the traditional outlook of the Old Brethren.

Disharmony, the beginnings of a more serious disunity had, indeed, already appeared among the Brethren by the eighties.[15] The points at issue were still in the realm of theological dogma; the controversy does not appear to have touched those outside the narrow circle of the Unity's priesthood and its lay leaders. A few years after Řehoř's death the age-old question as to the relative merits of justification by faith or by works had arisen among some of the better educated Brethren; and, after a little, the discussion began to cause considerable dissension, the priests and elders beginning to take sides. The old Unity, indeed, had put little value upon theological subtleties: their opponents among the clergy used to claim, it was said, that 'their faith was bad, but their works good.'[16] But now some members from their study of the Bible, and of St. Paul's writings in particular, began to feel that this emphasis upon works was likely seriously to endanger salvation. 'Christ [they said] is no longer of any avail for those who wish to be saved through justification by works (z skutkův spravedlnosti), and the justified can only be found in a state of sin. They blamed the primitive narrow way for all that was wrong, that

---

[14]   Goll-Krofta, op. cit., pp. 160, 161; Müller-Bartoš, Dějiny Jednoty bratrské, I, p. 153–55. Even Krasonický, for instance, after he had disavowed his early social radicalism, remained to the end 'a lover of the old simplicity' (Fiedler, op. cit., p. 227).

[15]   'Psaní jakéhos kněze Jana Appolinařského,' Časopis historický, 1882, no. 2, pp. 64, 66. This reprint contains the so-called Zpráva menší strany o rozmlouvání v Chlumci (1496). Here Matěj is reported as having said earlier that he began to have serious disagreements with Klenovský's party in the Inner Council 'sixteen years ago,' that is, soon after Řehoř's death. From the context this would seem to have been somewhere between 1475 and 1480.

[16]   Akta Jednoty Bratrské, IV (Opis), fol. 131.

from an overgreat straitness ... came the great evils of a vain religion, ... of trust in oneself and contempt for others.' Those who held to the old viewpoint on the other hand, writes Brother Lukáš, 'began to rise up against the defenders of this truth, praising ... the narrow way' and saying 'that reliance should not be placed on the merits of Christ, for in this manner, it seemed to them, have the Romans and others been corrupted.' A member of the Unity, they claimed, should be one who put into practice the ideal Christian way of life as portrayed with all its rigorism in the writings of Řehoř and Chelčický. The question had finally to be taken to the Inner Council for guidance.

At last Brother Prokop came forward with a compromise solution, which appears to have satisfied both sides for the time being. According to Lukáš's account, Prokop urged the importance of 'good will,' which would help to supplement the insufficiency of works done, and thereby help the Christian in his search for salvation. In this spirit 'a man should wish to believe simply, and to do faithfully, what God wishes him to believe and to do.' Prokop's formulation was welcomed with joy and relief by the contending parties who had not, indeed, allowed feeling to rise to such a pitch as later in the years of schism. Throughout, says Lukáš, 'they did not condemn, but rather served each other.'

Though remote from everyday life and confined within the narrow limits of the Unity leadership, this dispute was to form a prelude to the larger controversy in the nineties which split the ranks of the Brethren from top to bottom. The two parties which were to emerge during the ensuing struggle were already present, in embryo, in the supporters of justification by faith, on the one hand, and in those who urged justification by works on the other; and the consequences of the compromise reached through Prokop's intervention were to bear directly on the doctrines, which the Unity professed in political and social matters.

Those holding to the doctrine of justification by works who, according to Lukáš, 'interpretated justification immoderately and regarded it from too lofty a standpoint', appear at the same time to have held strictly to the old viewpoint on social doctrine. 'From a 'high' way of thinking and an immoderate interpretation of the scriptures [Lukáš goes on] they condemned in the Unity many faithful and good people, those in positions of authority or approving of such authority, those having estates and trades, with the pastors (zpráve) who ministered to them, as well as all those who had dealings with them.' In their view membership of the Unity, the personal salvation that all were seeking, entailed strict observance of the Unity's various testimonies against that participation in the affairs of state which the duties of citizenship were increasingly forcing upon the Brethren.

The other side, while still seemingly giving theoretical assent to these testimonies, was prepared to allow the possibility of salvation to those who did not – or could not – take the narrow path, provided they had the requisite faith or, according to Prokop, the necessary good will. Lukáš admits that this position in some cases led to a loosening of the old morality: some of its advocates 'went so far that they later strayed away into sins and the world and earthly affairs.'

But even Prokop's compromise, putting forward 'good will' as a meeting-place between the exponents of the two conflicting viewpoints, did not seem fargoing enough for young Lukáš who, though a mere neophyte among the Brethren, in his own words still 'a child understanding little or nothing,' remained inwardly dissatisfied with this solution. 'Although I did not then know how to speak up [Lukáš writes] it indeed seemed to me as if there should be something more than mere good will, ... but the time ... had not come for this.' His own conviction remained that it was only through 'God's love and the merits of Christ' that salvation could be attained.

If, on the one hand, Lukáš and those like him, who wished for the full implications of the doctrine of justification by faith to gain acceptance within the Unity, remained dissatisfied with any half-way solution, the other side, too, soon became equally perturbed by what they considered a falling-away from the old principles. Once more we are dependent on Lukáš for our information as to the ferment going on among those at the head of the Unity:

When there had been much writing and preaching concerning good will, some began to oppose it [urging] that ... good will without works, promise without fulfilment, leads to damnation. Fearing for works and seeing the shortcomings of some, as before ... they now claimed that it was from conceptions about God's love and the merits of Christ that sins came, as well as loose speech and licentious actions; and they spoke in like manner also about good will. ... Others recognized that God had granted good will, in like manner as to the poor, to the noble and those in authority also, and to many, too, in certain questionable (*nebezpečných*) trades, who had joined the Unity and wished to be instructed ... in their communities in regard to the office of alderman (*konšel*) and as to civil administration and many other things. ... Some denied that civil authority could be exercised, that anyone in authority could become a Brother. ... These strove after simplicity, equality, and poverty. Others, however, saw that in the early church, in the time of Christ and the apostles, equality in goods and in rank and in characters did not exist; and it seemed to them as if the scriptures, interpreted in too exaggerated a manner (*převýšeně nad to, než vznějí*), had been taken from the exposition of Petr Chelčický and of certain Utraquist (*českých*) priests, especially as regards the fifth chapter of St. Matthew.[17]

Thus what had originally been a theological dispute among the pastors and elders of the Unity broadened out into a controversy vitally affecting the lives of the humblest Brethren. It merged imperceptibly with the larger issues. What was to be the attitude of Unity members to the increasing demands which the state was making on them in their everyday life? What, too, was to be the attitude of the Unity as a whole to the problem of the influx of new members from classes of society, which could not so easily adapt themselves to a way of life suited to simple countryfolk of an earlier generation? The development of the controversy was symptomatic of the fundamental changes in the Unity's position in society that had been taking place during this period.

Unfortunately no precise dates are available either as to when the diversity of opinion first arose or when Prokop first propounded his doctrine of 'good will.' Lukáš, whose *O obnovení* is our main authority, is more than usually vague about the chronology of the events he is relating; nor is his account told in strictly chronological order. That the whole episode is contained within the period between Řehoř's death in 1474 and 1490, when the controversy over political and social doctrines first comes out into the open, is alone not open to question. Prokop's intervention, says Lukáš, came at an unspecified date after Brother Řehoř's death (*po smrti bratra Řehoře některé léto*), when he himself had already been a member of the Unity for four or five years. This would place it about the beginning of the second half of the eighties. But the whole controversy must have been brewing for a number of years before Prokop hit upon his compromise formula. The continuation of the controversy, even after agreement had apparently been reached on the basis of 'good will,' and its extension to political and social questions through the application of the doctrine of 'good will' to such matters – Lukáš merely says – lasted for 'several years' before 1490.[18]

---

[17] 'O obnovení,' fols. 89v–95 (quoted in Goll-Krofta, *op. cit.*, pp. 198–202). Cf. Goll-Krofta, *op. cit.*, pp. 165–171; Müller-Bartoš, *op. cit.*, pp. 152, 153, 160. It is not clear who were the Utraquist priests referred to here by Lukáš.

[18] 'O obnovení,' *loc. cit.* Both Goll-Krofta, *op. cit.*, p. 169, and Müller-Bartoš, *op. cit.*, p. 152, put the beginning of the controversy on faith and works about 1480, which seems quite probable. On the other hand, Müller-Bartoš's dating of Prokop's intervention in 1490 and the account there of the two controversies, the theological and the practical, as if they took place simultaneously instead of the latter leading out of the

By 1490, indeed, 'the pastors were once again split in two' not only now on the subtle problems of justification by faith or by works, but on the whole question of the Unity's attitude to society.[19] It was, therefore, to a deeply divided leadership, unable to come foreward with a programme acceptable to all, that the rank-and-file were to appeal for help in the solution of the problems which they were having to face daily in their relations with their neighbours and with the community at large.

It was the Litomyšl Brethren who appear to have been the first to have referred to Matěj and his Inner Council for a clear directive as to how they should meet the demands of the authorities in the numerous instances when these clashed with the established principles of the Unity. Litomyšl at that time was in the possession of a powerful noble family, who were for long to be members of the Unity and among its most staunch protectors. Jan Kostka of Postupice was the first to become a Brother; and when in 1486 his son, Bohuš, who was also a member of the Unity, succeeded to his estates, he continued to favour the Brethren throughout his extensive demesnes. Soon after, Bohuš founded a new quarter in his town of Litomyšl, the so-called New or Upper Town, to which in 1490 the king, on Bohuš's request, granted the same privileges as those enjoyed by the Old Town. The inhabitants of the New Town were drawn mainly from members of the Unity, attracted there by the favourable conditions which Bohuš's protection provided for them. Among the privileges they then obtained from their lord was freedom from the obligation of military service unconnected with the defence of the city itself and, in 1491, from all dues and taxes for a period of seventeen years as well. The Brethren, too, would of course be able to carry out their religious practices free from outside interference.[20] As a result Litomyšl became, in the words of Tůma Přeloučský in his *Cedule* to Jan Kostka the younger, 'famous for its inhabitants and its handicrafts; the empty places in the market square were filled up, and along the ditches and elsewhere [the Brethren] erected their houses.'[21]

Not only was the community of Litomyšl Brethren enlarged by an

---

former, does not appear to be borne out by the main source, Lukáš's *O obnovení*. This work is, however, remarkably obscure. Goll was led to antedate the beginnings of the controversy on the Unity's attitude to the state by attributing the tract *Psání o moci světské* to a member of the Minor Party, Říha Votický, who was supposed to have written it in 1485. In actual fact, as Bidlo has shown, its real author was Brother Řehoř and its date 1468–71. See Goll-Krofta, *op. cit.*, p. 171.

[19] 'O obnovení', fol. 95 (quoted by Goll-Krofta, *op. cit.*, p. 201).

[20] Müller-Bartoš, *op. cit.*, pp. 155, 156; Goll-Krofta, *op. cit.*, p. 174; Molnar, *Boleslavští bratří*, pp. 33, 34.

[21] Winter, *Život církevní v Čechách*, I, p. 54.

influx of fellow Brethren from the country or other townships. But a considerable number of craftsmen, traders and merchants, previously unconnected with the Unity, settled in the New Town, attracted in the same way by the favourable conditions offered to newcomers; and some of these non-Brethren in time came themselves to join the Unity, which was undoubtedly the most live religious influence in the neighbourhood. In other cases it was the reputation of the Unity as a vital spiritual force that in the first place brought those dissatisfied with the deadness of official Utraquism to settle in one of its main centres. A good picture of this process is to be found in the preface, written by Adam Bakalář, a later town clerk (*písař*) of Litomyšl, for Martin Kabátník's account of his visit to the East in 1491 in company with Lukáš and two other Brethren. During the eighties, writes Adam, Kabátník who was a cloth merchant:

Came from Prague to Litomyšl, because he had been unable to have an easy conscience through the services of the priests. He sought to see if he could attain this with the Brethren, who at that time enjoyed the greatest freedom under [Bohuš Kostka]. The latter was, indeed, of one mind with them and protected them so that they were free from oppression and injustice, for his father had been a Brother and his mother a Sister. And it came to pass that the above-mentioned Martin also became a Brother.[22]

Among the Brethren in Litomyšl, as in other congregations of the Unity, there were present many of the elements which were becoming restive at the constraints imposed by the narrow way of Brother Řehoř and the Old Brethren. There was, first, the nobility, several of whom like the lord of Litomyšl, Bohuš Kostka, were now either actual members of the Unity or its close sympathizers. Although Lukáš mentions, without giving their names, 'two important nobles, as well as some of the gentry (*zemané*) [who], wishing to become Brethren, were required to give up their estates,'[23] there must have been comparatively few ready to make such a great sacrifice; and the example of Bohuš Kostka shows that in some cases, even, it was already not demanded. For the young intellectuals, like Lukáš and Krasonický, whose numbers were increasing among the Brethren, the winning over of powerful protectors among the upper ranks of society appeared as one of the most urgent tasks before the Unity, while the rank-and-file, as the rapid migration of Brethren to Litomyšl clearly showed, welcomed with relief the advantages which their protectors were able to offer them. It was hard to refuse to accept the latter into membership,

[22]   Kabátník, *Cesta z Čech do Jeruzalema a Kaira r. 1491–92*, p.l. Kabátník appears to have been illiterate and dictated his story to Adam Bakalář.
[23]   'O obnovení,' fol. 95 (quoted in Goll-Krofta, *op. cit.*, pp. 201, 202). Cf. Chap. II, p. 98, note 56.

if they applied for admission; and, indeed, only through their full membership could the Unity be certain that the next generation would be brought up in the faith of its fathers, who had always been ready to befriend the Brethren. Only by complete association could there be a reasonable likelihood that the son would not reverse the policy of the father on succeeding to his estates.

Secondly, among the ordinary Brethren the new arrivals from the countryside were faced with a different way of life more difficult to square with the rigid principles which they had, with varying success, attempted to put into practice in their villages. The new demands, therefore, led them to grope after new solutions of their most urgent problems.

A third element of discontent, of potential revolt against the accepted principles of conduct, derived from those new recruits to the Unity who, previously unacquainted with its political and social doctrines, had been reared in an urban environment alien to the conditions which had given birth to the Unity.

But the loyalty of the Brethren to their church, the strong group coherence which welded the Unity together in the face of a hostile and persecuting environment, a genuine attachment to the old ideas, made them do their utmost to avoid open disobedience to the Unity's principles. It was in this spirit, therefore, that early in 1490 the appeal for guidance was made in the name of the Litomyšl Brethren to the highest authority within the Unity, to its bishop, Matěj, and his Inner Council.

They demanded 'advice and help' in two matters in particular. Their first difficulty arose, to quote the later report of the Inner Council, 'when the aldermen summon certain of you [i.e. Litomyšl Brethren] to the town hall and face you with some rather tricky questions: perhaps that you should give your advice or state your opinion or confer with the community.' They were concerned, secondly, with the fact 'that already they make aldermen of some of the Brethren, and you foresee that there will be more of them. If you wish to escape this, it is not permitted, for seemingly it is regarded as just ... since you live together with them in the community.' But the Litomyšl Brethren conclude in their own words: 'Even if we must suffer some material loss as a result, we intend to follow your counsel as far as we are able.'

The Inner Council considered the whole matter of such importance that they summoned a special 'conference of the teachers [i.e. the priests of the Unity], who came up from the provinces'; and this body issued a pronouncement (*výpověď*) which was to act as an answer to the Litomyšl Brethren's queries. This document, for the most part, avoided giving a clear answer to the points at issue; it was evasive, vague, and failed to satisfy anyone. It was evidently the result of a compromise between those who held to the old doctrines and the Brethren who wished to see these modified. But, unlike Prokop's earlier proposals to resolve the problem of justification by faith or by works, the conference's answer completely failed even temporarily to carry conviction. Its naivety, its failure to face the issues or to pronounce definitely for one or other course of action, its evasive style, indicate that it was not primarily the work of the reformers among the older or younger generations, for the imprint of Klenovský, Táborský, or even Prokop, not to speak of Lukáš or Krasonický, would surely have given the document a more decisive tone. It may have been a composite effort of the assembled priests, or it may have come from the pen of Matěj or one of the older Brethren vainly attempting to reconcile the two conflicting viewpoints.

The purpose of the document is given in its concluding paragraph, which in addition brings out the inability of the Inner Council to think out a clear cut policy on the issues at stake and its tendency to throw the problem back once more on to the individual member for him to find his own solution. 'These articles (kusové) are given [says the edict] as they came to mind during discussion, in order that some of them, or some part of them, may be chosen out for the instruction of those placed in office by the authorities and in that of alderman in particular.'

It marked, nevertheless, the first official recognition of the new opinions. For the first time the leadership of the Unity acknowledged not only that in practice some of the Brethren had failed to live up to the Unity's teachings in their everyday life, but it sought to find a partial justification for such backsliding from the old rigorism. Despite the hesitant terms in which it was expressed it can, therefore, properly be regarded as a victory for the opponents within the Unity of Chelčický's and Řehoř's teachings on political and social problems.

The edict dealt, first, with the summonses received by certain Brethren to attend the town hall.

Like you we, too, would be glad if you could avoid these in any way, but what else we can advise you in this matter we do not know at the moment. While as for the matters they may face you with, demanding an answer, some are easier, others more difficult, about which, indeed, advice cannot be given nisi generaliter. As far as you can perceive justice in any matter, declare it ... and do not give way to whatsoever is unjust.

An equally urgent problem was the increasingly frequent election of Brethren to the office of alderman.

It is difficult to give advice as to what you should do in this matter [replied the Inner Council helplessly]. If you should try to get out of it as, with divine assistance, you have done in previous years, the burghers will not often suffer this now, since there has been a considerable increase in the number of Brethren there [i.e. in Litomyšl]. And they are continually crowding in from other places and the lords or their officials accept them and refuse none. Some may say perhaps that they come on religious grounds, but it is mostly for material (*tělesné*) reasons.

Certain of these newcomers even, instead of attempting to avoid office as far as possible, wish to 'sit beside the foremost. Even though they do not seek the office of alderman, yet in this way they are soon led towards it (*se s ním potkají*).' All this is not happening only in Litomyšl, it is added, but 'they are also drawn into other towns for like things.' Some Brethren, again, are led to accept office through considering themselves wiser than their neighbours; and, once having accepted, their exalted position makes them have an even better opinion of themselves. The use of torture during the performance of their duties may, the Inner Council hope, 'open [their] eyes and give them a little understanding.' It was unfortunately very difficult to counsel such Brethren 'since they think they know best.'[24]

If, however, despite all his efforts to escape, a Brother was forced to take office, the Inner Council laid down that he should carry out his functions in the same spirit as a good member of the Unity performed other and less controversial duties. He was to seek justice and to avoid the snares of the unrighteous. Despite the fact that office-holding was only justified as a last resort after every effort had been made to avoid it, this was indeed a big concession.

A still bigger concession was to follow. 'Blessed are they which are persecuted for righteousness' sake,' the Inner Council quoted from the Beatitudes. But it was 'not [they went on to explain] that every unrighteousness had to be destroyed by [the Brethren], but that [they] should attempt to destroy it, though not indeed everywhere; at the very least they should not willingly succumb to it.' Even the obscurity of the original Czech cannot hide the fact that the spirit of such a passage is far removed from the simple negation of the state as an unqualified evil, which the Brethren had taken over from Chelčický.

---

[24] 'They have come to a certain amount of knowledge through certain Brethren,' says the edict (A. J. B., V. fol. 331v) of these overwise members of the Litomyšl community; and it is partly through this knowledge, it is hinted, that they are led to refuse all advice and admonition in the matter of taking office. The whole passage, as so often, is unclear; but it is possible that we have here an oblique attack on the protagonists of greater participation in the affairs of the world, inserted by those of the Inner Council and the priesthood who still held with varying degrees of firmness to the old views.

In indifferent matters, which it was neither a sin to avoid nor a virtue to perform, the Inner Council advised the Brethren to be careful, in cases where an element of personal gain might enter in, 'not to be forward in giving counsel and displaying their wisdom; for you indeed, better than others perhaps, should be able to realize that worldly people get little profit from you in their affairs, for it is a difficult enough matter for a Brother in a town to advise how the community should be administered so that its earthly affairs should prosper and endure.' But further difficulties, it was recognized, might easily arise for those Brethren who had accepted the office of alderman, trusting that they could preserve a clear conscience in the performance of their duties. These difficulties, however, the Inner Council was content to leave to be dealt with as they might arise.

The root of the trouble lay in the growth of a new type of Uniɩy member. The townsman, whether humble journeyman or prosperous trader, was not content with the meagre subsistence of a peasant. The accumulation of wealth was, indeed, one of the signs of virtue in the townsman. But this inevitably led to conflict with the principles of conduct which embodied the old relationship to society, suited to a peasant community. The reconciliation of theory and practice, which the Inner Council was striving for, resulted in effect in the pathetically indecisive terms in which the edict was couched. This is clearly brought out in the following passage:

Sometimes something may be [done] for such as wish to make sure both that, as regards business, their trades prosper everywhere and their earthly comforts are not greatly lacking, and that at the same time they may enjoy a good conscience and a certain assurance of salvation. But it is difficult to give advice in every instance and for every contingency.

In all doubtful cases the Inner Council had only one clear recommendation: let those with tender consciences return to the countryside. They admitted that such a change would probably bring material loss and that there would be some Brethren either unable or unwilling to make such a sacrifice. But this alone would bring 'a greater possibility of preserving a good conscience.' Already in such cases, they claimed, there were members of the Unity, who had 'changed their place [of residence] and accepted a diminution in trade, content with more modest needs.'

The Inner Council, in which the country element was still strong, condemned the movement on the part of the Brethren towards the towns. It was apprehensive, too, that any further concessions in this question oɩ the acceptance of the alderman's office would give it new momentum. If the Council were now to make such acceptance still easier, it argued, 'either with the taking of the oath or without,' or permitting kneeling

before the consecrated wafer, which was also often demanded of aldermen, then more Brethren 'would be enticed into the towns – persons who
had not previously had their living there, come now only to gain riches –
than ever abandoned the cities over the preceding years for the purpose of
attaining what is good.'

According to the evidence provided by the edict, the rank-and-file of
the Unity appear to have lost much of their earlier enthusiasm for the
radical negation of the world and its allurements that was embodied in
their church's political and social doctrines. The Inner Council complain:

Whenever we have done, either through incompetence or unawares,
something to their material disadvantage, they have long blamed us and
continue to blame us. Whenever [i.e. for the same reasons] we have done
or allowed to be done something to their spiritual disadvantage, if only it
be of material benefit, then likewise they have no difficulty in laying the
blame and the sin on us, saying: it is the Brethren [i.e. the Inner Council]
who have sanctioned it.

Such persons, however, may not have been typical of the average Unity
member, who continued to live out his life in the village of his birth
according to the old principles. It was, says the Inner Council, 'the
weaker people among the Brethren, those inclined to worldly things and
to bodily licentiousness and comfort above the measure of their own
needs, who have been – and are now – attracted to the towns.' All those,
at any rate, 'who may settle in the towns of their own free will, being able
to gain a living elsewhere, and there take upon themselves such dangerous
offices as the alderman's or the sexton's (kostelníčí) etc., such persons
– it may be said – have brought upon themselves the sins they have incurred
in this way.' Indeed, one of the reasons for issuing the edict, the Inner
Council adds, was to aid such persons, for 'they could escape all this if
they wished to listen' to the advice of their spiritual leaders.

Those in favour of taking office had used with the Inner Council the
argument that, 'through it, others might be directed towards righteousness (v spravedlnostech opravovati).' The Inner Council does not appear to
have been impressed by this line; since 'a great evil cannot be set aright by
a little good, for there are few Brethren who would have the opportunity
for this.'[25]

It is significant that the question of the validity of oath-taking among
Christians, around which so much controversy in the Unity was later to
centre, does not arise directly in the edict. It is not clear from the wording

[25] A. J. B., V, fols. 331–333 (quoted in part in Goll-Krofta, op. cit., pp. 196–98).

how far it actually sanctioned the oath. But it is difficult to see
how the acceptance of the alderman's office could be approved, even
though only in certain exceptional circumstances, without similar approval
being given to taking the oath which was demanded of everyone entering
upon office.[26] Opposition to oaths among some of the members of the
Inner Council was, however, probably still strong enough to prevent more
than tacit assent being granted to so revolutionary a step.

The documentary evidence gives no indication of precisely what sections
among the Litomyšl Brethren were responsible for the appeal to the Inner
Council: whether, indeed, the problems under discussion touched all the
Brethren equally, as a community, or whether certain members were more
nearly affected than others.

Two points alone are certain. First, the problem of accepting office and
of the attitude to be taken up towards the state in general was, as the
edict's advice to the Litomyšl Brethren to remove to the country shows,
one which weighed more heavily on the town communities than on the
village groups, though even here the problem might present itself for
solution.

Secondly, it was not by any means confined to the Litomyšl Brethren,
nor was it an entirely novel issue, which had not appeared before 1490.
Krasonický, for instance, writes that:

Everywhere, even in the villages, the Brethren were being placed in
offices, in that of judge or alderman or some other, and they were made to
take the oath on the boundaries. If they did not wish to do so, they had
to pay fines, which were imposed on them for not testifying to the truth
according to the custom of the land with the confirmation of an oath.
Likewise in regard to the alderman's and other offices, it was nowhere
permitted that, living together in the community as fellow citizens, they
should escape their duties.[27]

Another contemporary witness, Brother Lukáš, though one who, like
Krasonický, was also hostile to the old views, confirms the widespread
nature of the problem which the Unity was facing at the time. He writes
that 'when countless troubles from the nobility arose [i.e. for the Brethren]
throughout the Czech lands and in Moravia, because of the offices of
alderman and judge and of oath-taking, with imprisonment and torture and

---

[26]   Winter, *Kulturní obraz českých měst*, I, pp. 657–59, 730, 731.
[27]   'O učených,' fol. 18v (quoted in Goll-Krofta, *op. cit.*, p. 206). The oath on the
boundaries probably refers to the juryman's oath as to the boundaries of holdings
defined only by customary law. I am grateful to Professor R. R. Betts for this suggestion.

fines, they often sent up from the provinces to the elders of the Brethren for advice as to what to do; and the elders advised them to remove from the cities into the suburbs.[28]

The question as to the source of inspiration for the appeals made by the Litomyšl Brethren, as well as by communities from other towns, should perhaps be approached from another angle. Was the whole community equally liable for those duties and obligations demanded by the authorities which ran contrary to the religious principles of the Brethren? Was there a division within the town community between those Brethren who, finding the burden of continual refusal of the demands of the authorities insupportable, began to chafe more and more at the restrictions imposed by the old ideology and, on the other hand, those who, not being liable – at least in the same degree – for such services, would not have the same incentives to throw over the traditional viewpoint? In other words, can the origins of the two parties in the ensuing controversy concerning the Unity's political and social doctrines be traced back not only to the division between the town and country membership, between the educated and the simple Brethren, but also to the existence of social differences within the new Brethren communities in the towns, which were rapidly growing in numerical strength?

During the fifteenth century artisans were almost always obliged to become members of their respective gilds.[29] The grandmaster of a gild (cechmistr) on coming into office was required to take an oath, which was indeed demanded in offices of every kind; and his duties included various judicial and administrative functions of a semi-public nature. He could even in some cases sentence persons to imprisonment. But the grand-masters were elected, not by all the members of the gild, but only by the masters, that is, by the more influential and affluent citizens.[30] Conditions were much the same in regard to other municipal offices.

Aldermen on the other hand, of whom there were usually 12 in larger towns forming the town council in charge of municipal administration and jurisdiction within the city boundaries, responsible, too, for carrying out the death penalty on occasion, might theoretically be appointed from almost all townsmen possessing full citizen rights (právo městké). 'In fact [writes Winter] many such were excluded. Since the retiring alder-men always had influence on the election of the new ones, ... a virtual burgher aristocracy grew up, distinct from their poorer neighbours, who

---

[28]   Lukáš, *Odpis proti odtržencom*, fol. 45v (quoted *ibid.*, p. 212).
[29]   Winter, *Dějeny řemesel a obchodu v Čechách v XIV a XV století*, pp. 592, 593.
[30]   *Ibid.*, pp. 661, 663, 664, 666–76.

were not elected to the council and represented, therefore, a democratic element within the community.'[31]   Judges, too, exercising extensive authority within the township and combining judicial, police and executive functions, might be appointed from the ranks of almost all those possessing full citizen rights. But practice once again confined this choice to a narrower circle. The judge, in addition to his judicial functions, was responsible for the administration of the prison and was a participant in the torture of accused persons and convicted criminals.[32]

In addition to the full citizens, there also existed in most towns a class of inhabitants with lesser rights or no rights at all. There were, first, those who did not possess their own house, property ownership being an essential qualification for full citizenship. Secondly came the numerous inhabitants of the suburbs which grew up around most towns, those who had their houses or shacks outside the city gates. These consisted mainly of the poorest immigrants from the countryside, peasants and village artisans, fishermen and others who were unable or unwilling to bear the full burden of citizenship.[33]

The main offices in the city – the grand-masters of the gilds, the aldermen, and the judges – were, therefore, only open in effect to the richer and more influential citizens. The position of alderman, at least, was reserved for the very highest layer of urban society. At the same time, outside the ranks of the citizens privileged to a greater or lesser degree, there existed whole groups of inhabitants, the town poor and the dwellers in the suburbs, who did not enjoy any legal rights at all within the urban community.

It was with the validity of taking up office, of accepting that of alderman in particular, that the appeals for advice from the Litomyšl and other Brethren communities were mainly concerned; and it was these appeals that ushered in the controversy which was finally to transform completely the Unity's political and social doctrines. These facts would seem clearly to indicate that the inspiration for such appeals, the desire for a modification of the old principles, arose mainly among those Brethren belonging to the richer and more prosperous sections of the urban community. Among those Brethren who had settled in the towns, writes the Inner Council in its edict, 'sometimes, as in Litomyšl, the better sort are sum-

---

[31]   Winter, *Kulturní obraz českých měst*, I, pp. 633, 637–40, 643, 644, 647.
[32]   *Ibid.*, II, pp. 3, 4, 9, 757, 840.
[33]   *Ibid.*, I, 65, 70, 74, 75, 756. For the economic, social, and legal position of the poorest members of the town community before, and during the early stages of, the Hussite revolution, see František Graus, *Chudina městská v době předhusitské* (Prague, 1949), esp. chaps. II, IV.

moned to take office or their help in counsel is required.'[34] It was to be 'the better' Brethren who were to carry through the internal revolution which succeeded in transforming the Unity within a few decades.

Nevertheless, the problem of the relationship of the Unity to the state was one which, even though to a lesser degree, touched all its members, rich and poor, peasant and townsman. It was this that made so futile Brother Matěj's advice to those town Brethren troubled as to how to square the demands of the authorities with their consciences, to move into the suburbs or to remove altogether from the towns and return to the simple life of the village. For even the suburbs and the village communities had their own officials, aldermen, and judges as in the towns; though, it is true, their competence was much narrower and their functions less likely to conflict with the Brethren's principles.[35] Most fit male inhabitants of the country, however, might on occasion be liable for military service, even if only in the event of a direct threat to their own township or village; and it would be rather the poorer inhabitants of town and country who would be unable to buy a substitute, if chosen for service in the general levy (veřejná hotovost).[36] Anyone, too, might have to appear as a witness in court where the taking of an oath was obligatory.[37]

It is not surprising, therefore, that the Inner Council's edict failed to set at rest the doubts entertained by many Brethren concerning the attitude they should take up in such matters. Those who attempted to put its injunctions into practice found that its precepts did not bring relief from hardship and persecution. Lukáš has painted a dark picture of the situation at this period. When some had exchanged the town for the suburbs or the country, he writes:

It still did not help at all. Many indeed were quite unable to take this step; still others were faint-hearted and, being put to torture, [acted] against their consciences, taking unchristian oaths [i.e. oaths by the Virgin Mary or the saints] and accepting such like things.'[38] 'And when even that was sometimes of no avail they [i.e. Matěj and the Inner Council] advised them to buy themselves out or take some other employment. And that, too, was of no avail, for other persons also were trying to do the same thing, and it was not possible for many people to [escape] this way.[39]

---

[34]   A. J. B., V, fol. 333 (quoted in Goll-Krofta, op. cit., p. 198).
[35]   Krofta, Dějiny selského stavu, pp. 139–41; Winter, op. cit., I, pp. 75, 76.
[36]   Winter, op. cit., I, pp. 280, 299, 306; Dějiny řemesel a obchodu, p. 654; Krofta, op. cit., pp. 136, 137.
[37]   Winter, Kulturní obraz, II, pp. 659, 660.
[38]   A. J. B., IV, fol. 143v (quoted in Goll-Krofta, op. cit., p. 212).
[39]   Odpis, fol. 45v (quoted loc. cit.).

The mood among many of the town Brethren was rapidly changing from willingness to follow the counsel of the leaders of the Unity, even if this should mean continued hardship and suffering, to one of potential revolt, of openly expressed dissatisfaction. Krasonický has preserved for us the apt comment of one Filip the Soapmaker, a Litomyšl Brother, on learning of Matěj's advice to retire to the country: 'Cows won't give soap and, anyhow, the nobles appoint aldermen and judges there too.'[40]

The Inner Council, divided between the protagonists of the old principles and those wishing their modification, was thoroughly perplexed as to the right course to be pursued. Lukáš writes:

They held many meetings and sessions and discussions on this matter, with prayers and fasting, according to the scriptures, seeking God's will. And through the holy scriptures they came to realize that some believers in Christ had exercised civil power and taken oaths. From this they reasoned that such things were not everywhere and in all cases forbidden by the holy scriptures. Secondly, they realized that such prohibitions arose from an unmeasured and 'high' way of thinking as well as from twisting and misusing the scriptures.[41]

This, then, was the position when in the same year the Inner Council, in which at least a majority seems now to have become convinced of the need to relax the strict code of conduct hitherto prevailing among the Brethren, decided to call a general assembly of 'all the priests, deacons, assessors and assistants (*všech kněží, jáhnuov, soudci i pomocníkuov*).'[42] Such gatherings had been held only very rarely during the early years of the Unity's history, partly because of the difficulties of travel at that date. Indeed, between 1467 and 1490 an assembly of this kind does not appear to have been called at all.[43] The Inner Council's present decision to convoke a general assembly was, therefore, a measure of the concern which the growing dissension among the Brethren was evoking throughout the whole Unity.

Preceded by preliminary prayers and fasting among the congregations the assembly was held at Brandýs nad Orlicí, a well-established centre of Brethren activity. Its precise date is not known. The agenda of the proceedings had been circulated among the Brethren before the first session opened. Four questions were to be debated at the assembly. The

---

[40] 'O učených,' fol. 18v (quoted *ibid.*, p. 206).
[41] *Odpis, loc. cit.* It is not completely clear whether these words refer only to the period in 1490 between the composition of the Inner Council's reply to the Litomyšl Brethren and the general assembly held later in the year. But such an interpretation seems the most probable from the context.
[42] *Odpis*, fol. 46 (quoted Goll-Krofta, *op. cit.*, p. 212).
[43] Tapié, *Une église tchèque au XVe siècle: L'Unité des Frères*, p. 87.

first of these, however, which concerned the degree of authority a member of the Unity was to exercise within his own family, was of secondary importance. The main discussions were to centre around the other three items, all concerned with the burning question of the attitude of the Unity to the state and its demands.

What was to be the Unity's attitude to the acceptance of authority by its members, hitherto officially forbidden, or to the carrying out of the demands of the powers that be, which in so many cases conflicted with the old rigorism? Were the Brethren to permit worldly power among themselves 'actively and passively'? A further question, closely connected with the first two, concerned the much debated problem of the validity of oath-taking for those who – like the early Brethren – were trying to live out the Christian gospel in every detail in their daily lives. 'Did the Lord forbid the oath in every shape so that never, and in no circumstances, could one swear?' These were the knotty problems awaiting solution, which faced the Brethren when they gathered together at Brandýs.[44]

A significant feature of the conference, ominous indeed for the future of the Old Brethren's point of view, was the invitation extended to two noblemen, 'who were in sympathy with the Unity': Albrecht Rendl of Oušava and Liška. Their presence must have considerably influenced the discussions, weighing the scales in favour of a solution favourable to the new demands, since, even though they were almost certainly not at that time actual members of the Unity, they participated fully in the proceedings of the conference. Nothing is known for certain as to the identity of Liška.[45] But Rendl of Oušava is a well-known and rather sinister figure in Czech history. Sprung from the minor gentry, he was yet to rise to high office in the land, gaining a bad name in history as the protagonist of the nobility against the towns in their struggle for power during the early years of the sixteenth century.[46] He was a capable man, but ambitious and unscrupulous; his lack of principle made him a strange adviser for the devout Brethren and, as will be seen, disillusioned they were eventually to sever all connection with him.

Klenovský opened the proceedings on behalf of Matěj and the Inner Council. He asked the assembled Brethren to give their frank opinion as to how far civil authority was consistent with the Unity's principles. 'For [he had to admit] we simply do not know to what degree we should allow

---

[44] 'O učených,' fol. 18v, 19 (quoted *ibid.*, p. 206).
[45] See Goll-Krofta, *op. cit.*, p. 176.
[46] For Rendl, see Jireček, *op. cit.*, II, pp. 169–76; *Ottův slovník naučný*, XXI (Prague, 1904), pp. 552–54.

or prohibit these things.' Those knowing how to write, therefore, were to put down their views on pieces of paper with their names and place them in an urn. Those who were illiterate were to get someone knowing how to write to take down their opinion for them.

Then all those present – including the two noble sympathizers, Rendl and Liška, who were not indeed strictly entitled to do so – handed in their opinions (cedulki), with the exception of Brother Matěj. 'He was fearful [writes Krasonický later] lest through the acceptance of authority the Unity would be corrupted. And they earnestly urged him to come down on one side or the other in this matter of authority: either that it could be admitted among the faithful, or that it could not, as at the beginning they had accepted from Petr Chelčický's treatise.' From Krasonický's account, the only one left us of the actual course of the conference's proceedings, it would seem that the result was a forgone conclusion even before the urn with the Brethren's opinions was opened: otherwise Matěj's hesitation would have been pointless, if it had not already been fairly certain that some degree of approval would be given to a modification of the old viewpoint. Once again Matěj's lack of decision, his fear of going against the opinion of the educated members of his Council, even where his own convictions ran contrary to theirs, and his inability to give a lead in times of crisis, showed themselves at this critical moment. 'He did not dare [Krasonický writes] to remain alone and he, too, gave way, but not in his heart.'[47]

All the members of the Inner Council (starší) were agreed on assigning a legitimate place to civil authority 'among the faithful, both actively and passively.' Klenovský is said to have expressed himself during one of the sessions even more forcibly: 'If we forbid the Brethren to take part in the administration of justice (aby se nesoudili), we shall be placing an unbearable yoke upon the necks of our followers, which even our fathers were unable to bear.'[48]

Though not expressly stated, it is probable nevertheless that some of the ordinary Brethren present came out against any watering down of the Unity's previous doctrines. But the influence of such members as Táborský and Prokop, as well as of the non-member Rendl, whose

[47] Such passages show that Gindely's verdict on Matěj, op. cit., p. 66 – 'seine innerste Neigung galt der gemässigsten Partei, aber die Überzeugungen seines Meisters Gregor hatten noch immer ihre Kraft auf ihm nich verloren' – is incorrect. Matěj's innermost convictions lay rather with the doctrines of Řehoř and the old Brethren, but the superior will-power and learning of the opponents of such views among his nearest advisers was to gain an increasing influence on his policy.

[48] A. J. B., IV, fol. 51v (quoted in Goll-Krofta, op. cit., p. 226).

statements all came out definitely in favour of the acceptance by the Unity of a more positive attitude towards the state, proved of greater weight than the force of tradition. Prokop's statement was read out to the assembly on the recommendation of Brother Matěj and his council. Then the delgates were told that, if they had any objections to the contents of Prokop's statement, they should make these known, since 'it is not a matter involving a loss of life or honour and, if they do it out of a sense of duty and with love, they will be dealt with in their turn with kindness.'[49]

The Inner Council was entrusted by those present with drawing up at once before the delegates dispersed a new edict (*výpověd*), which would contain the decisions arrived at during the conference and a justification for the changes in doctrine. According to Lukáš's *O obnovení*, in order to save time (*abych krátkosti požíval*) the conference accepted as a basis for the edict the exposition of the Brother 'who had written well on good will,' and whose 'writing and commentary on the fifth chapter of St. Matthew concerning the higher righteousness' had seemingly also been read out and approved during the conference. This could only have been Brother Prokop, though neither of the works mentioned are any longer extant.[50]

Prokop's gift for finding a compromise solution broadly acceptable to both sides, as exemplified in his treatment of the controversy on justification by works or faith, makes his authorship of the edict most probable. He had already, in the period immediately before the conference at Brandýs, made effective use of a clever argument to counteract the tendency to regard the opinions of Řehoř and the Old Brethren as binding on the Unity for ever. Cross-questioning a gathering of Brethren about certain articles of their faith, and finding they held diverse opinions, he had then gone on to quote passages from the writings of the early Brethren, where they had condemned a lack of unanimity in matters of faith within any Christian congregation, holding that such diveristy was the mark of damnation and had advocated that such people be shunned by all true believers. 'Therefore [Prokop concluded triumphantly] I tell you in all sincerity that I do not know how to justify these passages; and if they

---

[49] 'O učených,' fols. 19–20 (quoted Goll-Krofta, *op. cit.*, pp. 206, 207).
[50] 'O obnovení,' fol. 95v (quoted *ibid.*, pp. 175, 202). According to Goll, Prokop's tract probably contained a commentary on the Sermon on the Mount, in which a differentiation was made between Christ's commandments (*přikázání*) and his mere advice (*rada*). The former was to be obeyed in all cases, the latter might to some extent be a matter of choice: in this way the severe code of behaviour of the early Unity, obligatory for all true Christians, was seriously undermined.

really are true, it would be right to depart from you and provide for one-self in some other way.' The Brethren, alarmed at the thought that their leaders might desert them, answered: 'Dear Brother Prokop ... do not leave us; we very much want to listen to what you recommend in this as in other matters and, indeed, in everything.' The incident, says Kraso-nický who relates the story, was a prelude to the Inner Council's taking under serious consideration the whole question of the Unity's attitude to the civil authorities.[51]

All this would seem to indicate that the actual composition of the edict of Brandýs was the result of Prokop's drafting. Nevertheless, Krasonický's narrative later implies that it was Táborský's statement (*cedule*), com-posed during the conference, and not Prokop's, that provided the basis for the edict.[52] This, too, would seem to be more in line with Lukáš's statement that two of the Brethren opposed to the old doctrines, 'making their excuses, did not take part in these matters [i.e. the passing of the edict] in order that it should not be said that the wise and the learned had brought them about.' One of these two men was definitely Klenovský; and the other has been identified by Goll as most probably Prokop.[53] But whoever may have been most reponsible for the drawing up of the actual text, its contents must almost certainly have been agreed upon beforehand among such leading figures as Klenovský, Prokop, and Táborský.

The edict of Brandýs, as this momentous document was called, refers back in its very first sentence to the question, first postulated by the Litomyšl Brethren, as to whether Unity members should accept office. It is again admitted that it is a difficult problem, and that the Brethren are most anxious to avoid anything that might be against God's will or against their own consciences. But necessity had forced them to come to some decision in the matter. They therefore recommend, in view of the countless temptations involved, that no Brother should 'of his own free will' accept office as an alderman, judge, or grandmaster of a gild, or become a tavern-keeper, or go to the wars, 'or ever be instrumental in torturing or putting to death a fellow-man accused of wrong-doing.' A

[51] 'O učených,' fols. 17v, 18 (quoted *ibid.*, p. 206).
[52] 'O učených,' fols. 19v, 20 (quoted *ibid.*, p. 207). Cf. Lukáš, *Odpis*, fol. 46 (quoted *ibid.*, pp. 212, 213), where it is merely stated that the assembled Brethren left it to the elders to draw up the exact wording of the edict, and that the final version, presented in the name of all the members of the Inner Council, was then unanimously accepted by the whole assembly as their own. Though it probably exaggerates the degree of unanimity, this account contains all that can be regarded as certain concerning the authorship of the edict.
[53] 'O obnovení,' fol. 97 (quoted *ibid.*, p. 203).

Brother should avoid as far as possible such occupations, repeating the words of the Lord's Prayer: 'Lead us not into temptation.'

So far, the edict followed closely the viewpoint of the Old Brethren. But what was to happen if all their efforts were in vain and the authorities demanded acceptance on pain of the most serious penalties? Here the edict was to make a concession, which constituted in essence a complete reversal of the Unity's official standpoint hitherto.

If a Brother should be forced by the civil authority, against his conscience, to accept any of these things, being unable to escape either through humble pleading or in any other way, he should according to [our] counsel submit to the authorities in whatever is not against God. ... For in such matters as these, although it is difficult to preserve a good conscience and shun evil, it is not impossible. ... We cannot give uniform instruction and teaching as to how one should conduct oneself [i.e., in such cases], on account of the divergence of cause, place, time, and persons. Those Brethren, indeed, throughout the whole country, to whom the task of oversight is entrusted, should consider the matter and discuss amongst themselves what counsel and teaching should be given those placed in such situations, as to how they should behave. And wherever the Brethren cannot agree on any matter, there is Brother Matěj in Rýchnov to appeal to in the more difficult and perplexing questions.

This perhaps is not formally a great advance on the reply sent earlier in the year to the Litomyšl Brethren. In the trickier cases the decision is left once again to the provincial congregations and the individual Brethren to make; and the injunction to comply with the demands of the authorities, where these cannot be avoided, 'in whatever is not against God' is extremely evasive. The point at issue was to determine exactly what was and what was not against God's will, or, in other words, to discover whether a certain line of action previously condemned by the Unity was not in reality quite consistent with Christ's teachings. The injunction to accept the duties of office in so far as these did not conflict with God's will, if taken literally, scarcely provided an answer to these questions. The general advice that 'in every class and in every rank, in all professions, at every time and in every place, let the scripture be fulfilled: 'Let every one that nameth the name of Christ depart from iniquity' [2 Timothy II, 19] and 'Let him eschew evil and do good' [1 Peter III, 11],' did not go far in defining exactly what tasks undertaken at the command of the powers that be were wrong for the Christian to perform.

Nevertheless, the tone of the new edict is more forceful, more authoritative, and the responsibility of Matěj and the Inner Council to give a definite ruling in difficult cases is expressly stated. Goll has pointed out that, although neither the question of the validity of oaths nor that of the admission of members of the nobility into the Unity was expressly dealt with in the edict, a positive answer was implicit in its decisions.[54] By the edict of Brandýs, therefore, the holding of office, a more positive attitude to the demands of the state, was officially recognized as being consistent with the Unity way of life, though such recognition was still hedged around with numerous provisos and restrictions.

It was laid down that not only were office and all forms of state service to be avoided if humanly possible if exemption were not to be obtained, or, at least those duties which directly conflicted with Christian morality should be refused. Under no circumstances, either, were the Brethren to call in the aid of the state in matters concerning Unity members alone. 'We should not permit civil authority with all its laws and punishments among ourselves.' Nevertheless, even here the edict gave a loophole for a further modification of the rule later on since, although the Brethren were urged to resist any attempt to have recourse to the law and the state in their own affairs, their opposition was to be carried on 'moderately until a further understanding' had been reached.

At the same time a conscientious objection clause was inserted in the edict for those among the Brethren who held to the old principles. All that was to be demanded of such persons was tolerance of those Brethren whose consciences directed them otherwise.

Anyone for whom it would be against their conscience to become an alderman, judge, etc. [the edict states] should not be constrained by the fact that the Brethren allow this with fitting reservations. Whoever would rather suffer should have the liberty to do so, on condition only that he does not vilify those who have approved this, and that he should not consider himself better than those who do not suffer.[55]

---

[54] Goll-Krofta, *op. cit.*, pp. 176, 177. Lukáš in his 'O obnovení,' fols. 95v, 96 (quoted *ibid.*, p. 202), states, however, that the edict expressly allowed 'nobles and those in authority' to be accepted into the Unity, under certain conditions, without renouncing their positions. He states here, too, that the edict also permitted members of the Unity to call in the aid of the law 'for their own defence,' a point which does not figure in the other versions; and, in addition, that it dealt with the subject of oaths and the types of employment permitted among the Brethren. It is most likely, however, that this account was not so much a précis of the edict's contents as a summary of the inferences drawn from it over the next few years.

[55] *Odpis*, fols. 46v, 47 (quoted *ibid.*, pp. 213, 214). The edict appears in several versions, apart from the one given by Lukáš in his *Odpis*. Goll-Krofta prints the more important variations from the *Zprava větší strany o rozmlouvání v Chlumci* and Lukáš's *Psaní proti těm, kteříž samými písmy bez zprávcův neb kněží zpravovati se chtějí*. There is also a shortened version in *O obnovení*, see note 54.

For a decade and more the edict of Brandýs was to be a bone of contention between the two factions within the Unity, a source of bitterness and
hatred between one Brother and another. For those who remained loyal
to the old political and social doctrines it meant a betrayal of their dearest
principles. The only motive for these changes, in their view, was a desire
to escape persecution. Through the edict their opponents 'had let the
looseness of the world' into the Unity; and it is, indeed, hard to avoid the
conclusion that, since holding office, going to the wars, condemning
criminals to death and participating in their torture and execution, and
the other actions hitherto officially forbidden to the Brethren, were still to
be avoided at almost any cost, a quite understandable desire to put an end
to the suffering involved in resistance was now in fact the main reason for
justifying conformity in the final instance. If objection were taken only to
those actions involved in carrying out such duties 'as were against God,'
why still advise Unity members to avoid the other and less reprehensible
duties altogether if this were at all possible?

The logic of the situation was finally to drive the Unity still further on
the road towards conformity. But for some years the opponents of the
Old Brethren continued flatly to deny any truth in such assertions. They
claimed that the Brethren had not ceased to be persecuted after the passing
of the edict, though they had to admit, indeed, that it was no longer their
attitude to the state which gave rise to such persecution. The recent
changes were due, they said, to the fact that they had now regained 'the
true interpretation of the holy scriptures.'[56] The demand for this had
come from below, from the rank-and-file Brethren; and, anyhow, from
the beginning the rigorists had not been consistent. 'Those who advocated not swearing, not accepting office etc. in reality were not themselves
constant in this matter.'[57]

The call to preserve mutual toleration was to remain only a pious hope.
Nevertheless the assembly had broken up in a conciliatory atmosphere.
Either on the same day as the edict was approved by the delegates or on the
day following – Lukáš's account is not clear on this point – a further
resolution was read out and likewise accepted by those present. The
decisions just taken, this said, had not been reached in a hurry, but over a
period of several years, as a result of lengthy consideration by Brother
Matěj and his Inner Council of the problems involved. They were not
light decisions but such as were forced upon them by dire necessity. The
leadership of the Unity, it was claimed, had done its utmost to show

[56] A. J. B., IV, fol. 143v.
[57] Ibid., fol. 28.

tolerance of all points of view. 'Therefore, if anyone has any objections [i.e. to the decisions taken], great or small, let him make them known before you depart.' But 'they all said that they approved and without more ado accepted everything as good.'[58]

There is much that is hard to understand in the story as related by Lukáš. It is certain that there were opponents of the viewpoint expressed in the edict present at the assembly: 'certain persons of the primitive 'high' way of thinking (*někteří z prvního vysokého smýšlení*),' Lukáš calls them. But it is hard to see why they 'hid (*zatajili*)' their opinions at this critical moment, especially when it is realized that both Amos and Jakub, the two future leaders of the opposition Minor Party, men who appear later as remarkably outspoken in the defence of their views, were delegates to the assembly.[59] Were they temporarily appeased by the recognition still accorded the old doctrines in the edict? Or were they perhaps overawed by the weight of opinion on the side of a change in doctrine and by the superior learning of their opponents? Or, even more likely, were they motivated by a combination of both these reasons, feeling that as things had turned out the best plan was to bide their time and wait until they had returned among their own people, before opening the attack against the innovations?

In view of the absence of documentary evidence these can only remain suppositions. What is clear, however, is that even though no one came forward to voice their objections to the edict, the leadership of the Unity was still apprehensive that the seeming unanimity would prove illusory, since they now brought forward still another supplementary resolution, which was forthwith passed unanimously:

If, after thinking things over or for any other reasons, anyone should still find any objections [it stated] he should neither speak nor act openly or in secret against this edict ... but coming in person – or writing – to Brother Matěj and his Brethren, he should inform them or that Brother who is in charge of the province. And Brother Matěj and his Brethren should take the matter into consideration, and arrange that without disturbance things should either remain as they are or something in them be changed. If, however, anyone should not observe what is here ordained ... having first been admonished, he should then be corrected. But if anyone, not out of weakness but from stubbornness and wilfulness, should be unwilling to accept correction, but should cause disturbances and dissension, then ... shall he first be excluded from the body and blood of the Lord and, should he remain obstinate corrupting others, he shall be expelled from

[58] *Odpis*, fol. 47v (quoted *ibid.*, pp. 214, 215).
[59] 'O obnovení,' fol. 96v (quoted *ibid.*, p. 202).

his congregation and, if he continue in his wickedness, from the Unity as well.[60]

This resolution was to figure prominently in the forthcoming controversy. It was to provide theoretical justification for the expulsion of the leaders of the Minor Party on the grounds, not of their opposition to the new regulations – for had not both viewpoints been granted toleration in the edict of Brandýs? – but because of their 'stubborness and wilfulness' and 'the disturbances and dissension' they were to inspire.[61]

The protagonists of the old doctrines had, indeed, committed a tactical blunder in not immediately coming out into the open with their opposition to the recent changes. They had given their opponents the opportunity to brand them as destroyers of the Unity's discipline, rebels against the properly constituted leadership. They had made it harder for themselves to act as if they were martyrs of conscience, suffering on account of their religious beliefs and penalized by their opponents for remaining faithful to the old doctrines of the Unity, even though this may not have been so very far from the truth.

---

[60]   Odpis, fols. 47v, 48 (quoted ibid., p. 215).

[61]   Krasonický in his 'O Učených,' fol. 20 (quoted ibid., p. 207), in line with Lukáš's account, says that neither Amos nor Jakub gave their formal agreement to what had been enacted during the assembly. This is not inconsistent, however, with their having given tacit assent to this proposal through refraining from any sign of open opposition. As Lukáš writes in his Odpis, loc. cit.: 'Being summoned to this assembly and having objections, they kept them to themselves and thus showed a lack of loyalty, for indeed they knew quite well that whoever holds his tongue in such matters in fact gives his consent to what is being enacted.'

IV

THE BEGINNINGS OF THE MINOR PARTY

The edict of Brandýs, however ill-defined its provisions may seem in comparison with the position the Brethren were later to take up in formulating their new approach to society, marks the first stage in the internal revolution within the Unity. This revolution was to transform it from an obscure sect of semi-literate peasants and humble artisans into a religious community, in which the aristocracy of birth and wealth as well as of learning and literature were to play their part in making it one of the most vital forces in the history of the Czech lands during the century preceding the battle of the White Mountain. But the victory of the reformers was bought at a great price. They were prepared to throw over almost all those doctrines of the early Brethren which signified their distinctive contribution to the history of political thought. They were ready to abandon the attempt to live out the ideal of the early Christian church not – as the medieval monastic orders had done – apart from the world, but within society.

The revolution, however, was not carried through without a struggle. The controversy which ensued was, indeed, marked by all the bitterness and rancour and verbal slander, which quarrels in the realm of theology or politics seem almost inevitably to arouse. But it was not until after the assembly of Brandýs was over that a well-defined party arose among the Brethren, which was eventually prepared to split the Unity and go into the wilderness rather than sanction any adulteration of the old doctrines.

The history of the Minor Party (*Menší strana*), as these Brethren are usually known,[1] is associated in particular with two names: Amos and Jakub (or Kubik) Štěkenský, both participants in the conference of

---

[1] Their opponents who, it was soon to become clear, formed the majority of the Unity were often known as the Major Party (*Větší strana*). The epithets, 'conservative,' 'progressive', 'radical,' etc., have been used by modern historians to describe both parties. This has led to some confusion and indeed begs the issue. Wherever possible I have avoided such terms.

Brandýs who now went back to their home district of Prácheň in south
Bohemia and immediately began a vigorous campaign against the new
trends in the Unity, and against the recently promulgated edict in particular. Soon after their return home the two composed a tract in defence
of the old doctrine which they then sent to Brother Matěj.[2] This was,
indeed, quite in accordance with the provisions of the edict of Brandýs.
However, they did not then wait for Matěj's answer, but began agitating
among their fellow Brethren against the decisions taken at Brandýs,
whereby they made themselves liable to disciplinary action from their
church authorities.

It is at the assembly of Brandýs that the names of the two future leaders
of the Minor Party are met with for the first time. In later controversy it
is Amos who figures most prominently. 'Among all the schismatics he
was first and foremost [writes Lukáš in 1527] being the source (*původ*) of
them all.'[3] Nevertheless, it was rather Jakub the Miller from Štěkeň in
the district of Prácheň, won over by Amos for the cause of the old doctrines about a year before the holding of the assembly of Brandýs,[4] who
at first assumed the leadership. Of Jakub's early career almost nothing is
known.[5]

Lukáš, however, has preserved several details about the activities of
Amos, his lifelong opponent, relating to the period before 1490. He had
been, says Lukáš, 'prominent in the Band of Love (*v rotě milovné*)' before
he joined the Brethren: by which statement Lukáš meant that Amos had
been one of those converted by Brother Řehoř to the Unity from the
Adamites. This may well be true. But Lukáš goes on to give some further
bits of information of a scurrilous nature, the truth of which is more than
doubtful. Amos, Lukáš claims, had been from the beginning a secret
enemy of Brother Řehoř, a kind of fifth-columnist among the Brethren;
he led, moreover, an immoral life and had amassed a large fortune through
various shady dealings. He was probably, it is true, always a somewhat
difficult character to handle, but the accusations of personal dishonesty
and immorality are unproven. Amos had originated from Uherský Brod
in Moravia and later became a trader in wax, an occupation permitted to
its members by the strict social code of the early Brethren and one which
must have brought him into contact with a wide circle of acquaintances in

---

[2] Lukáš, 'O obnovení,' fol. 96v; Krasonický, 'O učených,' fol. 20; Lukáš, *Odpis proti održencom*, fol. 48; Akta Jednoty Bratrské, IV, fols. 145, 145v (quoted Goll-Krofta, *Chelčický a Jednota v XV. století*, pp. 203, 207, 215, 216).

[3] A. J. B., IV, fol. 111 v.

[4] Šafařík, 'Br. Jana Blahoslava historie bratří českých,' *Č. Č. M.*, 1862, p. 107.

[5] Jireček, *Rukověť k dějinám literatury české*, I, p. 430.

different parts of Bohemia and Moravia. He now made his home at Vodňany in south Bohemia, not far from Chelčický's native village; and from here carried on a successful business activity.[6] He was also prominent locally in the church life of his province, being an assistant (*pomocník*) of the Unity clergy.[7]

It is impossible to say what measure of support Amos and Jakub possessed either before or after their return from the assembly of Brandýs. The followers whom they were to gather around them during the next few years were not, according to Müller, confined only to their own province of Prácheň, but were to be found elsewhere among the Unity congregations around Beroun, Lanškroun, Litomyšl, Klatov, as well as in Moravia.[8] Krasonický says that 'of the schismatics there were at the beginning only two,' Amos and Jakub.[9] This is certainly a gross exaggeration, but it may be true that they were at first the only ones ready to take an active lead against the innovators. They certainly had quite a number of supporters and sympathizers among the delegates at the assembly, as the whole course of the proceedings clearly shows; and Lukáš expressly states that 'Amos was present at this assembly with some of his supporters (*s svými některými*).'[10]

Devotion to the ideals of Brother Řehoř and the Old Brethren must have been widespread among Unity members throughout the country, despite the increasing hardships entailed in carrying them into practice. Support for them was forthcoming expecially from the older generation, as well as from the country Brethren and the poorest members in the towns, many of whom retained something of the uncompromising thirst after righteousness unsullied by contact with the world, which so strongly characterized the way of life of the Brethren during the first two decades of the Unity's existence. The rigorists were especially strong in south Bohemia, the country of Chelčický and the Taborites, whose inhabitants were familiar with the most radical traditions of the Hussite movement, with their roots in these parts stretching back to the obscure Waldensian sectaries of the period before Hus. It is not then mere chance that it was also from south Bohemia that the two leaders of the party which strove to maintain the tradition of social radicalism in the Unity came; and that it was here that their main strength lay.

[6]   A. J. B., IV, fols, 110v, 112v (quoted *ibid*., pp. 222, 223); *Odpis*, fol. 45 (quoted *ibid*., p. 212). Cf. Jireček, *op. cit*., I, pp. 14, 15; Krofta, *O bratrském dějepisectví*, p. 10.
[7]   Hrejsa, *Dějiny křest'anství v Československu*, IV, p. 129.
[8]   Müller-Bartoš, *Dějiny Jednoty bratrské*, I, p. 168.
[9]   Krasonický, 'Psaní proti Kalencowi o puowodu odtržencůw,' fol. 357v.
[10]   A. J. B., IV, fol. 110v (quoted *ibid*., p. 222).

It was, therefore, in the country around their native Práchen that Amos and Kubík now began to rally their supporters in defence of the old doctrines. The sources give scarcely any personal details about those whom they won over to form the nucleus of the future Minor Party. Krasonický writes that 'these two then sought to obtain the help of anyone they could persuade, chiefly such as the Brethren were to expel on account of their sins and their wilfulness and other evils.'[11] Once more this is mostly abuse. But it seems true that some of the more restless and fractious spirits in the Unity were drawn into the Minor Party, though the charges of loose living and immorality, brought by opponents such as Lukáš and Krasonický, must be treated with the greatest caution.

Only two names are known of these first disciples enlisted by Amos and Jakub for their cause. There was, first, Vodička, a tailor in Chlumec, who seems to have steered a rather erratic course in his spiritual life, changing his religious allegiance several times.

Another supporter Amos and Jakub were soon to find in Matouš the Weaver from Lanškroun, an even more unruly character stirring up dissension wherever he went, about whom Krasonický, who knew him well, writes in some detail. He was not one of those who, like Amos himself, had joined the Unity in its very first days; but apparently as early as 1488 he had been expelled from the Unity, allegedly for causing disturbances among the Brethren and for denying Christ's divine nature. But the exact reasons for his expulsion are somewhat obscure. They seem to have also been connected with disputes over such points of Unity belief as the attitude to be adopted by Brethren towards the state. He was evidently of an argumentative and self-assertive disposition, but with an interest in theological and ethical problems unusual in a simple layman. Prior to his expulsion he took an active part in the controversy over justification by faith or by works; and he disputed publicly as well with Krasonický, who was then visiting preacher in Lanškroun, on the weight to be put on the Old Testament. Matouš told Krasonický after the latter had used a quotation from the Old Testament in his address: 'What are you daring to assert? What have we to do with the Jews? We have the New, not Old Testament.'[12] Despite attempts on the part of Krasonický and the Brethren to convince him of the wrongness of his general position

---

[11]   Krasonický, 'Psaní,' fol. 358.

[12]   Matouš was to make a similar remark some years later during the conference (*rozmlouvání*) at Chlumec in 1496. See Chap. V, p. 172. As has been seen, both Chelčický and Řehoř were to emphasize the subordinate place which, in their opinion, the Old Testament should hold in Christian dogma.

he continued obdurate; and when in 1490 Amos and Jakub appeared on the scene, 'he immediately joined them and soon became one of the leaders' of their party. 'He was eloquent [Krasonický adds] and was fairly well educated.'[13]

But the old ideology must also have had its followers within the Inner Council. Brother Matěj, its head, was, as has been seen, himself in close sympathy with the old doctrines enunciated by his master, Brother Řehoř, and looked with considerable misgiving on the new tendencies in the Unity which aimed at setting these aside. Probably already in the very same year as that in which the assembly of Brandýs was held, a change in the composition of the Inner Council was made, whereby those members favourable to the recent changes retired, giving place to 'the good old Brethren.'

The circumstances in which the changeover took place are most difficult to ascertain. There are three accounts left by contemporaries: two by Lukáš and the third from Krasonický. In his *O obnovení* the former writes that Klenovský and his party within the Inner Council:

Seeing that assent had indeed been given, but that there was little realization and small understanding of its contents, decided, therefore, that the edict of Brandýs should be rescinded and a return made to the primitive doctrine (*první smysl*). And that those who felt unable to participate in this task should retire from the Inner Council, and those who would forward it should be elected in their stead. And it was all brought about with good intention and in the spirit of mutual service, so that those who imagined they knew [i.e. what was good] should discover from practical experience that in fact they did not know ... and afterwards be more peaceable and compliant.[14]

Krasonický's version adds several further details to this picture:

The old council, realizing that they would not achieve anything if they wanted to give practical effect to this edict [i.e. of Brandýs], but only create trouble, having come to their decision, it seems, after seeking God's will, gave over the reins to Brother Matěj ... and retired from the council, and each of them found himself a trade, saying that they were willing to obey Brother Matěj. ... And this greatly pleased him and he appointed a new council from the good old Brethren.[15]

[13] *Ibid.*, fols. 358–359v (quoted in part in Goll-Krofta, *op. cit.*, pp. 185, 187). It should be borne in mind that almost all the biographical information which has come down about the members of the Minor Party originates from extremely hostile sources.

[14] 'O obnovení,' fol. 97 (quoted *ibid.*, p. 203). Cf. *Odpis*, fol. 48 (quoted *ibid.*, p. 216), which is much briefer. The dating here of the change-over in 1492 is incorrect. The statement that many other Brethren besides Amos and Jakub 'gave very faint-hearted assistance' in carrying out the edict of Brandýs shows that the latter still had many potential supporters among Unity members at that time.

[15] 'O učených,' fols. 20, 20v (quoted *ibid.*, p. 207).

Do these accounts tell the whole story? Or was there a greater degree of involuntariness about the resignations? Modern historians are divided on this point; and, indeed, in view of the lack of positive evidence the truth can only be surmised. Gindely,[16] for instance, as well as Denis[17] later, held that the changes in the composition of the Inner Council and the rescinding of the edict of Brandýs were due rather to the strength of the party supporting the old doctrines, which was able to oust its opponents from office and return to the *status quo ante*. This, too, is the version given by the Minor Party, according to which Matěj removed Klenovský and his supporters 'from office as unworthy people ... and, having swept aside one council, appointed in its place another, which found favour' in his eyes.[18] Müller[19] and Tapié,[20] however, take Lukáš's and Krasonický's statements more at their face value. The most probable explanation is perhaps the one given by Goll: that, though Lukáš's account, written twenty years after the events described, is not consciously misleading, nevertheless other factors overlooked by Lukáš were present in the decision to resign, factors of a more involuntary nature.[21]

One such element was, besides the natural desire hinted at in Krasonický's account to avoid creating dissension among the Brethren, the further fact that Brother Matěj at this time made a successful attempt to escape from the dominating influence of Klenovský, who had been his close adviser for some years. Under Klenovský's guidance Matěj had given somewhat hesitant approval to the changes in the Unity's political and social doctrines that had recently been enacted. But he remained at heart attached to the old ideals; and even before 1490 he seems to have been apprehensive that, as he later confided to the leaders of the Minor Party, 'through Klenovský the Unity will become tainted' by contact with the world. At the same time his fears increased that the new tendencies would corrupt 'the thought and action of the Brothers and Sisters.' Many

[16]   Gindely, *Geschichte der Böhmischen Brüder*, I, p. 67: 'Allein so friedlich ging es bei dieser Veranlassung, wie alle sonstigen Berichte zeigen, nicht her; Lukáš selbst hält sich in eine absichtliche Unklarheit bei Erzählung der ganzen Begebenheit ein und war zu sehr bemüht, die frühere Zeit vor jedem grellen Lichte zu bewahren.' His statement, *ibid.*, p. 66, that another assembly was held later in 1490, at which a strong representation of the Old Brethren was present, and that during the course of this assembly Matěj dismissed the moderates from his council, is definitely incorrect.

[17]   Denis, *Fin de l'Indépendance Bohême*, I, p. 347: 'Le récit de Loukach est un apologie visiblement arrangée dans le but de rejeter tous les torts sur les rigoristes.'

[18]   'Psaní jakéhos kněze Jana Appolinařského,' *Časopis historický*, 1882, no. 2, p. 66.

[19]   Müller-Bartoš, *op. cit.*, pp. 159, 160.

[20]   Tapié, *Une église tchèque au XVe siècle: L'Unité des Frères*, p. 101.

[21]   Goll-Krofta, *op. cit.*, p. 178.

of the members of the Inner Council from Klenovský's party had at that time, according to Matěj, 'scornfully abused the old teaching and the old doctrine.' Matěj later claimed that he had defended the old doctrines against their attacks. 'But he was hedged around by Klenovský as with a fence and surrounded as with a wall and bestrown as with stones and arguments.'[22]

The two men, indeed, differed enormously from each other both in temperament and character, as well as in background and education. 'They are as alike as heaven and earth,' was the verdict of some one who knew both well. Klenovský was 'well versed in many matters; while Brother Matěj is a simple, guileless man.'[23] Perhaps just because of these differences the two men to some extent complemented each other. Certainly Matěj relied greatly on Klenovský's superior education and knowledge of the world; while, for the latter, Matěj's childlike simplicity provided an element lacking in his own character.

Their collaboration, however, was by no means easy. For reasons which remain obscure Klenovský had stayed in the background throughout most of the proceedings of the assembly of Brandýs.[24] Shortly after the assembly, feeling himself now strong enough to stand on his own, Matěj entered once more into alliance with the Old Brethren, whose convictions on the controversial issues of the day he shared to the full, even though he had not always had the courage to champion them. This brought a definite break with Klenovský. In a private interview between the two men, the latter demanded from Matěj a clarification of his still somewhat ambiguous position. 'You shall not leave the room, Brother Matěj [said Klenovský] until you have said which doctrine (smysl) you hold, that of the Old Brethren or the new doctrine, for you should realize ... that worldly authoritiy is pressing into the Unity and has indeed already gained admittance with all its rights, with the one possible exception of fighting in matters of religion.' In reply Matěj frankly avowed his allegiance to the old doctrines of Chelčický and Řehoř.[25]

This incident probably took place in 1490 after the assembly of Brandýs, though it is unclear whether immediately prior to, or just after the change-over in the Inner Council.[26] Indeed, very little is known at all about the whole period between the return to power of the Old Brethren

[22] *Čas, historický*, p. 64.
[23] 'O učených,' fols. 24v, 25.
[24] Goll-Krofta, *op. cit.*, p. 177.
[25] *Čas. historický*, p. 64.
[26] Goll-Krofta, *op. cit.*, p. 234.

and their final replacement by those representing the new tendencies at the assembly of Rýchnov in 1494. Of the members whom Matěj now appointed to seats in the Inner Council in place of the resigning members, only the names of two are known definitely: Jakub and Matěj Uhlíř, who later went over to Klenovský's party.[27] It is probable, too, that Brother Michal who followed Matěj in a somewhat hesitant loyalty to the old principles was also a member of the council during this period;[28] and several of the members of the previous council, who to some extent represented the traditional viewpoint, may also have continued in office after the more militant protagonists of the revised doctrine, like Klenovský, Táborský and Prokop, had resigned.

The old regulations prohibiting Unity members from participating in any form of activity connected with the state were once again put into force, though it is doubtful whether disciplinary action, though threatened, was ever actually taken against Brethren who did not fully observe them. The reversal of the decisions taken at Brandýs, however, now seemed complete. The official head of the Unity, Brother Matěj, had given his blessing to the changes, ordaining that 'whoever took the oath should be excluded from the sacraments,' while 'he who should be privy to the death of a fellow man should be expelled'; and he went himself to Štěkeň and the Prácheň area on a friendly visit to confer with Amos and Jakub and the other members of their party. During this visit Matěj 'reached complete agreement (*smlouvu s námi dělal*)' with the latter on the attitude which the Unity should adopt towards the demands of the state; and he 'condemned the recent innovations and decreed that they should return unanimously to the old doctrine and base their actions on it.' About this time, too, he wrote them several pastoral letters, strongly criticizing the previous council for its attempts to adulterate the purity of Unity doctrine and for the first time making public the doubts which had for long existed in his own mind as to the wisdom of their policy. His suspicions of Klenovský and his associates had started, he wrote, 'immediately after Řehoř's death when [he] succeeded to the leadership and dissension had broken out among the Brethren, one speaking contrary to another.' One of his letters was now 'read out before an important congregation composed of both sexes.'[29] These writings of Matěj were

[27] *Ibid.*, p. 245. The list of members given by the later Unity historian, Brother Jafet, in his *Meč Goliášův*, completed in 1607 and printed by Jireček, 'B. Jana Jafeta krátká zpráva o biskupích a starších Jednoty bratrské,' *Č. Č. M.*, 1861, p. 144, is probably almost entirely imaginary.

[28] *Ibid.*, p. 178.

[29] *Čas. historický*, pp. 64–66.

later to be brought up against him by Amos and Jakub as proof of his 'waverings' comparable to 'the perversity of [Pope] Sylvester.'[30]

The period of the Old Brethren's renewed predominance within the Unity were years of uncertainty, of seeking on all sides for guidance through the problems that beset the Unity. The struggle between the two different codes of social behaviour was not by any means settled once for all. Members on both sides were, indeed, assailed by doubts and hesitations as to the correct course of action.

It was perhaps in part as a result of the controversy on the Christian attitude to the state that the proposal may now have arisen to send a deputation to visit the churches in the East, in the birthplace of Christianity, in order to get firsthand information as to how far stories that the primitive Christian faith was still preserved in these lands in all its purity were true. The initiative seems to have come from the reforming party, anxious to see if they could get confirmation for their innovations among other Christian groups also attempting like the Unity to base their whole way of life on an uncompromising adherence to the ideals of their Master.

The congregation at Litomyšl was especially active in the project: the clash with the authorities over the Unity's attitude to their demands was, as has been seen, not merely of theoretical interest, but of practical significance for the townsfolk among the Brethren.

At this time ... the elders of the Litomyšl Brethren held frequent conferences with many important persons and, in particular, with [Bohuš Kostka, the lord of Litomyšl and a member of the Unity] ... enquiring all the time whether there existed anywhere in the world a people who still preserved the manner and order of the primitive church, ... desiring always to have communion with such people and not wishing to be schismatics and sectaries. And they decided that certain persons from their midst should be sent to foreign and distant parts in order that they might see with their own eyes and discover for themselves, for they did not want to rely on mere tales told them by persons coming to Bohemia from those countries.

The funds for the expedition were provided by Bohuš Kostka, who was also instrumental in obtaining letters of introduction from King Vladislav for the four Brethren chosen to make the journey. These were Mareš Kokovec, 'a worthy man of knightly rank'; Kabátník, the Litomyšl

---

[30]   A. J. B., IV (Opis), fol. 133 (quoted in Goll-Krofta, op. cit., p. 225). It is not at all clear from the scanty information given in the Zpráva menší strany and Jakub's first tract in what chronological order the events described actually occurred. From the phrasing in places it would almost seem as if Matěj wrote some of his letters (písmo a cedule) to the Prácheň congregations even before the resignation of Klenovský and his friends from the Inner Council or his own visitation of the south.

clothier who had participated in the preliminary conferences with Bohuš; a certain Kašpar, a former Waldensian from Brandenburg; and Brother Lukáš himself. The four men set off in March 1491, returning to Bohemia in November 1492. The details of the journey, some of which are recorded in the account which the semi-illiterate Kabátník dictated to his friend, Adam Bakalař, about ten years later, do not concern us here. Once again the Brethren experienced the same disappointment as in their earlier contacts with the Russian and Greek churches in Brother Řehoř's day, and as they were to do a few years later with the Italian Waldenses. They failed in each case to find the ideal Christian community which they were seeking.[31]

At home the trials which the Brethren were experiencing in their attempts to put their principles into practice in face of the hostility of the state, continued to increase. According to the *Historia Fratrum*, in 1492 the Inner Council devoted over a month, from 23 April until 25 May, to discussing the problems in general.[32] In the same year Koranda, the administrator of the Utraquist church and a former Unity sympathizer, addressed a special letter to Bohuš Kostka, deprecating the Brethren's refusal to take up office when elected. He entitled his epistle: *Že pigharti odpierají býti konšele.*

There have been and there still are [writes Koranda] certain people who refuse to accept office as aldermen or in any other capacity, seemingly because they do not want to administer justice, having regard to the scriptural passage: 'Judge not, that ye be not judged' [Matt. VII, 1] which they interpret in their own fashion.' 'But [he goes on to argue] since these Brethren consider themselves more perfect than the rest of us, then, being lovers of justice and truth, they should be able ... in positions of authority to deal out justice ... fairly and faithfully in order that righteousness and truth may be established and unrighteousness and wrongdoing be put down. ... It is a perverseness worthy of reprobation in these Brethren that they should ... regard [their fellow Christians] as pagans, for in this way they insult their neighbours by cutting themselves off from other Christians devoted to God's truth, trusting in themselves alone.[33]

Koranda's remarks serve to emphasize the point already made that, especially in the towns, the Brethren's refusal of office appeared to their fellow citizens more often than not as a dereliction of duty, as a desire to

---

[31]   Kabátník, *Cesta z Čech do Jeruzalema a Kaira r. 1491–92*, esp. pp. VIII, X, 1, 2. See also Gindely, *op. cit.*, pp. 67–69; Goll-Krofta, *op. cit.*, pp. 153, 154; Müller-Bartoš, *op. cit.*, pp. 161–63.
[32]   Quoted in Müller-Bartoš, *op. cit.*, pp. 159, 160.
[33]   Koranda, *Manualník*, pp. XVII, 141–43.

escape from the obligations of citizenship. Their conscientious scruples were mistaken for a device to dodge responsibility; and the fact that Unity members were now divided as to how far they might rightly accept such duties must have made it even harder to defend the rigorist position. That the Brethren in the towns continued for so long to endure hardship and persecution, even after many of them had begun to doubt the full validity of the ideas for which they were suffering, is, indeed, a tribute both to the loyalty of the ordinary members towards Matěj and the Inner Council and to the hold which the traditional viewpoint still had on all sections of the Unity, not excluding even those of the younger generation who could not remember the times of Brother Řehoř and the early Brethren.

The situation, however, was rapidly becoming unbearable. Some solution had to be found; and the Inner Council of the Old Brethren was proving itself incapable of steering the Unity through the troubled waters. Without either a mass exodus from the towns or a continued readiness to court martyrdom on the part of the town Brethren, it was difficult to see how a satisfactory way out could be found, consonant with loyalty to the traditional principles of the Unity. But it was extremely hard for the majority of the Old Brethren on the council to throw over so many of the ideals upon which the Unity had been founded, ideals which had been expecially dear to Brother Řehoř and his contemporaries in the Unity. The task could only be accomplished by younger men, unencumbered with any sentimental attachment to doctrines which seemed no longer to apply under existing conditions.

The period of the Old Brethren's return to power lasted over three years. Throughout, the Unity priests and provincial administrators were continually applying to Brother Matěj for advice 'concerning the alderman's office and oaths and the other offices, which they placed upon the Brethren in their communities.' Matěj, distressed beyond endurance by the sufferings of his fellow Brethren, even 'went himself to the lords or their officials or to the town hall and said to them: 'These people whom you are persecuting and torturing ... are innocent, for it is we who have instructed them in this. We implore you to let them go, for we wish to suffer in their stead'.'

After a little, 'having sometimes conferred together for several weeks about the same problem without coming to any conclusion,' several of the Inner Council began to realize their inability to provide the necessary leadership for the Unity. 'You have dismissed those with wisdom and understanding [they told Matěj] and put us fools in their place.' Many of the leaders of the Unity in the provinces sent in their resignations to Matěj, feeling themselves unable to advise their flock to resist the authorities any further.[34] The situation of the Unity was, according to Krasonický, 'like that of a house built on piles, when these piles are removed.'[35] Finally the members of the Inner Council, 'finding by experience that the task they had taken on was an impossible one and only led to a great deal of evil, unanimously recommended that they should ask to be set free again, since they were achieving nothing good, and that the Brethren of the previous council should take office once more, being more knowledgeable and experienced in the matter.'[36]

The first step to implement their decision was taken when Matěj 'with the Brethren' issued a circular letter to the membership, informing it of the forthcoming synod to be held at Rýchnov:

This is to tell you [he wrote] that it is our intention to meet with certain of the Brethren and discuss together the most important matters concerning the general good and to reach agreement, with God's help as well as with yours, on certain matters connected with faith and brotherly love and the hope of salvation. It is apparent, indeed, that there is no possibility in such things of unanimity and harmony in service together without fear of endangering salvation unless we hold some kind of deliberation in common. We are asking you, therefore, to help us with your prayers ... and with fasting ... so that the Lord may listen to the desire of His poor creatures. ... God willing, the Brethren will keep you informed on these matters according to your need, when they return from us back home again.[37]

The synod – obecný sněm valný, Lukáš calls it – was summoned for 5 May 1494 to discuss the two problems of the future leadership of the Unity and of its official doctrine in the questions under dispute. Four accounts written by participants of the synod – two by Lukáš and the other two by Krasonický and Jakub – are still extant. But, as usual, the chronology of the events described, and many of the incidents themselves, remain obscure. It seems that, shortly before the opening of the general assembly, probably more than one preparatory meeting was held between Matěj and the members of the retiring Inner Council, on the one hand, and Klenovský and his supporters, on the other; and the viewpoint expressed in the edict of Brandýs was once again accepted as the official doctrine of the Unity.[38]

[34] 'O učených,' fol. 20v (quoted Goll-Krofta, op. cit., p. 207).
[35] Ibid., fol. 24v.
[36] 'O obnovení,' fol. 98v (quoted ibid., p. 204).
[37] A. J. B., V, fol. 315 v.
[38] 'O obnovení,' loc. cit. Cf. Müller-Bartoš, op. cit., p. 165.

The only member to resist the forthcoming changes was the redoubt-able Jakub, who at the very outset had made clear his unrelenting oppo-sition to any wateringdown of the old principles. For several days Matěj and his colleagues on the council, as well as those of the opposing side, had argued with him, trying to persuade him to accept the compromise which they believed the edict embodied. At last Klenovský, his patience exhausted, exclaimed that 'even if I have to tear your soul from your body,' he would make him comply with their demands. Still Jakub stood his ground, asking that they should not try to impose their views on him. After that he 'got up from the council and walked out.' Thankful perhaps to rid themselves of so inconvenient a councillor, Matěj and the Brethren readily gave their consent to Jakub's resignation from the proceedings.

From Jakub's account it would seem as if the renewal of the edict of Brandýs occurred during one of the main sessions of the conference. 'They were glad of it [Jakub writes of his own withdrawal] expecting that it would lead to good.' The assembled Brethren, he goes on, after giving their consent to his resignation from the conference, sang a hymn; and 'it was resolved that the edict of Brandýs, which had been rescinded and set aside by Brother Matěj's orders, should be read out. And it was therefore read again, so that it might be observed (držána).'[39]

But Lukáš tells another story; and the personal details which it contains would indicate its authenticity. It is probable, indeed, that Jakub, whose version has no pretensions to historical method, telescopes into one all the incidents in which he was himself involved.

According to Lukáš, whose account is supplemented at times by Krasonický's, the delegates at the synod confined themselves to first examining and approving the request from Matěj and his council to accept their resignations, and then to calling on the members of the previous council to accept office once more. Matěj, on account of his failure 'to administer (spravovati)' the Unity successfully, had asked to be relieved of his bishop's office and begged to be allowed to continue to serve the Unity, if need be just 'as an ordinary Brother.' 'Brother Matěj and his [previous] council humbly submitted themselves in everything to the judgement [i.e. of the synod]; whatsoever should be decreed there, they were willing compliantly to accept.' Touched by this display of disinterest-ed devotion to the Unity, Táborský, one of the best educated Brethren, called out: 'Brother Matěj, you ask to be cast out on account of your ignorance. Know that we, too, have for long been without knowledge or

[39] A. J. B., IV (opis), fols. 132, 133 (quoted Goll-Krofta, op. cit., p. 225).

understanding. Should we also be cast out? Rather let us come together and help each other.'

Klenovský, Prokop, Táborský, and the other leaders of their party still continued for some time to hesitate to re-enter the Inner Council: *A stálo to tak chvíli drahnou*, says Krasonický. But finally some of the younger pastors, like Krasonický and Lukáš, succeeded in breaking down their resistance – which may anyhow have been more apparent than real. They all now yielded to the entreaties of the rest of the Brethren, with the exception of old Tůma Přeloučský, one of the three first priests of the Unity chosen in 1467, who continued in his refusal to return to the council. Some of the younger personalities, too, were called upon by the delegates to take a more prominent part in the direction of Unity affairs; and full authority was now granted the new council, 'on account of the numerous difficulties,' to take what steps it saw fit to safeguard the wellbeing of the Unity without the obligation of summoning another general assembly. With this the synod closed its sessions.

But in the evening of the same day [Lukáš goes on] when some of us had gone for a walk, the Brethren who had been dismissed from the Inner Council, conferring with certain of the other Brethren (*s jinými bez jiných*), summoned those near by, and in their presence renewed (*vyzdvihli*) [the edict of] the Brandýs assembly, saying: 'Since it has kept us apart, let it now join us together.' And I, returning from my walk, came to the door and said to the Brother who stood by it: 'So the Brethren are in conference?' And he replied that they were. Then I enquired what they were doing. And he replied somewhat unwillingly: 'Have you not heard that they have renewed [the edict of] the Brandýs assembly?' And I replied: 'What! Late in the evening! We have just passed several other ordinances, but nothing from the Brandýs assembly.' And I could not sleep at all that night pondering what might arise from this and how little understanding and forethought had gone into it; and with the fear of a fresh schism and trouble I took my departure.[40]

The resolutions of the synod of Rýchnov had thus, like those of the previous assembly of Brandýs, been intended as a compromise. The victorious party had evidently not wished to press their triumph too far, realizing perhaps that sympathy for the old views was still strong among many even on their own side and unwilling, too, to risk losing support among the waverers, chief among whom were now Matěj and almost all the members of his council of the Old Brethren. During the actual sessions of the synod no attempt was seemingly made to reintroduce the edict of Brandýs, which had now become such a bone of contention among

[40] 'O obnovení,' fols. 98v–99v; 'O učených,' fols. 20v–21v; *Odpis*, fol. 48v (quoted *ibid.*, pp. 204, 205, 207, 208, 216).

the members. The task of defining exactly what obligations towards the state might properly be undertaken by a member of the Unity had been left to the Inner Council. The resolution of confidence in the new Inner Council, proposed at the end of the synod by two Brethren, Martin Bydžovský the Chairmaker and Šimon Hranický, both themselves later to become its members, and passed unanimously, gave it full authority for this. Those present promised obedience to all its decisions, which might be taken 'without calling an assembly.' The council was empowered, 'as seemed to them fit, to alter or to decide upon and to enact what they recognized as needful for the Unity and for its continuance (*vzdělání*) in faith and grace.'[41] Klenovský and his associates were content, therefore, to see the replacement of the old council by one which would include themselves and a general recognition by the Unity that the old principles were no longer obligatory. Time might be relied on to bring their victory to completion.

More difficult to understand is the behaviour of the Old Brethren, who had just handed in their resignations from the Inner Council, in re-enacting the edict of Brandýs, which apparently not even the most ardent of the reforming party wished to see done.[42] A desire to put an end to further controversy by definitely accepting the point of view of their former opponents, the tendency of the recent convert to be the most zealous in his new-found creed, a wish to compensate for what were deemed past mistakes, may all have contributed to this most unexpected action.

The part which Lukáš himself played in these proceedings is also not at all clear. He had been present at the assembly of Brandýs; but, as he remarks, 'I made no contribution [i.e. to it], being occupied with other

---

[41] *Dekrety Jednoty bratrské*, pp. 32, 33; Goll-Krofta, *op. cit.*, pp. 180, 246. Cf. A. J. B., IV (Opis), fol. 132 (quoted Goll-Krofta, *op. cit.*, p. 225), where Jakub seems to imply that at least Bydžovský was largely responsible for the re-enactment of the edict of Brandýs; in which case he may have been one of the Old Brethren councillors, who were to return to the Inner Council after recantation of their former opinions and new-found enthusiasm for those of their opponents.

[42] Tapié, *op. cit.*, p. 104, notes the obscurity of Lukáš's account of this incident in his *O obnovení*. Gindely, *op. cit.*, p. 71, interprets the word employed, *vyzdvihnouti*, as meaning 'to reject.' It is undoubtedly with this meaning that Lukáš, for instance, uses the word in the same work in connection with the rescinding of the edict a few years earlier (fol. 97); and such an interpretation might appear more in harmony with the previously held opinions of the old council. Nevertheless, the context shows that Goll is right in giving it the meaning 'to re-adopt.' Though, as Tapié points out, both versions would explain Lukáš's fears as to the future of the somewhat shaky equilibrium between the two parties just reached at the synod with considerable difficulty and now endangered by this precipitate action. The events of the next few years show clearly that of the Old Brethren in the Inner Council. Jakub alone continued in open opposition to the new tendencies.

matters.' After the edict had been set aside by Matěj and the Old Brethren Lukáš claims that, during the period of the latter's supremacy within the Unity, he 'did not join either party.'[43] Again, as has been seen, during the synod of Rýchnov Lukáš presents himself rather as a neutral observer, as one who sought to bring about harmony between the two opposing sides and achieve a synthesis of their conflicting viewpoints.

However, in view of what is known of his later career, Lukáš in the role of a mediator in the controversy concerning the Unity's political and social doctrines does not carry complete conviction. Even in the earlier controversy concerning justification by faith or by works Lukáš had been unsatisfied with Prokop's compromise solution of 'good will': the young reformer wanted a more radical revision of the old beliefs.[44] He had been associated in the expedition to the East in 1491 with such noble members of the Unity as Bohuš Kostka and with the burgher Brethren of Litomyšl, whose dissatisfaction with the old doctrines had given such an impetus to the whole controversy. After his return, 'working with his hands' as was still the usual custom with the priests of the Unity, he had at the same time launched out on his career as a writer; and of the five works – no longer indeed extant – which he composed about the year 1493, at least two were concerned with such matters as the oath, the obligations of the various social classes within the Unity, and worldly power in general.[45] It would be extremely unlikely if in these works Lukáš did not take up a position favouring at least some degree of revision in the doctrines of the Old Brethren. Even his *Bárka* ('The Boat') composed at that time, which does not deal directly with social problems, was indeed, according to Molnár, with its attack on renunciation and suffering for their own sake alone, later to give the Unity a theoretical basis for its emergence from retirement from the world.[46]

Lukáš, therefore, despite his own assertions to the contrary, must definitely be reckoned among the members of the reforming party. His desire not to exacerbate the ill-feeling on each side was undoubtedly sincere; and, later, he was always to claim – in answer to the Minor Party's statements to the contrary – that he stood for mutual toleration of both points of view. His own belief in the validity of the new doctrine, recognizing in principle the claims of the state within the Christian com-

---

[43] 'O obnovení,' fols, 96, 97v (quoted *ibid.*, pp. 202, 203).
[44] *Ibid.*, fol. 93v (quoted *ibid.*, p. 201). Molnár, *Boleslavští bratří*, p. 35, would not seem to be justified in definitely connecting this passage with the assembly of Brandýs.
[45] *Ibid.*, fols. 97v–98v (quoted *ibid.*, pp. 203, 204).
[46] Molnár, *op. cit.*, p. 36. Cf. Müller-Bartoš, *op. cit.*, p. 164.

munity, and in the wrongness of its opponents was never in doubt from at least the beginning of the nineties. But he was still, according to his own words, 'young in years and understanding';[47] his views had perhaps not taken on the clear shape they were later to acquire, as was, indeed, also the case with the majority of the reformers; and finally, it was not yet Lukáš, but Klenovský and his two associates, Táborský and Prokop, who framed the policy, at first of the reforming party alone, but from now onwards of the whole Unity.

It had not been only Lukáš and Jakub who, though for different reasons, had left Rýchnov at the end of the conference filled with apprehension for the future. Jakub relates a moving story about Michal, the first Utraquist priest to join the Brethren and one whose memories stretched back to the very first days of the Unity's existence.

When already many of the Brethren had departed [Jakub writes] old Brother Michal turned to some of the leading Brethren who still remained: 'How many good men have suffered torture and persecution and the sacrifice of life itself for just this [i.e. for the old principles now set aside]. What have all our endeavours come to? We could almost have remained with the good priests [i.e. instead of founding a separate church].' Thereupon Klenovský answered him: 'Brother Michal, don't spoil things (nekaz).'[48]

Tůma Přeloučský, too, had left Rýchnov in an unsettled frame of mind, still adamant in his refusal to accept office again in the council. He was not, indeed, at any time to take a very active part in the controversy, since his residence at Přerov in Moravia, distant from the main centres of Unity activity, prevented him from doing this. But it might have been supposed that, as one of the three who had been chosen in 1467 to be the first Unity priests, he would have sided with the rigorists or at least have given the old views the vacillating sympathy shown them by Matěj or Michal. But just the contrary is true. He was evidently one of those Brethren in the Inner Council who had followed Klenovský in giving in their resignations in 1490, though there is no evidence to indicate when he first came to discard the pacifist anarchism of the old Unity. His standpoint is all the more surprising when it is remembered both that he was famed for his attachment to the primitive simplicity of the Unity of Brother Řehoř's day, later disagreeing strongly with Lukáš in such matters, and that, as will be seen below, he was a fervent champion of the rights of the poor and the oppressed against the claims of the socially privileged.[49]

---

[47] 'O obnovení,' loc. cit.
[48] A. J. B., IV (Opis), fol. 133 (quoted ibid., p. 225).
[49] Přeloučský, Spis o původu Jednoty bratrské a o chudých lidech, Sokol's Intro., pp.

The fact that he was one of the most learned of the Brethren, with a good knowledge of Latin – though his learning was, it is true, acquired by self-education and not in the university lecture-hall – may have influenced him in his decision to side with Klenovský and the 'learned' Brethren.

The presence of Tůma in the new council would naturally be a considerable asset. He was a wellknown figure throughout the whole Unity; he was respected by all for his simple piety and natural intelligence, as well as for the considerable amount of learning he had managed to acquire; and, above all, his open accession to the reforming party would serve to give it an added sanction, the vicarious blessing, as it were, of Brother Řehoř and the Old Brethren of his time. Tůma's membership of the council along with Matěj and Michal would go far to counteract the very plausible claims of Jakub and Amos that their party represented the real Unity tradition, from which the majority had fallen away.

What were the motives behind Tůma's continued refusal of office? The reason put forward by a recent biographer – that of Tůma's loyalty to the old principles of Řehoř's day[50] – though not impossible, does not seem very likely. Tůma had not been a member of the resigning council of Old Brethren: he had shown himself, as has been seen, an opponent of their viewpoint. Perhaps the most probable explanation – in view of the lack of positive evidence it must, however, remain a mere supposition – is that at the outset of the conference Tůma had been at one with Klenovský and his colleagues in their joint refusal of office: a refusal the reasons for which are once again obscure, but which was probably due, at least in part, to a reluctance to take up office again unless it was clear that they had the backing of the whole assembly. Once this was obtained the others abandoned their resistance; Tůma alone remained unconvinced, fearing the renewed outbreak of dissension among the Brethren.

Some of the leading delegates, before leaving Rýchnov, had first agreed to meet together shortly at Tůma's house in Přerov. The object of this second meeting, in addition to settling some important details of administration consequent on the changes decided upon at Rýchnov, was to make a final attempt to persuade Tůma to alter his mind. Again, the assistance of the younger members was called in. 'You want to put the burdens on the others [said Krasonický pertinently to Tůma] and not touch them yourself, even with your finger-tips.' Tůma at last yielded to

20–23; Měrka, 'Tomáš Přeloučský,' *Časopis pro moderní filologii a literatury*, III (1913), pp. 297–303; Krofta, *O bratrském dějepisectví*, pp. 15–17.
[50] Sokol, *op. cit.*, pp. 22, 23.

their arguments; and they were then able to go on to consider the division of duties among the new leadership of the Unity as well as certain theological and moral problems.

First, Brother Matěj was deprived of his powers as administrator responsible for the direction of the Unity's affairs; and this task was allotted to Prokop, who was given the title of judge (*sudí*). The former, however, was still left with his right as bishop of ordaining the new priests of the Unity. Among other appointments made at Přerov the most important were as follows: Klenovský as 'confessor (*zpovědník*)' throughout the whole of Bohemia and Moravia and Prokop's chief adviser; Táborský as pastor of the important congregation at Litomyšl and Klenovský's right-hand man; Lukáš as pastor of the equally important Mladá Boleslav; Eliáš Chřenovický as Klenovský's deputy in Moravia; and Krasonický as a kind of itinerant preacher (*já abych pomocník byl Jednoty, co bych rozuměl a v zbořích promlouval*). To Klenovský, in addition, was entrusted the significant task of 'seeing to the Unity sympathizers among the lords and holding converse with them.'[51] The second task of the Přerov meeting was to pass a series of decrees framed in the traditional spirit, dealing with such theological questions as the validity of sacraments administered by a sinful priest, the eucharist, and kneeling before the sacrament.[52]

In addition, an important decree was enacted aiming at providing an answer to the question as to exactly which professions and trades a Brother might properly carry on. With very few exceptions, of which the chief was usury, ran the answer, all were now lawful. Brethren, however, were advised not to take up commerce if they could get a living from their old occupation; but those already engaged in it, who would otherwise be without suitable employment, were to be permitted to remain, provided they did not engage in such deceitful practices as falsifying weights and measures. In every instance they were to observe exactly the Ten Commandments, and not swear 'false' oaths or tell untruths. In all their undertakings they were to honour God and love their neighbours. They were, too, and the women and young folk in particular, to avoid all luxuries in their apparel. 'This is to be the measure [the decree concluded] by which everyone must abide, who wishes to be saved through the Christian faith.' According to this decree the priests and elders were to advise their people. It was to be, indeed, the first of a long series of similar

---

[51] 'O učených,' fols. 21v–22v (quoted, *ibid.*, p. 208).
[52] Müller-Bartoš, *op. cit.*, p. 168.

declarations, by the light of which may be traced the Unity's gradual retreat from the rigorist position of the early Brethren.[53]

Klenovský was now undisputed leader of the Unity, with Táborský and Prokop as the two other most important figures. Matěj was in disgrace; Michal had lapsed back into obscurity; while Tůma Přeloučský was fully occupied in his Moravian outpost. Lukáš and Krasonický were, indeed, rapidly rising to prominence, but as yet their roles were subordinate to their seniors in age; while members, like Mikuláš Slanský for instance, though they figure in the history of the Brethren in other connections, did not take a particularly conspicuous part in the administration of the Unity. Some of the Old Brethren from the previous council were probably included as a conciliatory gesture in the composition of the new Inner Council; and among these may have been Eliáš Chřenovický, with Tůma and Matěj one of the three first Unity priests, and Matěj Uhlíř, who had definitely sat in the previous council. But their influence had now waned; and anyhow their previous conduct had shown that they completely lacked the capacity for strong leadership. Other prominent Unity priests – for instance, Tůma the Scribe, Tůma the German, Ambrož of Skuteč, or Bernard of Přibyslavice – were but shadowy figures, about whom often little more than their bare names is known.[54]

The only opposition to the acceptance of the new doctrines, and the rapid elimination of the old, came from Jakub and Amos and their supporters among the rank-and-file. The schism, long threatened, was now to become a fact.

---

[53] *Dekrety*, pp. 125, 126.

[55] See Goll-Krofta, *op. cit.*, pp. 245, 246; *Dekrety*, pp. 2, 38. Tapié, *op. cit.*, p. 104, remarks of the Unity in the period immediately after the Synod of Rýchnov: 'On peut se demander, toutefois, comment des gens, dont l'opinion venait d'être desavouée, conservaient la direction de l'Unité. On récit plus vraisemblable admet, qu'à côté des anciens membres, des partisans de 'l'interprétation large' entrèrent dans le Conseil.' This appears to be based on a misunderstanding of the character of the changes which had occurred. The sources show that the Old Brethren had resigned *en bloc* from the council and were then replaced by the representatives of the opposing party, though a few of the old councillors, having recanted their former opinions, may have continued to sit in the new council. Matěj's authority was relegated to the purely formal function of ordination.

V

THE SCHISM

Largely as a result of the decisions taken at the meetings held at Rýchnov and Přerov and the reconstitution of the Unity which ensued, the following year, 1495, brought two events which showed clearly that the struggle had now reached a new stage of development. The disciplinary action to be taken against Jakub and his followers, in conjunction with a new and important decree passed by the leaders of the Major Party, signified that the attempt to unite the Brethren of both parties on the basis of a compromise formula granting the validity of the positions taken up by each side had been unsuccessful.

Its failure had been due both to the unyielding attitude of Jakub and his followers in defence of the old doctrines and to the unwillingness of their opponents to accept these doctrines as still binding on the Unity membership; and for the same causes all further attempts at reconciliation were to come to grief. A middle party, centring round Matěj and certain of the Old Brethren whom he had called to the Inner Council in 1490, had collapsed. Its members had now, after a long period of vacillation, gone over, though perhaps with some reservations, to the Major Party.

Jakub's return from Rýchnov, like his return with Amos from the assembly of Brandýs four years earlier, marked the beginning of an active campaign on behalf of the old doctrines. His first step now was to issue an open letter to Brother Matěj (*První traktát Jakuba Štěkenského*, as it came to be called), defining his own position and attacking his opponents, and Klenovský in particular, in no uncertain terms.

The wisdom of God, in his view, was 'hidden from the wise and prudent,' by which he meant Klenovský and the Major Party. He went on to contrast the unanimity and godliness of the early days of the Unity with the present situation.

But now the Brethren say: Let us, therefore, open the gates of the fold in order to gather in more sheep. And when they have opened up the fold, the sheep that are already there run out and the wolves tear them to pieces. ... The gates are God's commandments and the prohibitions of Christ the strait path and the narrow doorway. And whoever broadens these, ... saying that a Brother may become an alderman and a judge, and take oaths, and exercise the bloody rights of the sword, is like unto a rogue and a thief who comes not in by the door.

Christ's commandments were absolute and no pleas of human weakness or the imperfection of this world could be allowed as an excuse for not keeping them to the full. 'For God does not revoke his commandments or change his will on account of men's difficulties.' But now even the leaders of the Brethren, claiming that the old doctrines were too 'high' for the ordinary members, had themselves made the way easy 'to amass wealth, ... to be just like other people, frequenting taverns and banquets and feasts and weddings.' Indeed could not many of the sayings of Christ and St. Paul be considered much more 'high' than anything Brother Řehoř ever advocated? 'Then why do you put all the blame on' him, Jakub asked, 'since he spoke much more moderately himself and merely confirmed the sayings of Christ and the apostles?'

A clear proof for Jakub that God did not look with favour on the new order in the Unity was to be found in the contrast between the spiritual peace of the early Brethren and the tempestuous heart-searchings and restlessness of the last few years. Another sure sign of disintegration lay in the different way of life led by the new generation of Unity pastors. They no longer went out into the world, Jakub complained, to preach the gospel like the early apostles. 'Now [they] have settled in one place and concern themselves with their parsonages ... leading a peaceful existence.'

Bishop Matěj had been witness of the slow rot that had set in in the Unity since Řehoř's death and had never raised his voice against the new tendencies. Even 'a swineherd would not have kept silent when such harm was being done to his herd,' wrote Jakub rather unfairly. 'After your death and ours [he concluded his attack on Matěj] your own words as well as the writings and letters you sent us in the Prácheň district [i.e. after his break with Klenovský in 1490] ... will witness against you. ... After your death good men and bad will regard your vacillation as they now regard [Pope] Sylvester's apostasy.'

Towards the end of his letter Jakub summed up the attitude of himself and his friends in regard to the changes recently made in Unity doctrine and the line of action which they intended to take up in the future:

I do not acknowledge the new tendency (*smysl poslední*), for I consider it to be both heretical and untrue; and so long as there are no Brethren holding to the old doctrine (*smysl první*) in the council, we shall not continue to obey your orders.[1]

This was both a challenge and a threat to Matěj and his new council; and as such it was regarded by them.[2] Jakub was evidently able to gather enough support in the neighbourhood for his point of view to cause the victorious party serious anxiety.[3] He and Amos were able to challenge the authority of the provincial leaders of the Unity, who had sided with the Major Party. Their supporters in Klatov, including some of 'the best' members of the congregation, refused to attend communion administered by the local Unity pastor, Jan Pořímský, so long as he refused 'to reform.' But their most fiery attacks were directed against Ambrož of Skuteč, the leading pastor in the province, a well-educated Brother who had been prominent in the Unity for many years. He had become a decided protagonist of the new tendencies only after the recent synod; and, thereby, he was brought into conflict with the leaders of the Minor Party.

He and Pořímský, on returning from Rýchnov, spoke and wrote on behalf of the new doctrines, claiming that the Unity had unanimously agreed to accept them. Ambrož especially attacked Jakub and Amos for refusing to accept the validity of oathtaking and, according to Jakub, declared that he was ready to accept 'everyone as a Brother, whatever he might do, so long as he was not excommunicated (*vyobcován*).' Jakub retorted angrily that 'in that case [he] would regard as Brethren such as were killed in the wars among the footsoldiers and those who were hanged and those who sat in the pillory for adultery.'[4]

Jakub also became engaged about this time in a lively controversy with

---

[1] Akta Jednoty Bratrské, IV (Opis), fols 129–34 (quoted in part in Goll-Krofta, *Chelčický a Jednota v XV. století*, pp. 223–25).

[2] The dating of Jakub's tract, however, presents a number of problems. According to Goll, *op. cit.*, p. 194, it was written after the synod of Rýchnov, probably in 1495, but before Matěj and Lukáš's visit to Štěken during Lent of that year. His statement, though, that it came after the decree concerning Řehoř's writings is not consistent with his dating this decree in the end of the year, *ibid.*, p. 180. Müller-Bartoš, *Dějiny Jednoty bratrské*, I, pp. 170, 171, dates it sometime after April and, at the same time, places it likewise beofre Jakub's tract. But it is possible that the references in the tract to the condemnation of Řehoř's writing refer not to the actual decree on this subject, but to the criticisms of the early Brethren which had often been made already by the leaders of the Major Party. Alternately, the tract may either have been written in fact after Matěj and Lukáš's visit, or the decree about Řehoř may have been made earlier. The evidence is in any case indecisive. The opinions expressed by Jakub, however, must certainly have been known to Matěj in outline before his visit.

[3] See Gindely, *Geschichte der Böhmischen Brüder*, I, p. 71.

[4] 'Psaní jakéhos kněze Jana Appolinařského,' *Časopis historický*, 1882, no. 2, p. 65.

Rendl of Oušava, the nobleman who had played such an important part
in bringing about the victory of the Major Party at Brandýs in 1490. Our
knowledge of their dispute is only fragmentary. It seems that Rendl was
a member of the same congregation as Jakub, though it is not completely
certain when the former actually became a full member of the Unity.
In 1491 he had been appointed Burgrave (*purkrabí*) of Prague Castle, a
post of considerable importance in the administrative hierarchy. His
admission to the Unity, therefore, would after this have seemed to
Jakub an even worse betrayal of its principles than before. Their dispute,
which probably arose sometime in 1494, may have been due to an attempt
on Jakub's part to have Rendl's application for membership turned down
or, if indeed he had already become a member earlier, to bring about his
expulsion for holding office contrary to the old regulations of the Unity.
Another source of conflict may have been the fact that Rendl, owing to his
position in society, was allowed to join the Unity as a secret member, an
innovation which, indeed, was not accepted for long even by the Major
Party.[5] Jakub's charges may have carried considerable weight in his own
congregation, but they could only add fuel to the flames of his dispute
with Ambrož.

For all these reasons the newly constituted Inner Council considered
the situation serious enough to send a deputation of three to visit the
turbulent province. Matěj, Lukáš, and a third Brother whose name is not
recorded arrived in Štěken in Lent 1495 to bring the rebels to heel. Both
sides were summoned to attend a meeting at which they were required to
state their case. The result was a foregone conclusion, since Jakub and
Amos were obviously unwilling to give up their opposition to the edict
of Brandýs; while the new leadership of the Unity naturally supported
Ambrož's standpoint in the dispute.

Accounts of the meeting, which took place in Jakub's home,[6] are
fragmentary. It seems that Lukáš defended with vigour the validity of
oathtaking. There were, he claimed, three different types of oaths. False
oaths and ones lightly taken were forbidden; but oaths which contained
the truth were not only permissible, but 'whoever is unwilling to swear on
truth, commits a sin and breaks the Law.' If he, Lukáš, was 'required to
take such an oath, [he] would regard it as a sin to refuse.'[7] The argument,
as reported by Jakub, is certainly more radical than in previous discussions,

[5]   Goll-Krofta, *op. cit.*, pp. 234–36.
[6]   *Čas. hist.*, p. 66.
[7]   A. J. B., IV, fol. 56v (quoted in Palmov, *Cheshkie bratya v svoikh konfessiyach*, II,
p. 156).

when oaths were to be taken only as a last resort and full freedom was granted those willing to suffer for continued refusal.

Lukáš had been backed up in his argument by Matěj, who indeed denied there had ever been any serious differences of opinion in the Unity in such matters. One of the Minor Party, therefore, asked him whether he was not acting from compulsion, pressure having been brought upon him to give his support. Matěj replied: 'I have come to the same way of thinking as Lukáš of my own free will and without any pressure.'[8] Another member of the Minor Party, an unlettered Brother called Blažek, attempted to defend the old doctrines and was informed that his words contained 'immoderate and overhigh accusations.'[9]

There was also an angry exchange of opinions between Jakub and Pořímský, who was told by the former: 'It was not in order to spread lies from province to province and create hatred among people that you were ordained priest.' This remark was probably in answer to Pořímský's accusation, repeated several times, that Jakub had been stirring up trouble among members of his congregation. This Jakub, however, stoutly denied, maintaining that the discontent was a spontaneous reaction on the part of those still loyal to the old doctrines.[10]

The discussion continued until late in the evening. The verdict of Matěj and the two visiting Brethren, therefore, was to be promulgated on the following day, Jakub and Amos promising to remain in the town until then. The two rebels, however, realizing that this decision would inevitably go against them, departed from Štěken secretly during the night. The verdict, calling upon them to abandon their opposition as well as to become reconciled to Ambrož and Rendl of Oušava, and to submit to the decisions of the Inner Council – Lukáš calls it *ousudek opravy* – had to be sent on to them in writing. Later Jakub made the rather ambiguous statement that, if he had known that Matěj would afterwards try to conceal the fact of his frequent changes of opinion, 'we would never have left [i.e. in the night], but instead have entered the congregation and proclaimed before both the sexes what had taken place between us.' Doubtless a feeling of having been outwitted coloured Jakub's version of what took place.[11]

As was to be expected, Jakub and Amos took no notice of their con-

---

[8]   *Ibid.*, fol. 51 (quoted in Goll-Krofta, *op. cit.*, p. 226). Cf. *Čas. hist.*, pp. 65, 66.
[9]   *Ibid.*, fol. 50v.
[10]   *Čas. hist.*, p. 65.
[11]   A. J. B., IV, fol. 57v. This seems to indicate that Matěj's decision on the following morning was read out before the whole congregation of Štěken Brethren.

demnation, continuing to proclaim their belief in the obligatoriness of the old principles on all the Brethren and to rally support, wherever possible, among the membership. 'And hence once again no little confusion arose within the Unity,' relates Lukáš, who maintains, however, that the eventual result was beneficial, since it relieved the Unity of many of its most fractious members.

The sources are not quite clear as to the exact date when disciplinary action was taken against Jakub and Amos. Its first stage was exclusion from the eucharist; full expulsion from the Unity only came several years later, after Amos had created about 1500 a separate priesthood for the Minor Party. The verdict of excommunication may actually have been taken at the Lent meeting at Štěken, or it may only have come afterwards as a result of the rebel's non-compliance with the decisions made there. Lukáš and the Major Party, indeed, were always to maintain that their opponents were not expelled for their views, but on account of the 'sin' of disobedience to the properly constituted authority of the Unity and their intolerance of those Brethren who did not share their opinions.[12] After the synod of Rýchnov, Amos and Jakub, wrote Lukáš, 'were not forced to anything opposed to their conscience; on the contrary, love was shown to them, so that they might continue to think as they had thought.'[13]

The ordinary members of the Minor Party were to be tolerated for the time being within the Unity, despite their disagreement with the new doctrines. It was probably hoped that the radical action to be taken against their leaders, and the letters sent to the Brethren of the Minor Party by Matěj during or immediately after his visit to Štěken, declaring the validity of oathtaking and participation in the state,[14] would put an end to the disaffection among the rank-and-file, who had not yet been guilty of acts of indiscipline against their spiritual superiors. As Matěj wrote in the letter he sent to Jakub and to Blažek, one of the Minor Party present at the meeting, to whom he handed it on leaving Štěken: 'In conversation with us you several times asserted that you cannot, and will not, submit in the matter of worldly power and the oath, even though in the opinion of others it is not against Christ's commandment. But we have a mind to suffer you for a suitable time.'[15]

The accusations which the Minor Party were constantly bringing for-

---

[12]   For Matěj's visit and its aftermath, see Lukáš, 'O obnovení,' fols. 99v, 100: *Odpis proti odtržencom*, fols, 45, 45v, 48v (quoted in Goll-Krofta, *op. cit.*, pp. 205, 212, 216); *Čas. hist.*, pp. 64, 65.
[13]   A. J. B., IV, fol. 145.
[14]   *Ibid.*, fol. 51 (quoted in Goll-Krofta, *op. cit.*, p. 226); *Čas. hist.*, p. 66.
[15]   *Ibid.*, fol. 57 (quoted *ibid.*, p. 227); fol. 33.

ward against Matěj, however, had probably touched him on the raw. In another letter, written in the name of the Inner Council and now sent to the Brethren of the Minor Party, he sought to rebut their assertions of treachery or at least to get them to moderate their tone. 'After much writing and direct talks with you, let me remind you of the duty of brotherly love.' Let them stop creating disturbances, 'since you are not forced by us in any way either as regards actions or thoughts ... we have throughout wanted to tolerate you if you had not committed other offences,' i.e. of indiscipline. Matěj now considered acceptance of office under certain conditions as scripturally justified. 'Therefore we beseech you to take care not to become offenders against God's commandments for the sake of the letter (*pro některá literní slova*) which, it seems to us, you do not understand.'

He was prepared, however, to make some concessions towards their point of view. First, the avoidance of office wherever possible was still considered advisable. The second concession was one which had not appeared before during the course of the controversy: 'We do not forbid you [wrote Matěj] to lead whomsoever you can of the wealthy towards voluntary poverty, ... to snatch them from offices, in which their souls are in much danger', and lead them 'towards a more perfect life and ... a closer imitation of Christ. But that is not for all men.' According to Christ it was indeed difficult, but not impossible, for a rich man to enter the Kingdom of Heaven. Some, too, who believed in Christ, such as the Roman centurion, were men placed in authority. The views of the Minor Party – which, of course, had been those of the whole Unity a few years before – were judged by Matěj to be unsound; and he concluded his letter with the threat of 'avoidance,' of a boycott by the loyal members of the Unity against the refractory.[16]

Soon after this, on the request of some of the pastors in the provinces, Matěj and his Inner Council sent out a strongly worded directive as to the attitude to be taken up towards the rebel leaders, 'wicked and bold men [they are called] who are unable to profit from any admonition or talks

---

[16] *Odpis*, fols, 54–55 (quoted in part in Goll-Krofta, *op. cit.*, p. 219). There is no clear indication of the dating of this letter. Goll rather vaguely puts it sometime before the conference at Chlumec in 1496; while Lukáš makes it precede the letter quoted in note 18, ordering the boycotting of those who remained in the Minor Party. It is equally difficult to place either letter in relation to Jakub's Second Tract; but they would both appear to have been written before its composition. Both the tract and the two letters served to give written expression to the opinions of the two parties during the period between the disciplinary action taken against the Minor Party after Matěj's Lent visit to Štěken and the Chlumec conference of the following year.

together. For whatever is said to them, they twist around ... to our detriment.'[17] Therefore, the pastors are advised to warn:

Their people and their assistants not to speak with them nor even to wish to listen to them, but to deal with them briefly, saying: 'We believe according to the Brethren [i.e., cf the Inner Council] in salvation in God; if you have anything against that, tell it to them.' For we are more aware of some of their lies. But if, despite the general warning, some continue to hold intercourse with them, then they should be personally admonished. If, despite even that, these should still appear to such persons more right and good ... let them have a taste, give them freedom. ... For most probably the same sort of persons will join them as they are themselves, people who would stick at nothing.[18]

In the same year as the partial expulsion from the Unity of the leaders of the Minor Party, Amos and Jakub, another step was taken towards the final eradication of the political and social doctrines of the Old Brethren. A second conference was held at Rýchnov to discuss the question how far, in view of the recent changes, the writings of Chelčický, Řehoř, and his contemporaries were now binding on Unity members. Unlike the conference of the previous year, which had included both priest and laymen, now only eighteen leading pastors were present, including all members of the new Inner Council and some, like Matěj and Michal, who had formerly been upholders of the old viewpoint. The object of the conference was to find means to counter the accusation, made by the Minor Party, that it was they who represented the true Unity tradition, while the present Inner Council had betrayed the ideals of its founder. Such arguments could obviously be used with great effect among the rank-and-file Brethren, especially those of the older generation used to regard the writings of Brother Řehoř as of almost equal validity with the scriptures.

The decree (svolení) which embodied the conference's findings opened by declaring that the Unity did not regard any previous sayings or writings of any of its members, past or present, as 'unalterable laws.' The arguments to the contrary of those presentday Brethren, by whom Amos and

---

[17] Odpis, fol. 55v.
[18] Ibid. (quoted in part in Goll-Krofta, op. cit., p. 219). For dating, see Müller-Bartoš, op. cit., p. 169. At Chlumec in the following year the Major Party accused Jakub and his friends of writing to Prague to incite the Utraquist Masters against them. The Minor Party, however, denied they knew any of the Prague Masters or priests, asserting, on the contrary, that it was their opponents, especially Táborský, who had written several times to Prague — seemingly in particular to M. Viktorín Kornel, the Unity's erstwhile friend and later opponent — to 'our and your great enemies.' The Utraquist priests, as a result, making use of their denunciations, had 'preached [i.e. against the Minor Party] in their sermons.' The references to these contacts in the Report of the Minor Party (Čas. hist., pp. 65, 66) are not at all clear.

Jakub were obviously meant though their names were not specifically mentioned, who interpreted these writings in such a way as to cause 'a general lack of trust' among members and 'even to bring about a schism,' were on no account to be given credence.

After a brief historical survey of the origins of the Unity in the year 1457, the writers of the decree went on to express themselves very critically concerning the opinions given vent to at that time. The Brethren then, it was claimed, were wont to view matters from an 'immoderately lofty' standpoint, which had been handed on to succeeding generations as the official Unity line. Among those responsible for the acceptance of such ideas, persons 'who praised what they themselves did not practice,' was Petr Chelčický, whose works were especially popular reading in Unity circles. Even though the Brethren found it extremely hard to live up to such principles, the attempt was made to base their way of life upon the doctrines of Chelčický and Řehoř and their like. New converts, too, were required to accept these principles as their own. The net result was, however, that the Brethren came to trust more in their own good works than 'in the cross of Christ.'

Countering in advance the accusation of disrespect towards the founders of their society, the authors of the decree pointed out that Moses in the Old Testament and the apostles, and especially St. Peter, all fell short of perfection and deserved admonishment for some of their actions. 'It was the same, also, with the founders of the Unity.' After some time it began to be felt that some of the doctrines accepted by the Unity were mistaken and even erroneous. Therefore, they had now come to acknowledge that the works of the early Brethren containing the official corpus of Unity doctrine 'were written with insufficiency.' Several of Brother Řehoř's writings were, indeed, specifically mentioned, though it is difficult to identify them exactly, as a result of the imprecise use of titles.

Owing to God's love and effective actions we have come to realize [the decree goes on] that certain matters have been treated without moderation and intemperately (nad míru a střídmost) ... We, therefore, both those who have been members from the beginning and those who joined later, have unanimously and with good intent decreed, after much heartsearching, that we should not be impeded by these things nor keep them for future guidance ... But that they should be reckoned among the Apocrypha, and that those writings for long accepted by all Christians, which are set out and contained in the Bible, are sufficient.

In the present dissension and controversy within the Unity on the attitude towards the state, their chief concern should be to strive patiently for the reformation of the wrong thinking and not to act simply from anger and hatred. Towards the end of the decree the writers called for the exhibition of a spirit of brotherly love. Their aim in making this decree, they claimed, was to put an end to the uncertainty and bickering which had existed hitherto, and to give a clear proof of the unity which existed on this subject among the leadership, between the younger members and those who had joined in Brother Řehoř's day.[19]

The decree of Rýchnov was a landmark in Unity history. The old political and social doctrines, as expressed in the writings of Chelčický and Řehoř, were not, it is true, entirely rejected. They were still to have binding force 'so long as they coincided with the holy scriptures and served the purpose of profitable edification.'[20] As the *Historia Fratrum* expressed it, the decree was designed to bring about 'a uniting and a harmonious calming of all the divisions, which had existed hitherto in the Unity of Brethren.'[21] But, in actual fact, it was to have the effect of re-placing the traditional ideology by one which was by degrees to come to accept the existing social order without any reservations. The appeal to the writings of Řehoř or Chelčický, therefore, was no longer to be an irrefutable proof of the rightness of any given opinion, though even among many of those who accepted the new standpoint the authority at least of Řehoř still had much weight.

This must, above all, have been true of Brother Matěj, bound by so many ties of affection and respect to Řehoř's memory. For this reason probably the Minor Party now sent one of their number, Beneš Vodička, to speak with Matěj while he was visiting Litomyšl, and to find out exactly what his views were on these subjects. Matěj's reply to the question whether he 'wished to stand by the early doctrine or by the present decree' was typical of his whole outlook: 'By both, since we tolerate both (*Že při prvním i nynějším, neb obému dáváme miesto*).'[22] It was also for the present the official attitude of the Inner Council.

About this time, too, Jakub, with the assistance of Amos and a third member of the Minor Party, Říha of Votice, composed a lengthy manifesto which puts forward in somewhat chaotic fashion, but with an almost fanatical earnestness and sincerity, the case for the Minor Party.[23] Jakub's

[19] Goll-Krofta, *op. cit.*, p. 209–11, which reprints the major part of the fuller version given in the *Historia Fratrum*. The version in *Dekrety Jednoty bratrské*, p. 2, is very much shortened.

[20] *Dekrety, loc. cit.*

[21] Šafařík, 'Br. Jana Blahoslava historie bratří českých,' *Č. Č. M.*, XXXVI (1862), p. 108.

[22] *Odpis*, fol. 54v (quoted in Goll-Krofta, *op. cit.*, p. 219).

[23] Goll-Krofta, *op. cit.*, p. 194.

Second Tract, as it is usually called, was to be of considerable importance in the ensuing stages of the controversy.

At the outset Jakub stressed, first, the virtues of suffering and poverty: 'From the beginning of the world the good people had had to suffer.'[24] Renegades, like Lukáš and Krasonický, had tried to prove that if a person 'suffers, being able to defend himself, his suffering is merely that of an ass or a beast.' But Christ had not taken this view. He had not hesitated 'to lay his yoke' upon his disciples 'for the sake of God's kingdom,' requiring that they should renounce property and family. His followers were found among the lowly and the poor, among servants, not rulers. 'For it is not the poor who rule the world but the rich.' Christianity, for Jakub and his like, was a religion 'which blesses the poor ... and apportions misery to the rich.' During the early years of the Unity, he writes, 'many people had renounced great estates, honour, fame and a luxurious life and with joy undergone great trials, hard imprisonment, cruel torture and some even death itself.'[25] Jakub mentions the names of some of these 'high and noble' persons who, upon joining the Unity, lived thereafter on the same level as the 'simple' Brethren: persons belonging to the Šárovec and Sudoměř families and Brother Votík, about whose lives however nothing further is known. These he contrasts with the type of person now recruited into the Unity, who 'has acquired estates, has become rich, gained honour and renown and the friendship of the world' and risen – and here Rendl of Oušava is probably referred to – to high office: all during the period when, as a neophyte, he should be doing penance for his former sins in the world.[26]

Jakub's second point was that the true Christian faith had been held throughout the centuries only by a small minority of the faithful. 'Whenever the number of people multiplied, they stifled the seed of faith; but God preserves it in a small company.'[27] It was better to be on the right path with the chosen few than on the wrong with the majority. It was to the small flock that Christ's words of comfort were directed. This Jakub illustrates by the contrast between the history of the official church since the Donation of Constantine and that of the Waldenses, a persecuted minority. But even the latter had finally departed from the teachings of their founder, for every movement, though 'begun in God, ... in the course of time undergoes a decrease and later a corruption through the

[24]   A. J. B., IV, fol. 50 (quoted *ibid.*, p. 225).
[25]   *Ibid.*, fols. 51v, 52, 53, 54, 56.
[26]   *Ibid.*, fol. 54v (quoted Goll-Krofta, *op. cit.*, pp. 226, 234, 235).
[27]   *Ibid.*, fol. 50 (quoted in part in *ibid.*, p. 225).

wicked enemy.' This, indeed, had now happened with the Brethren. 'Many people were saying, as they called to mind their early works and saw what they were doing at present, that the Brethren, having begun in the spirit, were ending with the flesh.' This was the result of the innovations of the Major Party.[28] They had, it was implied, abandoned the old doctrines to avoid persecution and to win over large numbers of people unwilling to make the sacrifices hitherto demanded on entry into the Unity.

Thirdly, the tract stressed the absolute binding force of every word of Christ, according to the interpretation given by the early Brethren. Christ would acknowledge only 'those who accepted His teaching, so cherishing it that heaven and earth would first pass away before the least of His words.'[29] This interpretation was of course the one given by Chelčický and Řehoř, which had been accepted until recently by almost all the Brethren.

For the first time in the polemical literature of the Unity the question of the oath comes to the fore, though it does not as yet take the central position in the controversy it was shortly to do. Jakub devotes considerable attention to it and quotes the words of Christ (Matthew V, 34–37) and St. James (James V, 12) to prove that every kind of oath is forbidden to the Christian. 'And when the prohibition concerning the oath is set aside [he writes] then the commandment to love one's enemies is broken too,' as well as all the other injunctions of the Sermon on the Mount. Any attempt, therefore, to lessen the force of one commandment was an attack on all the others.

The tract repeated the familiar arguments against the participation of the Christian in the work of the state. 'There is no proof whatsoever [wrote Jakub] that the civil power ever had any part in the unity of the holy church.' To mix the two would be like combining fire and water. Those Christian bodies, heedless of Christ's injunctions in the Sermon on the Mount, who have allowed their members to participate in the state, were in fact 'the legions of damnation'. Jakub rejected with scorn his opponents' claim that by the recent changes in doctrine they had not simply accepted the standards of the paganized Christianity of the world. He even accused them of hiding the full implications of their position from the ordinary members of the Unity. For him the edict of Brandýs meant, not only that the Brethren might now take office, swear and fight in the wars, but that 'a Brother might deliver up a thief to justice, to the rack and the scaffold, ... and do evil for evil.'

---

[28] *Ibid.*, fols. 51v, 52, 53–54, 56, 56v.
[29] *Ibid.*, fol 51 (quoted *ibid.*, p. 226).

Why had the Minor Party broken with their opponents of the Major Party? It was in the first place, Jakub replied, because 'you oppress us by force.' A second reason lay in the fact that they had no right to act as judges in the dispute, 'since you are yourselves one of the parties (*neb jste strana*).' Thirdly, it was impossible to continue to submit to 'your prostitution of doctrine, by which you corrupt the holy scripture' with the assertion that the former strict interpretation of Christ's commandments might be abandoned. It was in fact rather the Major Party which had split off from the Minor, since the latter alone held to the primitive faith of the early Brethren. The former were 'the devisers of new things and the defenders of new-fangled' doctrines. Jakub, therefore, flatly denied the Major Party's claim that the cause of the schism was not a dispute about doctrine, but a case of indiscipline among a minority of the members, whose conscientious scruples were to be respected, so long as the same toleration was accorded to the opinions of the majority.[30]

Much space in the tract was devoted to attacks on the leaders of the Major Party: Klenovský, Lukáš,[31] Krasonický and Tůma the Scribe. But the bitterest jibes were directed against Matěj, the turncoat, the renegade who only a few years earlier had confided in Jakub and his friends his distrust of Klenovský and his loyalty to the old doctrines. 'You are unworthy to be a bishop and pastor', Jakub told him. 'The same doctrine which we now hold, Brother Matěj held for many years; and we are minded to keep to this doctrine until we die, for it was observed for many years under Brother Řehoř and many Brothers and Sisters still hold it dear.' But now Matěj had 'of his own free will' deserted them, even going so far as to warn his congregations against contact with them, just because of their loyalty to principle.[32]

The tract is badly constructed. Its arguments are thrown together without much attempt at any logical sequence. The arrangement is completely muddled and personal abuse is often substituted for reasoning. But it is obviously the product of a personality which, however untrained,

[30] *Ibid.*, fols. 51–52v, 55, 56v, 57.
[31] In January 1496 Lukáš had issued a tract entitled *O příčinách oddělení sepsání bratrské* (A. J. B., III, fols 98–138) mainly for the purpose of controverting the Minor Party's thesis that the Unity separated from the Utraquist church as a protest against the moral corruption of its clergy. Lukáš, on the other hand, ascribed its origin to differences over theological and dogmatic questions rather than to a moral revolt, thereby weakening the emphasis placed by his opponents on the problem of moral behaviour in political and social matters. See Molnár, *Boleslavští bratří*, p. 43. Lukáš, on account of his literary activities and his increasing participation in the dispute, was now rightly regarded by the Minor Party as one of their most weighty opponents.
[32] A. J. B., IV, fols. 57, 57v.

possessed a deep moral seriousness. The atmosphere, with its continuous
emphasis on the narrow path to be trod by the small and lowly flock of
true Christians, is the same as is found in the writings of Řehoř or
Chelčický. Its author's burning anger, the feeling of frustration almost to
the point of inarticulateness, was due to his realization that not only were
the ideals of the Unity's founders being destroyed by those who claimed
to be the guardians of its traditions, but that among the latter were some
even who, like Matěj, had been Řehoř's closest associates. It must, too,
have become increasingly clear that the bulk of the membership was
prepared to stand by indifferent and see this happen, with many Brethren,
indeed, actively taking part in the controversy on the side of the
innovators.

Neither threats nor attempts at conciliation were to make the Minor
Party more ready to accept the existence within the Unity of any members
unwilling to keep to the strict moral code of Řehoř's day. The threats
only strengthened their conviction of the wrongness of their adversaries.
They scornfully rejected the limited toleration of their own views offered
them by Matěj. 'We are not in the least grateful to you [wrote Jakub in his
Second Tract] for suffering us in those matters, where we are in fact
fulfilling God's commandments. Therefore, we do not need your toleration.' Nevertheless, Jakub went on to hint that his party would welcome
another meeting for discussion, and to protest even that the disciplinary
action taken against himself and other members of the Minor Party was
especially unfair, in view of the fact that so far they had been refused a
further chance of expressing their standpoint.[33] Matěj and the Inner
Council also still appear to have been anxious to confer with Jakub and
his friends once more. The chances of a successful outcome to such a
meeting were, however, remote.

A conference (*rozmlouvání*) actually took place on 23 May 1496 at
Chlumec on the river Cidlina.[34] The object of the conference in the view
of each side was the same, to convince the other party of the wrongness of
its opinions: 'For the sake of putting them right,' as the Report (*Zpráva*)
of the Major Party put it. The immediate initiative in calling the conference seems to have come from the latter. 'The Brethren in the true suc-

[33] A. J. B., IV, fol. 57.
[34] Detailed accounts of the conference are given in the Report of the Major Party
(A. J. B., IV, fols. 26–33v), which is almost certainly by Lukáš, and in that of the Minor
Party (*Časopis historický*, 1882, no. 2, pp. 61–67, reprinted from A. J. B., IV), the
author of which was probably Jakub. The chronological order in which the discussions
are presented, though probably accurate on the whole, is in both reports sometimes
rather erratic.

cession (*v puovodu*) [as they called themselves] were unwilling to reply on paper to the writings' of the Minor Party, prefering 'to speak with them in person for the sake of a better understanding between the two sides. Therefore ... it was left for them to choose when and where they wished to come together for a conference.' The leaders of the Minor Party evidently chose Chlumec as being in the centre of the area where they had numerous supporters.

The delegates of the Major Party, Matěj, Prokop, Lukáš, Matěj Uhlíř, like Matěj a former protagonist of the old doctrines, and Bernard of Přibislavice from the congregation at Litomyšl, on arriving in Chlumec on the Saturday before Whitsun sent to ask whether the Minor Party still 'wished for a meeting; and where and according to what order of speaking and before what persons it should take place.' The Minor Party, in answer, designated the following Monday for the conference and the house of Beneš Vodička as its location. Vodička was a tailor and a prominent member of the Minor Party which, as already related, had sent him not long before on a visit to Matěj to find out exactly where the bishop stood in the controversy. The Minor Party also proposed that 'the rank-and-file Brethren of the neighbourhood (*bratří obecní, okolní y domacy*) should be summoned' to attend its sessions. Matěj and his colleagues agreed to this on condition that 'they provided accomodation and provisions for them.' But the Minor Party were not at first ready to fall in with their suggestion; nor did they give an immediate answer as to the rules under which the conference should be conducted, promising however to give this later.

On the Sunday evening Matěj again sent a messenger to the Minor Party asking for an answer, and also to find out whether they wanted a general conference of all the delegates or would prefer to elect several of their number for a more intimate discussion. It appeared, however, that the Minor Party had not at first understood the meaning of the questions put to them. They now answered that they wanted the conference to be conducted 'without squabblings and as a friendly discussion, and that they were ready to behave properly towards Brother Matěj.' But, they added, they were disappointed at the absence of Klenovský, whom they rightly regarded as the leading personality in the Inner Council. It is, indeed, quite possible that Klenovský kept away from the conference realizing that his rejection of the old doctrines, being more radical than that of some of his colleagues, might impede its success.

On the Monday morning the members of the local congregation gathered to hear the proceedings of the conference, some Brethren also arriving

from the neighbouring congregation at Nový Bydžov.[35] These onlookers
were present at the request of the Minor Party; and Matěj and his
colleagues, therefore, thought it advisable to have them warned, before
the session opened, 'that they should sit quietly in silence and not take part
themselves in anything.'

Then the disputants entered, Matěj and his colleagues being shown to
one table and the Brethren of the Minor Party to another. The latter
were well-represented, eleven of their number being present as against
only five from the Major Party. Jakub and Amos of course attended as
well as Beneš Vodička who acted as host. Their other delegates were:
Matouš the Weaver of Lanškroun, Ondřej the Cobbler, Jan the Miller
from Sušice, Říha the Weaver from Votice, Havel the Clothier from
Litomyšl, Jiřík the Cooper, also from Votice, 'a certain' Jan Cvilda, a
furrier, and Pavel, formerly a priest of the *Mikulášenci*.[36] They were
representative, it would seem, of the proletarian element in the Unity in
contrast to educated theologians like Prokop and Lukáš of the visiting
delegation. The greater size of the Minor Party's delegation was undoubtedly due to the fact that its members mostly came from the neighbourhood, where the Minor Party had strong support.

The conference opened in an atmosphere of mutual toleration, which,
however, was unfortunately not to be maintained for long. Even the
Report of the Major Party admits that some of the members of the
opposing delegation 'came with the object of promoting peace and conciliation'; and before the session actually opened, on Matěj's proposal,
both sides had stood in prayer together. Then all the delegates sat down;
and Vodička as host thanked Matěj for consenting to come, promising
that they would listen quietly to what he had to say.

Matěj spoke first, briefly outlining the reasons for holding the conference. He asked the Minor Party to state whether they still held to the
attacks made on him and his colleagues in Jakub's Second Tract, which
they seem to have distributed among both the members of the Major

[35] Cf. *Odpis*, fol. 49 (quoted in Goll-Krofta, *op. cit.*, p. 216), where Lukáš writes that
the conference was held 'before the local congregation and before many [Brethren]
gathered from the province of Hradec Králové.'
[36] For this sect, see Jireček, 'Mikulášenci,' *Č. Č. M.*, 1876, pp. 47–82. They apparently
did not share the early Unity's pacifist anarchism and were severely criticized by Jakub
for their collaboration with the civil authorities, A. J. B., IV, fols. 55v, 56. According
to Jireček, *op. cit.*, pp. 64, 65, they did not have priests of their own, but Pavel may have
been one of their elders who administered the affairs of the sect. Its members, including
the elders, consisted almost entirely of illiterate peasants and artisans. See also my
article 'The Weeping Brethren of Bohemia', *The Iliff Review* (Denver, Colorado),
Winter 1956, pp. 15—20.

Party and 'others' outside the Unity.[37] The Minor Party in answer protested that 'it is not right to speak first of your affairs ... we shall give you a proper reply concerning these in our own time. Let us rather talk first concerning holy matters, fundamental and essential to salvation.' They then turned to Matěj and asked him: 'Was the Unity at the very beginning built upon the foundation of Christ?' Prokop broke in to say that it was, 'but that there was insufficiency in the teaching of the original doctrine.' The Major Party however, he added, were ready to agree that the old doctrines (*první smysl*) were still to be tolerated within the Unity. The Minor Party tried to press them on this point: 'We thanked them that they had spoken truth and asked them why they had made a second new doctrine which could not be confirmed by the scripture, when one could be saved through the first.' The reply was the same as Matěj had given earlier to Vodička: that both doctrines might equally be held to. This however, with considerable justification, the Minor Party were quite unprepared to accept; for them 'the one was the contrary of the other, like water and fire.' They discoursed eloquently on the cruelties involved in putting the new doctrines into practice in the sphere of judicial admini-stration. 'How can you say that both doctrines can be adopted [their speaker ended with indignation] that one can hang a man with loving kindness (*aby mohl z lásky oběsiti*).'[38] 'They had [he said] been brought up in [the old doctrine], for its sake they had broken away from other religious societies and joined the Brethren, been baptised a second time and entered into the holy church. And it was for this doctrine that they had split off from the Brethren, when they came to realize the significance of the decree [i.e. of Brandýs] contrary to it.'

The two sides were in fact arguing at cross purposes. The Minor Party wished to centre the discussion on the scriptural validity of the old doc-trine. Matěj and his colleagues, on the other hand, wanted to make the whole question one of Unity discipline. Tolerance having been granted to the two points of view, it was a question, in their opinion, how far the Minor Party were prepared to accept the control of the properly con-stituted church authorities; whether they were willing to cease causing dissension, provided a guarantee was given that their conscientious scruples would be respected. For this reason perhaps, they again proposed to limit the conference to a smaller number of persons chosen by each side, which proposal the Minor Party had evidently turned down earlier;

[37] A. J. B., IV, fols. 26, 26v.
[38] *Čas. hist.*, p. 62.

and the decisions reached in this narrower circle were thereafter to be binding on both parties. But again the Minor Party refused.[39]

The Minor Party continued, indeed, to assert that it was for their loyalty 'to the old doctrine' that they had been disciplined. Their opponents answered: 'We do not exclude you because of your opinions, but on account of your sins' of indiscipline. Tempers began to rise, since Matěj and his colleagues, conscious perhaps that the views of the Minor Party were in fact not at all unconnected with the action taken against them, refused to enter upon any further details as to the exact nature of these alleged sins. Now, indeed, the local Brethren, probably mostly sympathetic to the Minor Party, who were sitting round as mere spectators, forgetting the adjurations given them earlier on no account to take part in the debates, began to murmur and demand 'that our sins [i.e. those of the Minor Party] should be named in front of them all.' The argument continued for some time to go round in a circle without either side showing any signs of yielding its ground.

When the Minor Party attempted to give a definition of the two rival doctrines, their opponents strongly disagreed with the remark that the new doctrine, as expressed in the edict of Brandýs and later decrees, was equivalent to accepting worldly conceptions 'even as far as the hangman.' Then Vodička got up and said that he was ready to prove this statement, not merely by the words of the Major Party, but by their deeds. The examples he went on to give, though undoubtedly his narrative was coloured by partisan bias, throw an interesting light on the practical application of the Unity's new attitude towards the state and the authorities.

His first illustration concerned a certain teacher (učitel), a member of the Unity called Vavřinec, who was himself present at the conference; and the incident presumably took place in the locality of Chlumec.[40] Not long before the neighbouring lord's official, on the news that a gang of thieves was active in the district, had called out the local inhabitants, many of whom belonged to the Unity, to hunt the thieves down. They chose Vavřinec as their captain (hejtman) and entrusted the greater part of those captured to his charge, 'knowing that he would best take care of them.' Vavřinec then delivered them over to the prison, where they were later hanged.

[39]   A. J. B., IV, fol. 26v.
[40]   Cf. A. J. B., IV, fol. 31, where it would seem, however, as if this incident may have taken place near Kunvald in north-east Bohemia. It does not seem possible on the existing evidence to identify this Vavřinec with Vavřinec Krasonický, who is not mentioned as being present at the conference.

His next example was taken from the near-by town of Nový Bydžov, from which a number of the onlookers at the conference came. The local inhabitants had taken into custody a man who had been condemned to torture by the lord of Chlumec. His official, gathering together the local peasantry, pursued the refugee from justice; but the men of Bydžov refused to give him up. Then the official said:

'Be prepared to defend yourselves.' And among the men of Bydžov there were many Brethren and among the men of Chlumec likewise. Among the men of Bydžov there was a Brother who was a teacher, and among those from Chlumec was his son, also a Brother. And they stood over against each other with their arms ready, prepared to fight and shoot: Brethren against Brethren, father against son and son against father. And the men of Bydžov had to deliver up the prisoner, for there were few of them. But they said: 'If there had been more of us, either they would have to have killed us or we them.' You tell us [Vodička went on with fierce indignation, turning to the representatives of the Major Party] that as yet you do not go to the wars. But is not that abominable and disgusting warfare? ... And in this way you confuse and muddle good people, until they do not even know what is good and what evil.

A third example was given by another member of the Minor Party, who asserted that the Lady Johanka Tovačovská z Krajku, later to inherit Mladá Boleslav where Lukáš had his congregation, 'your famous Sister, has more sentences carried out than many a lord in the rest of Bohemia.'[41]

These illustrations of how the rejection of the old principles worked out in practice were likely to carry considerable weight with the rank-and-file of the Unity. The two incidents described must have been familiar to most of those present at the conference; and the name of the Lady Johanka Tovačovská was well-known among the Brethren as a patroness of the Major Party.[42]

It was Lukáš who attempted to answer the accusations. He was himself a friend of Johanka and one of those who wished to see a more forthright acceptance of the duty of participation in the state: the tone of his arguments now appears to have gone somewhat further than the previous cautious statements of Matěj and Prokop. 'The civil power [he now stated] with its laws and punishments can be allowed in our Unity and in the holy church. A lord owning estates, castles, fortresses and towns may be accepted into our Unity without having to relinquish the sword, and

[41] *Čas. hist.*, pp. 62, 63.
[42] Molnár, *op. cit.*, pp. 41, 42, 77, points out that, though already a sympathizer, Johanka did not actually join the Unity until 1512. It is not known to what punishments the Minor Party were referring in the passage quoted above.

may become a Brother while continuing to order punishments and executions.' It was possible, he claimed, to hang a man having love towards him in one's heart. Acceptance of worldly power, civil authority, was not equivalent to acceptance of worldly values.[43]

It was only the abuse of authority that had been condemned by Christ and not its use in all circumstances. The reason why the Major Party advocated that Brethren should, wherever possible, avoid taking office, exercising authority, amassing wealth or participating in public activities, was 'not on account of power (*moc*) in itself, but because of the evils which are associated with power or riches or landed property.' It was, it was true, difficult to keep a clean conscience in such matters, but not at all impossible. The Minor Party, in advocating the Old Brethren's theories of the incompatibility of worldly power in any form and under any conditions on the grounds that this was forbidden by Christ during the Sermon on the Mount, was entirely mistaken.

But by what standards, indeed, was the scripture to be interpreted? 'It should be understood simply [replied Jakub] without any commentaries and glosses.' The Major Party, however, thought this impractical, and gave as an instance the muddled arguments used during the lengthy speech just made by Matouš the Weaver, who had once again been arguing against the validity of the Old Testament for the Christian. In his view the Ten Commandments had given place for the Christian to the Sermon on the Mount. The Major Party believed that their opponents, in taking such passages of scripture as the Sermon on the Mount 'simply,' were in fact applying their own interpretation to them, an interpretation which they believed to be erroneous.[44]

Several other matters were probably dealt with either still during the morning session or early in the afternoon.[45] Concerning tavern-keeping, for instance, Prokop is said to have remarked: 'Why should not people live as best they can.' Inevitably, too, the question of oaths cropped up. Lukáš seems to some extent to have retracted his forthright condemnation at Štěken of those who refused to swear if just occasion arose. But he vigourously defended the Major Party's position that oaths were not forbidden by Christ in all circumstances. The Minor Party, realizing the very close connection between the oath and participation in the state, now

---

[43] *Cas. hist.*, p. 63.
[44] A. J. B., IV, fols. 27v, 28. See chap. IV, p. 136, n. 12.
[45] It is almost always difficult, and often impossible, to determine whether or not the same argument is being described in both reports. It is difficult, too, to distinguish between direct reporting and later commentary.

claimed that the Major Party had been led to justify oath-taking 'in order that they might carry out every cruel punishment without fear or conscience . . . in order that [Brethren in office] might order the executioner to hang and quarter or break men on the wheel.' At that date, as has been seen, an oath was demanded of all who held office: permission for Brethren to take office would, therefore, have been a dead letter if they had been forbidden to swear.

At the afternoon session the Major Party consented to the reading of the edict of Brandýs, which the Minor Party had asked for in the morning, on condition that Jakub's Second Tract was also read out and discussed. Now, however, the Minor Party would not hear of this. 'What a strange business [the Major Party told Jakub and his friends]. First you are very insistent in demanding a reading; and when the Brethren agree, you then refuse.' The Minor Party reluctantly gave their consent. But it would seem that in fact only 'a couple of paragraphs' of the edict were read out, perhaps in order to save time. The Major Party proceeded to give their reasons for promulgating the edict, arguing that its conclusions did not conflict with Christ's teachings and that they had been reached as a result of careful study of the meaning of the scriptures.

They next went on to consider Jakub's Second Tract, which was read out 'word by word.' It then transpired, according to the Report of the Major Party, that several of the Minor Party's delegates had neither participated in drawing it up nor even approved of its contents. It had been almost entirely the work of three men: Jakub, Amos and Říha of Votice. According again to the Major Party, they seem to have made a rather poor showing in their defence of the tract, leaving this mainly to Matouš the Weaver, even though he had had nothing to do with its composition.[46] Lukáš, from the other side, took the lead in defending the position of the Major Party, not only against the personal attacks made on the absent Klenovský and in the obscure dispute over an alleged connivance by the Major Party at the loosening of the marriage bond, but also in regard to the more general accusations made by Jakub in his Second Tract.[47]

There was little that was new in Lukáš's argument, which he developed at great length, or indeed in that of his opponents. To the Minor Party's charge that the Major Party was attempting to conceal from the rank-and-file of the membership its real opinion on these questions, Lukáš replied that they wished to behave with discretion and confine the discussion of controversial matters to the right occasion. Lukáš did,

[46]   *Čas. hist., loc. cit.*; A. J. B., IV., fols. 28–30v.
[47]   A. J. B., IV, fols. 29v–33v.

however, stress that his party were against all forms of religious persecution by the secular arm: they were still one, therefore, with the Minor Party in condemning Sylvester for his alliance with Constantine. He repeated once again the assurance that his opponents would never be penalized because of their opinions.[48] He was able to claim with complete justification that, anyhow, the Major Party's views on the relationship of church and state were a great deal 'more moderate,' that is to say, still much closer to the old doctrines of the Unity, than those held by Wyclif or Hus or Matěj of Janov, whom the Minor Party had claimed as their spiritual ancestors, as 'the true source and origin of the faithful (*pramen pořádný puovodu věrných*).[49] Interesting, too, is Lukáš's argument that turning the other cheek may be obligatory for individual Christians, but not necessarily the duty of Christian communities or their rulers.[50]

Sometime during these debates – it is indeed difficult to ascertain at exactly what point – the delegates of the Minor Party launched forth on a fierce attack on poor Brother Matěj. 'We have never dared to tell you the truth directly on account of your dignity [they told him]. ... But the fulness of time has arrived for what has been whispered in the ear to be spoken out aloud (*aby na světle bylo praveno*).'

They brought up against him his former adherence to their point of view, the criticisms he had made of some of his present colleagues during the period of the return of the Old Brethren to the Inner Council, and the stand he was now taking in favour of the new views. He was, they claimed, excommunicating them for the very opinions which he himself had adjured them to hold to at all cost. 'If I myself should ever speak otherwise [he had told them] do not believe me'; though Matěj could not now remember having made this remark. But Vodička broke in to say that he had heard him make it during one of his visits to this very congregation of Chlumec. It was Matěj, therefore, who was the turncoat: they had but followed his instructions.

What you regarded as evil, what you wrote against, you are now in fact doing; while what you formerly described as good, what you praised with your lips, you now condemn. You revile us for these things. At the same time you put those in hope [i.e. of salvation], who against their consciences swear oaths and deliver men up to the executioner; and you admit them to communion.

Their own consciences were clear: they would be loyal to the principles

[48]   *Ibid.*, fol. 31.
[49]   *Ibid.*, fol. 31v.
[50]   *Ibid.*, fols. 32, 32v.

they had accepted on entry into the Unity, to the doctrines in which they had been brought up. 'Here we stand [said Vodička to Matěj] but you have not remained with us.' The Minor Party put obedience to God, Vodička went on, before allegiance to any earthly superior. The wretched Matěj was evidently reduced by their taunts to silence, if not to tears. 'We had a mind to ask Brother Matěj' several more questions, the Minor Party were to report, 'but we were sorry for him.'[51]

The light began to fail before they had finished reading Jakub's tract. The detailed discussion of the various points as they had arisen had taken up much time. Neither side had yielded an inch to its opponents. Both, indeed, had only been strengthened in their previous conviction that they were entirely in the right and that their opponents were schismatics or traitors to the faith. Both felt that the other side had been unable to answer the arguments put forward and each was later to claim a victory.

It is not suprising, therefore, that neither party was anxious to continue the debate next day; but no decision seems to have been taken that evening. Next morning Prokop and Bernard were sent by Matěj to speak with the delegates of the Minor Party. After some skirmishing about the number of the sacraments and about some of the accusations made the previous day by the Minor Party and various other disputed points, the two emissaries departed. They had tried, says the Report of the Major Party, to convince their opponents 'not to act in so angry a fashion, but rather to have regard to the matter on hand. They would not, however, be persuaded, but wished to speak as they had begun.'[52] It was thus in a spirit of mutual distrust and increased animosity that the conference, whose beginnings had augured so favourably, was now brought to an end.

There had indeed been little chance of a successful outcome in view of the irreconcilability of the two positions. Both parties, as has been seen, had come to the conference in a fairly conciliatory mood. The Major Party all along expressed their desire to tolerate their opponents as a minority within the Unity: while the Minor Party, from their side, claimed to be ready to amend their doctrine on whatever points they could be proved to be in error.[53] But, as the conference proceeded, the debate became more heated; abuse was often substituted for argument; and it became clear that neither side was in practice prepared to yield an inch, expecting the other party to make all the concessions. This was indeed only to be expected. The leaders of the Major Party were eager to make

[51] Čas. hist., pp. 64–67.
[52] Ibid., p. 67; A. J. B., IV, fol. 33v.
[53] Čas. hist., p. 63.

an even more clearcut break with the old principles than had been achieved by the edicts of Brandýs or Rýchnov, which to some extent represented a compromise between old and new. The Minor Party, on the other hand, was on the defensive, suspecting that every concession made to their opponents would be seized upon by cunning theologians, like Lukáš or Krasonický, to undermine their position still further.

Though the conference, therefore, was from the outset almost inevitably doomed to failure, it serves as an extremely important landmark in the history of the controversy. It marks the last serious attempt to reach a *modus vivendi* between the two parties. Owing to the fact that each side has left its own account of the proceedings, it is indeed possible to gain a clearer picture of their mental processes than usual. The conference of Chlumec reveals far better than the somewhat arid pages of their polemical tracts the workings of the minds of the human beings who played the leading parts in the drama.

The remaining four years of the century brought virtually no new developments in the controversy. It was only a matter of time before the schism, already existing in practice, was brought to its formal conclusion of a complete secession of the Minor Party from the reconstituted Unity.

This period in the history of the Unity's political and social ideology was marked, first, by the promulgation by the Major Party of a series of decrees, which gave detailed instructions on various points of practical conduct in connection with the attitude of the individual Unity member to the state and society. Synods were held each year: in 1497 at an unknown location; in 1498 at Přerov; in 1499 at Brandýs, when the full sessions were preceded by a meeting of the Inner Council at Prostějov; in 1500 at Přerov and at Rýchnov. The decrees passed during these conferences are extremely important as evidence of the state of Unity thinking on these subjects in the period of transition; since, however, the issuing of this series did not cease at the end of the fifteenth, but continued on into the early years of the sixteenth century, detailed discussion of their contents will be given in Chapter VII.

Secondly, in close connection with these decrees a cycle of polemical tracts was issued during these years, the most important of which were written about 1499 or 1500. They dealt primarily with the theoretical background of the controversy, the main discussion now centring on the problem of the validity of oathtaking among Christians. The cycle appears to have opened in July 1499 with a short tract, *Odpor smyslu druhému* (A Refutation of the New Doctrine), written in defence of the Minor Party's views and addressed to an unidentified Brother Beneš. It is a well-argued piece of work, clearly written and free from the usual personal abuse. Its unknown author was not a member of the Unity at all; the leaders of the Minor Party, feeling that their own literary talents were no match for their opponents, had evidently commissioned some educated sympathizer to write it in their name.[54] In the same year, too, both Lukáš and Krasonický took up the cudgels in defence of their party's position, elaborating their objections to the arguments of the Minor Party's new champion and their own attitude to the oath.[55] These works, however, extremely important for the light they throw on the theoretical positions of each side, will be treated in the next chapter in connection with a second cycle of polemical tracts, which issued out of the renewed controversy in the first half of the 1520's between Lukáš and Krasonický, on the one hand, and Amos and Jan Kalenec, his successor, on the other.

Thirdly, the last four years of the century were filled with several more abortive attempts to prevent a final and complete split between the two parties and some further fruitless discussions. This exchange of view, however, served only to widen the breach.

The chronological order of events during this period is, as Goll points out, even more confused than hitherto.[56] After the conference of Chlumec the controversy appears to have died down somewhat; at least it has left few traces in the records. In 1498 Lukáš made another journey abroad, this time to Italy when he visited the Waldenses. The Minor Party had expressed their admiration for this sect and stressed the Waldensian influence in the history of the Unity, frequently illustrating their arguments with the example of the adherence of the Waldenses to the same political and social principles, though in fact the latter had by now abandoned their pacifism and social radicalism. The name of the sect had several times cropped up during the conference at Chlumec. Though the imme-

---

[54] Hrejsa, *Dějiny křesťanství v Československu*, IV, p. 141, suggests that the anonymous author may have been in fact M. Viktorín Kornel, the famous humanist and earlier a sympathizer of the Unity. See A. J. B., IV, fols. 75v, 83, 93; Goll-Krofta, *op. cit.*, pp. 228–30.

[55] Both Krasonický and Lukáš wrote tracts entitled *Odpověd na spis proti přísaze*. In addition, Lukáš wrote about this time one called *O přísaze* of a less polemical nature. There exists also a fourth tract emanating from the Major Party entitled *Dodatek k odpovědi na spis proti přísaze*. Though Müller-Bartoš, *op. cit.*, p. 340, list this work as item 52 in their bibliography of Lukáš's writings, on p. 173 they follow Goll-Krofta, *op. cit.*, p. 230 – almost certainly correctly – in attributing it to Krasonický. *Spis proti přísaze* referred to here was of course the Minor Party's tract, *Odpor smyslu druhému*. Lukáš's physician brother, Jan Černý, also wrote a tract, no longer extant, which despite its title, *Dialog, že křesťanu nenáleží přísahati*, was probably, too, a defence of the Major Party's position, see *ibid.*, p. 231.

[56] *Ibid.*, p. 232.

diate reason for Lukáš's journey was his concern for the influence of the pagan humanist tendencies, which were finding their way from Italy to Bohemia, a secondary consideration may have been a desire to discover how far the Waldenses in their native Alpine retreat lived up to the ideal picture painted of them by the Minor Party. Lukáš, indeed, returned home disillusioned as to the existing condition of the Waldensian community.[57]

In the following year, before Easter, the Minor Party sent a deputation to Brother Matěj, still hoping perhaps to win him back to their side. He was asked whether he and his party 'wished to correct those matters which [they] had decided on.' Matěj put off giving an immediate answer 'until we have spoken with the Brethren in Moravia.' After Easter, having in the meanwhile seen the latter, Matěj sent back his answer, an uncompromising defence of the opinions of the Major Party.

Though he and his Brethren were willing to accept correction where they were shown to be wrong, they did not consider, he states, that the standpoint they had adopted was in any way contrary to scripture. In fact the Minor Party had completely misunderstood their position. As for the accusation, often repeated in the polemical literature of the Minor Party, that the new doctrine in allowing Brethren to participate in the execution of justice was throwing aside the teachings of the Sermon on the Mount, Matěj answered sarcastically:

We consider that all who love justice regard it as a good thing ... that thieves and marauders should not multiply. And even those who speak [as the Minor Party did] are glad that the higher power gives them peace, so that they may be the more safe both at home and on the highways. And those who thus approve are not far removed from those who actually do the work.

This did not mean, however, Matěj insisted, that the Major Party gave their approval to the present methods of justice, which were often lacking in mercy. It was the humanitarian aims of the state that they supported. It was not a sin, therefore, for a Christian 'placed in authority to give over the evildoer into the hands of the executioner, according to the order and command and judgement of God, as His minister. For to this end are the powers that be ordained of God ... to execute wrath upon him that doeth evil and praise the good' (Cf. Romans XIII, 1–5).

Individual members of the Minor Party had been circulating among other Unity members, as well as among non-members, slanderous attacks

[57]   Müller-Bartoš, *op. cit.*, pp. 178, 179; Molnár, *op. cit.*, pp. 44–47.

against their opponents. Blažek and Amos, Matouš the Weaver and Říha of Votice and others had all been responsible for writing various items. It was thus difficult, in Matěj's view, to distinguish what was composed in the name of their party from what was merely a private expression of opinion. 'Therefore, we would be glad if all together you would write something of how you think in these matters.'

Towards the end of his epistle Matěj gave a brief *resumé* of his party's standpoint:

We do not reject authority if, according to divine order, it has been purged from the errors and sins of the world for temporal use. For God does not reject those in authority and all authority is from him.

Matěj's final sentence, indeed, concluded on a conciliatory note. He was quite ready, he wrote, to change his opinion if it could be shown him from scripture that the Major Party's doctrine was incorrect, that in fact all civil authority was incompatible with the Christian way of life.[58] The contents of his letter, however, showed that the ageing bishop, whatever inner doubts and hesitations he may still have had, had definitely come down on the side of the Major Party. His expressions were identical with those used by Klenovský or Lukáš. The unknown author of *Odpor smyslu druhému* has described Matěj's state of dependence at this period on the more educated members of his party; 'he had [he writes] to follow after the others.'[59]

Three further meetings between representatives of the two parties took place after Easter. One conference was held 'before the congregation at [Mladá] Boleslav,' where Lukáš was pastor; and the other two at Prostějov and Hranice in Moravia.[60] The choice of places in Moravia may have been due to the fact that, during the last few years of his life, Matěj often resided in this part of the country or possibly to the fact that the Minor Party had many supporters there. However, no account remains of any of these meetings.

Matěj was already too ill to come in person to Hranice; and he therefore sent the delegates of the Minor Party a letter in which he called upon them to show a more tolerant attitude to their opponents.[61] 'I charge you not to condemn after hearing only one side on some one occasion, . . . but

[58] A. J. B., IV, fols. 41–42v, 147; *Odpis*, fols. 49–51v (quoted in part in Goll-Krofta, *op. cit.*, pp. 217, 218, 222).
[59] A. J. B., IV, fol. 74 (quoted in *ibid*, p. 229).
[60] *Odpis*, fol. 49 (quoted *ibid.*, p. 217). The chronological order in which the conferences were held and their dating are not clear. They probably took place during the latter half of 1499 or in 1500. For the Mladá Boleslav meeting, see note 64.
[61] Goll-Krofta, *op. cit.*, pp. 186, 218; Müller-Bartoš, *op. cit.*, p. 173.

to enquire further in regard to us ... whether we actually are [as you have pictured us or not]'. They needed to consult together further to find out if they were not perhaps mistaken in their opinions concerning their former brethren, whom they should be prepared to trust more than other men. He went on once again to defend in some detail the position taken up by the Major Party, repeating that no one in the Unity was being penalized for his opinions. 'If you cannot accept this doctrine in so moderate a form or believe' what the Major Party teach, Matěj concluded, 'still they are prepared gladly to suffer you and to live together in harmony with you. Only give over dissension and slander ... for they are greater sins than those about which you are quarrelling.'[62]

This epistle appears to have been Matěj's last public utterance. He died, aged 48, in January 1500 at Lipník, in Moravia. The last year of the old century saw not only the death of the Unity's first bishop, who had watched it develop from its obscure beginnings, but also the final completion of the schism. The death of Matěj had removed from the scene the one man of influence in the Major Party, who might possibly have been won back for the old doctrines. Through his influence, indeed, control of the Unity's destinies might conceivably have been regained once more by the Minor Party.

After Matěj's death, therefore, the more determined spirits in the Minor Party, among whom Amos was the chief, decided to follow the Unity's example in 1467 and establish a separate priesthood.[63] Jakub and several others, however, were unprepared for such a radical step and returned to the Unity.[64] By the end of 1500, therefore, the schism was complete.

The re-enactment of the edict of Brandýs in 1494, and the promulgation in 1495 of the decree depriving the writings of Chelčický and Řehoř of any special authority within the Unity, signified a definite break with the

---

[62] A. J. B., IV, fols. 147v–149v. But cf. fol. 85v, which seems to imply that disciplinary action could be enforced for wrong teaching about oaths.

[63] This final step was taken in 1500 or soon after, see Goll-Krofta, op. cit., pp. 186, 232.

[64] Krasonický, 'Psaní proti Kalencowi o puowodu odtržencůw,' fol. 357v (quoted in Goll-Krofta, op. cit., pp. 187, 232). After doing penance Jakub was received back as 'an ordinary Brother.' Vodička the Tailor left the Minor Party and returned to the Unity. But both men soon broke away again and died outside the Unity. Jakub, says Krasonický, was 'expelled for the second time on account of his frequenting taverns.' It is impossible to say if this accusation was true or mere slander. According to Lukáš's account, Odpis, fol. 49 (quoted in Goll-Krofta, op. cit., p. 217), it would seem to have been at the Mladá Boleslav meeting that Jakub and his associates returned to the Unity. In this case the meeting presumably took place after the final separation of the Minor Party.

political and social doctrines of the Old Brethren which, with one brief interlude in 1490, had been binding on Unity members since its foundation. The second half of the last decade of the fifteenth century, at the end of which the schism between the two parties within the Unity was carried to its logical conclusion of complete separation, was a period of indecision and half measures. Attempts at healing the breach collapsed, however, owing to the unwillingness of either side to compromise on essentials, on the points which were in fact in dispute. But during these years members of the Minor Party still nominally retained their membership of the Unity, though disciplinary measures had been taken against them by the party now in control of its affairs. The efforts of the Minor Party to win over a majority of the Brethren were unsuccessful. Even though the rebels enjoyed considerable support in certain parts of the country, the average Brother was either indifferent or actively supported the Major Party. Equally unsuccessful was the attempt to win back Brother Matěj who, as bishop of the Unity and one of its oldest and most respected members, might have brought with him a considerable section of the Brethren.

The fundamental reason for the failure of the Minor Party, apart from errors in tactics and practical leadership, lay in the fact that the character of the average member of the Unity, or at least of those sections of the membership which carried most weight in its affairs, was rapidly changing. The humble unlettered men, mostly peasants with a sprinkling of artisans, who had at first formed the overwhelming majority of the rank-and-file Brethren, and their simple self-educated leaders of the type of Řehoř or Matěj, were giving way to the burgher Brethren, some of whom had even managed through practising the virtues of frugality and thrift to amass not inconsiderable wealth, and to the university-bred leadership of the younger men like Lukáš or Krasonický. The ideology of an earlier generation could not be fitted satisfactorily to the needs of its successors without considerable adjustment. The process of readjusting the political and social doctrines of the Czech Brethren was, however, to amount to a revolution in theory and practice.

VI

THE BRETHREN,
THE CIVIL POWER, AND THE OATH

The controversy among the Brethren was carried on at two levels: the theoretical and the practical. How, first, was the Unity to interpret the teachings of Christ, which both parties were agreed on taking as the touchstone of conduct in political and social matters as well as in the more strictly religious? And, on the basis of this interpretation, what was to be the Unity's attitude to the often disputed problem of the relationship of the Christian to the state? What in fact was the Christian idea of the state? What, too, was the nature of a truly Christian community?

The second group of questions, while flowing from this fundamental problem, was more directly related to everyday life. How were the Brethren to react in practice to the concrete demands which the state was increasingly making for their services either as executors or instruments of its commands? What types of occupation might properly be carried on by members of the Unity?

The two groups of problems were, it is clear, closely interrelated. They were, indeed, rarely differentiated by those actually engaged in the controversy. Nevertheless, there do exist two types of sources which correspond broadly to the two categories of problems outlined above. There is, first, the series of tracts composed by Lukáš and Krasonický on the one hand, and by members or sympathizers of the Minor Party on the other, during the last few years of the fifteenth century and later, after an interval of twenty years, in connection with the outbreak of renewed controversy in the early twenties of the sixteenth century. The second category, more closely related to everyday life, consists mainly of the decrees issued by the Unity synods during the last few years of the fifteenth and the first few years of the sixteenth centuries in order to guide the membership on the practical problems, which now faced them in their relationship to society and the state. They gave practical expression to the new ideology which had won supremacy in the Unity.

The present chapter is concerned with the underlying theoretical problems, the debate on fundamentals. The more practical issues will be dealt with in Chapter VII.

I

The basis upon which the Old Brethren had built their theoretical negation of the state was their doctrine concerning 'the higher righteousness,' which Christ had taught in his Sermon on the Mount. In the interpretation accepted by the Brethren it precluded, as has been seen, any form of participation in the affairs of the community. The Unity remained a sect apart.

The Major Party – and its two leading theologians of the younger generation, Lukáš and Krasonický, in particular – sought to undermine this position by giving the words of Christ a completely different interpretation. The righteousness that Christ preached, writes Krasonický, was not intended to supplant the Law and the Prophets, but only to supplement them. These did not lose their validity because of Christ's teachings; rather did they gain new force, being purged from the accretions of the centuries. The righteousness taught in the Sermon on the Mount was, it is true, higher than the debased moral code observed by the scribes and pharisees: it was this corruption that was attacked by Christ and not the original law.

It was their teaching He commanded should be shunned. . . . And hence He told His disciples that if their righteousness was not higher than that of the scribes and pharisees – for He was not referring here to that of the Jews as a whole – they would not enter into the kingdom of heaven. . . . Therefore in this place He is not the creator of new commandments, but refers back to the old . . . in their purity. . . . Christ never said or intended that another Christian righteousness be contained in these injunctions . . . as [the Minor Party] blindly infer. . . . He never meant that Christian righteousness should be higher than the Jewish in these moral commandments, which are ever pure in themselves, for the will of God is eternal. . . . Christ never created any new commandments beside or above the old.

Christ had come, in his own words, to fulfil and not to destroy the Law and the Prophets though, indeed, he tempered these with mercy and love.[1]

In the Major Party's view, therefore, the books of the Old Testament were still valid for Christians 'for the purpose of instruction (k naučení).' They were of equal value to the New Testament and not to be set aside as of inferior worth, as the Minor Party had done. 'Like Christ and the

---

[1] Akta Jednoty Bratrské, IV, fols. 87–89v.

apostles [writes Lukáš] we have drawn our proofs not only from the New Testament, but also from the Old,' which contained in embryo Christ's gospel of love.[2]

For the Minor Party their doctrine of the higher righteousness had meant that the fact that God in the Old Testament had seemingly approved executions and cruel punishments, law-courts and prisons, wars both aggressive and defensive, could not be used as an argument in favour of these things in a community which strove to follow Christ's example. For them the Law of Christ had taken the place of the lower Mosaic law.[3] In the opinion of such writers as the Minor Party's champion, the anonymous author of the *Odpor smyslu druhému,* a literal interpretation of many passages in the New Testament, and of the Sermon on the Mount in particular, was the best guarantee of the correctness of such an attitude.

The reason why the Roman Catholic Church had strayed so far from Christ's original teachings was, the Minor Party's advocate claimed, because it abandoned the simple attitude of the first centuries. The Brethren of the Major Party were now themselves on the same slippery road of interpreting inconvenient passages away. Let them, therefore, cease to rely so much on people of 'worldly wisdom' and return to their former simplicity and literalist attitude. 'In my opinion [he went on] it would serve the Brethren best simply to believe Christ's words, putting aside deep interpretations, for in this manner the early church went astray; and in this way, also, the Brethren's primitive virtue is being lulled asleep.' No middle way existed, wrote Amos and Blažek in a letter to their colleague Jakub, between on the one hand carrying out Christ's commandments in their most literal sense and to the last letter, and conforming with the ways of the world on the other. 'Who is he who has discovered this mean and not strayed from God and yielded to the flattery

---

[2] Krasonický, 'Psaní proti Kalencowi,' fols. 360–361v; Lukáš, *Odpověd na spis Kalencuo,* fol. 3. It is interesting to note that a similar division of opinion occurred during the latter half of the sixteenth century among the Polish Arians on the very same subject of their attitude to the civil power. Those wishing to throw over the earlier social radicalism, in particular Szymon Budny who in his *O urzędzie miecza używającem* (1583) was the most forceful exponent of the new trends, relied very largely on arguments based on the Old Testament. On the other hand, those among the Arians who, like the Czech Minor Party, advocated a negative attitude to the state, tended likewise to relegate the Old Testament to a position of secondary importance compared to the New, which they interpreted along similar lines. See Kot, *Ideologja polityczna i społeczna Braci Polskich,* pp. 55, 57. Professor Kot brought out in 1933 a new edition of Budny's work, which he edited from the only surviving copy in the library of the Czartoryski Museum in Cracow.

[3] A. J. B., IV, fol. 68.

of the world (*pochlebník aby nebyl světu*)?[4] If the scriptures were given their simple, literal meaning, a later leader of the Minor Party, Kalenec, was to claim, they would never find in the New Testament any injunctions to the faithful to set up authority.

But was the simple interpretation really on the side of the Minor Party? Lukáš stoutly denied this, asserting that 'anyone with any understanding who reads our writings and yours will find those of the Brethren [i.e. the Major Party] much nearer simplicity. ... When you ... cannot get any proofs, then it is you take refuge in simplicity.'[5] 'It is proper to base simplicity not on the letter, but on the truth.'[6]

Though the Major Party could, and did, claim to be nearer in their new doctrines to the original teachings of Christ, they could not deny that their opponents were closer in the spirit and in the letter to the conception of the Christian church propounded by Brother Řehoř. It was for this reason, as has been seen, that in 1495 they had passed the edict of Rýchnov, declaring that the latter's writings were no longer binding on the Unity.

'We have always stood unanimously for the things for which this Unity was founded according to the doctrine of Christ,' claimed the Minor Party. 'For we take nothing new unto ourselves ... we follow the doctrine derived by Brother Řehoř and the others from His holy spirit.'[7] This conservative, fundamentalist attitude was challenged by the young reformers of the Major Party, who made little pretence of trying to square the new doctrines with those of the Old Brethren. The change, they claimed instead, had taken place only after much heartsearching and lengthy discussion and earnest prayer. The results of their deliberations were, they believed, 'better and more useful' than the old doctrines had been, nearer to the spirit of Christ and more likely to make the Unity an effective instrument to spread the gospel. The change had not come as a result of 'carnal freedom, but on account of Christ's words; and, through it, God had shown the doctrine introduced into the people by Petr Chelčický and others of their own wisdom to be unhealthy, and He has helped towards one more moderate and realistic.'[8] The Unity had rejected the teachings of its founders as unscriptural.

The Major Party, indeed, regarded the early Brethren's political and

---

[4]   *Ibid.*, fols. 66, 75, 75v.
[5]   Lukáš, *Odpis proti odtržencom*, fols. 24v, 25v, 26.
[6]   A. J. B., IV, fol. 83.
[7]   *Ibid.*, fol. 67v.
[8]   *Ibid.*, fols. 82v, 93, 94v.

social doctrines as an unwarranted perfectionism. The Christian church, the community of believers, could never in this world attain to the high standard demanded by Řehoř and his like: the saintly life was not for the multitude. 'That all members [i.e. of the church] should thus shine in truth . . . would be wonderful [writes Krasonický ironically]. But this in my opinion has never happened in the world, even among the flock at the time of Christ and His apostles.' Even then, everyone was to some extent seeking his own interest. 'Since this was so with the priests and pastors, what then about the ordinary folk? . . . The Brethren will be doing enough if they continue not to give way to open wickedness . . . without repentance.'[9] Lukáš, too, did not believe that everyone in a Christian community could be perfect, though seemingly some members might achieve this. 'The faithful could not exist among the unrighteous Christians,' he writes, unless they were protected by the civil authorities.[10] For the Minor Party and their predecessors, of course, 'an unrighteous Christian' was a contradiction in terms: a community in which force was needed to repress the evil tendencies in men could not, in their view, be called a Christian one.

The civil power for the Major Party was not an unmitigated evil or, rather, it was to be regarded as a necessary evil in a sinful world. It originated, according to Lukáš, in the Fall of Man, 'from the sin of Adam' which introduced evildoing among men. 'The source of the civil power took its beginning according to God's decree from repentance after the fall of' Adam and Eve, when God put the latter under the authority of her husband and their children later under the authority of the parents. The power of the father over his household was in the course of time extended over still larger groups. 'The householders came together in greater or smaller numbers, and through such gatherings villages and towns and cities arose in different parts of the earth . . . those who had come together were unable to exist in harmony and peace without order and authority.' Thus, from village community through city state, the need was felt to set up some form of government 'for common defence and the administration of the communal life and business.' Walls were built round the towns, rulers chosen from the commonalty and disturbers of the public peace put down. 'In the towns' there sprang up 'seats of government (rathúzy) and numerous defences, for the towns and cities could not exist for the wickedness of some men, for their power and cruelty.'

[9] Ibid., fols. 93v, 94 (quoted in part in Goll-Krofta, Chelčický a Jednota v XV. století, p. 230).
[10] Odpis, fol. 15v.

God had, therefore, instituted one man or one institution to control the evil tendencies in man. That, claimed Lukáš, was the origin of the office of every properly constituted ruler, from mighty emperor to humble alderman: that 'all should in an orderly manner be bound one unto another according to constituted authority, higher and lower.' The establishment of world empires had been intended by God as a means of keeping in order the lesser kings, continuously quarrelling among themselves, and of bringing the nations under one ruler. Governing according to natural law, the world emperors had ruled cruelly and wickedly: 'God had aroused [them] to punish the people of Israel.' This did not, indeed, alter the fact that God had instituted the civil power for man's ultimate well-being according to the written law of the Old Testament, which was later to be confirmed by Christ in the New.[11]

The Minor Party, on the other hand, held republican doctrines. Kalenec, for instance, tried to prove that, since Christ had refused the devil's offer of all the kingdoms of the world, it was therefore wrong for any Christian to exercise the functions of king. Lukáš naturally denied this, arguing that the incident proved only that Christ's kingdom was not of this world.[12]

In his concept of the state's origin Lukáš, therefore, differed fundamentally from the explanation put forward, for instance, by Chelčický in his *Sít' víry*, even though the latter gave a qualified approval to civil authority among non-Christians. But in their picture of the place which the civil power occupied in the early Christian community, both men drew very close in their ideas. The early Christians, according to Lukáš, lived together for some 300 years on the basis of the Law of Love (*zákon milosti*) alone. Though they remained subject to the powers that be in all matters not against conscience, they took no part in worldly affairs, which were left to the pagans. There were, indeed, a few rulers among the early Christians; however, 'believers were not ruled by them, but all together were subject ... to the spiritual administrators and, in addition, to the constituted civil power,' which remained outside the Christian church. The only sanction they employed was expulsion of wrongdoers from the community of Christians.

As time passed, the influx of new members from the ruling classes

---

[11]   *Ibid.*, fol. 4v; Lukáš, *Spis o mocy swěta*, fols. 4–7. In his conception of the original equality of man, and of the state as a result of, and at the same time a remedy for sin, Lukáš follows St. Augustine. For his acquaintance with the writings of St. Augustine and other church fathers, see Müller-Bartoš, *Dějiny Jednoty bratrské*, I, pp. 288, 289.

[12]   *Odpis*, fols. 18, 18v.

greatly increased. 'They did not exercise their secular offices over or among the faithful, but over the world,' says Lukáš. Chelčický's view however, obviously not shared by Lukáš, had been that in such cases the Christian convert should resign his office and renounce civil authority on joining the church. This, as has been seen, was the practice enforced by the early Brethren and still advocated by the Minor Party. For Lukáš, on the other hand, what was wrong and unchristian was not that those in authority retained their offices on becoming Christians or that Christians should accept authority in the outside world. It was the exercise of force in matters of faith, the use of the secular arm in spiritual affairs, that was the legendary 'poison injected into God's church.' The spiritual and the secular, in his view, should be kept strictly apart. But that did not mean either 'that civil power should not be brought under the faith' or that those in official positions, who had 'come to the faith, should not or could not be saved.'[13]

In his commentary, too, on the legend of the Donation of Constantine Lukáš's attitude is outwardly not dissimilar to that of Chelčický and the early Brethren. There is, however, this fundamental difference between the two writers: that whereas Chelčický saw in the story a warning against the participation of the Christian in all activities connected with the state, Lukáš merely regards the corruption of the church, which was said to have ensued from the Donation, as a result of the fusion of the secular and the spiritual spheres of life.

Like the Jews under their judges, writes Lukáš, a later generation of Christians 'demanded for themselves a king and civil power, that they should enjoy these things as other nations.' So God sent them Constantine, who helped to put the false Christians under Sylvester into power. The latter then proceeded to suppress all those who refused to acknowledge their supremacy in religious matters or to approve of their acquisition of authority and wealth. 'The Roman Emperor gave Sylvester power and authority over the earth, in order to promote the priesthood in this world, leading them to the seat of authority (na rathauz) as the devil led Christ to the temple and up onto the mountain.' The faithful few, who by an anachronism are pictured as having been at that time under the leadership of Pierre Valdo, remained behind in the forests, fleeing now from the additional persecution of a paganized church dressed in Caesar's 'robes.'[14]

[13] Spis o mocy swĕta, fols. 7v–10.
[14] Lukáš, 'O obnovení,' fols. 133, 135v, 214, 216. Lukáš does not always seem to have been consistent in rejecting the interference of the secular arm in spiritual affairs. Cf. the following passage from his Spis o mocy swĕta, fol. 27v: 'Whoever will not listen to

It was the existence of evil that, in Lukáš's eyes, justified the participation of Christian laymen in the affairs of the world.

Since evil and unrighteousness must, according to the scriptures, inevitably go on increasing in Christendom until the end of the world, God ...
has raised some men above others ... in order to put down evil. The
reason for His doing this has not grown less. He has not, therefore,
abolished power by the Law of Love, so that it should not be exercised
over the wicked and the turbulent; nor has He now made it a sin and
unrighteous because of the promulgation of this Law.

For this reason, therefore, God desired 'to have his own not only among
the commonalty subject to authority, but also among such of those placed
in authority as may be faithful to the gospel of love.'

What then, in Lukáš's view, was the nature of the Christian state?
Civil authority must, in the first place, deal only with 'earthly and
temporal matters, never with spiritual.' Wicked rulers were, indeed, to be
obeyed in secular affairs, but evil spiritual advisers, even if backed by the
authority of the state, were not to be heeded if they advocated
unchristian actions. Secondly, the civil power must be properly
constituted (zřízený) and directed only against wrongdoers and those who
infringed the civil law. It was to be exercised only to curb 'the refractory
and disobedient, the wicked and unjust and unrighteous, the unrepentant,
criminals and unpeaceable persons, for the sake of whom the law of the
civil power is set up to frighten and to punish.' The purpose of the law
was to punish evildoers and to protect the good, who would otherwise
perish from the resulting disorders. God, therefore, 'had not condemned
the lawcourt and punishments,' including even the death penalty 'for those
who would not repent, provided the judges themselves were without sin.'

Thirdly, the power of the state was not to be unlimited. There were
cases where subjects should refuse obedience to their rulers, though such
disobedience should always be passive. True Christians must suffer the
consequences of such disobedience, where to obey would be against their
consciences. Lastly, Christian rulers should strive after the welfare of
their subjects, 'desiring out of fatherly love to be their benefactors.'[15] The
just and benevolent lawgiver careful for the well-being of his people, the
lord conscious of his obligations to society, had in the new social ideology

---

the church should be considered a sinner and a publican. Over such a person, the civil
authority and the law have the power to use force, to command and to punish, for such
are no longer under the Law of Love which has been set up for the penitent and the just,
but under the law of fear and vengeance which has power over them.' But he may have
been thinking here mainly of moral offences rather than any kind of heresy.

[15] Spis o mocy swĕta, fols. 10v–13, 24v, 25, 29v, 38–40v.

of the Major Party an equal right to be considered good Christians as the common man of Chelčický's ideal, free from all active association with the machinery of government.

The participation, likewise, of Brethren in courts of law was not wrong in itself, nor was their co-operation in the punishment of wrongdoers. According to Lukáš, law courts were introduced among Christians in the time of the apostles (1 Corinthians VI, 1–7). His opponents had alleged that St. Paul had given his approval to them merely as a temporary measure. But, argued Lukáš, if it had been a sin St. Paul would never have permitted their establishment even for a short time. Indeed, the necessity for them was, on the contrary, likely to last for ever. Christians 'will always have to have courts; the more they have increased in numbers the more differences have arisen.'[16] Secular courts were nowhere forbidden in the New Testament.

Those who denied that the machinery of justice could have any place in a Christian community, were themselves usually guilty in spirit of all the bad features allegedly involved in the administration of the law. 'Whenever some wrong occurs [Lukáš writes] they are the most offended, getting angry, aggressive, censurious, breathing forth threats of vengeance, etc. It appears to them that if they do this outside the court then it is no sin.' It was true that at present courts were conducted in an unchristian fashion; and it was difficult to escape contamination. But it was only such kinds of courts that Christ condemned in the Sermon on the Mount (Matthew V, 40) and not all courts; since, Lukáš adds, 'without them it would be impossible to live, not only in the world, but in the church, for they are carrying out God's work: the settlement of disputes and the reconciliation and bringing into harmony of persons, who would not of themselves be able to reach this state.'[17]

A Christian, Lukáš went on to maintain, was perfectly justified in demanding a restitution of his property, though he added the somewhat ambiguous proviso that it should be done 'without sin or the chance of worse evil' arising and without cruelty. Christ had certainly taught his followers to love their enemies. But it was still necessary to punish persistent evildoers even, if necessary, with death itself. The execution of justice, provided it was tempered with mercy, was not inconsistent with loving one's enemies. Lukáš wrote in justification of his point of view: 'God loves ... just and good men; and because of them he hates the sins of the wicked, so that the former might live in peace. But he loves, too,

---

[16]   *Odpis*, fols. 28, 28v; Lukáš, *Odpowĕd na spis Kalencuo*, fols. 5v, 6.
[17]   *Spis o mocy swĕta*, fols. 33v–35, 37, 38, 56. Cf. *Odpowĕd na spis Kalencuo*, fol. 5.

the sinful even while he punishes them, for thus he prevents them from further sinning.' With this attitude Lukáš contrasts that taken up by Chelčický and Řehoř and the Brethren who followed their teachings. 'Those who take the part of wrongdoers [he writes scornfully] urging that they should be loved, do not show love for peaceable folk or for widows and orphans.' It was one thing to love one's personal enemies and to forgive them their evil deeds committed against us personally: it was quite a different matter, Lukáš urged, when people set in authority in the course of their duties protected the innocent by punishing criminals.[18] Arguments similar to those used by Lukáš were, indeed, frequently to be brought forward during the course of subsequent controversies on the subject.

Not only might Christians attempt by due process of law to recover what had been unlawfully taken from them; they were justified too, in the opinion of Lukáš and the Major Party, in using force in the defence of life and property. For their opponents of the Minor Party, on the other hand, such doctrine seemed the antithesis of the Christian gospel; for them spiritual warfare – the *boj duchovní* of Chelčický – was the only battle in which the follower of Christ might participate. In the Sermon on the Mount, they wrote in one of their tracts, the right of 'self-defence is taken away as is all revenge.' 'For when God forbids killing he not only excludes brigandage (*lotrovství*), which is not even allowed according to the declared laws, but he also warns against those things which are justified in men's eyes.'[19] Theirs was the uncompromising doctrine of complete non-resistance.

Lukáš started with a more historical interpretation of the Fifth Commandment: 'Thou shalt not kill.' In his view, it was not an absolute prohibition of killing under any circumstances as Chelčický and his successors maintained. It meant only that 'whoever spilt human blood without proper authority and contrary to God's law and justice' was guilty of a great sin. This naturally did not exclude either the death penalty or just wars or self-defence; and Christ, who had come to fulfil and not to destroy the law, had not altered its validity. If he had, 'anyone committing murder would have no fear of judgement and sentence.' Indeed, Lukáš considered Christ himself had made a distinction 'between legitimate killing, permitted by God, and the forbidden forms of killing which are called murder.' It was not a sin for the magistrate or those

---

[18] *Spis o mocy swĕta*, fols. 41, 41v, 42v, 44, 44v, 45v.
[19] A. J. B., IV, fols. 62–63v, 65.

enforcing the law or defending the state to kill 'the unrepentent wrongdoer and other unrighteous persons.'[20]

The official Unity position was put forward as follows in one of their confessions of faith, written in 1507:[21]

The fifth [commandment] is fulfilled, when anger leading to revenge is wholly renounced and vengeance against the objects of one's dislike and in one's own cause is taken away, and ... also blasphemy and contempt which, too, are the causes of both bodily and spiritual murder. And in addition to anger envy, hatred, malice, backbiting, secret condemnations, treachery, lying, slander, etc. are forbidden. For, in acting in this fashion, the scribes did not realize that they were going against the commandment: 'Thou shalt not kill.' It is also being fulfilled when mercy, goodness, pity are taught, ... when vengeance on wrongdoers is taken out of the hands of the common people. Hence it proclaims the order of the civil power as just when performed without anger and unrighteousness, with moderation and love in punishment and discipline. This commandment is also fulfilled when it ... teaches the judge not to judge according to outward appearance (*ne podle tváři*), nor according to his ungovernable inclinations, but justly and lovingly.[22]

The positive injunctions of Christ given mainly in the Sermon on the Mount, which were quoted by the Minor Party in defence of their doctrine of non-resistance, were also subjected by Lukáš to similar interpretation. Such injunctions were, for Lukáš, merely an elaboration of the truths already enunciated in the Law and the Prophets, a return indeed to the pristine purity of their doctrine. There was no contradiction between the two.

'Resist not evil,' for instance, was an attempt to counteract a too great insistence by the Jews on retribution for wrong done. Christ's words meant only that his followers were not 'to resist evil from anger, from an inordinate desire for revenge in one's own cause, without judgement by those put in authority and without pity or mercy.' It was not intended as an attack on the civil power, whether Christian or pagan, acting 'not for vengeance, but to bring about peace or a proper reformation' of the wrongdoer. In an ordered society, in the kind of society where Christian principles were put into practice, Lukáš argued in a passage which brings to mind modern political theory, resistance to evil was not left to the

[20]   *Spis o mocy swĕta*, fols. 21–24, 50v.
[21]   Palmov, *Cheshkie bratya v svoikh konfessiyach*, I, p. 273. The confession was entitled *Spis dosti činijcy z wijry, kterýžto latijnskau řečij Apologia slowe, w Normberce prwe imprymowán, počijná se sst'astnĕ.*
[22]   *Ibid.*, II, p. 293.

individual citizen as in more primitive communities, but entrusted to the properly constituted authority.[23]

Turning the other cheek, too, could not be explained literally. In his lengthy tract on the civil power Lukáš gives this passage (Matthew V, 39) a far-fetched and complicated metaphorical interpretation by which he sought to refute his opponents' claims to find here a clear justification of their point of view. 'The right cheek [he says] is the truth. ... The left is the wrong or fault of the one who must suffer for it.' There was no obligation for Christ to turn his other cheek since he had committed no sin; he suffered for truth's sake alone. 'Christ offered his right cheek for our left, for the innocent suffered for the guilty.' Turning the left cheek meant either to endure injury 'from one against whom you have yourself done wrong, or patiently to suffer the penalty of the [civil] power and of the court and humbly make amends.' Lukáš further interpreted it to mean that Christians should not take it upon themselves to avenge their own wrongs, but should leave this either 'to God or the order set up by God,' in other words to the state.[24]

The injunction to love one's enemies, which the Minor Party had regarded as a prohibition not only of warfare and the death penalty, but of the whole state system and the apparatus of justice, did not apply, in Lukáš's view, to the collective activities of men. Forgiveness of injuries was possible only for the individual Christian. While people in authority should temper justice with mercy in cases where there were extenuating circumstances or where the wrongdoer manifested genuine repentance, they could not fail to take the requisite action against breakers of the law. Anyhow, claimed Lukáš, 'to kill and destroy the enemies' of the Lord, provided it was done 'justly and without hatred,' was not inconsistent with showing at the same time love towards them.[25]

Lukáš in fact, convinced as he was from practical observation of the rightness of Christian participation in the state, was forced to adapt even the most refractory of Christ's sayings to this conception. The Minor Party, on the other hand, persuaded by their reading of the New Testament, as well as by the works of Chelčický and the early Brethren, of the immorality of such participation, were led to take up a wholly negative position in regard to every aspect of the functioning of the civil power.

The use of force, the Major Party maintained, was in fact justified in two sets of circumstances. First, Christians might carry some sort of

[23] *Spis o mocy swĕta*, fols. 31–32.
[24] *Ibid.*, fols. 32v–33v.
[25] *Ibid.*, fols. 30v, 51–52.

weapon for use in personal self-defence, or the defence of one's property, in cases where the law was unable to afford protection. They must, however, be careful to avoid such weapons as might lead persons of a fiery temperament to commit bloodthirsty deeds. 'There is need of moderation in this matter [writes Lukáš] but I cannot properly regard it as wrong to go about with daggers.'[26] Members of the Christian community, in the second place, might call in the aid of the civil power to assist them in defence of their temporal interests:

It is one thing [writes Lukáš again] to defend the church by the sword lawfully in regard to its material welfare, and quite another to do this in regard to spiritual matters. The former may rightly occur when those set in authority defend the temporal welfare of the church or its members, since for this purpose was the [civil] power instituted and the faithful have made use of it to this end.

But Christians, contrary to the accepted practice of the official church since the Donation of Constantine, were never to call upon the temporal power in the purely religious sphere, to enforce right belief on heretics or to impose Christianity on non-Christians. For a Christian to spread the faith by the use of the sword 'against pagans' was to act 'unlawfully and to stray from the path (svodně).'[27] Christians fighting against the Turks, even though such participation in warfare might now be permitted the Brethren under certain circumstances, were not justified in calling themselves martyrs for the faith, since God had in fact sent such enemies as a punishment for the misdeeds of the official church with its great 'wealth and power.' Besides, Lukáš added, the Turks did not make converts by force to their religion.[28]

The complete separation of church and state, in its consequences one of the most revolutionary of the tenets of the early Brethren, was therefore still advocated by the Major Party.[29] But this separation of the functions of church and state did not mean, as Chelčický's school of thought argued, that members of the church could not take part in the state, the direction of which must be left to non-Christians or nominal Christians. As has been seen, the Major Party made frequent use of the argument that from the beginning practising Christians, like the Roman centurion for instance, who had not been told by Christ 'that he must resign his authority for the

[26] *Odpowěd na spis Kalencuo*, fols. 4v, 5.
[27] *Odpis*, fol. 10; 'O obnovení,' fol. 186.
[28] Vlček, *Dějiny české literatury*, I, p. 376, quoting from Lukáš's *Výkladové na knihy, jenž slovú Apokalypsis* (1501).
[29] A. J. B., vol. IV, fol. 31.

faith's sake,' had taken office 'without harm to their salvation.' Indeed it had often been their duty to do so. 'Even though they might receive payment and money here from their service with the civil power, for this reason they were not cut off from the faith'; rather might they expect to be rewarded in heaven for their good deeds in succouring the poor and the oppressed.[30]

Among his contemporaries Lukáš observed two erroneous viewpoints on the relationship between Christianity and the state: 'the high and the low,' as he calls them. There was, first, the position of his opponents in the present controversy, who regarded church and state as mutually opposed to each other. Then there were those who extolled the civil power 'inordinately, in wondrous fashion twisting and falsifying the scriptures.'[31] A middle road between the two extremes seemed to Lukáš to be the soundest doctrine, the one most consistent with Christ's teaching.

In spiritual matters the Brethren had separated themselves from the other Christian churches of East and West when these were all found wanting. In regard to the civil power, however, Lukáš writes:

We have not cut ourselves off, nor have we the intention, as the Taborites and others have had, of taking up the sword in defence of the faith ... It is only that some of our members are engaged in administering the civil power in courts and in offices ... We participate in this, but without taking part ... in any unrighteousness; and there is, indeed, no scripture that runs contrary to this, since it happened even in the early church.

In exactly what circumstances might 'the faithful,' members of the Unity of Brethren, exercise temporal power and enter the service of the state? 'Those [answered Lukáš] who have already joined us or who would like to do so, being set in authority and unable to escape from it,' should be allowed to remain in office. Secondly, 'those who, not of their own free will, are forced to perform some lesser functions and activities of this authority' should not be considered to have infringed in any way the moral code of the Unity.[32]

Despite the very measured terms in which these conditions are formulated, with their recommendation to attempt first to avoid collaboration with the work of government, Lukáš's intention is quite clear. Obstacles in the way of gaining new converts from among the nobles and gentry, whose influence and protection was much needed by the Unity to secure it from renewed persecution, were to be removed; and at the same time

[30] *Odpis*, fols. 2, 5, 8.
[31] *Spis o mocy swĕta*, fols. 13v–14v.
[32] *Odpis*, fol. 2v, 14.

the path of the town Brethren, growing in affluence and influence but drawn thereby into increasingly close contact with the judicial and administrative machine, would be made smoother.

God of his love has delivered us [writes Lukáš] from these errors [i.e. of the Minor Party concerning the civil power]. He has permitted us to think through to a sound conception of the civil power in Christendom ... Therefore some members of our Unity have become aldermen and judges and mayors (*fojtové*). And if their conduct has been worthy of it, some of these have also been [our] teachers ... These aldermen and mayors, who have acted rightly and justly, have been serving not two masters, not Mammon, ... but the one God and His Law, bearing others' burdens and thus fulfilling Christ's teaching.[33]

The Major Party, as has been seen, continued to grant the doctrines of the Minor Party, sanctified as they were by the approval given them by Chelčický, Řehoř and the Old Brethren, the right to exist as a minority position within the Unity.[34] The theoretical reason for this limited tolerance, which Lukáš and his party were ready to grant their opponents, lay in their view of what constituted the essence of Unity doctrine (*původ Jednoty*). Kalenec, for instance, claimed on behalf of the Minor Party that, in throwing over the political and social ideology of the Old Brethren, the Major Party had abandoned the fundamental principles on account of which the Unity had originally broken away from the Utraquist church.[35] The Minor Party, writes Lukáš in reply, 'consider the doctrine on [civil] power and the oath as the origin' of the Unity. But in fact such ideas arose 'from the flesh... and not from God'; they had never belonged to the essential tenets of their faith. Such doctrines should never be made a touchstone of salvation, since 'the scriptures proclaim other things as the origin and foundation of belief and salvation, ... and it was for them we separated and set up our own organization. Since, therefore, we are in every way closer to the scriptures,' we are ready to accept 'as fellow Christians people of goodwill; and neither censure nor condemn those placed in authority.'[36] In like manner they were prepared to retain within the Unity, if they were willing to remain, those who still held to the old doctrines.

But the Minor Party, with their eyes fixed exclusively on one issue, 'regarded the disparagement of the [civil] power and the oath (which in

---

[33] *Odpowĕd na spis Kalencuo*, fols. 7v, 8.
[34] *Odpis*, fol. 3v, 56, 56v.
[35] Cf. the similar sentiment expressed by Brother Michal at the conclusion of the Conference of Rýchnov (1494), see Chap. IV, p. 149.
[36] *Odpowĕd na spis Kalencuo*, fols. 9, 10.

actual fact were instituted by God and brought to fulfilment by Christ in His higher righteousness) as alone constituting the gospel of Christ.'[37] They were not even consistent, Lukáš went on, since not only did they consider that Christ's condemnation of the civil power left pagans still free to exercise it, but in practice they themselves 'made use of this power which they despise.' Why indeed did they remain within the Christian community enjoying the benefits of citizenship, while not prepared to undertake its obligations, asked Lukáš sarcastically: 'Why did you not rather go out among the pagans, where you might enjoy their protection,' according to your own principles and those of your master, Chelčický? With a strange ignorance of the early history of the Unity Lukáš denied that there had ever been a single martyr for the anti-state views of the Minor Party, though indeed, he continued, neither suffering nor smallness in numbers were sufficient in themselves, as the Minor Party seemed to consider, to show where the right lay.[38]

For their uncompromising attitude, Lukáš claimed, Chelčický was largely responsible; and in later life the former was to have little good to say for the teachings of the man whose writings, more than anything else, had helped to bring him as a young man to the Unity. Doubtless the continuous quoting on the part of the Minor Party of Chelčický's example made Lukáš anxious to destroy his standing with the Brethren of both camps. Indeed, considering the central position which his pacifist anarchist ideas have in Chelčický's general philosophy of life, it would have been hard to continue to hold his works in the same high esteem, while at the same time rejecting in practice the core of his teaching.

Apart from attacks of a personal character accusing Chelčický of not living up to the high ideals which he preached in his writings, Lukáš's main assault is naturally directed mainly against the former's views on state and society. Lukáš admits that there was 'much that was useful in his writings.' But at the same time he considered that Chelčický's rejection of the civil power, his denial of the need for any coercive action in a Christian community, his overemphasis of the virtues of suffering and poverty and the rustic life, could not be accepted without danger of undermining the framework of civilized society. Such views, thought Lukáš, arose from the conditions in which Chelčický had lived, from contemplation of the abuse of the name of religion during the fratricidal warfare of his time. They arose in him 'by reason of the warlike Taborites, in connection with the evil use of the [civil] power; and, being disgusted by all this, he con-

[37] *Ibid.*, fol. 4v.
[38] *Ibid.*, fols. 7v, 9, 17; *Odpis*, fols. 13v, 18, 37; *Spis o mocy swĕta*, fol. 3.

demned and despised it as unchristian.' Therefore, 'no one should conduct himself according to [Chelčicky's] writings, for he himself was not
under the rule of salvation.'[39]

Thus the wheel had come full circle. The Unity which had taken the
political and social teachings of the village philosopher as its own, seeking
to model the community of the Brethren according to the pattern found
in his writings, had now not only ceased to give these doctrines any special
place in their society, but it had replaced them by a set of principles
approving the very way of life, which Chelčicky and his disciples had
always regarded as the antithesis of the Christian way. It was Lukáš who,
more than any other leader of the Major Party, was able to provide the
new Unity with this theoretical justification of the revolution which had
taken place in their midst.[40] For, indeed, the period of the Old Brethren
and the new epoch which was now beginning in the Unity's history were
divided by a deep gulf, both in theory and in practical behaviour. It was
to be the question of the validity of taking oaths that was to become the
symbol dividing the two parties.

II

The question of the permissibility of oathtaking for true Christians had,
from the middle of the last decade of the fifteenth century onwards, come
more and more to dominate the whole controversy between the Major and
Minor Parties in the Unity. In its scope it overlapped both the theoretical
problems and the more practical issues, forming a connecting link between
the two categories.

It was just this problem that the individual Brethren in their relationship
to society had most frequently to grapple with in their everyday lives.
It was a question which almost all might sometime be called upon to face.
Oaths were demanded upon entrance into the most humble offices: refusal
might mean severe and repeated punishment. Since, therefore, a refusal

[39] *Odpowĕd na spis Kalencuo*, fol. 6v; *Spis o mocy swĕta*, fols. 2v, 14; *Odpis*, 28v, 29
(quoted in Jireček, 'P. J. Šafaříka studie o Petru Chelčickém', *Č. Č. M.*, 1874, pp. 104,
105). Cf. Palmov, *op. cit.*, II, p. 225; Krofta, *O bratrském dĕjepisectví*, p. 24.
[40] The literary historian, Vlček, *op. cit.*, pp. 374–76, has pointed out that, despite his
renunciation of Chelčicky's theories, several even of Lukáš's later works, both in form
and in spirit, are reminiscent of Chelčicky. Their approach, for instance, to the Roman
Catholic church, which both men regarded as an institution irreparably corrupted by
its alliance with the powers that be, was very similar, as was their idealization of the way
of poverty as peculiarly appropriate for the practising Christian. But both ideas were,
indeed, common to the medieval sectarian tradition represented by the Waldenses.

of oaths was involved in almost every point in dispute between the two parties, since, too, it was the one question which overlapped all the other problems, it quickly came to be accepted as a party slogan easily understood by the most simple. The Major Party, therefore, became the 'juror' Brethren; while the Minor Party were often known also as 'the non-jurors.'[41]

Earlier, indeed, the problem of oathtaking had remained in the background. But Chelčický and Řehoř, though they rarely dealt with the question in their writings, had followed the Waldenses in rejecting oaths as unchristian; and the early Brethren had likewise refused on principle to take oaths when these were demanded of them. The problem, however, as has been seen, did not possess the same urgency during the early years of the Unity's existence as it was to have later, when the number of Brethren settled in the towns had greatly increased.

With the outbreak at the beginning of the nineties of the controversy over the Unity's attitude to society and the state, the problem came more and more to the fore.[42] From an issue of only secondary importance it was to become a party cry in the bitter ideological strife which eventually split the Unity. The struggle over the oath, however, was not a barren theological dispute over a formality; it represented a radical cleavage of opinion over some of the most fundamental issues which have faced men in their relationship to society. Acceptance by the Brethren of the oath meant in essence a reconciliation with the existing condition of society, an abandonment of the Unity's separation from the community, of its passive negation of the state. A continued rejection of the oath, on the other hand, signified a return to the simple life of an agrarian society, which had been enjoyed by an earlier generation of Brethren. It was in part a reflection of the age-old conflict between urban and rural societies.

Both parties wrote at considerable length on the subject of oaths. As might be expected from university-trained theologians, leaders of the Major Party like Lukáš and Krasonický presented a better argued and a more systematic presentation of their attitude. The Minor Party's case, as given in the polemical tracts of Jakub and Amos, or later of Jan Kalenec, is a compound of passion and righteous indignation, mingled with somewhat chaotic argument based primarily on a literal interpretation of Christ's words in the Sermon on the Mount [Matthew V, 33–37].

It was, therefore, the Major Party which attempted in the first place to define the nature of an oath. 'An oath [writes Lukáš] is the confirmation

[41] Müller-Bartoš, op. cit., pp. 172, 173.
[42] Goll-Krofta, op. cit., pp. 227, 228.

[i.e. of a statement] in a process of law by God's knowledge and testimony, in other words, that God knows that what is said or done or to be done is the truth, and that He is able to avenge a lie. . . . It is to call upon God as a witness.'[43]

Both Lukáš and Krasonický frequently quoted cases of oathtaking in the Old Testament, done either with God's approval or even at his express command. First, writes Lukáš, in those times the Jews were permitted to take oaths to avoid the sin of idolatry involved in swearing by strange gods. All false oaths or oaths taken in the name of any lesser being than God himself were strictly forbidden. They were only to 'swear by His name' [Deut. VI, 13]. A second justification made in the Old Testament for oath-taking lay in the fact of human imperfection which, on account of the frequent occurrence of false witness, often made men loath to believe even the truth unless backed by an oath. An oath, therefore, was justified 'for the confirmation of the truth, when one might be compelled by the fear of the person who summons a witness, he anxious lest he be considered a liar and a perjuror (křivý přísežník).' Lastly, oaths were also justified in the Old Testament 'in order to reconcile differences between people.'[44]

The Minor Party, indeed, did not attempt to deny that the Jews had been permitted by God to take oaths. But, they said, Christ through his teaching of 'the higher righteousness' had forbidden his followers to swear under any circumstances, as he had forbidden them to use evil means to combat evil. 'The oath [writes their anonymous champion in his *Odpor smyslu druhému*] is forbidden by Christ to Christians; for pagans it is allowed on all occasions; while for the Jews it is permissible on some occasions ... If Christians may swear, in what manner is the Christian righteousness higher than the Jewish?' If Christ had meant Christians to swear, he would have left the Jewish commandments as they were and not mentioned them at all. It was only such matters as needed correction that Christ dealt with in his teachings. First he had given the old Jewish doctrine on the matter and then, in the succeeding verses, he showed how his own differed from it [Matthew V, 33–37].[45]

Lukáš and his school, on the other hand, put a completely different interpretation on these passages. For them Christ's intention had not been to change or supplement the teachings of the Old Testament, but only to purge them of the abuses which in the course of the centuries had

[43]   A. J. B., IV, fol. 154 (quoted by Palmov, *op. cit.*, II, p. 165). Cf. Krasonický's similar definition, fol. 90v.
[44]   *Ibid.*, fols. 77–78, 96, 154, 154v.
[45]   *Ibid.*, fols. 73, 73v (quoted in part in Goll-Krofta, *op. cit.*, pp. 228, 229).

grown up around them. He had come to fulfil and not to destroy the Law and the Prophets.

The scribes and the pharisees had not observed either of the two commandments concerned with oathtaking [Exodus XX, 7, 16], for they had imagined that God's 'prohibition' applied merely to the external character of the oath and not at all to its actual contents. They thought, therefore, that so long as the matter witnessed was true, and the intention of fulfilment was present, then the oath was thereby justified, regardless of the moral nature of its contents. Secondly, they were prepared to swear in the name of things created by God, taking the commandments to apply only against swearing by pagan gods.[46] It was such an attitude that Christ sought to rectify. 'Christ [writes Krasonický] taught nothing in regard to the moral commandments, which was not contained in embryo in the natural or in the written law.' His teachings were designed to put this law in a clearer light and to remove the imperfections which later interpreters had introduced. 'He could not possibly put on one side that which had been commanded to the Jews.'[47]

The Major Party were obliged to give certain passages a rather forced interpretation in order to fit them in with their viewpoint. The main stumbling block lay in the words: 'Swear not at all' [Matthew V, 34], where the Minor Party, like the Mennonites and the Quakers and certain other post-Reformation sects in later centuries, followed the example of the early Brethren, and the Waldenses before them, in giving these words a literal interpretation.

Lukáš and Krasonický, both classical scholars of a sort and wellread in the Latin church fathers, had recourse to the Vulgate. The words used there – non iurare omnino – they interpreted as meaning: 'Swear not in all things,' i.e. not in every instance where an oath may be demanded.[48] They were intended by Christ, it was claimed, to counteract the custom of the scribes and pharisees 'to take an oath in every matter which was true.'[49] They did not preclude a follower of Christ from swearing under certain clearly defined conditions.

This was strongly denied by the Minor Party. Not only had Christ meant to forbid his followers to swear under any conditions; he had also shown them the way they should behave in such circumstances. Had He not said: 'But let your communication be, Yes, yea; Nay, nay: for whatso-

---

[46] Spis o mocy swĕta, fols. 58v, 59. Cf. A. J. B., IV, fols. 80, 155v.
[47] A. J. B., IV, fol. 81v.
[48] Ibid., fols. 79, 83, 91, 156, 157. The phrase in Czech was nepřisahati ovšem.
[49] Spis o mocy swĕta, fols. 59v, 68.

ever is more than these cometh of evil' [Matthew V, 37]? This was the pattern to be followed. Quoting Cyprian in support of the Minor Party's position, the author of the 'Odpor smyslu druhému' gives a well reasoned presentation of their case against what they considered the sophistries of their opponents.

It is my opinion [he writes] that, if these words were considered without ... undue license, there would be no need for so many useless interpretations. For, where the words themselves are simple, they do not need interpretation. But he who seeks out explanations in simple matters, may be suspected of inserting there something of his own devising. ... In this way the Brethren have now begun variously to interpret the Latin word *omnino* ... with the aim, it seems to me, of allowing the oath ... following the Roman interpretation that ... the Latin meant ... *non in omni causa* and the Czech ... 'not for every reason.' But in my opinion, although I do not possess a great deal of classical learning, *omnino* may be paraphrased in Latin as *nequequam* ... in Czech *nikoli*. ... But I believe, indeed, that simplicity, about which they used to talk much in their congregations, would serve the Brethren best. ... If they once enter upon explanations of words they will have little success among simple people. There will be as many interpretations as there are glosses; and even if they did want to embark upon [this] ... few of them are fit for coping with such a task.[50]

The Major Party, it is true, did not countenance every kind of oath. They attempted to define the type of oaths which it was permissible for Christians to take. In all cases they were not to infringe any of the rules laid down in the Old Testament. Besides this, first, the right must be on the side of the person taking the oath: the matter in question must be 'just, righteous, useful and necessary, taking away nothing that is anyone else's or giving anyone anything that is not his.' There must be no question, either, of any harm arising out of the oath. Christians, in the second place, should be certain that what they were swearing contained the whole truth and only the truth. Thirdly , oaths should be taken only in cases of dire necessity, never lightly, 'without extreme need either of oneself or one's fellows.'[51]

To the objection brought up later by Kalenec in the 1520's that, 'if it was not a sin to swear under pressure, then no sins would harm people if committed under compulsion,' Lukáš replied that this would be true only of an unrighteous oath. 'The oath is not sent from God like his other commandments to be used freely without compelling need from someone else. ... The commandment concerning the oath is given on account of

---

[50] A. J. B., IV, fol. 73v (quoted in part in Goll-Krofta, *op. cit.*, p. 229).
[51] *Ibid.*, fols. 78–81, 96, 96v, 156v, 157, 158, 159v.

human imperfection for the confirmation of truth and for the sake of harmony.'[52] The object of permitting oaths in a Christian society, in Lukáš's opinion, was 'to help faith and the hope of fulfilling promises and testimony. ... It is essential for putting an end to disagreements between people and reconciling conflicting viewpoints.'[53]

Oaths, however, were never to be used between one Brother and another, by members of the Unity among themselves. 'Among the faithful [Lukáš explained] there is no need of the oath, since they are all members of one another, simple children of God who should order their affairs according to the Law of Christ, so that their communication be, Yea, yea; Nay, nay.' Oaths were only justified in the larger Christian community because of the presence there of 'bad people ... and lovers of the world,' who were not accustomed to speak the truth and, therefore, suspected others of not doing so either.[54] The old Brethren idea of restricting the conception of a Christian community to those who followed literally the strict rule laid down by Christ in the Sermon on the Mount is here abandoned; and for it is substituted the current medieval idea of two levels of Christian living. In the Catholic Church the higher way of life was to be followed only by monks and, to a lesser degree, by the secular clergy. In the ideas now current in the Unity this higher way of life was to be restricted to the dealings of the Brethren among themselves. It was not to preclude either conformity to a somewhat lower standard in their relations with the outside world or to granting a limited recognition to that world.

True Christians should never in their private disputes demand oaths of others. It does not make any difference, says Krasonický, 'whether you think he will swear truly or falsely.'[55] But this prohibition did not of course apply to those whose offices entailed the administration of oaths in the course of their legitimate duties.

The Major Party maintained therefore that, though oaths might be taken by members of the Unity under compulsion in certain circumstances, there were many kinds of oaths which were still forbidden to the Brethren. In addition there were, for instance, various cruelties and evils connected with the imposition of oaths which were nevertheless in accordance with the law of the land.

One of the faithful, therefore, who takes an oath is not bound to do and

[52] *Odpis*, fols. 34, 34v.
[53] *Spis o mocy swĕta*, fols. 66, 67v.
[54] *Ibid.*, fols. 69, 69v; *Odpowĕd na spis Kalencuo*, fol. 8; A. J. B., fol. 158v.
[55] A. J. B., IV, fols. 97, 98v.

fulfil whatever is contained in civil and municipal laws contrary to God's laws and judgements; nor indeed should these laws, if they are well made, lead to this. ... But wherever the civil laws coincide with God's justice and are not contrary to Christ, in this spirit may an oath be made and kept.[56]

In cases of doubt the Brethren should consult with their spiritual advisers to ascertain whether the oath demanded might rightly be made. For oaths, says Lukáš, were neither good nor bad in themselves: it depended on the conditions in which they were taken. Those whose job it was to advise the Brethren should first be sure in their own minds what kinds of oaths were permissible for Christians. Secondly, they must enquire into the exact circumstances of the oath in question.[57]

The Minor Party had accused their opponents of allowing oaths for the same reason as they had justified participation in the state: to escape persecution and to obtain certain material advantages for the Unity. Their attitude, it was claimed, was simply one of expediency.

They want God's commandment [wrote the author of *Odpor smyslu druhému*] to go in line with their own needs. ... So long as the Brethren were not faced with the need to swear, so long were oaths wrong; but when the necessity arose, then this evil was transformed into a good and just thing.

This was vigorously contested by Lukáš and his party. They still held, the former wrote, that where some act was definitely forbidden by God, the Brethren must suffer imprisonment and death rather than obey. But they had now come to believe that the taking of oaths, like participation in the state, was a necessity in view of the general wickedness of mankind, that it was allowed by God to prevent still greater evils from arising.

Just as the civil power [wrote Krasonický] while having its origin in evil, is nevertheless set up with a good intention and a good aim, and he who so administers it does not sin, but carries out the Lord's will and serves God, in like manner may the oath be taken for good or for evil. Indeed, a good act done because of evil is not itself evil, but it is an evil act which arises out of evil that is wrong.[58]

Historically, however, it is hard to deny the force of the Minor Party's assertion that it was the changed circumstances in which the Brethren found themselves, where it was increasingly difficult to escape the obligations of office and oathtaking, that had brought about the change in their views on these subjects. This is brought out by Lukáš himself, who

[56]   *Ibid.*, fol. 103 (quoted in Goll-Krofta, *op. cit.*, p. 231).

[57]   *Ibid.*, fols. 83v, 160v. Cf. fol. 74 (quoted in part in *ibid.*, p. 229).

[58]   *Ibid.*, fols. 74v, 84, 99v.

later wrote that, 'when many years before certain [of the Brethren] encountered great difficulties in connection with the oath, many appealed to the Brethren with scriptural proofs, while the lords who sympathized with the Brethren [appealed] with threats.'[59] Pressure from above and below was in fact largely responsible for the internal revolution, which was to sanction oathtaking along with many other political and social actions hitherto forbidden to the Brethren. At the same time, the accusations of hypocrisy and personal cowardice which the Minor Party brought against the leading theoreticians of the Major Party may be discounted.

In the controversy over the oath, the leaders of the Minor Party had shown themselves bad tacticians in allowing their main attention to be centred on a single issue, one moreover which could in fact only be solved by a learned theologian or philologist. Discussion over the exact meaning of the words used by Christ was not likely to keep alive for long the enthusiasm of their simple followers. Even more significant was the fact that the problem of oathtaking, which had originally served merely as a symbol of a whole philosophy of society, of the negative attitude to the state which had been inherited from Chelčický and Řehoř, and as a rallying cry for those who continued faithful to the doctrines of the first generation of the Brethren, became before long the main point of difference between the two parties. The real stakes had become overlaid in the minds of the protagonists by a secondary issue. The Minor Party had substituted a symbol for reality, argument over the literal interpretation of certain passages of scripture for the struggle for a whole political philosophy.

Concurrently with the theoretical controversy on the validity of the oath and the civil power in a Christian community, changes, too, of a more practical nature had been taking place within the Unity that were to transform it from an obscure sect existing on the fringe of the community into one of the three leading denominations in the land and a force of first-rate importance, as well, in the political and cultural life of the country. Through these changes, however, the Unity was largely to abandon its character as a protest against social injustice and its passionate advocacy of the rights of the common man. The members of the Minor Party, which continued to uphold the ideals of the early Brethren, were at the same time forced out into the wilderness. By the middle of the sixteenth century the social philosophy for which they stood had disappeared almost completely from Czech national life.

[59] *Odpowĕd na spis Kalencuo, loc. cit.*

VII

THE NEW UNITY

The thirty years between the death in 1498 of Klenovský, the original leader of the revolt against the ideals of the Old Brethren, and that of Lukáš, his successor and the virtual refounder of the Unity, in 1528, saw the revolution in the Unity's political and social doctrines brought to completion. In the second half of the last decade of the fifteenth century these doctrines had been the subject of fierce controversy among the Brethren; and this controversy fills the pages of the Unity's history for this period. Thrity years later they were almost forgotten and the very memory of the struggles which rent the Unity was already falling into oblivion.

This period has been well named by Müller 'the era of Brother Lukáš,'[1] for it was his personality more than that of any other man, which imprinted itself on the history of the Unity and controlled the direction it took during these years so vital for its future evolution.[2] They were years, indeed, of considerable difficulty for the Unity, of great strain and stress. With the marriage of the impressionable Vladislav II to Anne de Foix-Candale, a great enemy of heresy, a time of renewed persecution ensued. Legislation against the Brethren culminated in 1508 in the so-called *Mandát Svatojakubský*, by which all the Unity's churches and congregations were to be closed and its communion services prohibited, its books confiscated and its printing presses shut down. Severe measures, too, were ordered to be taken against the Unity priesthood. Though several Brethren during this period suffered death for their faith and many more imprisonment, the fact that conditions were easier in Moravia

---

[1] Müller-Bartoš, *Dějiny Jednoty bratrské*, I, p. 175.
[2] Around the turn of the century death had removed a number of the leading personalities in the Unity: Táborský (d. 1495); Klenovský (d. 1498); Matěj (d. 1500); Michal (d. 1501); Eliáš (d. 1503); and Prokop (d. 1507). Even Krasonický (d. 1532) and Tůma Přeloučský (d. 1518), who were active during all or the greater part of the period of Lukáš's supremacy, played a very subordinate role in comparison with the latter; and this was even more true of the remaining Unity leaders.

enabled most members of the Inner Council to find refuge there until the death of Vladislav II in 1516 and the succession of his son Ludvík, a minor who spent most of his time in his other Kingdom of Hungary, brought the persecution to an end.

The ten years of young King Ludvík's reign saw further momentous changes in the Unity's evolution. In the period 1518–24 leading Brethren were in friendly contact with Luther and Erasmus; and although Lukáš to the end of his life stoutly maintained the Unity's completely separate identity and much of the old traditional outlook in the purely religious sphere, the Unity of Brethren, like the official Utraquist church, was, as its subsequent development was to show, by no means untouched by either of the new currents of thought: the religious Reformation or secular Humanism.

It had been Lukáš who had been responsible for carrying through, and completing, the revolution in the Unity's attitude to state and society, begun in the nineties under the leadership of Klenovský, Táborský and Prokop. The Unity for the last century of its existence, before its suppression during the reaction which followed as a result of the Battle of the White Mountain, was largely the creation of Brother Lukáš. This is nowhere more true than in the realm of political and social theory and practice.

The theoretical apologia for the new doctrine, which was contained in the series of theological tracts composed by Lukáš and, to a lesser degree, by Krasonický, was supplemented by a number of practical decisions taken by the Unity, once again under Lukáš's inspiration, to instruct its members as to how they should conduct themselves in everyday life under the new dispensation. The theoretical arguments were probably destined mainly for the priests and the leading laymen of each party; it is unlikely that these learned tracts were read by the rank-and-file of either side, though the gist of their arguments must have been known to many at second-hand.

But the schism in the Unity had originally arisen on a practical issue: the right attitude to be taken up by the Litomyšl Brethren in face of the various demands of the authorities for their collaboration. The controversy during subsequent years, too, remained very largely on the plane of practical behaviour: it dealt primarily with the relationship of the individual Brethren to society as a whole.

As has been seen, by 1496, with the failure of the Conference of Chlumec, the new doctrines had definitely won predominance in the Unity. At once the need was felt to work out their detailed application;

and through a gradual process of evolution the full consequences were to be drawn from what had at first been stated only hesitantly and half-heartedly. From 1497 onwards, a series of decrees was promulgated by Unity synods or by the Inner Council, which attempted to regulate the new code of social behaviour incumbent on Unity members.

Unfortunately these decrees have not come down in their original form nor are they arranged in chronological order. Few of them are indeed dated, though it is clear that the most important group originated in the last three years of the fifteenth century and the first few years of the sixteenth.[3] All those under discussion here, however, were promulgated during Brother Lukáš's lifetime; they give expression, therefore, to the revolution in ideas which he and the other leaders of the Major Party effected during this period.[4]

The general purpose of this series of decrees and other similar documents was described by Lukáš himself in 1523 in the following words:

Be it known that this [civil] power is not permitted to members of the Unity ... except under guidance from the Lord's words. The noble, the rich, the mighty, officials, judges and the rest possess ... written instructions (*zprávy*) regarding the reservations and conditions under which they may exercise such power. The Brethren have these full instructions for all classes and ranks, for all trades and professions and all walks of life ... and each, according to his ability, should order his life by them.[5]

---

[3] Müller-Bartoš, *op. cit.*, pp. 183–91.
[4] *Dekrety Jednoty bratrské*, pp. VI, VII. Cf. Goll. *Quellen und Untersuchungen zur Geschichte der Böhmischen Brüder*, I, p. 36: 'Leider besitzen wir diese Dekrete bis 1530 nicht in ihrer ursprünglichen Fassung; erst mit dem Jahre 1531 folgen in der Sammlung die vollständigen Texte in chronologischer Ordnung. Der Sammler, der in 17. Jahrhunderte auf Grund eines Synodbeschlusses v. J. 1617 die Arbeit unternahm, legte für die ältere Zeit ein Werk zu Grunde, *Zprávy kněžské* genannt, das bereits zur Zeit des Lukáš von Prag entstanden war. Die Dekrete bringen die Beschlüsse der Synoden und des Engen Rathes bis 1531 nicht in chronologischer, sondern in systematischer Ordnung: ihr erster Theil enthält eine Ubersicht der Lehre und Verfassung der Unität zur Zeit des Lukáš. Es ist bezeichnend, dass jenes Dekret, durch das im J. 1495 den Schriften Gregors eine bindende Autorität abgesprochen wurde, das ganze Werk eröffnet. Der Geist der alten Unität ist in diesen Dekreten nicht mehr zu finden.' The *Zprávy kněžské*, which was the work of Brother Lukáš, was printed in 1527; and much of the same matter was used earlier in the *Dekrety* and in Lukáš's *Odpis proti odtržencom*. A small amount of material dating back before 1495 was also included in the collection of decrees. See Müller-Bartoš, *op. cit.*, p. 341; Goll-Krofta, *Chelčický a Jednota v XV. století*, p. 196; Dobiáš, 'Hodnocení Lukášových Zpráv kněžských,' *Křest'anská revue*, XX, 1953, pp. 84–90.
[5] Lukáš, *Spis o mocy swěta*, fol. 57. A role, somewhat similar to that of the decrees of the Czech Unity, was played among the Polish Arians by the discourses given by their leader, Faustus Socinus, at Raków in 1601 and 1602. These discourses which marked

On the other hand, as seen from the viewpoint of the Minor Party (which is given in the report of the Utraquist priest, Jan Bechyňka), the Major Party were to be condemned for now advocating in these decrees:

That a brother may be a civil official, alderman, judge, etc.; that he may take an oath, participate in courts of law, go to the wars, deliver up criminals to be put to death, deal in strong liquor and trade generally; ... that he may with love in his heart hang, imprison, chain up, ... collaborate with the world as far as the executioner; ... that civil power with its laws and punishments may find a place in the Unity; that a lord, having castles, fortresses and towns, may join the Brethren and continue to deal out vengeful punishments; indeed, that the Brethren may inflict every manner ... of penalty so long as they are not responsible for the death of an innocent person; that there is no reason why men should not earn a living as best they can, even from usury; that anyone unwilling to take an oath to confirm the truth is committing a sin and that the Law is being fulfilled by [swearing]; that so long as he has not actually been excommunicated (*vyobcován*), every member is to be looked upon as a Brother, regardless of his deeds.[6]

This hostile summing up of the new doctrines, which Bechyňka calls 'the articles of the new dispensation (*artikulové nového svolení*),'[7] was indeed somewhat tendentious in tone, though correctly reflecting the attitude of the Minor Party to the changes taking place. In essentials it gives an accurate, if unsympathetic, picture of the views of the Major Party as they found expression in the series of decrees passed under Lukáš's inspiration, defining for the future the rights and obligations of Unity members towards society.

The virtue of patient suffering had, in the Major Party's opinion, been exaggerated by the Unity in the past: it had formed the kernel of its doctrine of non-resistance, of its negation of state and society. 'It seems [announced one of the decrees] that there was insufficiency; and suffering was valued more highly than was warranted.' The injunction not to resist evil was meant by Christ only for 'the common people, who hold no civil office.' For those whose duty it was to enforce the law, it was a sin not to carry out their obligations, provided they acted for the public welfare and not to revenge personal wrongs. The justification of active resistance to evil on the part of the properly constituted authorities, and the policy

---

a definite break with earlier social radicalism ranged over a number of subjects, including self-defence and war, oaths, courts of law and the death penalty, civil office, property and usury, standards of living and church discipline in general. See Kot, *Ideologja polityczna i społeczna Braci Polskich*, pp. 80–85.

[6] 'Psaní jakéhos kněze Jana Appolinařského,' *Časopis historický*, 1882, no. 2, pp. 67, 68.

[7] *Ibid.*, p. 67.

of state affirmation which went with it, was reflected in all the decrees issued over the thirty years during which Lukáš virtually controlled the destinies of the Unity.

A Christian ruler, then, was not a contradiction in terms. Those Brethren who held office, and those holding office who wished to become Brethren, were confirmed in their positions by a decree of 1499 which, indeed, did little more than repeat in slightly less ambiguous language the decisions of earlier synods.

Concerning the civil power [it was stated] according to previous judgements we also acknowledge that ... those lords or officials, aldermen or judges who are engaged in this for suitable reasons and cannot get out, provided they steer clear of other sins ... and use their power properly to the end appointed by God, may have a place among us.[8]

Detailed instructions were laid down as to the manner and spirit in which such a Christian office holder should carry out his duties. He was not to seek his own glory through entry on office nor was he to consider himself superior on that account, remembering always that all those set in authority were only 'God's servants, who must give account to Him for what has been entrusted to them' and that men were 'naturally equal.' They must not be idle or self-indulgent, corrupt or cruel, or use their office for their own profit. Their aim must be impartial justice towards all. They must never seek 'revenge in their own quarrel.' In the view of the Unity, the purpose of civil authority was the welfare of the ordinary citizen. Those summoned to take office, therefore, 'should realize that they have been called to this work in order to serve and that, through service to the people, they were acting rightly.' The aim of their administration was to enable their subjects to 'live out their lives in peace, carrying on their occupations ... not harming each other and free from disturbers of the peace.' Their ultimate object was to fulfil God's will on earth.[9]

A separate set of instructions was issued for officials of the lower grades, who executed the commands of their superiors and were for the most part in direct contact with the ordinary populace. As elsewhere there was the inevitable repetition of the injunction to avoid office where possible, a remnant of the old ideology which was to lose all meaning with the passing of time. Officials were, in the first place, enjoined to take service only 'with a lord loving righteousness and with a hatred of injustice with its avarice and cruelty.' By this, presumably, not only actual members or sympathizers of the Unity were indicated, but those lords who had a

[8] *Dekrety*, p. 87.
[9] *Ibid.*, pp. 90, 91; *Odpis*, fols. 57, 57v.

reputation for treating their tenants well and seeking a fair administration of justice on their demesnes. Officials who were members of the Unity were to serve their lords loyally and honestly, to deal justly with the people and not to oppress them. They were, therefore, not to consent to anything 'against justice and their own conscience' or to be privy to anything 'contrary to their salvation,' either 'in the acquisition of profits or in the government of men.' They were, too, to remain unswayed by any personal motives in the administration of justice and never 'to accept gifts, which blind and hide up righteousness.' They were not to be haughty in their bearing and to concern themselves not merely with their lord's profits, but also with the welfare of his tenants. Finally, they were to 'observe the obligations and customs of the Unity and not to be ashamed of their Brotherhood.'[10] The high moral standards which the Unity imposed on its members made them, indeed, extremely sought after both by the owners of landed property in order to manage their estates or townships and by their fellow citizens in the larger cities as their elected administrators.

Every official, whether representing crown, city or feudal lord, was closely concerned with the carrying-out of a system of justice, which was often harsh and crude and sometimes extremely cruel in the punishments inflicted. This had been one of the chief considerations leading Chelčický and the early Brethren to reject the whole state system as inconsistent with the Christian way of life. But now that collaboration in the working of that system was within certain limitations allowed even the strictest member of the Unity, it became necessary for the Unity to issue some rules of conduct for those Brethren who were engaged therein.

The first duty of a newly appointed official, as has been seen, was to take the oath of office. An undated decree, summarizing succinctly the whole position in regard to oaths which, as we have seen, was to be propounded at much greater length in the works of Lukáš and Krasonický, declares that:

At first it was held that under no circumstances was [an oath] to be made, since it was an unchristian thing. The Unity has altered this: that is to say, that when a man, avoiding any unrighteous and unjust act, intends ... to speak the simple truth and do justice, and provided he neither demands the oath himself nor compels anyone to it, then, being forced by one who is not a member of the Unity to confirm ... the case ... by

---

[10]   *Ibid.*, pp. 92, 93; *Odpis*, fols 58v–59v. It is interesting to note that, where the *Dekrety* adjures officials to 'obey their lord in everything,' the *Odpis* qualifies this by adding the adjectives 'just, honest and good.' The latter is possibly an older version more in harmony with the earlier doctrine abandoned only several decades before.

calling upon the name of God, he does not break God's commandments by doing this with the solemnity of a judgement and on truth and justice.[11]

In practice only two kinds of oaths were still forbidden the Brethren: those sworn on the saints or by the Virgin Mary. To swear by these was to incur 'the sin of idolatry'; and therefore it was right for the Brethren openly to resist such a demand – which was indeed fairly frequent in the Czech lands at that period – and to suffer the consequences of their refusal.[12] These remaining reservations against oathtaking were thus devoid of any social content, such as had largely inspired the objections of the Old Brethren to swearing as part and parcel of the unchristian civil power.

A second important function of most officials was to participate in some capacity in courts of law trying cases of varying significance. The Unity had now granted the legal system a definite place within the Christian community: its functioning, it was claimed, had the sanction of the scriptures behind it. It had been instituted 'so that the subject people might carry on their livelihood in peace and live together in society ... without harm to each other and freed from disturbers of the peace.'

Special advice was given to those who actually served as judges in the courts. They were to have a clear understanding of the purpose of courts of law, which was to distinguish 'between one case and another through hearing each side, enquiring and weighing up correctly the circumstantial evidence (*příčiny okolostojící*) without any improper bias.' They were not to give judgement until they had heard all the evidence, first taking into consideration 'who, what, when, why, by whose help, etc., as well as the time, place, person and reason' of the offence. They should not be swayed at all by outward appearances or fine words or by the acceptance of any bribe or by any personal predilection or ties of friendship, or be overawed by the position or influence of any of the persons concerned. They were to remember that they would finally have to account before God for all their actions; and, therefore, they should endeavour to 'bring the civil laws ... into line with God's commandments and judgements, so that they may not be opposed to each other.' Otherwise, 'through their own lack of knowledge or the stupidity' of the civil law, they might condemn someone who was innocent in the eyes of God. They were, therefore, to take care to be responsible for the deaths of none save those unrepentant criminals, 'whom God will not suffer but gives over to vengeance.'

An illustration of the humanitarianism which was to distinguish the political thinking of the Unity, even after its social radicalism had been

[11] *Dekrety*, p. 87.
[12] *Ibid.*, p. 82. See also *Odpis*, fol 64. Cf. Kot, *op. cit.*, p. 83.

discarded, is to be found in the distinction to be made between the motives which led to the commission of an offence. Crimes which arose 'from inadvertence or from excessive passion or from incitement,' from accidental circumstances rather than from an evil way of life, were to be treated more leniently, where contrition was shown, than deliberate and calculated misdeeds. 'But these matters [the decree rather helplessly adds] are very unclear and, therefore, a man should, wherever possible, steer clear of having to give judgement concerning them.'[13]

Further regulations defined more specifically the duties and functions of those Brethren who were chosen to be village magistrates (rychtáří) or aldermen (konšelé). First, the relevant decree lays down that such offices should be filled by 'a suitable person, uncorrupted by anger and greed ... and with complete control over himself.' He was to excel others in wisdom and prudence and to be capable of sound judgement. The remaining injunctions are mainly elaborations, more detailed versions of those given in general to those who had to act on occasion as judges.[14] Lukáš adds an interesting item in his Zprávy, where such judges and aldermen as were members of the Unity were required to seek to act like arbitrators in a dispute and, wherever possible, to lead both parties to accept a mutually satisfactory conclusion. In this way 'they can preserve love and friendship,' which was the Christian solution. But the course most in line with Christian doctrine, Lukáš also says in this Advice, was to avoid such offices altogether 'on account of the many dangers which generally accompany them.'[15]

The main objects of the modern judicial system are twofold: the protection of the innocent and law-abiding by the infliction of various punishments on the wrongdoer and, secondly, the reformation of the wrongdoer himself by making him once more a decent member of the community. With the latter aim the Minor Party and their teachers could have had no quarrel. But the first purpose was, they would have claimed, not only unchristian; in the case of harsh punishments and the death penalty it was actually in conflict with the other alleged aim of justice. It was punishment rather than reformation that, in their view, dominated the legal procedure of their day. The validity of a third motive for instituting courts of law – the settlement of disputes between otherwise law-abiding members of society – was also denied by those who thought like the Minor Party. This was natural in a pagan community, they said,

[13] Dekrety, pp. 91, 93, 94.
[14] Ibid., pp. 95, 96.
[15] Odpis, fol. 61, 61v (quoted in part in Goll-Krofta, op. cit., p. 221).

but it had no place in a social order which claimed to be Christian; though even Chelčický, for instance, was prepared to allow arbitration within the church.

It was above all the problem of legal punishment, and of the death penalty in particular, that continued to vex the minds of Unity members even after they had discarded the strict application of the old doctrines. The note of hesitancy and uncertainty as to how far the new doctrine might be carried, apparent indeed in most of the decrees issued on social questions during the period immediately following the schism, is especially strongly marked here.

The judge were first to endeavour, if possible, to effect the reformation of the criminal. Milder forms of punishment were recommended, such as holding the wrongdoer up to public censure or reproving him in private. The motives on account of which the offence was committed were to be taken into consideration; and with these in mind punishment was to be administered 'with moderation and prudence.' Heavier punishments might take three basic forms: deprivation of property, of honour, or of liberty or life and limb. In the first case, care was to be taken that no desire for personal profit entered into the sentence of confiscation, but only the wish to see justice done. The punishment, too, must fit the crime: no more might be taken in compensation than an equivalent of the injury done, as had been taught in the Old Testament.

But it was the severer penalties involving corporal punishment and the loss of liberty, limb and even life, all common at that time, that were most difficult to square with the Christian gospel.

Concerning punishment by bodily torture, beating, imprisonment, starvation, shackling [says one of the decrees] they may only be practised upon ... those who can be deterred from their evil doing neither by exhortation nor by shame nor by a fine, but alone through dread of this. As to deprivation of limbs, and even more of life, it is proper to know God's judgement as to whether he deserves it by reason of this crime or not ... and whether he cannot be led away from his evil doing by some other means. ... In connection with every punishment it is proper to avoid cruelty, anger, revenge, hatred and other forms of unrighteousness and to do justice with mercy ... [civil] power, too, should be exercized neither against the prohibitions of the Old and New [Testaments] nor in support of spiritual concerns.[16]

There are several interesting variations in the different wordings of this decree; of interest, too, are various additional injunctions on the same

[16] *Dekrety*, pp. 91, 92.

subject to be found in other decrees. They all serve to bring out the underlying disquietude which continued for some time among the Brethren as
to the Christian character of the penal system of their day.

The decree on the duties of village magistrates and aldermen, for
instance, advises these officers, 'as regards the death penalty, to act
circumspectly (*bázlivě se míti*) and as far as possible to have nothing to do
with it, so that above all they should not occasion it by will, mind, speech
or action; since such a matter needs a judgement from God, for it is His to
kill.'[17] Lukáš in his *Zpráva soudcim světským* recommends 'the penitent
(*kajicý*) man to escape from this judgement [i.e. of death] where he may...
and not to be present at executions of his own free will.' In another place
he advises against 'excessive cruelties' in the infliction of certain punishments. The death penalty was not, for example, a fitting punishment for
common thieving provided this was not accompanied by violence. Brethren in office, therefore, 'should take care not to judge always according to
the letter of the law alone, especially when this is cruel, merciless and in
some respects unjust.'[18] But it is clear that the Unity's earlier testimony
against the death penalty and the brutalities of the penal system of the day
had on the whole been abandoned, even though this system was not yet
accepted in its entirety without a certain amount of protest.

Apart from appearing as judges or in the capacity of accused – this last
a very unlikely circumstance in a member of the Unity, except in connection with religious persecution, and one which would otherwise have
entailed expulsion – the Brethren might now also participate in courts of
law either as litigants in civil suits or as witnesses or in the role of lawyers.
Calling in the aid of the authorities, recourse to the law, was not now
forbidden the Brethren provided it was not a question of a purely religious
matter.

Concerning the temporal affairs of this life the Brethren may for sufficient
reasons have recourse to [the authorities] in their defence, where this
would promote justice and may be done without further hurt. They must
bear in mind that they should put their neighbours' salvation before the
things of the flesh ... they should be acquainted with the Christian rule
that it is sometimes better to endure an injury ... as Christ says: 'But
whosoever shall smite thee on thy right cheek, turn to him the other also.
And if any man will use thee at the law, and take away thy coat, let him
have the cloak also.' [Matthew V, 39, 40]. Indeed we are not to make
use of the civil power in those matters which affect salvation, so that some
should heed us through fear of it. All should have a free will in this matter,

17 *Ibid.*, pp. 95, 96.
18 *Odpis*, fols. 60–61 (quoted in part in Goll-Krofta, *op. cit.*, pp. 220, 221).

either to be with us or ... to leave ... or, if they have been disciplined by us for disobedience to the church, they should be treated as ... open sinners, then left in peace; and the aid of the [civil] power should not be sought ... There must always be heresy in order that some may be tried.[19]

The conditions under which the Brethren might go to court were, as was usual with all their contacts with the outer world, discussed in several of their decrees. Once again, too, the language in which these are framed is so loose, the thought so unclear and the conclusions so often contradictory, that it is not always possible to be sure of the exact meaning intended by those who originally drew them up.

Disputes, however, between one Unity member and another were, as under the Old Brethren, to be kept out of the courts and submitted instead to a panel of arbitrators appointed from among fellow members. In other cases, or if two Unity members were unable to find suitable arbitrators within their own society, a Brother should, especially if he was of an intemperate disposition, first be quite certain that the right was on his side and that the quarrel could not be settled amicably out of court – or at least early in the proceedings – before taking the decision to proceed. If these conditions were satisfied, in the last resort legal proceedings might be instituted with a clear conscience, so long as 'humility, calm, obedience and patience are preserved, and calumny and slander, vengeance and threats eschewed.' But even should the cause be a just one, it was not right to take the matter to court if it was of a trivial nature.

If a Brother was summoned to court 'from anger and revenge,' he was to conduct himself throughout in a becoming manner, bearing in mind Christ's injunction to repay good for evil and ready to suffer loss and injury, and even life itself, rather than break one of God's commandments. He was not to press for the punishment, still less if this involved the death penalty, of the one who had injured him, though presumably the fact that his suit might end in this way was not necessarily a reason for not proceeding with it. In any case the decision of the court, even if it went in favour of the other party, was to be accepted without ill-feeling. In all instances where legal action might be taken, whether between one Brother and another or with someone outside the Unity, 'the faithful should be aware that they must not proceed to court without the advice of the elders,' who would judge of the necessity in the light of the particular circumstances.[20]

[19] *Dekrety*, p. 88.
[20] *Ibid.*, pp. 94, 95; *Odpis*, fols. 62v–63v (quoted in part in Goll-Krofta, *op. cit.*, p. 221). Once again the *Odpis* is slightly nearer the spirit of the old Unity than the version

Brethren might also appear in court as witnesses. Before reluctantly consenting to bear witness, however, they were to take advice, presumably from one of their elders, as to whether their evidence contained 'an actual certainty or something heard or a vague supposition from something seen, heard or assumed.' Since there was much that was unclear (*mnohé nejistoty běží*) in such matters, the best course was to refrain from giving evidence at all. But, if one was forced to do so or was compelled by a sincere desire to be of assistance to one's neighbour in distress, care must still be taken that greater evil should not arise than that which it was intended to avoid. Brethren must be on their guard for any hint of bribery or avarice or flattery, for any lack of charity or bloodthirstiness in their readiness to act as witness. They must distinguish clearly in their evidence between what was merely hearsay and what they had observed themselves; and on every occasion they must refrain from taking an oath or requiring others to do so 'unless this was actually required by law.'

The third capacity in which Brethren might appear in court, apart from that of judge or judged, was in that of an advocate (*řečník*). 'No one [it says in the *Dekrety*] may become an advocate by profession under penalty of ecclesiastical censure.' But if the law requires one of the Brethren to take on this job, he is as usual first to consult with the elders. If they allow him to go ahead, he must still make certain that 'he whose lawyer he is to be has justice on his side. If not, he must lay it aside; he is not in any way consciously to make out an unjust [case] to be just.' In court a member of the Unity when acting as a lawyer had to observe a fairly strict code of professional behaviour.' 'He was to refrain from all unnecessary, libellous or vindictive speeches. He was to hear out the previous speaker to the end and not interrupt his speech or make difficulties.' He was to behave honestly and soberly and 'not cause trouble to the judge.' Finally, he was to conduct his case so that 'friendship or love' would result.[21]

Equally abhorrent to Chelčický and the Old Brethren had been a second function of the state which, together with the administration of the police and judicial systems, formed one of its most important activities. This was the waging of war against external enemies. The old Unity, as has been seen, prohibited its members from participating in any form of warfare, defensive or aggressive, whether against non-Christian or between the nominally Christian; and one of the major difficulties in which loyalty to their previously accepted principles had involved the Litomyšl Brethren

---

of the *Dekrety* which has come down to us. Its prohibition of Brethren taking disputes between one another to a civil court is more definite in its wording. Cf. Kot, *op. cit.*, p. 81.
[21] *Dekrety*, pp. 96, 97.

about 1490 had been, for instance, what to do in the face of the repeated demands from the authorities and their fellow citizens to take a share in the defence of the town or in certain circumstances in that of the state as a whole. The decree defining the attitude to be adopted by Brethren conscripted for war service (*zpráva na vojnu jdoucím*) brings out, perhaps even more clearly than the other decrees dealing with political and social behaviour, the radical break with tradition which the new standpoint signified, despite the fact that, as in the new Unity's other official pronouncements, this break was often concealed here too by the indecisive manner of presentation.

In this decree the Brethren were, first, admonished to avoid participation in war altogether wherever possible. At the outset, however, a distinction was made even here between just wars of defence and unjust wars, though the conditions of a just war are nowhere laid down with anything like the exactitude, for instance, of Catholic theology. A just war was merely defined as one where:

the king or lord seeks and follows peace and does not give occasion for fighting, but he or his subjects suffer cruelty and hurt from another [ruler, who] ... continues in his wickedness and will not agree to any truce. The one against whom this happens is forced, with approval from on high, to take up arms to defend justice and his own people; ... and to assist him in this he may call upon the subject people, among whom may be some of the faithful.

'Such a thing [the decree goes on] appears more tolerable ... than' participation in a war in which the right is on the opposing side. An unjust war, on the other hand, was defined as one where:

The matter over which the war is fought is from the side of the one who summons to it unrighteous and unjust, arising from pride only or greedy desire, anger, cruelty, wrong or some spiritual matter for which it is fitting to suffer patiently, since a Christian may not be a partaker in unrighteousness under the cover of justice.

In the second place, the Brethren were forbidden to enrol as mercenaries even in a just cause. But curiously enough they were at the same time advised, wherever possible, to hire a substitute, if conscripted, to take their place in the army. If, nevertheless, this was not possible and there was no other way out, a further set of instructions was issued for those forced to serve in the wars.

The Brethren conscripts were, first, to try to get appointed to non-combatant duties, to those tasks 'in the army where it would be suitable for them, by the waggons or in other services, or at home where they might stand guard in the castle or fulfil other duties.' But, if even this did not prove possible and they were compelled to take an active part in battle, they were to:

Avoid pushing themselves forward as well as the acquisition of glory through bravery, since excessive bravery as well as cruelty and looting and booty and avaricious desires and other unrighteousness were to be shunned. They were not to proceed willingly to these things [i.e. war service and its concomitants] but only under compulsion with the wish to be free of them. They were to beseech God to deliver them from evil, for in war many evils come to pass.

Men died in battle in a state of sin or killed others – the decree uses the word 'murdered' – in a state of sin; and fighting brought with it a multitude of attendant evils. War, therefore, was still to be regarded as in itself an evil 'contrary to the natural, Jewish and Christian laws.'[22] On whom, then, fell the guilt for the wrong which inevitably arose as a result? 'Whoever starts a war [so runs the Advice] and compels the people to it, is primarily responsible for whatever evil results contrary to God and justice, and not the subject and obedient people.' Less evil, too, was likely to result from war waged 'against the infidel Turks, unrighteous and unjust men,' than against fellow Christians. Of all wars civil war 'against men of the same language' was most to be deplored.[23] But whatever the nature of the particular war, the main burden of guilt was to rest on the shoulders of the ruler who started it without just cause and on any who, from love of renown or desire for gain, might volunteer their services. The least amount of blame attached to 'those who being under compulsion cannot escape, yet have no thought of murder ... nor of any unrighteousness.'[24]

It is, indeed, rather strange for the modern reader to find no mention made of any who might volunteer for war service out of conviction of the rightness of the cause. But the decree on the subject was in effect a compromise between the earlier absolute pacifism of the Unity, which was still palely reflected in its pronouncements, and the somewhat hesitant formal expression of its abandonment in practice. A second reason for such an omission lay in the nature of the composition of the armies of the day, which consisted mainly, as far as the lower ranks were concerned,

---

[22] *Ibid.*, p. 97.
[23] *Odpis*, fols. 65, 65v (quoted in Goll-Krofta, *op. cit.*, p. 222).
[24] *Spis o mocy swĕta*, fol. 51. Cf. the similar process of discarding their earlier pacifist tenets which took place early in the seventeenth century among the Polish Arians, see Kot, *op. cit.*, pp. 78, 79, 82, 95, 99, 121, 122, 134–36.

either of mercenary soldiers serving for profit and without any fixed principles, religious or national, or of peasants and townsmen conscripted for the purpose. Voluntary service in defence of the fatherland was on the whole left to the nobility; the ordinary citizen's horizon normally did not stretch much further than the defence of his village or township. Thirdly, the experiences of the religious wars which plagued the Czech lands during a large part of the fifteenth century, bringing home the devastating effects of war on the life and economy of the country, made the soldier's profession unpopular among many sections of the population who were unaffected by the pacifist scruples of the Old Brethren or, like the new Unity after the schism, had consciously abandoned them.[25]

In the theoretical system of Chelčický and the Old Brethren a society based on violence and war, which found its highest expression in the organized oppression of the state, was largely due to the failure of professing Christians to eliminate class inequalities and to replace an unjust social and economic order with one more in line with Christian principles. It was natural therefore that, as a result of the changes in doctrine which took place in the 1490's, the leaders of the victorious party in the controversy should devote considerable attention to formulating in concrete terms the new attitude to these problems.

The old Unity in principle had not acknowledged the existence of class differences among the Brethren, especially where these were associated with the exercise of administrative or judicial power. As has been seen, they had usually demanded of those from the upper ranks of society who desired to join the Unity that they should first renounce all that was associated with such functions, with the result that very few members of the nobility were to be found among their number during the early decades of the Unity's existence. The degree of sacrifice, the magnitude of the break with society which membership in such cases entailed, had meant that of the many potential recruits from the upper classes, attracted to the Unity by its high spiritual and moral tone contrasting with the deadness of the contemporary Utraquist church, there were in fact few ready to take the final step. It was on account of their continued adhesion to the strict views of the early Brethren that the Minor Party were accused

---

[25] Nevertheless, quite a cult of Žižka was to arise among the Brethren. In their second letter to Dr. Augustin Käsebrod in 1508 the Unity write that: 'If Žižka had not driven [the Roman Catholic crusaders] from Bohemia and Moravia with his flails, communion in two kinds even to-day would not have been possible.' – Palmov, *Cheshkie bratya v svoikh konfessiyakh*, I, p. 289. Cf. Lukáš in Akta Jednoty Bratrské, IV, fols. 114v, 115 (quoted in Goll-Krofta, *op. cit.*, p. 59); Přeloučský, *Spis o původu Jednoty bratrské a o chudých lidech*, pp. 38, 47–49, 52.

by their opponents of preventing 'the penitent from entering' the Unity. 'What our predecessors once held to be wrong and a sin according to the scriptures, [the Major Party] advocated as a proper means to increase the numbers in the Unity.'[26] Through their wealth and influence the presence inside the Unity of comparatively large numbers of 'the rich and well born,' to use the words of the decrees, would, it was hoped, afford the Brethren as a whole protection in times of trouble and a better standing in the community.

The victory of the Major Party signified a departure from the perfectionism of the Old Brethren, a step towards accomodation with the world. It was in this new spirit that the decree regulating the reception into the Unity of members of the nobility, of the rich and educated, was framed.

It seems only right that we should love as our own whomsoever from the rich, noble and learned ... is able to receive the teaching of Christ or the apostles ... whenever they submit to, and are bound by, instruction and admonishment ... and are ready to comport themselves on an equal footing with the poor and the unlettered, undergoing shame and danger with us. ... Since even in the most humble trades, among spinners and weavers for example, danger lurks, and falsehood and deceit are to be found, since it can be among the poor that there is carousing, voluptuousness and pride, licentiousness and readiness to take offence, while among the rich, well-born and learned humility, patience and obedience can exist, it is therefore proper to leave the separation [i.e. of the wheat from the tares, as in the parable] to the angels at the end of the world. ... Even in Christ's day and under the apostles there were good as well as bad [in the church], and rich as well as poor; it was the same when we came together at the beginning, being still few in numbers.[27]

There has been a subtle change of emphasis here. The Old Brethren regarded the exercise of any form of civil power as a sin in a Christian; and since such power was an inevitable concomitant of rank and wealth, the possession of these was thereby automatically rejected. The new Unity, having discarded its testimony against the exercise of civil power, was now free to acknowledge that the Christian virtues might be found among high born rulers as well as among lowly craftsmen and peasants.

Only one condition was now imposed on neophytes from the upper ranks of society, that is, provided they possessed the necessary moral and religious attributes of a member of the Unity. 'In 1503 it was decreed that everyone should openly acknowledge his membership of the Unity and not keep this hidden.' This resolution was directed in particular against Rendl of Oušava who, on account of his unwillingness to declare publicly

26   A. J. B., IV, fol. 67v.
27   *Dekrety*, pp. 64–66.

his allegiance to the despised Unity, was thereby excluded from its fellow-ship.[28] His influence on the momentous decisions which the Unity took at the Assembly of Brandýs in 1490 has already been mentioned. During the first few years after the Major Party's return to power in 1494 the new leadership had evidently not felt itself strong enough to demand an open declaration of membership from new recruits among the ruling class. By the end of a decade, however, the situation was improved enough for them to put forward the open accession of the nobility as an essential precondition of their acceptance into the Unity. In this way, too, un-scrupulous and ambitious politicians of the same type as Rendl of Oušava would have less scope for using the Unity as an instrument for the furtherance of their own private ends.

Members of the nobility, whether born into the Unity or Brethren by convincement, were required to behave in their station according to certain principles which are outlined in several of the Unity's decrees and advices. They were, first, not to consider themselves superior to their fellow Brethren on account of their birth:

But to recognize that they were on an equality from the point of view of nature with the poor people, for whom the most noble of all, Christ, ... gave himself ... even unto a shameful and ignominious death. He called them brothers and sisters, so that the others might know that they are to imitate Christ in humility and not puff themselves up with pride.

Secondly, the privileges of their birth had been granted them in order more easily to fulfil their social functions and serve those put under their care and protection. Therefore those nobles in the Unity who had no estates to administer, no tenantry to care for, for whom the *raison d'être* of their privileged position had in fact disappeared, were especially enjoined to show a humble spirit, to earn their living by their own hands 'along with the rest of the people,' and not to mark themselves off from the working people by finer dress or style of living. In the Unity's view it was only the obligations of rank that justified its privileges. 'For when someone has no [subject people], even though he was born of a noble stem, he does not achieve the end of his nobility.'

Brethren from the nobility were, in the third place, warned against conforming too closely with the worldly display of their class. They were to show 'their nobility not by their clothes or their idle entertainments, but through virtue, high morals, honesty and work ... on behalf of their

---

[28]   *Ibid.*, p. 82. Rendl, however, continued to favour the Brethren even after he had severed all formal connections with the Unity, see Goll-Krofta, *op. cit.*, p. 236; Müller-Bartoš, *op. cit.*, pp. 215, 235.

neighbours.' They were to disregard the opinion of the world, not take offence quickly or lightly at any slight to their dignity, and steer clear of any tendency to show off their wealth and power in dress, ornament or manner of life.[29]

Nowhere, indeed, were class distinctions at that period more easily noticeable than in the matter of clothing. The Unity was to issue several decrees impressing on its members the necessity of dressing soberly and without undue ostentation or any tendency to arouse lasciviousness, and warning Brethren engaged in the clothing industry that those conniving at the production of luxurious or immodest garments would be held equally responsible by God with those who actually wore them. But in addition to the natural differences due to sex, age and function, the Unity was now ready to admit that inequalities in social rank, too, might rightly find expression, even among the Brethren, in different styles and qualities of clothing worn. The noble and wealthy were, it is true, warned not to 'oppress the poor or their people' in order to obtain money to dress themselves up in finery and live on a lavish scale. But, as a decree of 1506 says, 'there is one kind of raiment proper to the peasant, another to the burgher and still another for the nobleman, etc.' An undated decree from about the turn of the century gives an even clearer illustration of the degree to which the Unity was now ready to come to terms with existing society:

Those persons who come to repentance from the noble, gentry or burgher classes, and who are accustomed to different food and clothing from the common people, should, it is apparent, be indulged in these matters ... since it can help them to continue in their repentance. The common people, however, from the lower orders should not copy their example, but should be instructed that they must behave as is proper in such matters and, indeed, a more simple apparel and cut is appropriate for them.

Then follows the threat that if Unity members from among the ordinary people did not follow this advice, which had found expression 'in many ordinances (od mnohých svolení),' they were liable to incur disciplinary action. The egalitarian ideas of the Old Brethren in this connection were now regarded as 'a failing (nedostatek)' which it was necessary to put aside.[30]

The picture of the ideal Unity nobleman which emerges from the decrees and advices and other contemporary documents of a similar character is one of patriarchal benevolence, of a consciousness of the obligations of the class to which he had been born and bred towards those whom God had pleased to place in a lower station in life. There is, indeed, a recog-

[29] Odpis, fol. 58 (quoted in Goll-Krofta, op. cit., p. 220); Dekrety, pp. 97, 98.
[30] Dekrety, pp. 89, 90, 127.

nition of the natural equality of all men in the eyes of God; but the note
of protest against manmade inequalities, so prominent a feature in the
writings of Chelčický and the early Brethren, has gone completely.

Noblemen who joined the Brethren were reminded that they were to use
their wealth and privileged position for the good of the community.
'They are to avoid vain show and extravagant expenditure ... on themselves, their wives, children and servants, and not pour out money on
their houses and horses and worldly ornament, but to give rather to the
poor among their people.'[31] 'They are not to keep superfluous servants,
horses, or other things, only for showing off or for pride or vanity, but
rather should they spend their wealth on necessities serving the good of
their tenants.' They were, wherever possible, to administer their estates
themselves and not as absentee landlords through their bailiffs. They must
act as protectors of their tenantry and not as their oppressors, succouring
the needy and helpless, acting as a father to the servants, and not bur-
dening their tenantry with excessive dues and labour services. The nobility
had been set by God in authority over them:

So that they may serve them, and in exchange they may receive respect
and dues for their sustenance, ... But for this they will have to give an
account to their ... Lord. ... Therefore ... they are not to imagine that
they [i.e., their tenants] are theirs to do with as they please; they are theirs
to govern and preserve and defend. In reality they are God's, particularly
when they are a Christian people.[32]

Nobles were not to justify acts of oppression against their tenantry by
saying that:

They have bought them and they are inscribed in the land books (ve
dckách) and in the registers and have been in the possession of their forefathers from time immemorial. ... Also nobles belonging to the faithful
should willingly provide food and drink for poor persons, who work for
them ... they must not cheat them of any part of their wages ... nor
take by force children from their parents or money from orphans, but
provide the latter, as is just, with guardians.

In regard to their fellow Brethren of inferior station, nobles in the Unity
were to make use of their greater opportunities to forward their common
interests. 'They were not to summon them to offices or to services against
their conscience ... they were to be obedient to the elders.' They were
also to consult the elders in important business, such as appearing in
court. As regards members of their household who likewise belonged to

[31]   *Odpis*, fol. 57v.
[32]   *Dekrety*, pp. 98, 99.

the Unity, they were to hold divine service together with them.[33] 'They are not to put any obstacles in the way of their attending services, but as they themselves keep fast-days, Christian holidays and festivals, and Sundays, they should encourage them too to fulfil their religious duty.'[34]

At a period when, with the laws passed by the Bohemian diet in 1497 and 1500, the peasantry were rapidly losing their free status and sinking to the position of serfs bound to the land, while the towns were becoming increasingly dependent on the landed aristocracy, in an era when the laws were still enforced by the landowning class, as well as by royal officials, with great cruelty on the subject population, the Unity had abandoned its protest against the whole system of class differentiation and contented itself henceforth with the attempt merely to ameliorate that system's most blatant injustices. In the Minor Party's view its aim was now to justify 'in Christian lords a separate way of life and customs from those of the ordinary people,'[35] in exchange for which, it might pleaded, members of the ruling class who adhered to the Unity were to devote their lives to the people's welfare and protection.

The Unity had in fact returned to the Wyclifite conception of 'the threefold people,' against which Chelčický had directed some of his bitterest and most effective invective. The 'happiness' of the 'faithful nobles' was not to lie in the renunciation of their position and authority, as in the earlier days of the Unity, but in fulfilling the duties of their station, dealing out punishment to the wrongdoer, though with mercy and conscious of their ultimate responsibility to God for their earthly stewardship. 'We consider [Lukáš wrote about 1498] such Christian nobles or kings to be happy, with the hope here and in the future' of eternal bliss.[36]

As late as 1512 the problem of what members of the nobility should do with their estates and their feudal rights of jurisdiction on joining the Unity was threshed out again by the Inner Council at their meeting in Brandýs in November of that year. The position was complicated by the fact that the person around whom the debate revolved was a woman, Johanka z Krajku, whose name has cropped up in connection with the

---

[33] *Odpis*, fols. 58, 58v (quoted *ibid.*). Cf. with Chelčický (Chapter I, p. 64).

[34] *Dekrety*, p. 99.

[35] A. J. B., IV, fol. 63v.

[36] *Ibid.*, fol. 62 (quoted in Molnár, *Boleslavští bratří*, pp. 47, 48). This short statement is accompanied by the comment from an unknown member of the Minor Party that 'here the Major Party, that is, Lukáš and his fellow Brethren, cuts its cloth to suit the nobles (*Tuto větší strana, Lukáš s svými bratřími panuom skrojují vhod plašt'ek*).' Its contents give an excellent picture of what the Unity now demanded from its noble members. Cf. Dobiáš, *op. cit.*, pp. 84–86.

discussions during the conference of Chlumec (1496). The Lady Johanka
was the wife of Jan of Šelmberk, one of the Unity's protectors from among
the Catholic nobility, and herself for long its close sympathizer before
actually joining. As the owner also in her own right of a vast network
of estates around Mladá Boleslav and Brandýs, she 'took counsel with
the elders whether she should leave her castle, having renounced the use
of her estates, or continue to enjoy them.' After lengthy discussion it was
decided that in principle there was no reason why she should not continue
as before to keep possession of her estates. The Inner Council, however,
despite the serious position in which the Unity was then placed through
the persecution which it was undergoing about this time, and undeterred
by the fact that Brandýs itself where they were confering was on Johanka's
property, still felt strong enough to lay down some fairly stringent conditions before confirming Johanka in membership. These followed in
the main the general principles outlined above concerning the conduct of
Brethren from the nobility. One interesting variation, however, due
probably to the fact that it was a woman who was involved, was that
Johanka was not herself to administer her estates; she was to 'install her
brother in her place to manage and govern' according to these principles.
In the following year the Lady Johanka did in fact sell her estates to her
brother, Kunrat Krajíř z Krajku, who, together with his wife, was also a
member of the Unity.[37]

The same conception of stewardship was present in the decree defining
the duties of those Unity members, whether from the nobility or untitled
burghers, who had either inherited wealth or acquired it by their own
efforts. First, it was asked, had they come by this wealth by just means
and, if so, were they in the second place putting it to good use? No clear
definition, however, was given of precisely what means were to be considered as justifiable or exactly how wealth justly acquired might rightly
be expended.

It should not have been obtained, it was said, 'by sinful means or any
kind of unrighteousness or as a result of wrong done to one's neighbours'
or by robbing and oppressing the poor and defenceless. Restitution was
to be made in such cases to the injured party or, if this were impossible,
atonement was to be by giving to the poor. Improper use of wealth

---

[37] *Dekrety*, pp. 88, 89; Molnár, *op. cit.*, p. 77. Molnár regards the Unity's intervention,
as in this case, in the material affairs of its magnate members as one of the last vestiges
of the old radical demand for social justice once voiced by the Taborites, as distinct
from later recommendations merely to exercise charity. He does not consider that
Johanka interfered in the life of the important Unity congregation established in her
town of Mladá Boleslav and under the spiritual care of Brother Lukáš. – *Op. cit.*, p. 42.

occurred when, instead of devoting it to help the poor and needy, it was expended on luxuries and riotous living. Forgiveness for such sins could only be earned 'by almsgiving' and 'by coming to realize that, in regard to their wealth, they are only God's stewards according to His will and . . . the Lord will demand an account.' Wealth was not a justification for any appearance of superiority over the less wealthy; and the wealthy were always to bear in mind that riches by themselves would not help them to enter the Kingdom of Heaven.[38]

There were, indeed, very occasional glimmers of the old communistic doctrines with which the Unity started; as, for instance, when it was stated in one of the decrees that 'the earth . . . produces for all alike; and in vain do some consider themselves guiltless, when they take to themselves the common good things which they have from God and do not distribute them.' But the conclusion drawn is not any form of communism of goods, even among a limited circle as at the very beginning of the Unity or among the monastic orders of the medieval church. It is merely an exhortation to give alms.[39]

The way was now open, therefore, for Brethren in the towns to launch out into enterprises which were to bring an increasing accumulation of wealth into their hands. In the future the only limitation placed by the discipline of the Unity was the observation of certain moral standards as well as the obligation to exercise charity on behalf of the poor. Indeed, such high moral standards, enjoining honesty in business and the avoidance of superfluous expenditure on articles of luxury, might themselves serve, as they have since done with other religious sects elsewhere, to bring success in the affairs of this world.

While one set of regulations sought to define the general principles of conduct for the rich and noble and those in authority, a further series dealt with the rights and duties of Brethren who derived from the working people, peasants and artisans and servants, the poor and the needy. The latter were above all urged to display a spirit of obedience in all things lawful and of patient endurance of wrong. The element of resistance, albeit passive, and of protest against an unjust social order largely disappeared from the official utterances of the Unity in the period after the schism.

The peasantry as tenants of the nobility and gentry, and subjects in general in relation to their rulers, were instructed that as members of the Unity:

[38] *Dekrety*, pp. 99, 100.
[39] *Ibid.*, p. 123.

They should realize that the world order is ordained by God for their own good; they should know their place, and that the servants of the world [i.e. those in authority] are set up for their good also and to preserve them from evil. They must be subject to them not only out of fear but for conscience' sake, since God wills this. They should be obedient, ... never exercise authority not properly entrusted to them but rather endure suffering; they should show a readiness for every good deed ... neither swear nor curse, pay their dues and taxes and show love towards good and faithful lords. They should refrain from striving after equality ... but surpass them in honesty, ... gladly suffer wrong knowing that the Lord has said: 'Vengeance is mine: I will repay' [Romans XII, 19]. ... The Brethren are to be taught to suffer things patiently if ever in any community (*v obci*) more is imposed upon one person than upon the others.[40]

Even though, in the words of Brother Matěj written at the end of the fifteenth century, 'there are none in our lands less free than those who may be sold and settled under the nobles,' yet the peasants 'must be subject in the fear of the Lord according to the apostle's teaching.'[41] Any hint of stirring up the peasantry against their masters was to be avoided at all costs, any suggestion that the Brethren were carrying on the radical social traditions of the 'Picards' or the dreaded Taborites.

We do nothing against the government of the world, against its lands and kingdoms [states an untitled Unity confession *dán na rathauz* in 1507] we are subject to His Majesty the King and our lords. We are not wicked disturbers of the peace, malefactors, thieves or traitors, ... we seek after peace and harmony between men, not taking the vengeance of wrongs into our own hands; instead we either suffer or look to the law for rectification, ... we pay [tithes] to the priests where we are settled, even though we do not make use of their services. Why then are we to be harried?[42]

Their acceptance, as a result of the changes in Unity doctrine, of the framework of the existing social order had given the Brethren the opportunity both to rebut charges made by the central authorities of anarchy and plotting and, at the same time, to put forward a body of social teaching that would not frighten away likely converts among persons of rank and influence.[43]

[40] *Ibid.*, p. 98. Cf. *ibid.*, pp. 128–30; *Odpis*, fol. 59v (quoted in part in Goll-Krofta, *op. cit.*, p. 220), where the duty of submission to social superiors is enjoined on artisans, apprentices, and the servant class respectively. The moral dangers connected with service in the houses of the nobility made it advisable, it was urged, to avoid such work. But if this was not possible, Brethren were at least not to imitate the frivolities and luxurious way of life of their masters.

[41] A. J. B., IV., fol. 41v. Cf. *Odpis*, fol. 50 (quoted *ibid.*, p. 217).

[42] Palmov, *op. cit.*, II, p. 277.

[43] Cf. Denis, *Fin de l'Indépendence Bohême*, I, p. 340: 'Une part de responsabilité dans la révolution qui s'accomplit alors en Bohême ne revient-elle pas aussi à l'Unité?

The majority of the Unity's following, however, continued to be drawn from the poorer sections of the community, and in particular from the peasantry, even though this class no longer set the tone of its social creed. The Minor Party, following in the footsteps of Chelčický and the long line of Czech reformers both before and after Hus, naturally still regarded the peasant's and the artisan's calling as the only way of life really consistent with true Christianity; for them one of the signs of a follower of Christ was his 'consorting with peasants (*s sedláky obcování*).'[44] But something of this idealization of the peasant, of this cult of the common man, continued to find expression in the writings of the Unity's new leadership during the first few decades following on the schism, despite the increasing conservatism which coloured most of its utterances on social topics.

Lukáš, for instance, in one of his most lengthy and elaborate treatises, *O obnovení církve svaté*, is continually inveighing against the oppression of the poor by the rich and powerful. He frequently emphasizes, quite in the style of the Old Brethren, the superiority of that poverty and simple piety which predominated in the early Christian church – as in his opinion it still did among the Brethren of his day – over the riches, power and learning of this world. The Brethren, he writes in phrases reminiscent of Chelčický, unwelcome in high society, were really at home only among the lower orders of society, 'with beasts, that is, among the despised, downtrodden people without significance in the world. The proud and the mighty, regarding these as beasts without understanding, treat them harshly and brutally as if they were animals, frequently oppressing them with unlawful *corvées* and dues.'[45] Elsewhere he writes that in the early church, even before Constantine's day, as the numbers of its adherents began to increase 'many of the well-born and those in authority turned to it and rested in the shade' of the church, thereby corrupting its pristine purity. A similar process, Lukáš was ready to admit, could easily take place within the Unity if extreme care were not taken to prevent it, since 'once more the devil had tried to instil the vanity of the world into the Unity through persons of birth and high rank,' decked out 'in sumptuous and immodest apparel.'[46]

Among the leaders of the Major Party an even more ardent advocate of the earlier simplicity was to be found in old Tůma Přeloučský who,

En prêchant aux paysans l'obéissance et le sacrifice, n'a-t-elle pas énervé leur force de résistance et facilité l'établissement général du servage?'

[44] A. J. B., IV, fol. 64.
[45] Lukáš, 'O obnovení,' fol. 27. Cf. Chelčický, *O trojím lidu*, p. 71.
[46] *Ibid.*, fols. 124v, 133.

indeed, differed from Lukáš, especially, on many matters touching the increasing use of ceremonial in the Unity. In his open letter 'to the noble lord, Lord Albrecht of Šternberk,' composed in 1502, Tůma comes forward as a champion of the rights of the semi-serf peasantry and of the poor in general. His object, he writes, was to examine:

How [the peasants] are treated by their lords, since God from of old has diligently commanded kings, princes, lords and all who rule over the people to act justly towards them ... God grant that His Majesty and his council ... may, as is the obligation of their office, look to the princes, lords, knights and squires, from the highest to the lowest, to see how they treat their poor folk. ... His Majesty would then discover that they have burdened them with numerous unjust *corvées* and extraordinary dues recently contrived, over and above ancient justice, and raised the customs duties, so that on that account it is difficult for them to travel. ... And these things are continually increasing from one day to another; and their number grows greater like river water after rain, so that now the poor people do not know what to do for such oppression. ... But if ever they should turn in their distress to the king ... and the king after listening to their humble petition should give them a letter to the lords exhorting these to leave them with their just rights, and they prepare to return home joyfully under the impression that their plight will be alleviated, then, when they have presented the letter [i.e. to the lords in council] ... these thereupon revile them, calling them varlets (*chlapi*) and traitors and make out a lengthy indictment, how they have accused their lords before the king. Thus they go hence in sorrow and, instead of amendment, something quite different results, for at home their lord is awaiting them to throw them into prison; and some he strips as one does a lime tree (*a nĕkteré odře co lípu*). And later it is twice as bad as it was before.[47]

Tůma attacked in biting language the priests, and the mendicant orders in particular, for not coming forward in support of the oppressed commenalty against the rich and the powerful, for flattering the latter instead, in order to obtain some share of their wealth and power. 'In this way they act quite contrary to the apostles.' 'It would be better [he concludes] for a man to be buried at the crossroads as a righteous person without any offering, so long as his spirit were carried by the angels to Abraham's bosom' to be with Lazarus, than to be given a fine church burial if, despite the ministrations of the monks and friars, his soul were thereupon to lodge for eternity with Dives in hell. Tůma acknowledged the validity of 'just tithes ... for service,' but at the same time he denounced those Utraquist or Catholic priests who levied excessive tithes or demanded them on unoccupied or uncultivated ground.

[47]   Cf. Krofta, *Dĕjiny selského stavu*, pp. 143–50. Přeloučský, in using the simile of the limetree, is echoing Chelčický, *loc. cit.*

He was equally unsparing in his denunciations of secular lords who had fallen short in their role of protectors of their people. Šternberk, the nobleman to whom Tůma's letter was addressed, was told quite frankly: 'Under Your Grace, it is said, there are many grievances.' The princes, nobles and wealthy of the realm, instead of putting the major portion of their burdens on 'the poor people' in the form of additional taxation and compulsory enlistment for military service, were exhorted themselves to make enormous contributions in men and money for the defence of Christendom, 'for if ever there was a time since the beginning of the Christian faith when it was necessary to fight against the Turks, it is now.'[48]

In spite of Tůma's zeal for social justice, his genuine sympathy with the depressed peasantry whose status in society was steadily worsening, and his championship of their rights against the oppression of the landlords, his position is in fact more akin to Štitný's, for instance, than to that of the Unity's spiritual founder, Chelčický, who denounced alike war, social inequality and the whole framework of contemporary society. The underlying assumption throughout Tůma's treatise, on the other hand, is the recognition of class divisions and inequalities even within a Christian society; he demands merely that the lords should observe their agreements and fulfil their obligations, not requiring more of their tenants than custom and law had previously prescribed.[49] Like his contemporary, Lukáš, or the earlier Czech reformers or the Englishman, Wyclif, he accepts the existing order of society as compatible with Christian principles, wishing only to reform or eliminate the abuses that had grown up within it.

The basic acceptance of the existing society, so different from the passive dissent of Chelčický and the early Brethren, comes out especially clearly in the new Unity's whole attitude to the problem of poverty. The division into rich and poor is accepted as equally natural for a Christian society as for a non-Christian one. The poor of the Unity were counselled to show patience and contentment with their lot, not to be envious of their wealthier neighbours and to place their hopes in happiness in the next world, where 'the future life eternal in heaven is full of every delight without any kind of imperfection (*beze všech nedostatkův*).' They were not to expect assistance as a right from those better placed materially, but to show gratitude for any help given. On the other hand, they were not to 'become flatterers of the rich for the sake of what they could get out oɪ them,' but to 'serve them faithfully.' 'They were neither to seek to be

[48] Přeloučský, *op. cit.*, pp. 30, 31, 59–67.
[49] *Ibid.*, p. 39.

unjustly enriched ... nor to ask for, or take, anything not theirs ... nor were they to commit any sin on account of their distress.' They were, too, never to ask for assistance unless it was absolutely necessary and to make good use of what they did receive in alms, not frittering it away in wasteful expenditure. Instead, they were to be industrious and frugal, ready themselves to be of assistance to others.[50]

The more prosperous Brethren, likewise, had duties towards their fellow members who were less well situated. But almsgiving, not the transformation of society, was now the obligation of Unity members. Detailed instructions were laid down for those who were entrusted with the task of caring for the funds destined for distribution among the poor, and the requisite qualifications for such an office were enumerated. The almoners appointed for this purpose were to keep strict account of every transaction; 'no one may either receive or disburse on his own, but only by agreement' with his fellow almoners. 'One is to have the coffer, a second the key and a third the pen or register.' They were to 'visit the poor, the orphans, the widows, the sick and the indigent ... and having indicated what was needed, they were to distribute clothing, money or other material according to the advice of the elders.' 'At Easter and on St. John the Baptist's day the Brethren in each congregation are to be exhorted to give alms; and at a given time the almoners must render account to the elders.' Those unwilling to give as they should were to be referred to various scriptural texts on the subject and, if this still failed to move them, 'for such often a reminder of death and future judgement is helpful.' The miserly were to remember, too, that they were sinning against God in refusing assistance to those in need, since all wealth was only held on trust from on high.

More detailed advice followed concerning the actual method of distributing alms; and pains were taken to avoid any hint of condescension or of a patronizing or moralizing manner. The almoners were to be frank and sympathetic, realizing 'that what they were giving out was not theirs but the Lord's.' They were, therefore, to act as careful stewards, choosing as recipients of their charity only those who really deserved help. The Brethren who drew up these decrees were particularly concerned to put the distribution of relief, the succour of indigent members, on a systematic basis. Brethren, therefore, were admonished not to give indiscriminately and immoderately (*nerozšafně*) and to avoid acts of charity done solely with the aim of being taken for great benefactors of their fellows.[51]

[50]   *Dekrety*, pp. 100, 122.
[51]   *Ibid.*, pp. 121–23.

A separate decree was enacted regulating the conditions under which legacies might be left for the use of the poor. Such endowments were to be administered only by lay members, presumably since, if the priests were to take responsibility for this task, they might become too involved in mundane affairs. 'Whatever may be left privily for the poor (*tajně na chudé*) should be placed in the coffer of the whole province, unless there be some immediate case of crying need.' Should a legacy be left to a Unity priest, he was immediately to consult with the elders as to what was to be done with it.[52]

In their attitude to the problem of economic inequality, therefore, the Brethren had abandoned entirely their former social radicalism. The organization of charity which they worked out in such detail applied, understandably enough, primarily to members of their own congregations, since their feeling of group responsibility, or indeed their material possibilities, did not extend to the wider community. Nevertheless, in the methods they adopted for alleviating material distress, the Brethren may rightfully be considered among the pioneers of organized social relief, even if their horizons were still limited to the narrow circle of their co-religionists — while the wider vision of a classless society, which had appeared fitfully to Chelčický and the Old Brethren, had disappeared.

This vision was the creation of a thinker who had identified himself with the lowest strata of society; and it had been the peasantry and the urban proletariat who had filled the ranks of the early Unity and coloured its social thinking until the schism in the nineties. Thereafter, the well-to-do trader and shopkeeper, and to a lesser degree the landowner and the university-trained theologian, were to predominate, if not in numbers, then at least in influence.

A special series of decrees was indeed issued at the very beginning of the sixteenth century, regulating the business practices of those Brethren engaged in trade and manufacturing and attempting to define which occupations were permitted to members of the Unity.

Among those callings forbidden in the decrees were 'dicing, gaming, juggling, painting, prophesying, fortune-telling, witchcraft, usury, alchemy, pimping, prostitution, music.'[53] Painting seems to have been condemned on account of its close association with the decoration of Catholic or Utraquist churches, and secular music because of its connection in the villages with the kind of merrymaking frowned on by the Unity which, nevertheless, was a great patron of various forms of church

[52] *Ibid.*, p. 58.
[53] *Ibid.*, p. 128.

music.[54] The condemnation of the remaining occupations, with the exception of usury the denunciation of which was indeed common to all medieval theology,[55] was on purely moral grounds devoid of all social significance.

The list of allowed professions is more interesting. They include 'farming, fishing, agricultural and building crafts, the production of articles of food and drink and clothing and other necessaries ... which people cannot do without, ... when they are not accompanied by display, unrighteousness, adornment, luxury and injustice.'[56] The superiority of the agriculturalist and the simple craftsmen is still clearly emphasized; but the way is now left open to pursue other more lucrative occupations and for a gradual amelioration of the old suspicion towards the growing urban economy.

Honesty in trade, fair business practice, was the main content of the new Unity doctrine in this field. Avarice, the desire to enrich oneself at the expense of just dealing and the welfare of one's neighbours, was deprecated in the strongest terms. Avarice was defined as 'an uncontrolled and insatiable lust for wealth,' and 'avaricious desire is the root of all evil.' Its signs among those who carried on trade, commerce or industry were enumerated. First came 'the covetous acquisition of wealth with the omission of things needful for salvation, its immoderate increase, and excessive preoccupation with business.' Brethren must, secondly, not strive to add 'one trade to another, when one was sufficient for a living,' nor change from a useful occupation to one less beneficial to the community, unless there was no other alternative. Thirdly, they were to avoid 'the acquisition of possessions' if accompanied by 'scandal or hurt' to others or outbreaks of anger as a result of misfortune in business, which might easily lead to litigation and disputes. A fourth sign of an avaricious attitude lay in the practice of depreciating the value of goods in order to buy cheap, then inflating it in order to sell dear. The final 'medicine against avarice' for use against any of the Brethren who continued in such practices after all milder remedies had failed, was to be expulsion from the Unity as an example to show 'that we allow no place amongst us to such blatant evil.'[57]

[54] Müller-Bartoš, op. cit., p. 189.
[55] Cf. Lukáš in his Spis o mocy swĕta, fols. 42, 42v, and his somewhat older Utraquist contemporary, Koranda, in the tract O lichvĕ (printed in 1493). Krofta, 'O spisech Václava Korandy mladšího z Nové Plzně.' Listy filologické, 1912, XXXIV, pp. 228, 229.
[56] Dekrety, loc. cit.
[57] Ibid., pp. 124–26.

But even when both the desire for illicit gain and any tendency towards unfair practices were absent, Brethren must take care that they did not cause anyone material loss through carrying on their business, however legitimate in itself. In the same decree they were also reminded that:

They should not hold on to justly obtained wealth in miserly fashion, with hardness of heart and to the detriment ... of wife or children or those in need, ... nor were they to waste their wealth ... in riotous living, on luxurious or delicate or unnecessary foods and drink. The tightfisted were to attend to their own needs and those of their kin and to put aside for, and lend to, the poor.[58]

Articles produced by Unity craftsmen must be such as would serve the good of their fellow men. The 'just price' was to be observed; there was to be no falsification of weights and measures; and all products were to be of good quality (pravě dělána). In trade and handicrafts, 'avaricious and bodily desire and worldly vanity' arising from such occupations as tavern-keeping or the production of fashionable garments of immodest cut or pandering to 'gluttony, feasting, drunkenness and lechery,' were to be shunned altogether.[59]

Indeed, even after the schism the Unity for long retained much of its earlier suspicion of all forms of activity connected with the amusement and recreation of the people, associated as these usually were with drunkenness and coarse humour. Brethren were neither to attend country wakes (posvícení) nor to allow their households to do so nor to hold them themselves, explaining to their neighbours that such was not the custom of their sect. 'But if a Brother has a wife, who is not at one with him in her thinking, and she, wishing to invite friends [i.e. for such a purpose], will not hear of anything else, for the sake of peace he may give way to her, provided she conducts things decently; while he can, if he wants, keep out of the way himself.' Heavy drinking, feasting and carousing and luxurious living in general, attendance at popular entertainments and junketings were forbidden to members of the Unity. Fairs and markets were also to be avoided whenever possible, especially if held on a Sunday.[60]

But the existence of class distinctions even among the Brethren was here once again given official recognition. According to a decree of 1506 concerning 'measure in the taking of food and drink,' 'the requirements of one's class (potřeba stavu)' were among the factors which were to be taken into account in governing the standards of behaviour to be observed

[58] Ibid., p. 128.
[59] Ibid., pp. 126–28.
[60] Ibid., pp. 90, 96, 125, 129.

in this respect.[61] A nobleman or rich burgher, therefore, who was also a member of the Unity, was not now expected to conform to the same modest standard of living as his Brother from the peasantry or artisan class.

Innkeeping and brewing, which had been frowned upon in the days of the Old Brethren, were now given qualified approval. Indeed, this overt recognition by the Major Party of a banned occupation was, as has been seen, one of the counts made against their opponents by the leaders of the Minor Party. The former, it is true, only permitted it to Unity members if they had no other means of gaining a livelihood. They were to sell wholesale by the barrel rather than carry on retail trade; but this, too, was allowed 'to travellers in need' of refreshment or to their neighbours in their own homes, so long as they did not sell to them 'on tick (*na řad nedávali*)' or themselves become 'servants of drunkenness' or in any way give encouragement to evil and disorder.

After the schism the same type of qualified recognition was granted also to commerce in general. 'All commerce is dangerous [says the decree on the subject] it is better to be clear of it if one can find another way of earning a living,' especially when the articles traded were mainly luxury items. It was just from such forms of commerce that 'traders eat and drink and lodge well, living in idleness.'

But necessary and useful commerce which is the result of labour, although dangerous, is however more tolerable; ... in salt, for instance, or in iron or other necessities, which are not to be found locally in the province, but must be brought with effort and danger. Local trade ... which demands little or no effort is unsuitable. ... [Traders] are to be admonished not to seek excessive or quick returns in the acquisition of wealth, not to oppress the righteous, nor to buy falsely, to have correct (*spravedlivé*) weights and measures, not to lie nor take oaths, to shun drunkenness and other wickednesses while journeying, ... and suffer losses patiently and not inflict them on others on the way.[62]

Not only were traders and tradesmen given a recognized place within the Unity, but what would to-day be known as the intelligentsia was now also more numerously and securely represented in the ranks of the Brethren. Even after the schism, however, the Unity still continued to regard higher education with considerable suspicion, but university trained men were to come more and more to hold leading positions in it; the common notion, assiduously propagated by its enemies, that the Unity consisted entirely of semi-illiterate artisans or rustics was of course quite erroneous.

[61] *Ibid.*, p. 89.
[62] *Ibid.*, pp. 130, 131. The injunction not to swear was presumably given on the understanding that oaths were allowable within the conditions laid down elsewhere.

There was at first, however, little contact with the new humanism which was making its influence felt in the cultural life of the country. The intellectuals of the Unity such as Lukáš, for example, looked inside the Unity for the source and inspiration of their ideas. Certain humanist writers none the less, such as Řehoř Hrubý of Jelení [63] or M. Viktorín Kornel and later the great Erasmus, adopted a friendly position towards the Brethren; and in one respect, in their attitude towards the education of women, the latter were more advanced than most contemporary Czech humanists.

In the history of printing in the Czech lands, too, the Brethren played a notable part from the beginning of the sixteenth century. In 1503 the Unity set up its first printing press on Bohuš Kostka's estate at Litomyšl; and during the first quarter of the sixteenth century nearly a third of all the books printed in the Czech lands were produced at one or another Unity press.

Education at all levels remained on a strictly practical basis; the teaching of Latin, for instance, was not considered necessary either for the layman or candidates for the priesthood. Even Lukáš, though himself well acquainted with Latin and, through the various catechisms and hymn-books which he compiled, a great promotor of popular education, adopted on the whole a conservative position in regard to education, defending the Unity in the 1520's against Luther's chidings on account of the general ignorance shown by its priests of the Latin, Greek and Hebrew tongues. [64] The works of the church fathers and doctors, says one of the decrees for instance, though they might sometimes be read with profit, were not to be placed on a level with the Bible, which alone was to be the touchstone of all conduct. Care was to be taken, the decree went on somewhat smugly, especially with more recent writings such as those of Thomas Aquinas, to distinguish the true from the false in them. [65] But even so, the Unity had of course moved far from the original attitude of Chelčický and its founders or from the negative position still taken by the Minor Party.

Apart from a growing number of educated Brethren from the ranks of the nobility or the richer burgher families, the priesthood of the Unity formed its main intellectual class. The obligation encumbent on every priest of working with his hands still remained in force. 'Those who are active and strong [says one of the decrees] should undertake manual work

[63] For similarities of view between Hrubý and the Unity, see Hrejsa, *Dějiny křest'-anství v Československu*, IV, p. 182.

[64] Urbánek, *Jednota bratrská a vyšší vzdělání*, pp. 34–46.

[65] *Dekrety*, pp. 59, 60.

to avoid idleness and indifference or as a relaxation.' But this was to be done 'without detriment to their office'; manual work, therefore, was to be performed rather as an example to others than as the chief means of gaining a livelihood. Trade and the medical profession were altogether forbidden to Unity priests. They were not to accumulate money or possessions 'above their need': for all legitimate purposes these would be provided for them by their congregations.

They were in theory to continue to hold all things in common after the model of the primitive Christian community, as they had done from the foundation of the Unity, and to limit their needs to the bare necessities of life. In this way, unencumbered with the things of this world, they would be the more ready to suffer persecution and, if necessary, death itself. At first, too, priests of the Unity had been celibate, but in 1498 their marriage was expressly allowed. This had opened the way for a watering down of the old principle of community of goods among the clergy and of the strict observance among them of apostolic poverty. To the question: 'Should priests save money?' – a positive answer was now given.

If they can save anything from their earnings they may do so and, likewise, if they are left anything by friends. But single men, especially when any of them should have acquired money through service and faithful labour, are not to leave anything except to their helpers in the work among their fellow Brethren [i.e. fellow priests], unless they get permission to do otherwise.[66]

The acquisition of special community houses, containing under one roof rooms for religious services and for a training school for candidates for the priesthood as well as accomodation for the priest himself and his assistants, marked a further stage in the approximation of the life of the Unity priest to that of his Catholic and Utraquist counterparts. These houses were usually presented to the Unity by sympathetic landowners; the first of a number of such donations was made at Tovačov and Mladá Boleslav in 1496 by Adam of Cimburk.

The earlier Unity ideal of the wandering priest without any fixed habitation, moving round among the faithful and preaching the gospel to all who would hear, the ideal which the Minor Party still clung to, had given way to a more rigid church organization. In the rules for the priest's office, issued in 1501 under the title *Řád či agenda týkající se ordinování či řízení kněží bratrských*, it was laid down that a priest 'may not visit other provinces or congregations for the purpose of preaching or pastoral work

[66]   *Ibid.*, pp. 54, 56, 57, 100, 101; Goll-Krofta, *op. cit.*, pp. 189–91.

(*k zprávě*) without permission from the elders or the administrator (*zpráce*) of that province where his assistance may be needed.'[67] Nevertheless the unendowed, 'poor' priest still remained the Unity ideal even after the schism, when the severity of the rule of poverty was to some extent relaxed. As Lukáš wrote:

[God] has not attached property and maintenance to the offices of the Unity, so that in this way they should not be sought after and the devil worshipped in them; but He has given spiritual poverty, so that [priests] may take the scriptures as their guide, ... seeking not the glory of the world, but living humbly and patiently.[68]

In the decrees, then, the ordinary Brother or Sister might find for his or her use a detailed code of social behaviour. There were specific regulations for members of each section of the social hierarchy from noble and ruler to serf peasant. There were regulations, too, to instruct members how they should react to the various demands society might make on them. However, the Catholic historian, Gindely, was not far from the truth when he wrote of these decrees that in regard to their social teaching: 'Sie sagen am Ende gar nichts, was nicht schon längst die Kirche ihren Gläubigen gesagt hatte.'[69]

The new Unity no longer rejected the state power with its concomitants of lawcourts and oaths, punishments and wars; it no longer regarded the social order, with its class distinctions and division into rich and poor, as incompatible with the Christian faith; it no longer viewed the urban way of life, trade and commerce and book learning, with as deep a suspicion as before. Chelčický's vaguely communistic dream of a classless, non-violent federation of peasant communities had given place to a qualified acceptance of the existing structure of society, with the emphasis on the virtues of honest dealing and thrift in business relations, integrity and justice in public service, respect for the established authority, a charitable spirit towards the poor and the unfortunate, and simple piety in private life.[70] The century and a quarter which remained before the Unity's

---

[67]   Winter, *Život církevní v Čechách*, pp. 476–79; Goll-Krofta, *loc. cit.* In his *O obnovení*, fols. 122v, 123, Lukáš mentions the refusal by the Unity of an offer of a village for the Litomyšl congregation on the grounds that this would 'corrupt the church.' Goll-Krofta, *op. cit.*, p. 191, quoting this passage, dates the refusal to the period before the schism, when Jan Kostka was lord of Litomyšl.

[68]   'O obnovení,' fol. 123v.

[69]   Gindely, *Geschichte der Böhmischen Brüder*, I, p. 85.

[70]   Cf. Troeltsch's penetrating remarks about the two main divisions in Christian social thinking in ancient and medieval times: 'Christianity seems to influence social life in two ways: Either, on the one hand, it develops an idealistic anarchism and the communism of love, which combines radical indifference or hostility towards the rest of

suppression after the Battle of the White Mountain was to see the almost complete integration of its social ethos with that of the rest of the community.

---

the social order with the effort to actualize this ideal of love in a small group; or, on the other hand, it develops along social-conservative lines into an attitude of submission to God and His Will, so far as the world is concerned, combined with a strong independence of an organized community which manages its own affairs, which, as its range of influence increases, finds that it cannot ignore secular institutions, but that it must do its utmost to utilize them for its own purposes. The first ideal is the source of ever-renewed radical social plans for smaller or larger groups of people, while the second ideal produces the conservative principles of patience and suffering within the world, whose ordinances are permitted by God, whose possibilities Christians use for their own ends, and whose continuance they endure, because inwardly they are unaffected by them.' – *The Social Teaching of the Christian Churches*, I, p. 82. The schism in the Unity of Brethren was in fact an example of a transition taking place within a Christian community from the first way of thought to the second.

VIII

THE DECLINE OF THE OLD DOCTRINES

With its establishment at the beginning of the new century of a separate priestly order the Minor Party had broken once and for all with the victorious majority in the Unity. It continued to exist in obscurity for almost another half century, but it ceased to have any influence on the further evolution of the Unity or to play a significant role in the religious life of Bohemia and Moravia. With the final disappearance of the Minor Party in the middle of the sixteenth century, the social radicalism which the Unity had represented for almost half a century disappeared too from the political thinking of the Czech people. A few comparatively unimportant remnants of this earlier radicalism, however, lingered on in the theory and practice of the reformed Unity right up to its final suppression in the years immediately following the national disaster of the White Mountain. Thereafter, until the reawakening of national consciousness during the nineteenth century, the earlier political and social doctrines of the Unity of Czech Brethren, as well as the teachings of their spiritual founder, Petr Chelčický, were relegated to almost complete oblivion.

I

With Jakub's return to the Unity as a result of his unwillingness to see the schism brought to completion by a formal separation from the main body, the leadership of the Minor Party from 1500 onwards passed to the more resolute Amos, whose followers on that account were usually dubbed 'Amosites' by their opponents.[1] Very little is known, however, of the

---

[1] The Major Party, regarding the schism as due solely to the obstinacy and personal ambitions of their rivals, also frequently referred to the Minor Party as 'the schismatics (*odtrženci*).' For a reasoned defence of such a nomenclature, see Krasonický, 'Psaní proti Kalencowi o puowodu odtrženców,' fols. 356, 356v.

history of the Minor Party during this period, which lasted until Amos's death about 1522.[2]

Amos's decision to separate was probably precipitated by the election in 1500 of four new bishops of the Unity, all decided opponents of the old doctrines, to take the place of Matěj who had died at the beginning of that year. None of the Unity priests had joined the Minor Party; and it is not known in what manner Amos and several more of his followers received their ordination.[3] Likewise, the sources give no indication of the numerical strength of the Minor Party at any stage of its existence. It evidently had sympathizers scattered throughout Bohemia and Moravia; but apart from Prague it was only in south Bohemia, in the country around Prácheň and Klatov where religious radicalism had always been influential, the home country of Amos and Jakub, that the Minor Party seems to have been strongly represented. At first quite a number of enquiring spirits both within and outside the Unity may have been attracted towards the rebels by their uncompromising sincerity, as well as by their loyalty to the traditional principles of the Unity.[4] But, as the lack of information in the sources concerning any widespread activity on the part of the Minor Party would seem to indicate, its numbers, never large, must have decreased over the two following decades, until by the time of Amos's death the tiny sect showed little signs of life. Its temporary resuscitation by Jan Kalenec during the mid 1520's resulted from the efforts of one who was, indeed, new to the body.

The character of the Minor Party as a proletarian movement, as one of the last expressions in the Czech lands of the expiring tradition of social radicalism, is well brought out by Krasonický when he writes that it was the aim of its leaders to 'inveigle the common people into it in order to be ministers and teachers over them.'[5] With the exception of a certain Izaiáš *u pana Jastřebského*, 'a good Latin scholar,'[6] no member of the Minor Party appears to have possessed much education. This, indeed, comes out clearly in those of their polemical tracts which they composed without outside help.

[2]   Müller-Bartoš, *Dějiny Jednoty bratrské*, I, pp. 173, 270.
[3]   Lukáš, 'O obnovení,' fols. 100, 100v; *Odpis proti odtržencom*, fol. 49 (quoted in Goll-Krofta, *Chelčický a Jednota v XV. století*, pp. 205, 217). Hrejsa, *Dějiny křesťanství v Československu*, IV, p. 150, suggests that ordination may have been obtained either from Pavel, the former priest of the *Mikulášenci*, or from Cvilda. The four new bishops elected by the Major Party in 1500 were: Tůma Přeloučský, Ambrož Skutečský, Eliáš Chřenovický, and Lukáš.
[4]   Odložilík, 'Jednota bratří Habrovanských,' *Č. Č. H.*, 1923, XXIX, p. 12.
[5]   Krasonický, *op. cit.*, fol. 356v.
[6]   Urbánek, *Jednota bratrská a vyšší vzdělání*, p. 23.

At first the dissidents caused the Unity considerable trouble. According to Lukáš and Krasonický, in 1503 the leaders of the Minor Party wrote a private memorandum to King Vladislav, accusing their opponents of the Major Party of treasonable designs against the crown, and of having changed their doctrine concerning 'the exercise of the civil power with all its laws and punishments' expressly for this purpose. On hearing of this the king was said to have burst out angrily: 'So now they wish to act like Žižka (*žižkovati*); we will look to it that that does not come to pass.' Then, says Krasonický who gives most detail in his account of the incident, the king 'ordered all Brethren on his lands and on lands mortgaged to such nobles as [Krištof of] Švamberk to be burnt; and to the towns of his kingdom he wrote to order them to unseat [the Brethren] from office and expel them, and likewise he wrote to the Prague masters and to the Administrator to tell all their priests how [the Brethren] should be dealt with.' As a result of the renewed persecution, in November six Brethren were burnt by the Lord of Švamberk in his town of Bor (near Plzeň).[7]

The Unity, however, stoutly denied the least taint of disloyalty;[8] and the *Oratio excusatoria* which it sent to the king in the same year, though it did not deal specifically with the question of civil authority, was undoubtedly in part intended to refute any such suggestions.[9]

On the other hand, the account given by the Major Party, in face of the lack of evidence from any other source, cannot be accepted without reservation. It is probably true that the Minor Party presented some kind of document to the king, in which perhaps they pointed out the evils arising, in their opinion, from their opponents' abandonment of their previous negative attitude to civil authority. This information may have served to inflame the anger of the king against the hated 'Picards.' But that it was a case of conscious delation to the authorities, or the sole or even the main cause of the renewal of persecution against the Unity, is not proven.

A year later a second incident occurred which, though without immediately dangerous consequences, showed that, even in the minds of the

---

[7] Lukáš, *Spis o mocy swĕta*, fol. 57v; 'Odpowĕd na spis Kalencuo,' fols. 4, 15; Krasonický, *op. cit.*, fols. 359v, 360. Cf. Müller-Bartoš, *op. cit.*, pp. 205, 207, 208; Goll-Krofta, *op. cit.*, pp. 215, 216.

[8] Cf. Macek, *Husitské revoluční hnutí*, p. 175, who, in alluding to this incident, misinterprets the attitude of the two parties in the Unity to the nobility.

[9] Lukáš in his *Spis o mocy swĕta, loc. cit.*, writes: 'The Brethren, having ascertained that it was from the memorial [of the Minor Party] that their troubles arose, drew up a statement (*počet vydávajíce*) concerning the civil power as to what they hold and think on the basis of the holy scriptures.' It is not clear exactly to what document Lukáš is referring here. Cf. Müller-Bartoš, *op. cit.*, p. 211.

well-informed, the tenets of the two rival sections of the Unity, and the nature of the schism which had taken place, were not clearly comprehended. Jan Bechyňka, a famous Utraquist preacher and an ardent defender of his denomination against both Catholics and Brethren, sent a copy of the Report on the conference of Chlumec (1496) composed by the Minor Party to the Lady Krescencia Zmrzlíkova, a member of the Major Party in the Unity and one of its most powerful patrons, in order to convince her of the wickedness and errors of her sect. He describes the Report as 'their treatise written by their own hand against themselves,' and 'in reading it [he tells the Lady Krescencia] you will be able to discover what sort of people they are and what they are aiming at.'[10] Angry at the use made by an outsider of the charges brought against the Major Party by their opponents during the recent controversy, the Lady Krescencia herself sent a detailed reply to Bechyňka. Her answer, however, is not free from the probably wilful confusion which marked the priest's original letter. She first denied altogether the existence of any schism or even of any division of opinion within the Unity; and then went on to give roughly the same version of recent events as can be found in the other writings of the Major Party.[11]

After these two isolated incidents at the very beginning of the century the Minor Party virtually disappears from view, until in the early twenties Kalenec's activities gave it a new, if brief, lease of life. During the intervening period writers such as Lukáš devote little attention to the Minor Party or a refutation of its doctrines: a sure sign that it was no longer considered a menace to the security of the Unity or the maintenance among its members of a positive attitude to the state and the demands of contemporary society; and a clear indication also that after a few years the Minor Party must have fallen into a state of semi-inactivity.

After Amos's death the leadership passed to Kalenec, with whose name the revival of the Minor Party is associated, though once again the amount of information which has survived is scanty. Kalenec, a Prague cutler, had been born a member of the Utraquist church and at first was a follower of the prominent neo-Utraquist preacher, Jan Poduška, rector of the famous Týn Chruch in Prague and a great admirer of Luther. At some unspecified date he came into contact with the Unity, visiting their congregations at Brandýs and Boleslav, where he talked with Brother Lukáš. But his independent spirit was unable to find spiritual satisfaction amongst

[10] 'Psaní jakéhos kněze Jana Appolinařského,' *Časopis historický*, 1882, no. 2, pp. 61, 68. For Bechyňka, see Jireček, *Rukovět k dějinám literatury české*, I, pp. 54, 55.
[11] Akta Jednoty Bratrské, IV (Opis), fol. 351.

the Brethren – or possibly a sufficiently promising field for his desire for leadership. (Lukáš, indeed, afterwards rejoiced 'that such a one kept clear of us and the Unity.'[12]). Kalenec then returned to Prague where he found a ready welcome there among the tiny group which had remained faithful to the Minor Party. The leader of the sect, the aged Amos, bestowed priestly orders on him,[13] and shortly before his death, about 1522, appointed him his successor.

In 1524 the Prague group appears to have been quite active as a result of the new impetus given it by Kalenec. The meetings which it held *na Oujezdě*, and the fact that the number of its adherents was increasing, now came to the attention of the authorities, who took prompt action against the group. In December Kalenec was arrested, branded on the face and, after being publicly whipped, expelled from the capital. Thereafter he settled at Letovice in Moravia, where he established a small congregation made up of his former disciples and those newly converted. In the years 1526–27, as a result of a short-lived conservative Utraquist reaction under Havel Cahera, the Prague group appears to have been finally suppressed: three of Kalenec's followers, two women and a man, were condemned to be burnt for heretical views concerning the Lord's Supper, and others suffered lengthy imprisonment.[14]

The revival of the activities of the Minor Party brought with it a renewal of the controversy with the Unity on the civil power and on oaths, which had been carried on with so much bitterness during the 1490's. Many of the leading protagonists on each side were dead. But Lukáš, now an old man, was still there to champion the viewpoint which had prevailed among the Brethren; and he was assisted as before in this task by his contemporary Krasonický, who composed during this period a short tract against Kalenec. Of the leaders of the Minor Party all were either dead or no longer active; so that Kalenec, a man who – as Krasonický expressed it – had no personal knowledge of 'the origin of these schismatics,'[15] was left to defend the minority position alone. Personal antagonism, as well as fierce ideological differences, combined with the lack of restraint usual in most contemporary polemical literature to give

---

[12] 'Odpowěd na spis Kalencuo,' fol. lv, 2v.
[13] The other three priests of the Minor Party were: Amos himself, Cvilda who figures in the controversies of the 1490's, and Mikuláš Vřetanář who was burnt in Prague in 1526.
[14] 'Kronika pražská Bartoše Písaře,' pp. 208–19; 'Paměti o bouři pražské roku 1524,' pp. 339–42 in *Fontes rerum bohemicarum*, VI. Cf. Müller-Bartoš, *op. cit.*, pp. 270, 271; Hrejsa, *op. cit.*, IV, pp. 297–300; V, p. 7.
[15] Krasonický, *loc. cit.*

the controversy the same bitter and angry tone in which the earlier debate had been conducted.

Since the early years of the century Lukáš had written little on the subject of political and social theory. In 1512 he had composed a treatise against the Amosites entitled *Psaní proti těm, kteříž samými písmy bez zprávcuo neb kněží zpravovati se chtějí*, which he had circulated in manuscript. Now fearing perhaps that the increased activity of the Minor Party might undermine the allegiance of some of the Brethren or serve to discredit the Unity in the eyes of the outside world, Lukáš set about the revision of two earlier treatises on the subject of civil power and oaths, neither of them any longer extant: *O přísaze a stavích, řádích a potřebách rozličných*, dating right back to about 1493, and, secondly, his *Psaní bratrské o zřízeném spasení i o moci světské též i o přísaze i o poživání její*, originally written in 1500 and extended and revised in 1513. These labours resulted in a comprehensive work, which he completed by July 1522 and had published at the Unity press in Mladá Boleslav in February 1523 under the title *Spis o mocy světa*. The book gives a reasoned apology for the Unity's change of opinion and its new attitude to the state and its demands; and in the preface Lukáš directs his attack specifically against the Amosites, in particular against their new leader, Kalenec.[16] His object, he writes, was to show 'that we have not permitted anything to enter into our midst, which is against the Law of Love or the teachings of Christ, and that we have no intention of doing so,' to show, too, 'what is allowed by the Law of Love and how far, and what is not permissible.'[17]

Kalenec then answered Lukáš with what the latter calls, in the words of the title of the work which he in his turn composed in reply to Kalenec, 'a treatise which he has scurrilously and in a very unchristian manner, without any fear of God, filled with his unrighteous notions. In it [Lukáš goes on] he brazenly condemns all and sundry to damnation, especially the Brethren, and Lukáš in particular.'[18] But neither this treatise nor two others, which Lukáš says Kalenec composed on the same subject,[19] are now extant, though extracts are sometimes quoted by Lukáš in his works.

Lukáš, indeed, replied to Kalenec in two stages. First, a shorter work was published at the Unity's press at Litomyšl in July 1523 under Lukáš's own name; by the end of the year, however, he had completed a fuller rejoinder, which he issued at Mladá Boleslav in January 1524 under the

[16] Müller-Bartoš, *op. cit.*, pp. 275–77, 340.
[17] *Spis o mocy světa*, fol. 14v. Cf. *Odpis*, fol. 65v.
[18] 'Odpowěd na spis Kalencuo,' fols. 1, 1v.
[19] *Ibid.*, fol. 13v.

title *Odpis proti odtržencom*. This tract is divided into three sections. The first part consists of a detailed refutation of the arguments recently put forward by Kalenec; in the second, Lukáš goes on to give his own version of the events which led up to the schism, taking as a basis for his account the treatise he composed against the Amosites in 1521; and he ends with a section in which he prints a number of decrees (*zprávy*) on political and social issues taken from his own writings and the official declarations of the Unity. Before they came to any judgement as to the rights and wrongs of the case, Lukáš appealed to those who were acquainted only with Kalenec's version to read carefully first both his original treatise on the civil power and oaths as well as his present reply to Kalenec.[20]

Kalenec's expulsion from Prague in the following December seems to have temporarily brought the controversy to an end. Nearly three years later, however, shortly before his death, Lukáš delivered a last broadside against the Minor Party in his treatise on the origins of the Unity, composed sometime in 1527. It is in the form of an answer to an earlier work attributed by Lukáš to Amos, which was probably written about 1496 and circulated in manuscript by Kalenec after the latter's death. It appears to have reached Lukáš's knowledge only several years later. Amos's thesis was, briefly, 'that the most certain beginning of our gathering together was at Kroměříž with the priest Štěpan';[21] in other words, the birthplace of the Unity was in fact the south Bohemian province where the Minor Party was strongest, since it was here that the followers of Štěpan finally settled and here that they came into contact with Brother Řehoř in 1458-59.[22]

The first section of Lukáš's answer was devoted to a detailed refutation of the Minor Party's arguments and a bitter personal attack on Amos himself.[23] Lukáš writes of Amos's tract:

The schismatics puff themselves up by deriving themselves from [the Klatov Brethren] and by claiming that their lineage ... is ancient. In this way the writer of the tract tries to show that another body of Brethren, more sure in their origin, existed before Brother Řehoř ... [and that]

---

[20] *Odpis*, fol. 4v.
[21] A. J. B., IV, fols. 106–109v.
[22] For the wanderings of the followers of Štěpan and their settlement in Klatov, see Chap. II, p. 76. Lukáš's verdict (A. J. B., IV, fol. 111) that Amos's tract does not correspond in the main with historical truth is modified by Goll-Krofta, *op. cit.*, p. 58, who considers this unjustified. Amos's main error, according to Goll, was merely to overemphasize the importance of the Klatov Brethren's contribution to the Unity tradition.
[23] A. J. B., IV, fols. 110–113.

only some time later Brother Řehoř joined them in Klatov and united with them.[24]

Lukáš then went on to give his own version of the foundation of the Unity to prove that the true succession rested with the main body of Brethren.[25]

This second period of controversy between the two parties concerning their political and social doctrines brought little to the debate that was original. For this reason the theoretical content of its literature has already been dealt with in a previous chapter in combination with a discussion of the earlier polemical literature, the arguments of which it serves to elucidate and amplify. Neither side was now productive of new ideas.[26]

Lukáš still preserved his outwardly conciliatory attitude, maintaining that, throughout, his party 'had behaved in a fatherly fashion towards' their opponents, whom they were even willing to tolerate within the Unity provided they ceased their campaign of abuse.[27] But they had again revived all their old slanders, says Lukáš in 1521. 'Therefore he was writing to warn the faithful, so that they might recognize that these people are of the same spirit as their fathers, from whom these lies came.'[28] On the other hand Kalenec, on whom Amos's mantle had now fallen, denied, according to Lukáš, that anyone who disagreed with him on the subject of the civil power or oaths could attain salvation.[29] Lukáš, too, accused Kalenec of inconsistency both for following Chelčický in his view that civil power was permissible among pagans — Christ's prohibition

[24]   *Ibid.*, fol. 110.
[25]   *Ibid.*, fols. 113v–122v.
[26]   Cf. Krasonický's verdict in his 'Psaní proti Kalencowi,' fol. 357, as to the lack of originality in the arguments used by Kalenec. The same, however, might also be said about those of the Major Party. It is, indeed, difficult to do full justice to Kalenec, since so few fragments of his writings have come down in comparison with the copious works of his leading antagonists, Lukáš and Krasonický, to whom, moreover, we are indebted in their citations from the tracts of their adversary for what little of Kalenec's writings has survived from this period.
[27]   It is interesting to note that over 250 years later, during the American War of Independence (1775–1783), somewhat similar arguments were used by the so-called 'Free Quakers,' a small section of the Society of Friends who demanded tolerance for those accepting the right of self-defence and the duty of military service in defensive wars. But in this case the overwhelming majority of members held to the old rigorist viewpoint; and it was its opponents who were forced to leave the Society. After attempting to discredit their adversaries with accusations of disloyalty to the state the 'Free Quakers,' like the much earlier Minor Party, were to disappear within half a century. See Margaret E. Hirst, *The Quakers in Peace and War* (London, 1923), pp. 411–13.
[28]   A. J. B., IV., fol. 151; *Odpis*, fol. 3v; 'Odpowěd na spis Kalencuo,' fols. 2, 10, 10v.
[29]   'Odpowěd,' fol. 14.

being interpreted as extending only to his own followers, who might continue to live under the protection of pagan rulers so long as they themselves did not collaborate actively with the state — and for allowing the taking of oaths in spiritual matters unconnected with the machinery of state and administration.[30]

But at this date it was not so much the opinions that Kalenec put forward, which prompted Lukáš to reply with so much vigour and at such length. Although the latter with considerable exaggeration alleged that the views of the Minor Party, and the disturbances which ensued upon their propagation, were such 'as were never before heard of in Christendom,'[31] it was rather the use that might be made of Kalenec's attacks by the enemies of the Unity, eager to seize every opportunity to discredit it in the eyes of the authorities, public opinion and its own members, that provided the chief motive for him to take up his pen once again in defence of the Unity's new position. 'Certain prominent persons [he writes], both lay and clerical, enemies of the Brethren, have praised [Kalenec's tract] and made use of it against the Brethren, even wishing to get it printed.'[32] As far as is known, however, no work by a member of the Minor Party ever actually appeared in print.

After Kalenec's expulsion from Prague at the end of 1524 when he settled in Moravia, and the suppression of the tiny group in the capital in 1526-27, the Minor Party was apparently confined solely to the remnant which gathered round their leader in Letovice. But they and their attacks on the 'learned' persons whom they considered had corrupted the Unity were still considered important enough for Krasonický about 1530 to compose a special treatise, which goes by the name *O učených*, in order to prove that such 'learned' men had played a prominent part in the Unity from the beginning.[33]

The Letovice group, however, gave few signs of life until the early forties. In 1542 Kalenec issued an open letter, *Proti wšem*, written in

---

[30]   *Odpis*, fols. 5, 18, 41v. Lukáš, *ibid.*, fol. 21v, also counters Kalenec's attempt to find support in Luther's writings for his own views as to the impermissibility of Christian participation in warfare. Kalenec, writes Lukáš, had obviously never read Luther properly on this subject. If he had, he would probably 'inveigh more even against him than against me,' putting Luther in the same category as 'hangmen, murderers, bastards, false prophets, etc., and depriving him of every virtue as well as of salvation.' The reference to Kalenec's qualified approval of certain kinds of oaths is not at all clear, since elsewhere his rejection of oaths appears to be absolute.

[31]   *Spis o mocy swěta*, fol. 56v.

[32]   'Odpowěd,' fol. 2.

[33]   Krasonický, 'O učených,' fol. 2, 2v; Goll-Krofta, *op. cit.*, p. 58; Krofta, *O bratrském dějepisectví*, p. 28.

collaboration with Pavel of Hořice, one of his elders, defending the views of the Minor Party and fiercely attacking all who disagreed; and in the following year he composed a second letter, addressed this time to the leading figure in the Unity, Jan Augusta. Kalenec's attitude towards the civil authority, oaths and the administration of the law, towards all methods of punishment as well as all kinds of warfare, remained unchanged. He attacked, for instance, the Swiss reformer, Zwingli, and his followers for resorting to arms against the counsel of St. Paul that 'the weapons of our warfare are not carnal, but mighty through God to the pulling down of strongholds' [2 Cor. X, 4]. The antitrinitarianism, which from the outset found expression in such members of the Minor Party as Matouš the Weaver, had become by the forties a dominant motif in its doctrinal system, together with the continued espousal of the anarchist pacifist position of Chelčický and the Old Brethren.

Sometime during the first half of the 1540's, in spite of its extremely small membership, a split took place within the Minor Party as a result of disputes concerning 'unchristian professions and the use of costly stuffs and ornaments.' Kalenec now called himself 'senior of the Lesser Brethren of the Minor Party.' The last mention of Kalenec or either of the branches of the Minor Party occurs in 1546; and Kalenec himself must have died soon after this date.[34] Thereafter, the name of the Minor Party disappears from history. It had, indeed, been due largely to the energy and remarkable powers of leadership shown by Kalenec that the life of the expiring sect had been prolonged for another quarter of a century after Amos's death.[35]

Despite its small numbers and the fact that after the completion of the schism the Unity itself apparently remained impervious to all its rival's efforts to win over at least some of the Brethren to its point of view on political and social matters, the Minor Party was not without influence in this respect among several of the radical minority groups, which appeared in the Czech lands during the first half of the sixteenth century. In a rather ambiguous passage in the preface to his treatise on the civil power of 1523

[34] Müller, Geschichte der Böhmischen Brüder, II, pp. 100–02; Hrejsa, op. cit., V, pp. 97, 98; Odložilík, op. cit., pp. 14, 351–57.

[35] According to Odložilík, op. cit., p. 356, though Kalenec did not receive a good education in his youth, he was remarkably wellread in the theological literature of his time, and he was even acquainted with Greek. For another favourable estimate from a modern historian of Kalenec's character and achievements, see Hrejsa, op. cit., p. 98. Cf. Krasonický, 'Psaní proti Kalencowi,' fol. 357, who describes Kalenec as one possessed with 'over-much zeal without understanding (je příliš horlivý bez umění).' But Krasonický, unlike Lukáš, was not apparently acquainted with Kalenec personally; he shared to the full, however, Lukáš's dislike and contempt for thier less educated rival.

Lukáš speaks, indeed, of 'this doctrine concerning the [civil] power and the oath, which we as well once held, and many to this day from the Czech party [i.e. the Utraquists], both priests and laymen, still maintain, deriving it not from the writings of God's Law according to the true conception intended by the Holy Spirit, but from Petr Chelčický.'[36] It is not clear from the context to whom exactly he is referring: whether to specific individuals among the Utraquists, or to a vague general sentiment both within this church and outside as to the unchristian character of the state as an institution.[37]

There is, however, clear evidence concerning the contacts between the Minor Party during the period of Kalenec's leadership and at least two other religious sects with similar political and social tenets. In the case of the Moravian Anabaptists, on the main issues each side had already reached the same conclusions quite independently: there was, therefore, no question of one accepting its views from the other. But in the second and more important instance — the contacts of the Minor Party with the so-called Habrovany Brethren — the latter were definitely influenced in formulating their social creed by Kalenec's teachings.

The Moravian Anabaptists were recruited from the local German population as well as from Swiss exiles, who about 1526 found a refuge from persecution near Mikulova on the estates of two noble brothers, the Barons von Liechtenstein. The brothers had granted the Anabaptists religious freedom in their settlements. Owing to the great power wielded throughout the Czech lands by the nobility, the Liechtensteins were able to give the Anabaptists adequate protection against attempts at coercion, in the same way as the noble patrons of the Unity of Czech Brethren were able to do for their *protégés*; and in return they hoped to benefit from the economic ability for which the settlers were already renowned. The newcomers brought with them from Switzerland a number of radical religious and social doctrines. Among these the chief were adult baptism and anarchist pacifist beliefs akin to those of Chelčický, which they too may have in part derived from the Waldenses.

---

[36]   *Spis o mocy swĕta*, fol. 2v (quoted in Hrejsa, *op. cit.*, IV, p. 298).
[37]   Cf. the remarks of the young Catholic humanist, Bohuslav Hasištejnský of Lobkovice, writing in 1489, concerning the prevalent Utraquist attitude towards the death penalty: 'It is extremely rare for a criminal to be punished by death in this town [i.e. Prague]. For, at the instigation of their priests, they have become imbued with the conviction that it is wrong and contrary to God's law to kill a man, be he the greatest criminal.' – Hrejsa, *op. cit.*, IV, p. 87. But these scruples in regard to the death penalty, which were earlier entertained even by the Taborites, were not of course equivalent to a general objection to the civil power or to warfare, such as Chelčický had maintained.

But soon dissension broke out on this very subject. The followers of Balthasar Hubmaier, mainly native converts from Lutheranism and called the *Schwertler* on account of their positive attitude to Christian participation in the state and warfare, were pitted against the disciples of Hans Hut and Jacob Wiedeman, mostly exiles from Switzerland and the Tyrol and later known as the *Stäbler*, the staff symbolizing their rejection of the state and all forms of violence. Hubmaier and Hut soon disappeared from the scene but the division of opinion remained; and a third source of dissension, an innovation which soon came to be associated with the name of Jacob Hutter, now appeared in the form of communistic doctrines which found concrete expression in a series of *Brüderhöfe*, households of persons practising community of goods, living under strict moral discipline and, for the most part, abstaining at the same time from all participation in the state or the life of the society around them. In 1535, however, the year in which the chiliastic Anabaptists of Münster met their end, all the Moravian Anabaptists were expelled from the land. But the Hutterites at least gradually filtered back again during the next few years; and they were to remain on in Moravia until forced to emigrate once more as a result of the Catholic reaction which followed the Battle of the White Mountain.[38]

It was presumably with the non-resistant group of Anabaptists that Kalenec established contact sometime after settling in Moravia at the end of 1524. Kalenec himself was in favour not only of adult baptism but also of the communism of the *Brüderhöfe*. In a letter to them he writes: 'We rejoice at the fact that you have condemned infant baptism, baptising a second time in faith, and also that you have attained the equality of the First Kingdom, that is, of the Church, where none may say: this is mine.' But the attempts at a *rapprochement* appear to have broken down owing to the lukewarmness and exclusiveness of the Anabaptists.[39]

Both sides, as has been seen, had reached a similar position on such subjects as the state, war and oaths independently. In regard to adult baptism, however, and even more as regards community of goods, it was Kalenec who was probably indebted to the Anabaptists for his acceptance of these tenets. But it is interesting to note the possibility that the Anabaptists from their side may have been following the example of the Minor Party in their adoption of the stave as a symbol of their non-violent creed. In 1523, that is, several years even before the appearance of the Anabaptists in Moravia, Lukáš in one of his attacks on the Minor Party

[38] Smith, *The Story of the Mennonites*, pp. 49–63, 346, 367–70.
[39] Odložilík, *op. cit.*, p. 357.

writes of the latter as follows: 'I highly disapprove of these vain pharisees wandering around with staffs (*s holmi*), who display their righteousness, angrily and poisonously condemning other people and upsetting men's minds.'[40] The carrying of staffs instead of swords, therefore, was evidently a practice of the Minor Party at this period.

The influence of the Minor Party on another contemporary religious community, that of the Habrovany Brethren, was both more palpable and of greater extent. Founded in 1528 by a Moravian Utraquist nobleman, Jan Dubčanský, this sect was recruited from the native Czech population in the neighbourhood of its patron's estates at Habrovany and Lileč. Its theological doctrines were largely derived from those of the Swiss reformer, Zwingli, which were finding adherents at that period in the Czech lands. Its social creed however, which included the theoretical rejection of the civil power, oaths and war, seems to have come from a reading of the works of Chelčický and the Old Brethren, as well as from personal contact with Kalenec and his tiny group of disciples who had settled not far away.[41]

Neither of the two modern historians of the Habrovany Brethren have indicated which of the sects' leaders was responsible for introducing the element of social radicalism into its midst. It would seem most probable, indeed, that this was due to Václav of Lileč rather than to Dubčanský himself, who with Matěj Poustevník, an independent minded Utraquist preacher, formed a trio directing and inspiring the sect's activities and thought. Václav was a former rector of the Vilemov monastery;[42] and it was here that in 1521 the Minor Party had had Chelčický's *Sít' víry* printed, primarily for use as a weapon in their controversy with the Major Party in the Unity. Vilemov, moreover, was situated in the province of Prácheň, Amos's home country and the area where the Minor Party was strongest, and the monastery itself was under the latter's influence.[43] Václav, therefore, must already have been in close contact with the Minor Party, if not an actual sympathizer with its ideas, even before his collaboration with Dubčanský and his Brethren.

---

[40] 'Odpowěd na spis Kalencuo,' fol. 5. The habit of wearing a wooden sword, as practised by the Polish Brethren (Arians) during the period of their early social radicalism, was derived from direct contacts with the Moravian Anabaptists. But it is possible that Biernat of Lublin, one of the precursors of the Polish Brethren in their rejection of the death penalty, may have come under the influence of the Minor Party. See Kot, *Ideologja polityczna i społeczna Braci Polskich*, pp. 5–11,15, 19.

[41] Hanák, 'Bratří a starší z Hory lilecké,' *Č. M. M.*, 1929, LIII, pp. 11, 37, 38.

[42] Odložilik, *op. cit.*, p. 39.

[43] Tobolka, *Tisk Chelčického Síti víry z roku 1521*, pp. 7–10. Cf. Preface (*předmluva*) to Chelčický, *Sít' víry*, pp. 1–4.

Concerning the precise views held by the Habrovany Brethren on political and social matters there is indeed some confusion in the sources. No treatise on the subject emanating from their circle has come down; and it is probable that they never formulated their views in systematic fashion. Reliance has to be placed, therefore, on chance allusions in their other writings, mainly of a polemical nature, and in the works of their opponents. Furthermore, in practice Dubčanský, for instance, certainly did not observe the non-violent, anarchist position which his Brethren appear to have held in theory.[44]

After its foundation the sect soon entered into personal contact with Kalenec's group, but attempts at fusion broke down despite agreement on almost all points. The Habrovany Brethren were unwilling to accept Kalenec's condition of adult baptism, which also prevented them from coming to an understanding with the Anabaptists; and they disagreed too with his antitrinitarian views. From their side they put forward a demand for obedience, which seemingly Kalenec refused.[45] The two sects, however, continued to exist side by side without any violent polemics until 1542 when Kalenec and Pavel of Hořice issued a letter directed against the Habrovany Brethren, reproaching them for their approval on the basis of certain sayings of Christ and St. Paul of various harsh forms of punishment, and also for following their master, Zwingli, in giving a qualified support to war. According to Kalenec the Habrovany Brethren, 'as regards marriage, dress, occupations and offices are to some extent on an equality with [the Major Party] in not keeping to the rule of Christ.'[46] But, in view of the absence of direct evidence, it is difficult to judge how far Kalenec's accusations may have been exaggerated.

Differing views on the civil power, war and oaths certainly figured prominently in the controversy which broke out between the Habrovany Brethren and the Major Party in the Unity after various attempts at reaching some kind of *rapprochement* had broken down.[47] Odložilík suggests that one of the reasons for Dubčanský's theoretical acceptance of

---

[44] Odložilík, *op. cit.*, p. 344; Hanák, *op. cit.*, 1928, LII, pp. 115, 116. Odložilík considers that this inconsistency may have arisen from a division of opinion among the elders who controlled the sect; and he points at Matěj Poustevník as the chief exponent of the Minor Party viewpoint. For the reasons given above, it would seem more like, however, that this role was played by Václav of Lileč.

[45] Müller-Bartoš, *op. cit.*, p. 283.

[46] Odložilík, *op. cit.*, p. 357; Hanák, *op. cit.*, LII, pp. 61–63, 115, 116.

[47] For the contacts between the Habrovany Brethren and the Unity, see Müller-Bartoš, *op. cit.*, pp. 279–83; Müller, *op. cit.*, II, pp. 93–100. The Unity also engaged at this period in some fruitless negotiations for fusion with the Moravian Anabaptists, see Müller-Bartoš, *op. cit.*, pp. 283, 284.

the Minor Party's political and social doctrines may have been the use that could be made of them against the official Unity.[48] Undoubtedly it was their lack of success in trying to win over the Minor Party that had led the Habrovany Brethren to turn their attention to its opponents of the Major Party.

In 1531 the Habrovany Brethren issued an attack on the Unity, showing 'the deficiencies of the elder Brethren of the Major Party as well as their rudeness towards us' and attacking them, among other things, for their acceptance of office in the state and for approving the taking of oaths; and they developed their arguments in several further polemical treatises. The debate culminated in a meeting between representatives of both sides, held at Kyjov in February 1535.

In their discussion of political and social questions the Habrovany Brethren accused the Unity, in the first place, of dividing their community into two halves. To their clergy they forbade all participation in the activities of the state which, none the less, was permitted to laymen. The Habrovany Brethren, on the other hand, made no distinction between priest and laymen. Secondly, they argued, it was wrong for either as Christians to hold office, though here the Unity was able, with a reference to Dubčanský's example, to taunt them with inconsistency. The Unity was also able to indicate some confusion in the thinking of the Habrovany Brethren on this subject; for they appear to have agreed with the Unity that the civil power even in a Christian society could be ordained by God, and that he might look with favour on those who acted loyally towards him in fulfilling their official duties. Though from other passages quoted in Unity writings it would seem as if the Habrovany Brethren, disregarding the teaching of Zwingli on this point, condemned Christian participation in state activities altogether, the somewhat anomalous position of their leader and patron, Dubčanský, as the owner of landed property, and the executor of the law therefore in regard to his tenantry, may have led to such inconsistencies in defending their position. 'Your chief bishop and elder [the Brethren write of Dubčanský] being on oath ... administers the laws with an oath, and by their means quarrels and holds forth in a court of law (*k právom přísežným stavá soudem se skrze ně sváří a řečnuje*).' In the third place, the Habrovany Brethren apparently accepted – at least in theory – the Minor Party's interpretation of 'the higher righteousness' as a ban on every form of activity which involved killing and violence against a fellow human being or the taking of an oath; and the arguments, and sometimes the very wording, of their attacks on the Unity are

[48] Odložilík, *op. cit.*, p. 344.

strongly reminiscent of similar passages in the polemical writings of the Minor Party earlier on.[49]

The Habrovany Brethren existed as an organized sect for a much shorter time than the Minor Party. Their organization was seriously jeopardized by the arrest of Dubčanský in 1538. After his release from prison he lost most of his earlier energy and his sect began to disintegrate. It had been largely his special creation, and it was on his estate in Moravia that its members found refuge. Its fate, therefore, was bound up with that of its patron and protector. Another cause of decline lay in the fact that, despite Dubčanský's efforts to spread its principles, it never got firm root among the masses of the population. Its numbers always remained small and, with Dubčanský's death in 1543, it gradually died away.[50] The last mention of the existence of the Habrovany Brethren occurs in 1558, long after it had ceased to play a significant role in the religious life of the country.[51]

With the final disappearance of the Minor Party in the 1540's and of the Habrovany Brethren in the following decade, social radicalism, too, vanished almost entirely from the religious thought of the Czech people. It remained alive, indeed, among the Moravian Anabaptists, a group of largely alien origin living their own community life apart from the life of the people among whom they dwelt. It was through one or other branch of the Anabaptists that that socio-religious radicalism derived, which was to find expression, for instance, among the Polish Arians, and afterwards among such denominations as the Dutch Mennonites, the English Quakers and the German Dunkards, who still to some extent maintain these teachings to-day. But neither party among the Czech Brethren was to exercise any direct influence on their historical evolution.

In the course of the sixteenth century the Unity, having shed its earlier radicalism, did its best to remove all traces of such doctrines from its ideology. The Minor Party, on the other hand, was too small and obscure to exert any influence outside the very small circle of its adherents and sympathizers. It lacked the inner dynamic power and the depth of religious thought, which had enabled Řehoř and the Old Brethren to surmount all obstacles in the way of making the Unity a force to be reckoned with in the religious life of the country and, finally, a movement which has left its mark in the history of central Europe.

[49]   Odložilík, *op. cit.*, pp. 307, 343, 344; Hanák, *op. cit.*, LII, pp. 64, 72, 79, 346; LIII, p. 37.
[50]   Odložilík, *op. cit.*, pp. 346–51.
[51]   Müller, *op. cit.*, II, p. 100.

II

During the period between the death of the last Jagiellonian king at Mochács in 1526 and the opening of the Thirty Years War, which was to bring the suppression of both national independence and of the Protestant religion, the Czech lands were governed successively by five monarchs of the House of Habsburg. Though the rule of the great nobles, who preserved intact their power and privileges gained at the expense of crown, town and peasantry, continued as before, Ferdinand I, who had succeeded to the throne in 1526, began the process towards a stronger centralized government and closer ties between the various Habsburg dominions under his sway: a process which went on during the remainder of the period before the Battle of the White Mountain. From the beginning, too, Ferdinand's hereditary claims to the throne had been acknowledged by the diets of Moravia, Silesia and the Lusatias, despite the fact that the Bohemian Estates would only recognize him as king by election.

The first years of Habsburg rule in the Czech lands were marked by the ever present threat from the south-east of invasion by the Turks, who had already overrun most of Hungary, as well as by the spread from the west of Lutheran and Calvinist doctrines. During these years the Unity of Brethren was comparatively free from persecution, except for a period after the defeat of the league of Protestant Bohemian noblemen, who had joined together in 1547 during the War of Schmalkalden in defence of their liberties. Then the Brethren were made a scapegoat for the king's anger against the insurgents. While their leader, Jan Augusta, was kept in prison for some sixteen years, many Brethren were forced to go into exile in the following years. This migration led to the foundation of the Unity's branch in Poland, where most of the emigrants eventually settled.

In the second half of the century two events – the Peace of Augsburg of 1555, which established peace in Germany between Protestant and Catholic on the principle *cuius regio, eius religio*, and the Counter Reformation, initiated by the Council of Trent and carried out largely through the instrumentality of the Jesuits, whom Ferdinand I had invited to Prague in 1556 – in great measure moulded the course of history in the Czech lands as in the other Habsburg dominions in central Europe. Czech Protestantism, however, was to be greatly strengthened by the promulgation in 1575 of the Czech Confession (*Confessio Bohemica*), representing a compromise between Calvinist, Lutheran and Unity doctrines. It guaranteed full freedom of worship to all Protestants and set up fifteen *Defensores* to watch over their interests. Towards the end of the century the old conservative Utraquist party merged imperceptibly with the Catholic Church; while the main body of Utraquists came to form in effect a Lutheran denomination. Though the Unity grew close in doctrine to the Calvinists, it retained its separate identity to the end. The battle waged between the two greatest figures in the history of the Brethren in the period after Lukáš's death, Jan Augusta, the supporter of fusion with the general body of Protestants, and Jan Blahoslav, the advocate of continued separation, was won by the latter.

The gains achieved by the Protestants at the time of the Czech Confession were enshrined in the famous Letter of Majesty issued in 1609 by the Emperor Rudolf II in his capacity of King of Bohemia. The Letter of Majesty, and the subsequent Agreement drawn up between Protestants and Roman Catholics, guaranteed freedom of religion to all classes of the population. Each confession was given the right to build churches or schools wherever these did not already exist. It was, indeed, the infringements of the Letter of Majesty perpetrated by the royal officials that eventually led to the famous Defenestration of Prague on 23 May 1618, the subsequent deposition of the Habsburgs from the Bohemian throne, and the outbreak of war between Protestant and Catholic throughout the Empire. The defeat on 8 November 1620 at the Battle of the White Mountain of the combined forces of Frederick of the Palatinate, who had been chosen King of Bohemia in place of Ferdinand II, and of the Protestant Czechs spelled the end of the country's independence and religious freedom. With the suppression of all forms of Utraquism in 1627 by the returning Habsburgs and with the victory of the Counter Reformation, the Unity of Brethren was driven underground or into exile.

The character of the Brethren's community had, indeed, changed greatly during the last century and a quarter of its existence. By the end of the sixteenth century, although the royal decrees issued against the Unity had not in many cases been officially suspended, the Brethren had become a power in the land with many influential adherents among the great nobles and the landed gentry. In the cultural sphere their translation of the Scriptures known as the Kralice Bible, completed between 1579–93, was one of the greatest achievements of the golden age of Czech literature; and the successes in the field of educational theory and methods of the last and greatest figure in the Unity's history, Jan Amos Komenský, whose main work however was done during his long exile, brought him lasting international fame. At the time of its suppression the Unity had become a prosperous, cultured and highly respected and influential community, whose position was at last safeguarded in the laws of the land: a religious body far removed in spirit from the social radicalism of the period before Brother Lukáš and his friends had carried out the internal revolution of the 1490's.

After the schism the Brethren of the victorious party in the Unity had not been able, indeed had not wished, to reject at once all their former political and social doctrines. The process of elimination was a slow and gradual one; and the Battle of the White Mountain came before the evolution was completed. On the other hand, it is true that the internal revolution carried through at the end of the fifteenth century was a thorough one; and what survived from the earlier period was of secondary importance. The main pattern of thought had changed.

The death of Brother Lukáš in 1528 marked the end of an era in the history of the Unity. More than any other of its leaders he had been responsible for completing the revolution in social theory and practice which his older colleagues had initiated. This revolution had been successful. It had come at a time when the Unity was temporarily free from pressure from outside. As Lukáš remarked: 'If martyrdom had come at that time I do not know what would have happened to many' of the Brethren.[52] The quality of the leadership displayed by the Major Party, its intellectual level and comparative moderation, proved superior to that of its opponents, who made their main appeal to literalism in Biblical interpretation and the sentiment of tradition. Above all, it was the support of the new elements in the Unity, the town Brethren, the 'learned' Brethren and the noble sympathizers, as well as new conditions of life which affected almost the whole membership, that had enabled the Major Party to carry through its programme of changes.

But even after Lukáš's death, a certain tension continued to exist among the leaders of the Unity between those like Martin Škoda (d. 1532) for instance, on the one hand, who strove after the old native simplicity and, on the other, the younger men like Jan Roh who looked with more favour on the new tendencies emanating from the German Reformation. It was the latter group which soon gained predominance; and later, under the leadership of Augusta, the Brethren were for a time to draw very near to the Lutheran camp.[53]

With the support of Krasonický, the new generation of young Unity priests now sought to obtain for their calling a higher standard of education more in line with the times. Lukáš indeed, like the other apologists of the Unity before and after him, had always been ready

[52] O obnovení, fol. 101.
[53] Müller, op. cit., pp. 2–5.

during his lifetime to submit all his writings to the approval of the whole body before circulating them; and shortly after his death, at a synod held in April 1531, the Brethren ordained that his works, which included some written from a standpoint hostile to humanist education, were not to be regarded as binding on future generations. It was also decided at this synod, contrary to Lukáš's view, to recommend a more thorough training for those boys intending to enter the ministry.

But a few years later in the forties, both Augusta and Roh, disillusioned by what they had learned of the lax morality prevalent at the Lutheran universities in Germany, took up a more suspicious attitude towards education in general reminiscent of the Unity's earlier standpoint. Both men were self-educated, Augusta working in his father's trade as a hatter, while Roh was a linen-weaver; and their social background undoubtedly helped to form such an attitude. Writing in 1567 Blahoslav says of Augusta: 'Est enim ... bonus vir misomusos et aliorum studia contemnentium dux et fautor.' As early as 1532 Augusta himself in his anonymous dialogue *Rozmlauwanie gednoho muže učeného czest a rozkoš swěta wiece nežli boha milugijcyho, druhého neučeného ačkoli sedlského, wssak boha a spasenie znagicýho člověka*, the very title of which brings to mind something of the cult of the simple man of Brother Řehoř's day, makes his peasant say to the scholar: 'We are not shy of receiving wholesome teaching ... even from one who works with his hands. The Lord Jesus did not seek out wise and ... learned men to preach His holy word, but He chose for that purpose fishermen and other artisans without any book learning.'

It was Augusta's rival, Blahoslav, who in his writings during the first two decades of the second half of the century finally reconciled the Unity with the new humanism. This in turn led to a definite relaxation of the old tradition of simplicity, which had for long after the schism continued to carry weight among the Brethren—as is shown, for instance, by the frequent recurrence of testimonies to this effect in the obituaries of eminent Brethren given in Vavřinec Orlík's *Kniha úmrtí* (The Book of the Dead).[54]

Most of the social content originally associated with this tradition of simplicity had vanished at the beginning of the century. But certain traces still remained as part of the life of the Unity.

The obligation for its priests to engage in some form of manual work was perhaps the most striking of these survivals. Throughout the whole

[54] *Ibid.*, pp. 2–5, 8, 9, 78–81; Urbánek, *Jednota bratrská a vyšší vzdělání*, pp. 32, 35, 46–55.

of its existence the Unity never officially withdrew this demand, though in time it moderated the breadth of its application; and latterly the Brethren did not require their priests to live entirely from the proceeds of their work. From a full-time employment manual labour became for the priesthood a part-time occupation.

During the sixteenth century and the early decades of the seventeenth, there are frequent references to this practice. In 1531, for instance, Konrad z Krajku, an influential nobleman who had joined the Unity in the previous year, defending his action in allowing a furrier to preach in his church at Brandýs, explained that the Unity was only following the example of the apostles in requiring its priests to work with their hands for a living.[55] In 1542 in the *Listové děkana na Horách* it is laid down that 'a Brethren priest must work with the flail in the barn, with the scythe on the meadows or go out [i.e. to fish] in a boat on the pond, thus keeping himself by his own labour.'[56] In the following year Augusta, replying to the taunts of the Utraquist priests that he was only a hatter, stated proudly: 'Because I may be a poor man and an artisan of scant importance in the world, can I not still serve the Church of God and His saints? Is it indeed a sin to know a trade and work with one's hands, and not rather a virtue and worthy of praise with God and all sensible men?'[57]

In 1555 a Unity synod recommends that priests 'should with greater willingness turn from work on the land or in the vineyards to some craft.'[58] But now, even the practice of handicrafts was not demanded if a priest was occupied fully in tasks considered more essential; for, as the *Osvědčení bratři* of 1558 stated, 'a loving people should not allow this.' The tradition continued none the less, despite a relaxation of its obligatory character. As late as 1610 Jan Fridrich of Žerotín, a powerful noble member of the Unity, granted to any Unity priest assigned to a congregation situated within his lands and both capable and willing to carry on some handicraft, the right to do so without hindrance. This privilege shows that the custom had by no means died out even during the final period of the Unity's existence.

---

[55] Müller, *op. cit.*, p. 60.
[56] Winter, *Život církevní v Čechách*, pp. 484, 485.
[57] Müller, *op. cit.*, p. 9. But cf. Kalenec's criticisms, certainly exaggerated, of the Unity priests' way of life at this period: 'You lead a life of idleness like prelates and, being able to succour the more indigent from the surplus, you erect instead fine meeting houses and weigh down your ordinary Brethren with various contributions.' It was only the deacons who did any work, he claimed, the elders doing next to nothing. – Odložilík, *op. cit.*, p. 355.
[58] *Dekrety Jednoty bratrské*, p. 178.

The life of the priesthood remained to the end a humble and simple one. Even when a priest inherited money from friends or relatives, it was his superiors who decided how much he might keep for himself and what proportion must be devoted to the charitable undertakings of the Unity.[59]

At least during the fifteenth century manual work had been regarded as the major source of a priest's income. This was closely connected with the fact that the Unity of Brethren, at least as far as the Czech lands are concerned, never became an established church recognized as such by the authorities. The major Protestant bodies which emerged as a result of the Reformation, not differing in this respect from their Roman Catholic adversaries or the earlier Czech Utraquists, were soon adopted in places as the state religion enforceable on all the prince's subjects. The Unity, however, continued to stand for the separation of church and state and for religious tolerance, a point of view shared at that time only by the equally unpopular German Anabaptists and Polish Arians, as well as by a few other minor radical sects. As Augusta wrote in 1541 to Bucer in Strasbourg:

The civil power is insufficient and, indeed, not suited to build Christ's kingdom. Only our king, the lord of souls, can do this, not through civil authority but through the Holy Spirit and His word made manifest. ... Thus one ... cannot expect the renewal, perfecting and edification of His Christian church to come about through the exercise of civil authority. ... If our forefathers ... had not placed their hopes in this power of God in Christ, then the edification of our Unity in faith and in the pure truth to this very day would not have taken place. ... It seems to us that through such an exercise of force [i.e. in the field of religion, as Bucer in fact advocated] much more harm than good can come to the church.[60]

But in Poland, where the Brethren fled in large numbers in 1548 to escape from the fierce persecution of the Unity in their home country, their congregations settled on the estates of powerful noble protectors, mainly in the province of Great Poland around Poznań, came to approximate

---

[59] Winter, *loc. cit.* Unity priests were not permitted to become officials, doctors or traders (see *Dekrety*, p. 216). It is interesting to note, too, that the Polish Arians also adopted at first the custom of requiring their priests to carry on some kind of manual work, see Kot, *op. cit.*, pp. 20, 55. The presence in the Polish Commonwealth of groups of Czech Brethren from 1548 onwards may have influenced the Poles in this respect, in addition to their contacts with the Moravian Anabaptists. The Unity in Poland, however, was apparently more lax in enforcing the obligation of manual work on their priesthood. Łasicki in his *Historiae de origine et rebus gestis Fratrum Bohemorum liber octavus*, Chap. XVIII, 'De Fratrum laboribus manuariis,' p. 94, writes: 'Habent Ministri in Polonia fundos, quos vel ipsi sua cum familia excolunt, vel horum loco certam a Dominis agrorum seu pecuniam sue annonam, capiunt.'

[60] Müller, *op. cit.*, II, pp. 119, 120, 155.

more and more to a state church.[61] Although the Polish Protestant nobles denied the accusations of their opponents that they used compulsion towards their tenants in religious matters, yet there was undoubtedly some pressure exerted on the latter to accept membership. In the case of noblemen belonging to the Unity its church was often the only one allowed to be erected on the estate. Thus even the Brethren's testimony against the use of force in matters of religion was considerably watered down among at least certain sections of the Unity.

But the revolution in ideas which had taken place at the end of the fifteenth century was perhaps most apparent in the change of attitude among the Brethren in the sphere of social and economic distinctions in the community. Even here however the old ideas, as in other matters, were never entirely eradicated.

In the sixteenth century the Unity came to a compromise with the capitalist economic system, which was just beginning to arise and formed the environment in which many of the most influential Brethren, those settled in the towns, carried on their lives. Possessions, property, ownership, according to the new doctrines were, as Smolík notes, 'morally neutral'; and in this view the new Unity was, indeed, not far removed from the Old Brethren. Riches, it was still recognized, were a source of much temptation. The Brethren were always to be careful in their conduct of worldly affairs to see that they were not being motivated by a desire for personal gain. 'Is it from real and unavoidable need [asks the *Napomenutí učiněné všechnem věrným* of 1584] that they are carrying on so much business, or from avarice and greed, or perhaps in order to lead an easy and luxurious life and enjoy plenty in all things, lacking nothing?' To use wealth for God's glory, says Augusta for instance in his *Kázání o stavu manželském*, is not wrong.

But it is a sin [he goes one] neither to realize that this has been given to one from God, nor to thank God for it and give Him the praise, but to use it for sins forbidden by God ... and not be ready to comfort and help others with these gifts, keeping them for one's self, hiding them away and not using them or giving to others.[62]

In other words the mere acquisition of wealth, which had been frowned on, though never definitely forbidden, in the Unity of the fifteenth

---

[61] *Ibid.*, III, pp. 68, 69. The Polish branch of the Unity continued as a separate religious community until the end of the eighteenth century.

[62] Smolík, 'Sociální působení Jednoty bratrské,' *Theologia evangelica*, 1948, no. 2, pp. 92, 93.

century, was quite consistent with the Christian life. It was only its use that was still to some extent regulated and circumscribed.

Even the ban on usury was relaxed. In June 1540 during the synod held at Mladá Boleslav, a decree on the subject entitled *O lichvě soud bratrský*, was enacted, which expressly sanctioned in certain circumstances both the lending and borrowing of money at interest. There had previously been, it was said, innumerable discussions as to the rights and wrongs of usury 'until they were weary of it (*až do tesknosti*)'; and in practice the Unity had evidently permitted two categories of newly joined members to continue to deal in loans at interest until they could satisfactorily dispose of such business. There were, in the first place, certain noblemen part of whose estate was tied up in money invested at interest. The second category consisted of poor persons, whose only means of livelihood was the lending of money to the rich in need of ready cash. Such persons had been required, on joining the Unity, to sell up their businesses and buy land. 'But before this could be done, a long time might elapse in some cases.' These exemptions had resulted in confusion, as well as criticism from certain quarters 'that we have permitted usury to the Brethren.'

This in fact was exactly what the synod with their decree then proceeded to do. As a result of their examination of the scriptures the Brethren, it was stated, had come to the conclusion that 'God has both disallowed and, at the same time, permitted' usury. There were in principle three kinds of usurers. First, there were poor persons who borrowed at interest on account of their poverty. In this case it was those who exploited them that were the sinners, deserving the name of 'robbers and plunderers of the poor.' Those who indulged in usurious dealings unnecessarily in order to acquire wealth, motivated by 'unappeasable avarice and desire,' formed the second category mentioned in the decree. The crimes of such persons were depicted in the darkest colours and their activities condemned *in toto*. Persons of wealth with money to spare should not turn usurer, but instead help to set up in business 'poor working men, artisans and peasants, those who work to gain their bread.' Though to make such an investment without requiring interest was to be regarded as equivalent to 'loaning to God on interest,' nevertheless the taking of interest in such cases does not seem to have been definitely forbidden. On the whole, it was agreed, the best medicine against avarice and greed among the members was a good example set by the Unity priesthood. But there was still a third class of persons who lent money at interest: 'lonely widows and aged people, the sick and the halt and such others as are not fit to make a living by their own efforts.' The taking of interest by these persons was not forbidden, if they made their loans to the rich and not to needy artisans for whom repayment would only be a further burden and if, above all, they really had no other means of supporting themselves. Even then they were to realize, as a later decree of 1553 states, that they were 'not altogether without sin.'

As late as 1612, however, Brother Konečný in his *Kniha o povinnostech křesťanských* strongly criticizes the practice of usury, though he makes the now customary exceptions to the general rule.[63] In the contemporary Church Government, a book of discipline drawn up after the Letter of Majesty of 1609 and in 1616 presented to, and approved by, the general synod at Žeravice in Moravia, the wording is even more forcible: 'That they shun Unlawful and Suspicious wayes of seeking Subsistence, abstaining altogether from Usury, because of the Divine Threatenings, and the several Iniquities concurring therein.'[64]

Nevertheless, in general, so far as the daily life of the average Brethren of the sixteenth and early seventeenth centuries went, the biting words penned by Kalenec in the early 1540's, though undoubtedly exaggerated, were not without foundation. He writes:

You permit the carrying on of various trades [i.e. previously forbidden]: usury and buying cheap and selling dear. Many of your Brethren, who could exist on a single craft, pursue freely several trades; moreover, they add one field to another, gardens, meadows and vineyards, and buy up one house after another and even village after village.[65]

The Brethren were still a closely knit community, sharing much in common and bound by a voluntarily accepted faith. But their fellowship had lost much of its former egalitarian character: it had become almost patriarchal in outlook. The Church Government referred to above, for instance, has a chapter treating 'of the Domestick Order of the People,' in which it is laid down 'that according as God has called every one, and placed them either Master or Mistress of a Family, or Son or Servant, so they should keep their own station in the fear of God.'[66] The relationship

[63] *Ibid.*, p. 94; *Dekrety*, pp. 160–62, 164, 174. Cf. Müller, *op. cit.*, II, p. 127.
[64] *Primitive Church Government in the Practice of the Reformed in Bohemia . . . with some Notes of John-Amos Comenius*, p. 41. For a reprint of the original Czech and Latin versions, see 'Řád církevní Jednoty bratří českých (Ratio disciplinae ordinisque ecclesiastici in unitate fratrum bohemorum)' in Komenský, *Veškeré spisy*, XVII (Brno, 1912), the introduction to which contains an account of the work's origin and a list of the various editions published. The English version is a somewhat free translation, first published in 1661.
[65] Odložilík, *op. cit.*, p. 354.
[66] *Primitive Church Government*, p. 40.

between employer and employee was to be one of mutual trust, free on either side from any taint of exploitation for personal profit. Journeymen and apprentices were to be treated by their masters as members of the family; a just wage was to be paid; and the religious life of the whole household was to be cared for. On the other hand, 'the journeyman who works with a pious employer [says the *Napomenutí* of 1584] should willingly suffer want and insufficiency in some things, so far as his bodily wants go,' rather than leave his master. Employers who were members of the Unity were not to entice apprentices away from other masters. A primitive form of labour exchange was even set up by the appointment of certain Brethren to act as officers (*bratří soudce*) responsible for arranging for the employment of apprentices belonging to the Unity. Otherwise, it was thought, there would be a danger of their drifting away from the Unity if they found work at such an impressionable age with an employer unsympathetic to its ideals. A similar scheme was operated for female servants with Sisters in the role of employment officers.

The organization of society was not conceived by the Brethren entirely in static terms. Change of employment, for instance, in order to avoid some kind of temptation or moral harm was permissible. But any tendency, such as had existed under the Old Brethren and had lingered on long after the schism, towards the idealization of the lowly and unlettered as against the educated and those in authority, of the country as against the town, had gone by the early years of the seventeenth century. Konečný writing in 1612 divided the various kinds of occupation into two groups: the one represented by those engaged in spiritual work, like the priesthood, or in the work of government or in the realm of learning or the law, and a lower group formed from those who gained a livelihood from more ordinary occupations.[67]

In the same way the moral obligation encumbent on Unity members to give alms freely, a survival from the early days of the old egalitarian ideology, was not now conceived in any way as an attempt to level out social differences. It was merely, as in the other branches of the Christian church, a medicine against avarice, an act of personal piety. It might even be a method of expiation for sins committed, a sop to set at rest the consciences of the rich and powerful, as comes out in the Advice in the *Napomenutí* of 1584; 'Lords should repay their riotous spending (*marnotratenství*) by almsgiving.' Such charity was naturally confined mainly to members of the same community, to the needy Brethren. But the Unity

[67]   Smolík, *op. cit.*, pp. 89–91.

gave a fine example by the way in which it cared for its own poor.[68]

The Church Government has some interesting instructions, which give a picture of the way in which charity was organized during the early years of the seventeenth century. In the section treating 'Of Alms' we read:

1. These the People bring as Voluntary Oblations into the Church Treasury, according as they are willing, for the Use of the Poor among the Faithful,
2. As this is free to every Man, when he pleases, so there used to be no joint Collections but on the days of Prayer, and Fasting, and the Holy Communion, and if any extraordinary Necessity fall out,
3. These used to be given out and distributed to the Poor, according to every ones Necessity, either by providing for some of them Food and Raiment in Hospitals, or by affording some Help to those who are worn by Age or Sickness.

The task of administering the funds collected in this way was allotted to a number of 'almoners,' described in the Church Government as:

Prudent Men, Conspicuous for Vertue and Fidelity, to whom is committed the Care of the Treasury, (into which any of the People put in, when and what they think fit, that the Left Hand may not know what the Right is doing,) that, when need requires, they may take Money out of it, record it in Books, and dispense it to the Poor, the Pastor in the mean time being acquainted therewith. For, as much as is possible for us, we prevent Beggary in any of ours, according to God's Command. It is their Office also to see to the Orphans, the Widows, the Sick, and those that are banished for the Gospel, that they be not destitute of all Help.[69]

Begging, says a decree of 1562, is forbidden to any members of the Unity. Every able-bodied Brother or Sister was expected to work or attend to household responsibilities. But if anyone, through no fault of his own, was in need of assistance, and the local congregation was unable to provide this, the elders were to have recourse to 'other more wealthy congregations.' But that the Unity felt no responsibility for the destitute outside its own community, that its social conscience had not developed widely enough to embrace society as a whole, comes out clearly in the

---

[68] *Ibid.*, pp. 96, 97.
[69] *Primitive Church Government*, pp. 5, 6, 36. Cf. *Dekrety*, p. 149, which shows that in 1534 the same principles concerning almsgiving were in operation. These date back in fact to the previous century. Kautsky in his *Communism in Central Europe in the Time of the Reformation*, p. 88, seems to be putting a rather forced interpretation on the words 'as much as is possible for us, we prevent beggary in any of ours (*aby se pokudž nejvýš možné žebroty nedopoustělo*)' when he writes: 'they now . . . went so far as to tolerate mendicity . . . hence there was no longer an unconditional obligation among the Brethren to help each other.'

same decree. 'On no account may letters [i.e. of recommendation] be given to strange beggars [it states] nor should ... pleas be made on their behalf in the congregations, for it is not fair on our part either to be generous at another's expense or to rob our own in order to hand it over to knaves from outside.'[70]

The early Unity's radical social ethic, therefore, had been replaced by a strict puritan moral code. In line with this, while indeed they advocated days of rest from labour, the Brethren remained rigidly opposed to the common sports and pastimes of the people. They continued to condemn all forms of dancing, card games, dicing, draughts, stage spectacles, country-wakes and other seemingly innocent recreations, in addition to the more clearly immoral varieties of human pleasure.[71] On the other hand, according to a decree of 1538 tavern-keeping and brewing, though frowned on as in earlier pronouncements, were no longer considered 'a sin in themselves.' Thus, provided such a trade was carried on without entailing drunkeness or immorality, it might be pursued by those Brethren who either had no other means of gaining a livelihood or were under compulsion from the authorities. Detailed regulations, partly incorporating the findings of previous decrees, were then laid down as to the manner in which such undertakings should be run so as not to conflict with the principles of the Unity.[72]

The Unity in theory still maintained its testimony in favour of simplicity of dress. But it is obvious from the repeated injunctions against finery and exaggerated modishness alone, that a continual struggle had to be kept up against the insidious effect which riches and position had upon many Brethren from the upper and middle classes.[73] According to the somewhat unreliable Kalenec, writing in the early 1540's: 'Brother Lukáš had been wont to exhort clothiers, dyers and tailors ... to repent of the vanity and wickedness of the world.' But now, he writes further on accusing the Brethren of indulging in showy apparel and sumptuous houses, 'your Sisters likewise according to your example wear costly robes laced with velvet, having underclothing of lawn variously embroidered ... and dresses decorated with silk of gold.'[74] But the leader of the Minor Party was in fact only echoing in his rather more colourful style part of the contents of a decree passed in 1538, which attacked the wearing

---

[70] *Dekrety*, pp. 215, 216.
[71] *Ibid.*, pp. 156, 158, 216, 236, 240, 241; Smolík, *op. cit.*, pp. 91, 92.
[72] *Dekrety*, pp. 156–58.
[73] Eg., *ibid.*, pp. 90, 98, 127, 156, 178, 240.
[74] Odložilík, *op. cit.*, pp. 354, 355.

of 'immodest apparel' in men and women and enumerated disapprovingly the various forms of finery then in fashion, particularly as regards female attire. It is obvious that such garments were by no means unknown among members of the Unity.[75] Indeed, in 1544 Augusta himself felt called on publicly to warn the young, especially, against this excessive luxury in dress styles which had become not uncommon even among the Brethren.[76]

The sumptuous way of living, against which Unity divines fulminated in vain and Unity synods composed angry decrees, was in fact the inevitable outcome of the compromise the Unity had reached with the contemporary world. It was part and parcel of the life of the nobility of the day, a class which had come to play such an important role within the Unity, and of the wealthy burghers who aped their manners and customs.

Already at the beginning of the sixteenth century members of several powerful families – Kostka of Postupice, Žerotín, Tovačovský of Cimburk, Krajíř z Krajku, for instance – had joined the Unity.[77] Though Lukáš in 1523 was still able to claim that there were then 'very few of the powerful and well-born' in the Unity,[78] the confession presented to the king in 1535 on behalf of the Unity was signed by 12 lords and 33 knights. Forty years later in 1575 a petition was sent to the Emperor, signed this time by 17 lords and 142 knights.[79] This gives some idea of the growth in numbers and influence of the nobility and gentry inside the Unity. Some of the most outstanding Brethren of the last years of the Unity's existence – Karel of Žerotín, for example, or Václav Budovec of Budov – were at the same time typical representatives of the Czech nobility and the spokesmen of their class in Bohemia or Moravia.[80]

Members of the nobility were still, indeed, subject to Unity discipline, which was not merely a dead letter but enforced in practice.[81] A decree of 1555, for instance, states: 'The subject of avaricious lords and their oppression of their tenantry was discussed ... They should be dealt with according to the findings of the Brethren; and, should they be unwilling to submit, disciplinary action must be taken against them.'[82] The Unity

[75] *Dekrety*, p. 156.
[76] Müller, *op. cit.*, II, p. 181.
[77] Müller-Bartoš, *op. cit.*, p. 198.
[78] 'Odpowĕd na spis Kalencuo,' fol. 6.
[79] Müller, *op. cit.*, II, pp. 71, 454, 481–85.
[80] Denis, *Fin de l'Indépendance Bohême*, I, p. 339, attributes the notable part played by the Unity in Czech political life in the sixteenth and early seventeenth centuries to its connection with the important section of the nobility which gave it their adherence.
[81] *Dekrety*, pp. 125, 238, 239.
[82] *Ibid.*, p. 178. Cf. Augusta's words of reprimand written in 1548 to Bohuš Kostka the

continued, too, to consider that the advantages of birth entailed equivalent obligations. When, therefore, it was found that 'many lords, on account of age or the lack of obedience among servants or because of debts or to avoid common burdens or because they had no heir, were anxious to sell their estates and lead a more comfortable life in the town, living off money invested at interest,' a synod of 1591, held at Lipník and composed of representatives from Poland as well as from Bohemia and Moravia, advised strongly against such a course of action. 'Lords should remain lords and on no account escape from their calling.'[83]

But even if in moral matters the Unity continued to the end to make severe demands on its members from the upper classes,[84] it must not be forgotten that in social doctrine it had long tolerated the different standards of life and conduct, which were entailed by its acknowledgement of social inequalities. Arising logically from this basic compromise with the existing state of society which came with the victory of the Major Party at the end of the fifteenth century, the Unity's attitude towards such manifestations of civil authority as courts of law and oathtaking and war, which had once been totally condemned as unchristian, showed a progressive accommodation to the ideas of the rest of the community.

Participation in the working of the law either as judge, legislator or executor, lawyer or litigant, was now considered as quite consistent with the calling of a Brother. Disputes between fellow members of the Unity which could easily arise especially in minor matters were, however, still to be settled if possible out of court. In the second decade of the seventeenth century the Church Government advises the Brethren 'that they be not hasty to go to law, but rather take up friendly the differences that fall out, either by the Eldership or chosen Arbiters.'[85] Lawyers were expected only to take on 'just cases,' according to a decree of 1572, which also expressly permitted the taking of lawyers' fees, 'provided it was not done with a

---

younger of Postupice, a member of the Unity, for his obedience to the king's orders to carry out punitory measures against the Brethren. In his letter Augusta refers to Christ's words concerning the difficulties in the way of a rich man entering into the kingdom of God [Mark X, 23–25]. – Müller, op. cit., II, p. 217.

[83] Dekrety, p. 246.

[84] Of Petr Vok of Rožmberk, a member of one of the most powerful and wealthy Czech noble families, who joined the Unity in 1582, largely through his wife's influence, Müller, op. cit., III, pp. 197–99, writes: 'War er für die Brüder ein schwieriges Kirchenmitglied, zumal auch sein nicht einwandfreies ausschweisendes Privatleben Differenzen mit den Brüdern hervorrief.' It is doubtful whether half a century earlier such a man could have long remained a member of the Unity.

[85] Primitive Church Governmet, p. 41. The original Czech makes it clear that recourse to a court of law was permissible, even among Brethren, if arbitration was refused. Cf. Dekrety, p. 156 (from 1538).

desire for gain and the oppression of the needy.'[86] In regard to oaths, by 1540 the complicated and hair-splitting differentiations and provisos which abound in the writings of Brother Lukáš and in the earlier decrees on the subject have already vanished. The permissibility of oaths is stated plainly; several biblical texts are quoted in support of this; a definition of an oath is then given; and false oaths and swearing in the name of any of God's creations are expressly forbidden. But there is now none of the hesitancy with which at first the Major Party approached the question.[87]

In regard to participation in warfare, the similar note of indecision disappeared perhaps even earlier than with oaths. A proof that by 1530 many Brethren were actively, and sometimes even voluntarily, participating in military service was the official publication by the Unity in that year of a book destined for Unity soldiers captured by the Turks, and instructing ɯǝɥʇ how they should behave during a long captivity. The book, probably the work of Brother Jan Roh, was written in the years immediately succeeding the defeat of the Hungarians at Mohács in 1526, when there was imminent danger of an invasion of the Czech lands. But its repeated reprinting shows that it continued to be regarded as the official doctrine of the Unity.[88]

If called upon to take part in defence against the Turks, the Brethren were to do so willingly; and if in the course of their duties they were forced to kill some of the enemy, they were to put aside all qualms. The Turks were crueller and more bloodthirsty than wild beasts, against whom it was the obligation of all to fight. To fall in battle for such a cause should be regarded by a Brother in the same light as to die from some illness.[89]

In 1559, when the subject of war came up during a conference of elders at Žeravice, the delegates were once again referred back to the Instructions of 1530 as providing Unity members with suitable advice on the proper line of behaviour in a war emergency. A promise was given, however, to issue some kind of supplement, which would be for the use of the pastors rather than the ordinary Brethren. At the same time, the assembled elders

[86] *Dekrety*, p. 239.
[87] *Ibid.*, pp. 162, 163.
[88] Müller, *op. cit.*, II, pp. 36, 37; Winter, *Kulturní obraz českých měst*, I, p. 343. Its full title was *Zprawa a naučenj křesťanům wěrným, gakby se w těchto časých nebez-pečných při spasenj božjm řjdíti zprawowati a w něm růsti měli: ano y při těžkostech nyněgssjch přicházegicých od násylj tureckého gak se mjti a zachowáwati magj.*
[89] Müller, *op. cit.*, pp. 37, 38. The Unity was rebuked by the Habrovany Brethren for issuing such instructions. But both sides in the controversy accused the other of participation in warlike expeditions. – Odložilík, *op. cit.* p. 344.

expatiated on the horrors of war and the moral and physical dangers to which soldiers were exposed on campaigns. War was, indeed, 'a scourge of God' with which Unity members were to avoid getting mixed up. But to die in defence of the faith or the fatherland was the duty of a true Christian, especially when the aggressor was the heathen Turk, with whom, it is added, only the pacifist Anabaptists were ready to make peace at any price. Therefore, the elders decree, the Brethren should be:

Most earnestly entreated to be ready ... with a clear conscience to suffer and die. ... If they are called up for the militia (*na veřejnost*), they should conduct themselves in all things obediently, submissively and humbly ... so that they be not reckoned as traitors or Anabaptists, who say: 'I don't know; let this Turk come if he must, etc.'[90]

The Unity, as Smolík has pointed out, during the century and a quarter after the schism never attempted, any more than it had done in the first half century of its existence, to work out in systematic fashion its political and social philosophy.[91] Nevertheless, this period saw an almost complete withdrawal from its former position. What remained survived by chance, not by design.

A certain tendency continued to extol, at least on paper, the virtues of simplicity in the things of the mind as well as in more mundane affairs such as dress, food, shelter and recreation. The duty encumbent on the able-bodied priests to engage, at least part-time, in some kind of manual work remained, too, as a relic of the Unity's proletarian origins. The stand which it never relinquished in favour of the separation of church and state was, indeed, a notable contribution to the history of religious toleration and freedom of thought. The privileges of wealth and rank, conceived as being held on trust from God, were never completely divorced in the eyes of the Brethren from the duties which these entailed; the unrestrained and unlimited acquisition of power and riches was condemned; and all members of the Unity continued to be subject to a strict moral discipline. In the face of God all men were equal; and the Unity never quite lost sight of this principle which had inspired so much of its earlier thought, even though the obligation of helping a neighbour in distress was now restricted for the most part to the distribution of charity within the narrow circle of the poorer Brethren. The idea of the Unity, of all Brethren of high and low degree, as one large family never ceased to have some reality. Even in their attitude to the law and the military, the two fields where compromise appears to have been most complete, the

[90]   *Dekrety*, p. 202.
[91]   Smolík, *op. cit.*, p. 88.

Brethren never came to accept without qualification the current outlook.

But true as it is that the process was never completed, the victory of the Major Party in the 1490's had none the less initiated a series of doctrinal changes which, both in theory as well as in their practical effect, were to alter entirely the social character of the Unity. The underlying truth of the words written by Anton Gindely a hundred years ago remains unchanged to-day, despite the subsequent researches of several generations of historians. In his classic history of the Unity he writes as follows of the transformation which the Unity underwent after the schism:

Aus den böhmischen Puritanern, ... die zu Peter von Chelčic mehr wie zu Hus hielten, die nach Paulinischer Lehrweise die Ehelosigkeit verzogon, keine Eide schworen, kein Amt verwalteten, keinen Luxus sich gestatteten, keinen Reichthum duldeten, nicht auf Zinsen liehen, den Kreig verabscheuten, waren ganz wohlhabende Kapitalisten, ganz ehrbare Ehemänner, ganz geschickte Gewerbsmänner, ganz anständige Bürgermeister und Geschworne, ganz tüchtige Generäle und Staatsmänner geworden.[92]

[92] Gindely, *Geschichte der Böhmischen Brüder*, II, p. 312.

CONCLUSIONS

The political and social doctrines of Chelčický and the early Czech Brethren represented the most radical position taken up during the Middle Ages towards the ever recurring problem of the relationship of the individual towards society in its organized form of the state. They were concerned, therefore, with questions which have lost none of their interest for our generation.

How far was the community entitled to use force to coerce its individual members? In what circumstances, on the other hand, were the citizens of a state justified in disobeying the authorities, and was such disobedience to be active or passive? Was not perhaps the ideal society the one which possessed no government at all, ruled by moral suasion alone? What was to be the proper relationship between church and state? Was the death penalty ever justified for serious crimes and, even more vital, might the Christian participate in warfare and bloodshed under certain conditions? And if these were in fact forbidden, how should he behave in the face of oppression and wrongdoing? What, too, was to be the right property relationship in a well-ordered society, and was there any place in it for class differences? Could equality be put into effect in the economic as well as in the political and social spheres? What place should be granted to superior talents or education? Did certain occupations possess a greater social value than others and was, for instance, an agricultural economy ethically superior to an urban one?

The body of Unity doctrine concerned to give an answer to questions such as these was, moreover, not merely the product of a single philosopher like, for instance, the daring political theories of Marsilius of Padua, created in isolation from the community, theories which had little practical effect on the daily lives of ordinary men and women. They were not destined either, as the social radicalism of the medieval church had been, only for a select few living a celibate and secluded life, without application for the rest of society or of purely theoretical validity for the ordinary citizen. The Czech Brethren, on the other hand, tried to live out, in the world as it then was, the political and social theories which they had accepted from their teacher, Chelčický. Their history for the first half century of their existence tells the story of this attempt; and the schism which arose in the 1490's is, indeed, so full of interest to-day just because it reflects the problems and difficulties which were encountered in the effort to bring the theories of the political philosopher into the realm of practical living.

Social radicalism of varying shades had found expression throughout the Middle Ages in a long series of sects leading up to the widespread activities of the Waldenses. But neither the Waldenses, nor their numerous predecessors, nor even the later Lollards in England, appear to have worked out their attitude to society in anything approaching the detail which Chelčický and the early Brethren lavished on the problem. In addition, the main sources for the former's life and thought are to be found in the reports of their opponents: other documentary evidence is extremely scanty, especially when contrasted with the numerous treatises touching on political and social problems which have been left by Chelčický and the early Brethren.

Hus and his predecessors and successors in the Czech reform movement, as well as the Taborites and the Adamites, were all concerned to some extent, too, with political and social questions. A large literature directed against various social abuses had resulted. But, apart from the brief chiliastic period, no serious attempt was made even in theory to remould the existing order so as to bring it more in line with the Christian gospel of justice and love. The aim was merely piecemeal reform, not a radical transformation of society.

For all his originality Chelčický, of course, did not arise as an isolated phenomenon in the history of political thought, without precursors or uninfluenced by his intellectual environment; nor was the social radicalism of the early Unity without close parallels elsewhere in succeeding centuries, despite the fact that it came to be disclaimed by a later generation of Brethren. While, therefore, from one point of view the appearance of Chelčický and the early Brethren marked the culminating point in the development of the social radicalism of the medieval sects, at the same time it ushers in the new social radicalism of the left-wing of the Protestant Reformation. Though the genetic connection is slight, the social thought of a number of post-Reformation sects presents many close parallels with that of the earlier Czech Brethren. In the German and Dutch speaking lands there were the Anabaptists and the Mennonites and their offshoots; in the Slav world there were the Polish Arians and, later, Tolstoy who in his turn influenced the Hindu Gandhi, as well as many Russian sectaries; in England there were the Quakers and several lesser Nonconformist bodies.

Two features have been characteristic of the social doctrines of almost all these sects. There is, in the first place, a strongly emphasized utopianism, a perfectionism which strives to realize in the present the maximum moral potentiality of which the human race is capable. Secondly, there is the Christian framework; the ultimate source of authority for the social teaching, as for the more purely theological, lies in the example of Christ and his apostles as portrayed in the New Testament.

In addition, the social origin of the majority of the sectaries has derived from the humbler sections of the community. They have mostly been, at least at the beginning, peasants and artisans and petty tradesmen; and this has been reflected in the character of their communities' social ideology. In every case this ideology has to some extent, therefore, been a gospel of revolt and protest, albeit passive, against the existing social order.

In the West historians of political and social ideas, in tracing back the origins of modern democracy or of contemporary movements like socialism and anarchism, have usually ignored the great contribution, which during the fifteenth century the Czech people made to their development in the form of the political and social doctrines of Chelčický and the Unity of Brethren. Nevertheless, the importance of these doctrines, as of the attempt to give them practical application in everyday life, reaches far beyond the borders of the Czech lands. They deserve, indeed, a fitting place in the history of European political thought.

APPENDIX

THE OLD DOCTRINES IN UNITY HISTORIOGRAPHY

The significance for the history of the Brethren's social radicalism, and of the schism which resulted in the 1490's, of the works of those historians of the second half of the sixteenth and of the seventeenth centuries who, whether members of the Unity or only friendly observers, dealt with the early period of the Unity's existence, does not lie so much in what they wrote but rather in what they omitted from their writings.

The controversy between the Major and Minor Parties within the Unity provided indeed the incentive for the Brethren's first efforts at history writing.[1] But the works which resulted from the pens of Lukáš and Krasonický or their opponents of the Minor Party, first-hand sources for the events related in the previous chapters and invaluable for this history as primary works, were produced in the heat of the struggle. With the possible exception, in so far as these dealt with the beginnings of the Brethren's history, of Krasonický's *O učených* or Lukáš's work on the origins of the Unity, they made little pretence to a cool historical narration or any attempt at a considered analysis of the events described.

Indeed, the whole spirit of contemporary historiography, as Krofta has pointed out, was coloured by the passion aroused by the controversies of the day, which were mainly of a religious nature; and this was nowhere more true than in the historical works written on the Unity throughout the period before its final suppression.[2] Nevertheless, the works produced after the death of those like Lukáš, Krasonický or Kalenec, who had actually taken a prominent part in the controversy over the Unity's political and social doctrines, could make greater claims to impartiality than anything written while the battle was on. On the other hand, while to the very end such works might still contain important details preserved

[1] Krofta, *O bratrském dějepisectví*, p. 24.
[2] *Ibid.*, p. 8.

in Unity circles by oral tradition, they naturally lacked the value of an eyewitness account possessed by the earlier writings.[3]

The most outstanding of the Unity historians was Jan Blahoslav (1523–1571), the man who contributed most towards, though he did not initiate or complete, the compilation of that great collection of documents relating to the history of the Brethren known as the Acts of the Unity of Brethren. He was also the author of two narratives which deal with the period of the early Brethren.

The first work, a treatise in Czech on the origins of the Unity of Brethren based largely on Krasonický's earlier work *O učených*, and to a lesser extent on writings by Lukáš as well as on various other original documents and on oral tradition, was composed early in Blahoslav's career between 1547 and 1551. It was destined for an unknown individual Brother and not for general circulation among Unity members. It contains little that throws light on the Unity's early social ideology, nor indeed was this subject closely connected with the main theme of the work.[4]

Even more striking, however, especially considering that Blahoslav had access to many of the original documents dating from the period which ended in the schism, is his neglect of the whole subject in a second work, also unpublished. The *Summa quaedam brevissima collecta ex variis scriptis Fratrum, qui falso Waldenses vel Piccardi vocantur, de eorundum Fratrum origine et actis* was written in 1556 with the object of defending the Unity against Flacius Illyricus's assertion that the Brethren were identical with the Waldenses. In his efforts to prove Flacius Illyricus wrong Blahoslav, indeed, goes too far when he writes of the founders of the Unity, who had previously been disciples of Rokycana, that: 'nulla fuerant commercia cum Waldensibus, immo ... vix quisquam Waldensium visus fuit. Nam illi latitabant iis temporibus dispersi per regiones istas circa Boemiam.' This playing down of Waldensian influence on the development of the Unity, while at the same time overemphasizing the part played by Rokycana and the Utraquists in bringing the Unity to

---

[3] Owing to the difficulties which prevented me from carrying out my research in Prague in person, and the practical necessity of restricting requests for microfilms to the more important sources, I have not had access to several works of later Unity historians which have remained in manuscript, such as for instance the bulky *Historia Fratrum*, which certainly makes passing reference to the early political and social doctrines and to the schism (see Šafařík, 'Br. Jana Blahoslava historie bratří českých,' *Č. Č. M.*, XXXVI, 1852, part I), or the writings of Brother Jafet. I have had, therefore, to rely here on references or extracts in secondary works.

[4] Odložilík, 'Bratra Jana Blahoslava Přerovského spis O původu Jednoty bratrské a řádu v ní,' *Věstník královské české společnosti náuk*, 1928, esp. pp. 1, 6–10; Yastrebov's article with similar title in *Č. Č. M.*, VIII, 1902, pp. 55, 61, 62.

birth, is also accompanied by the purposeful omission of Chelčický's powerful influence on the formation of the early Unity's thinking.[5]

Krofta, indeed, suggests that the reason why Blahoslav passed over in complete silence the epochmaking controversy between the Major and Minor parties and the events that led up to it, may have been his reluctance to dwell on internal differences in a work designed for circulation abroad.[6] This may in fact have been one of the considerations in Blahoslav's mind in treating in such a tendentious manner the early history of the Unity. But Goll is probably nearer the truth when he connects Blahoslav's attitude with the tendency to be found among all the historians of the Unity who followed him of ignoring the whole subject of the schism; and he goes on to find the reason for this in the revolution in the Unity's political and social doctrines at the end of the fifteenth century, which made it seem desirable to later generations to push the whole subject into the background. The rapid disappearance after this date of the traditions connected with the early Brethren's social ideology, with the result that these ideas were soon quite forgotten among almost all except a handful of scholars, was linked up with the victory of the Major Party and the complete elimination by the middle of the century of the Minor Party.[7]

The historical works of Blahoslav, unoriginal though they were as far as the history of the Unity in the fifteenth century is concerned, profoundly influenced the writings of later historians such as Camerarius, Łasicki, Jafet, Regenvolscius, and even Komenský.[8]

The first systematic history of the Unity did not come from the pen of a member, but was written by a sympathetic German Protestant scholar, Joachim Camerarius the elder (1500–74). Camerarius was a professor at Leipzig University, well known as a humanist and a follower of the theologian Melanchton. His work is based in part on original authorities

---

[5] Goll, *Quellen und Untersuchungen zur Geschichte der Böhmischen Brüder*, I, pp. 49, 53–56, 114–28; Palmov, *Cheshkie bratya v svoikh konfessiyakh*, I, p. 407. According to Blahoslav Jan Černý, his mentor, wrote that: 'Fratrum Unitas nomen Waldensium nolit agnoscere, ac veram originem Fratrum a Hussio, Rochezana, Lupaczio etc. debere deduci.' Černý in 1555 had also written to Flacius Illyricus to this effect. For another example of the current tendency on the part of the Brethren to seek their origins in the general Utraquist tradition rather than in Chelčický or the Waldenses, see the *Osvědčení Jednoty bratrské proti nářkům nestřídmým* of 1558, quoted in Winter, *Život církevní v Čechách*, I, p. 36.

[6] Krofta, *op. cit.*, p. 103.

[7] Goll-Krofta, *Chelčický a Jednota v XV. století*, pp. 59, 60. Cf. Kautsky, *Communism in Central Europe in the Time of the Reformation*, p. 88.

[8] Yastrebov, *op. cit.*, pp. 52–55, 62, 66, 67.

and, in treating of the early history of the Unity, he seeks to link up the Brethren with the remnants of the Taborites. Although he devotes considerable space to the early period of the Unity's history, he manages however to avoid making any mention of the old political and social doctrines or of the schism in the 1490's. His book was first published in Heidelberg in 1605, over thirty years after his death, in an edition brought out by his grandson. There was added, as an appendix to the volume, an essay written by Esrom Rüdinger in 1579 entitled *De Fratrum orthodoxorum in Bohemia et Moravia ecclesiolis narratiuncula.* This, however, is not in fact a complete history of the Unity in miniature, but rather an essay on its Hussite and Taborite origins.[9]

The next historian to deal comprehensively with the history of the Unity likewise came from outside its ranks. Jan Łasicki (1534–1602) was a Polish Protestant nobleman, who spent much of his life compiling a history of the Czech Brethren from their beginnings in the previous century. His first draft was considered unsatisfactory by the leading Brethren, though they had allowed him access to their archives for his research; and even his revised version, finished in 1599 three years before his death, has remained in manuscript, except for the eighth book, which Komenský printed at Leszno in 1649 with an introduction by himself as well as a summary of the whole together with certain selected passages from the other seven books. Without being able to consult the original manuscript it is impossible to speak with certainty concerning the whole work. But it is significant that neither in Komenský's summary of Books II and III, which dealt with the fifteenth and early sixteenth centuries, nor in the extracts from them which he published, is there any mention of the Brethren's early radicalism or of the schism.[10] If Łasicki did in fact treat of these subjects, Komenský evidently did not consider them important enough for insertion in the published work.

Like Łasicki Brother Jan Jafet (d. 1614) never lived to see any of his historical works appear in print. His writings are of a more distinctly polemical nature than those of the Pole, and were composed for the most part to defend the Unity against the attacks of the Counter Reformation. Perhaps for that reason, in order to be forearmed against any possible accusation of holding subversive opinions concerning the social and

---

[9] Camerarius, *Historica narratio de Fratrum orthodoxorum ecclesiis in Bohemia, Moravia et Polonia, passim.* See also Krofta, *op. cit.,* p. 171; Yastrebov, *op. cit.,* p. 62.
[10] Łasicki, *Johannis Lasitii, nobilis Poloni, historiae de origine et rebus gestis Fratrum Bohemorum liber octavus . . . Adduntur tamen reliquorum VII librorum argumenta et particularia quaedam excerpta . . .,* esp. pp. 176 ff. See also Krofta, *op. cit.,* pp. 173–76.

political order, Jafet in several of his works does deal, though somewhat perfunctorily and with a complete lack of sympathy or understanding, with the doctrines of the Old Brethren and their renunciation at the end of the fifteenth century. In his *Meč Goliášův* finished in 1607, for instance, he includes an account of the schism which he describes as having arisen 'because of the treatises of Petr Chelčický'; and, he writes, in the place of such erroneous notions the Unity henceforward acknowledged 'the right doctrine concerning the civil power (*dobrý smysl o vrchnosti světa*).' In another work, *Historie o původu Jednoty bratrské*, written in 1614 in answer to earlier attacks on the Unity from a Czech Jesuit, Václav Šturm, Jafet in passing again makes a few brief, but uncomplimentary references to Chelčický and the Minor Party.[11]

The triumph of the Counter Reformation throughout the Czech lands, which came as a result of the Battle of the White Mountain in 1620, did not immediately put an end to all interest in the past of the Unity. Concern for its history lived on among the Brethren who went into exile, as well as among their Polish co-religionists who, in spite of the many tribulations which the troubled middle years of the century brought them, continued to exist as an organized body.

The Polish branch of the Unity, the weakest in numbers and influence of the four main Protestant denominations in Poland, did not produce any important works dealing with the early history of their church. But a leading Polish Protestant historian and preacher, Andrzej Węgierski (1600–49), writing under the name of Adrianus Regenvolscius, produced a large volume devoted to the history of the church in the Slav countries. His book, which was published in 1652 in Utrecht after his death, contained a number of chapters devoted to the history of the Brethren. But in none does he touch on the subject of the Unity's political and social ideology or of the schism in the 1490's, thus following the example of most of the historians who preceded him.[12]

The story of the Czech branch of the Unity culminates in the many-sided activities of the greatest figure in its history. The life of Komenský indeed, the greater part of which was spent in exile after the seemingly complete destruction of the Unity in the land of its birth, belongs as much to the history of Western culture as to the more limited field of the annals

---

[11] Jireček, 'B. Jana Jafeta krátká zpráva o biskupích a starších Jednoty bratrské,' *Č. Č. M.* XXXV, 1861, pp. 144, 145; Goll-Krofta, *op. cit.*, pp. 236–47; Krofta, *op. cit.*, pp. 146–56.

[12] Regenvolscius, *Systema historico-chronologicum ecclesiarum slavonicarum per provincias varias*, esp. Book I, Chap. VIII, and Book II, Chap. VIII. Cf. Krofta, *op. cit.*, p. 176.

of the Brethren. Nevertheless Komenský was throughout his life profoundly interested in the history of his church and devoted to the task of preserving for posterity the record of its achievements. To Komenský, in addition, later historians are indebted for handing down the last surviving memories, dating back to the time of the Old Brethren, which the living tradition of the Unity still retained.

Komenský was at least in part responsible for two historical works on Unity history, which covered the early period. Both were largely based on such writers as Camerarius, Łasicki and Węgierski; and the later of the two, which was first published in Latin in Amsterdam in 1660 and dealt, like Węgierski's history, with the whole Slavonic church, omits all mention of the early Brethren's social radicalism and the whole controversy on this issue.[13] The earlier work, however, a record of the trials through which the Christian faith had had to pass in the Czech lands, does contain a passing reference to the old doctrines in the following passage:

In the year 1503 the most gentle King Wladislaus did again suffer himself to be transported against the brothers, insomuch that he gave order that they should be delivered to the Magistrates, imprisoned, and at pleasure afflicted. The causes of this were not only the open enemies raging against the little flocke according to their manner, but certain false brothers. For a certain question being propounded concerning the secular power, whether it were lawful for a Christian with a safe conscience to govern as a Magistrate, or to use the sword, or to give, or to exact Oaths, many were of the negative opinion as they are now in this Anabaptist age, but the greater part affirmed that it was lawfull. The discent [sic] did so greatly increase, that those of the negative opinion did separate themselves, and had by themselves a peculiar meeting at Prague, accusing the other that they did admit of the sword and propounded to defend themselves by outward force. This Calumny being greedily received and brought to the king's ears, was the reason that the king said, *What do they think do they think, to bring back Zisca again to us. We shall take a speedy course to suppresse this insolence.* The brothers hearing of it, did write a new Apology to the king, giving him an account of their faith, and removing from themselves the later accusations and the blasphemies attributed to the Piccardins.[14]

---

[13]   The Latin title of the work is *Ecclesiae slavonicae brevis historiola*, which was translated into English as 'A Short History of the Slavonian Church' and published in London in 1661 as the introductory section of *An Exhortation of the Churches of Bohemia to the Church of England*, which was dedicated to Charles II.

[14]   [Komenský], *The History of the Bohemian Persecution*, pp. 66, 67. This English translation was published in London in 1650. In the Latin original, first published three years earlier under the title *Historia persecutionum ecclesiae bohemicae*, this passage appears on pp. 78, 79. See also Krofta, *op. cit.*, pp 181–99.

The most striking fact about this passage, which is based on the story found in Lukáš and Krasonický,[15] is that, while it is true that Komenský does mention the existence of the schism, he gives no indication either here, or elsewhere in the same work, that the standpoint of the 'false brothers' had some fifteen years before been the acknowledged creed of the whole Unity. From his account it would seem as if the old doctrines were an innovation introduced into the Unity sometime after its foundation. It would appear as if, by Komenský's time, the realization had disappeared that for nearly forty years these doctrines had been an integral and very important part of the Unity's whole philosophy of life and, indeed, had had no more ardent champion than the Unity's founder, Brother Řehoř himself.

With Komenský's death in 1671 the long line of historians, who had written of the early history of the Brethren from the standpoint either of actual members or fairly close sympathizers of the Unity, came to an end. The thread of genuine research into the history of the Unity was not to be taken up again until the second quarter of the nineteenth century.

For almost all later historians, no longer eyewitnesses of the events described, the Unity of the period up to the death of Brother Matěj in 1500 was, to use the apt simile of Brother Vavřinec Orlík writing in the second half of the sixteenth century, 'like a child beginning to speak.'[16] The negative attitude which the Brethren then adopted towards the magistracy and the sword was regarded as evidence of its immaturity. Later writers tended to cover up as far as possible all traces of Chelčický's influence and the contacts with the Waldenses, endeavouring instead to link up the Unity with the general Hussite movement, with the official Utraquist church on the right and, on the left, with the more radical Taborites. In a remarkably short time the very memory of their early radicalism began to grow dim among the ordinary Brethren and was to be kept alive only among the scholars of the church, who themselves finally ceased to be aware of its proper significance.

It is not necessary to attribute deliberate bad faith to such men as Blahoslav, for instance, or Komenský. Nevertheless the desire to avoid giving prominence to, indeed the impulse to omit altogether, any discussion of ideas and theories long ago discarded, but liable to be regarded as subversive by the authorities, was undoubtedly one of the motives which, in its treatment of the problem, dominated the historiography of the Unity during the last century of its existence. Lukáš and Krasonický

[15] See Chap. VIII, p. 243.
[16] *Todtenbuch der Geistlichkeit der Böhmischen Brüder*, p. 220.

had been forced by the propaganda carried on by the Minor Party to devote considerable attention to the Unity's attitude to state and society. Freed from attacks from this quarter the Unity historians of subsequent generations felt no necessity to concern themselves with such problems.

NOTE ON SOURCES

The sources for a history of the political and social doctrines of the Unity of Czech Brethren in the fifteenth and early sixteenth centuries are scattered over a number of works in several different languages. The primary sources are mainly in Czech, supplemented by a few printed texts in Latin. Most of the secondary authorities are naturally in Czech too. But there are also a number of books or articles in German, as well as several in Russian, French, English and Polish, which throw some light on the subject.

The bibliography given below lists all the works bearing directly or indirectly on the history of the Brethren's political and social doctrines which I have used in this study. The object of this note is to deal only with the more important sources, both primary and secondary.

The doctrines of the Old Brethren, as has been seen, were largely taken over from the writings of Petr Chelčický. Though patient research over a century has succeeded in discovering comparatively little concerning the events of Chelčický's life, his written works, most of which have now been published in at least one edition, provide an abundant source for tracing his social and religious ideas. For the former his *Sít' víry* taken in conjunction with the earlier *O trojím lidu* are most useful, even though numerous scattered passages in his other works contain much, too, of interest and significance for his political and social philosophy.

The rediscovery of Chelčický as a writer and thinker during the second quarter of the nineteenth century, after two centuries of almost complete neglect, was an event of first-rate importance in the history of Czech literature and political thought. Scholars of the calibre of Palacký and Šafařík, Gindely and Goll, and later of Smetánka, Krofta, Urbánek, Bartoš and many other of their compatriots, as well as of the Russians Annenkov and Yastrebov, the Croat Jagić, the Germans Müller and Vogl, and the Frenchman Denis, have all made important contributions to our knowledge and understanding of this great Czech political thinker.

For nineteenth- and early twentieth-century Czechs, struggling to assert their nationhood, Chelčický was especially valued for the freshness and directness of his writing with its roots close to the life of the ordinary Czech people of his day, as well as for the proof it gave of the vitality and strength of the national culture at so early a date. On the other hand, in the writings of Russian scholars, whose interest in Chelčický was aroused during the 1890's, Chelčický was admired as a Slav, whose original though somewhat unorthodox genius was yet another example of the great cultural heritage of the Slav peoples.

Though as the present century advanced, Chelčický's social radicalism, and even more his outspoken pacifism, was not so much in accord with the mood of important sections of his nation, especially after the achievement of independence,[1] the interest of Czech scholars in his life and works continued unabated. But despite critical editions of individual works and numerous studies on particular aspects of his life and ideas, no definitive treatment of his philosophy taken as a whole has so far appeared. Knowledge of Chelčický outside Czechoslovakia, too, has remained extremely meagre.

Since the last war the changes in the political and economic structure of the country have brought with them equally far-reaching changes in the methods of writing history. In regard to Chelčický there seem at present to be two conflicting tendencies at work. The first attitude is that expressed, for instance, on the dust-cover of the modern Czech edition of *Sít' víry*, which attempts to present Chelčický almost in the light of a Marxist before Marx. On the other hand, the opposite view, that is, that Chelčický by his pacifism and attacks on the Taborites was, despite his demands for a radical change in the social order, in fact helping to bring about the victory of the forces of counter-revolution, has recently been voiced by a young Czech scholar, who backs his opinion with quotations from Gottwald's writings.[2] Nevertheless the figure of Chelčický, whether drawn as a precursor of Marxism or as an unconscious reactionary, will remain to be reckoned with by all serious students of the history of Czech culture in the fifteenth century.

Since the last war, too, there has been considerable interest in the social teachings of the Unity of Brethren among Czech Protestant historians and theologians. But, so far, the emphasis appears to have been put on the later period after the schism of the 1490's. The socially progressive

---

[1] See Pitter, *Chelcický, Tolstoi, Masaryk, passim.*
[2] Macek, *Husitské revoluční hnutí*, p. 181; *Tábor w husitském revolučním hnutí*, II, pp. 170–74. The first volume of the latter work was not accessible to me while writing.

features which remained in the later doctrines have been stressed; and the tendency has been to play down the fact that the victory of the Major Party meant in effect a basic compromise with the existing social order.

The sources for the political and social doctrines of the Old Brethren are, indeed, much more scanty than for those of Chelčický. Most information is to be found among the tracts and treatises in the two volumes of the Unity's Acts, which have been published by Bidlo with a lengthy and very informative introduction in the first volume. Most of the material, however, does not deal specifically with their social ideology, which is scattered among a number of separated passages.

With the outbreak of dissension in the 1490's the number of the primary sources which have survived increases. For the period of the schism these may be divided roughly into at least four categories. There is, in the first place, the polemical literature produced by the Major Party in the heat of the conflict before the end of the fifteenth century and, secondly, there come the less numerous products of their opponents of the Minor Party or its sympathizers. The works of neither party were intended for publication; and they have remained to this day for the most part in manuscript in the great collection of the Unity's Acts. The third group consists of those works which were composed in the sixteenth century, also of a strongly polemical nature but written less from the point of view of the immediate situation and with, therefore, a rather more considered approach. With the exception of Lukáš's *O obnovení* of 1510 they were all composed in connection with the outbreak of controversy between Major and Minor Parties in the twenties, and were mostly written either for publication or for circulation among a wider circle than the earlier cycle. They almost all come from the pen of Brother Lukáš, to whom, too, we are indebted for preserving lengthy extracts from the contemporary writings, now lost, of Amos and of Kalenec, his successor as leader of the Minor Party. But there are also two important manuscript treatises by Lukáš's friend, Krasonický, which belong in the same group.

In special categories of their own come two further works. Tůma Přeloučský's treatise, *Spis o původu Jednoty bratrské a o chudých lidech*, until recently in manuscript, throws an interesting light on the social thinking of the Unity at the outset of the sixteenth century. Even more important is the collection of Unity decrees published by Gindely nearly ninety years ago. For the period prior to 1531 they are unfortunately not arranged chronologically but somewhat arbitrarily according to subject. They form, however, an invaluable source for the state of the Unity as it emerged from the period of the schism, as well as for the later period of its history.

The most important epoch in the evolution of the political and social ideology of the Unity had undoubtedly been the years of schism. For this period it is the numerous writings of Brother Lukáš which give the most information. It is a pity, therefore, that in addition to the very decided bias common to all controversial literature of the period, which makes it not infrequently impossible to accept his statements at their face value, his works are written in a style remarkable mainly for its obscurity. This characteristic was commented on by Blahoslav.[3] Later Gindely, too, speaks of its 'Dunkelheit, der sich bis zur theilweisen Unverständlichkeit steigert. ... Man klagte allgemein über ihr schweres Verständniss';[4] and Goll remarks on the difficulties often to be met in determining the exact meaning of his narrative.[5]

After Lukáš's death, however, interest in their previous social radicalism rapidly declined among the Brethren. The reasons for this, and its significance for the history of the Unity in the sixteenth and seventeenth centuries, have already been discussed in an appendix.

It is true that the historiography of this period produced no work which adds more than a few minor details to our knowledge of the political and social ideology of the earlier period, and often omits any mention of it at all, or treats it in a very tendentious manner. Nevertheless it is primarily to the labours of the Brethren of the second half of the sixteenth century that we owe the existence of the Acts of the Unity of Brethren, which constitute the main source both for the history of its political and social doctrines, as well as for most other aspects of the Unity's history to the end of the sixteenth century.[6] Apart from the two volumes published by Bidlo, which cover the period of the Old Brethren, and Tůma Přelouč-ský's Spis o původu Jednoty, one of the manuscripts of which is included in the third volume of the Acts, it is the fourth volume which has proved most useful for the present work. This volume is mainly devoted to writings composed in connection with the schism in the 1490's; and includes works emanating from both sides in the controversy.

The titles of the individual items included are, for the most part, not

---

[3] Krofta, O bratrském dějepisectví, p. 26.
[4] Gindely, Geschichte der Böhmischen Brüder, I, p. 69.
[5] Goll-Krofta, Chelčický a Jednota v XV. století, p. 195.
[6] For the character, origins and subsequent history of the Acts, see Bidlo's introduction to Akty Jednoty bratrské, I, pp. 8–29. See also Müller, Geschichte der Böhmischen Brüder, I, pp. 578–604, which includes a list arranged chronologically of all items in the Acts written during the period up to 1528.

those used by the actual writers: they have been added later either by the sixteenth-century Brethren scribes who recopied the Acts or by modern historians. Their contents, too, are copies of the originals which date in some cases to a century earlier or even copies of copies. Nevertheless, the fact that they reproduce faithfully opinions and doctrines long since regarded as anathema by the Unity has inclined modern historians to accept them as trustworthy from the historical point of view, though it is obvious that spelling and certain grammatical forms have to some extent been adapted to the current usage of the mid-sixteenth century.[7]

After Lukáš's death in 1528, and the final disappearance of the Minor Party within a couple of decades, interest declined in the political and social doctrines of the Old Brethren and the controversy which raged around them. With the Battle of the White Mountain (1620), and Komenský's death some fifty years later, the very memory of the Czech Brethren grew dim in their home country. Abroad it was kept alive among the small group of their Polish co-religionists and an ever lessening number of religious exiles, until in the eighteenth century interest revived after the foundation in Germany of the church of the Moravian Brethren, which claimed spiritual descent from the earlier Unity. But the historical works on the history of the Czech Brethren which resulted, either from the pens of members of the Moravian Church or from sympathizers in the German Pietist movement, are now completely superseded.[8] It was not, indeed, until the rediscovery, beginning in the 1830's and 1840's, of the Czech sources for the history of the Unity that studies based on serious research could be attempted.

Meanwhile in the Czech lands, as a result of the national revival which was already in full swing, increased interest was being taken at this time in the history of the Unity. It is to the Czech Protestant Palacký, the Slovak Šafařík and the German Catholic Gindely, writing roughly a century ago and making use for the first time of a number of forgotten Czech sources, that we are indebted for the beginnings of modern research in the field of Unity history. Even Gindely who, of the three, devoted most attention to the history of the Unity has, however, now been superseded in many details as well as in his general approach, especially where he is dealing with the earlier period. But his work, together with that of Palacký and of

---

[7] Müller-Bartoš, *Dějiny Jednoty bratrské*, I, p. 354. The original manuscript of the Acts was kept at Herrnhut in Saxony. In the second half of the nineteenth century a very reliable transcript was made for the use of scholars in Prague, which was deposited in the Zemský Archiv, see Palmov, *Cheshkie bratya v svoikh konfessiyakh*, II, p. I.
[8] For a brief account of these works, see Müller-Bartoš, *op. cit.*, pp. III–VI.

Šafařík, whose researches were left at his death in an unfinished state, has remained the starting point for all subsequent study.

The century which has elapsed since they produced their main works has seen the creation of an extensive literature of varying quality, dealing directly or indirectly with the origins and development of the Unity in all the stages of its history. It has seen, too, the publication of a number of original sources bearing on this history and the detailed examination of many more which have remained in manuscript. Studies of particular aspects of Unity history or of its leading personalities, as well as general histories embracing the whole period of its existence, have been written. Nevertheless, no systematic account has so far been given of the Unity's political and social doctrines during the period of its social radicalism.

Among secondary works, most information on this subject can be found in the writings of Jaroslav Goll, especially in his fine book on the Unity in the fifteenth century. In the chapter on the schism in the 1490's, an essay of only 35 pages, he gives the best account hitherto of the momentous events of this period, an account notable for the sympathy and understanding with which the standpoint of the Minor Party is treated, especially when contrasted with the verdicts of both earlier and later historians.[9] His book, too, must be reckoned as a primary source on account of the extensive extracts from some of the most important contemporary material, printed and unprinted, which are given in a number of appendices. Goll's book, however, only takes the story down to 1500.

Next in importance comes the first volume of the history of the Unity, covering the period to the death of Brother Lukáš, the fruits of a lifelong study by the German Moravian historian Müller. The work has been translated into Czech and edited by F. M. Bartoš; and it is this edition that I have chiefly used. While its treatment of the Old Brethren's social radicalism and of the schism is briefer and less sympathetic than Goll's, it incorporates the results of later research and carries the story on into the sixteenth century.

Other general works on Unity history which have been found of value include those by two Frenchmen, Denis who wrote in the last century and Tapié in this, as well as the many-volume history of the church in Czechoslovakia by the veteran Protestant historian, Hrejsa, which is especially useful for background material, and the standard histories of Czech literature by Jakubec and Vlček with their detailed bibliographical information. Krofta's study of Unity historiography, published after the

---

[9] See esp. Goll-Krofta, *op. cit.*, pp. 192, 193.

last war, provides a convenient introduction to the study of the primary sources as well as to the later historians of the sixteenth and seventeenth centuries. The Russian, Palmov, has also made a notable contribution to Unity history in his unfinished work on the confessions of the Brethren, which prints in full many of the primary sources. But his book bears less directly on their political and social doctrines.

A considerable number of other books and articles throw some light, directly or indirectly, on the history of the Unity's social ideology, though their main concern is with other aspects of its life and doctrines. Full details of these are given in the bibliography. But several should perhaps be mentioned here. The numerous articles by Bartoš, mainly on the origins and background from which the Unity sprang; the comparative study by Cedlová of the religious ideas of Chelčický and Brother Řehoř; the recent researches of Molnár into the life of Brother Lukáš and of Smolík into the Brethren's social ideology in the period after the schism; the two weighty tomes by Peschke on the Brethren's theology in the fifteenth century; Urbánek's brief but penetrating study of the Unity's attitude to higher education; the many volumes produced by Winter on the religious, cultural, social and economic background of fifteenth-century Bohemia and Moravia; the exhaustive studies of the Habrovany Brethren by Odložilík and Hanák; all these have something to say of value for the history of the Unity's political and social doctrines during the early period.

The main contribution in modern times to the study of the Unity of Brethren has come, as might be expected, from Czech and German scholars. But Russians, Frenchmen and Poles have also taken a share in revealing the Unity's past achievements. There has unfortunately been an almost complete absence of writers on the subject from either England or the United States, that is, from scholars using the English language. There are, of course, passing references to the Unity in general histories of the Czech people, such as those of Count Lützow or C. E. Maurice or, more recently, of R. W. Seton-Watson or S. Harrison Thomson, or in the chapters dealing with Bohemia in the *Cambridge Medieval* and *Modern Histories*. But only two books have been written within the last century which deal specifically with the story of the Unity: the bulky *History of the Unitas Fratrum* written in 1885 by Edmund de Schweinitz, a bishop of the American Moravians, and the slighter, but more readable *History of the Moravian Church*, covering also the revived church of the eighteenth century, by an English Moravian, J. E. Hutton. Neither writers knew the Czech language: their works, therefore, are now of little value to the serious historian, although they succeeded in filling a gap at the time. Both de Schweinitz and Hutton, who indeed are mainly concerned with the Unity's later history, give only scant attention to the early Brethren's political and social doctrines.[10]

These, therefore, have remained almost unknown in English-speaking countries, even to scholars dealing with the history of political thought during the period of transition from medieval to modern times. It has been my aim in the previous pages to attempt, however inadequately, to give some account of this important but neglected subject.

---

[10]   At least Hutton, p. 60, shows a clear realization of the epoch-making consequences of the schism for the future history of the Unity. 'We are [he writes] justified in regarding the year 1495 as a turning-point in the history of the Brethren. The revolution was thorough and complete.'

BIBLIOGRAPHY

(I) PRIMARY SOURCES *

(a) Manuscript

Akta Jednoty Bratrské: **
  Vol. IV, Zpráva větší strany o rozmlouvání v Chlumci (fols. 26–33v).
    Psaní bratra Matěje odtržencům (fols 41–42v).
    Druhý traktát Kubikův (fols 50–58).
    Listy větší a menší strany (fols 62–63v).
    List Blažka a Amosa Kubíkovi (fols. 63v–67).
    List odtrženců (fols. 67v, 68).
    Odpor smyslu druhému (fols. 73–75v).
    Odpověd na spis proti přísaze (fols 76v–85v).
    Vavřinca Krasonického Odpověd na spis proti přísaze (fols 86–95).
    Dodatek k odpovědi na spis proti přísaze (fols 96–103v).
    O původu Jednoty bratrské (fols. 105–122v).
    Psaní proti těm, kteří samými písmy bez zprávcův neb kněží zpravovati
      se chtějí (fols. 130–151).
    O přísaze (fols 154–160v).
  Vol. V, Vydán starším (fols. 260–263v).
    Výpis ve věci rýchnovské synody (fol. 315v).
    Rada o konšelství městském (fol. 331–333).
Akta Jednoty Bratrské (Opis Zemského Archivu v Praze):
  Vol. IV, První traktát Jakuba či Kubíka Štěkenského.
    Odpověd paní Krescencie Zmrzlíkové etc. daná knězi Janovi od svatého
      Appolinaříše na jeho psání k ní učiněné.
Brother Lukáš. Spis o obnoveni cýrkwe swaté; a duowodowé slaužicy k dowěrnosti
  že gest se w Gednotě bratrské konečně stalo učiněny od Bratra Lukasse starssjho
  w Gednotě zpráwce zboru Boleslawského muže mocného w slowu y w skutku,
  Letha páně 1510. [Pražská Universitní Knihovna, MS. XVII E 31]
Krasonický, Vavřinec. O učených. [Knihovna Národního Musea, MS. V F 41, fols.
  2–28]
——. Psaní proti Kalencowi o puowodu odtržencůw. [Knihovna Národního Musea,
  MS. V F 41, fols 356–361v]

---

* Secondary works given below which also include original documents are marked with an asterisk.

** At least until the end of the last war the unique manuscript of the Acts was kept in the Archiv der Brüderunität, Herrnhut (Saxony). I have had at my disposal a microfilm of portions of the original manuscript made for me in Prague by the Národní Museum and the Kabinet filologické dokumentace při Ústavu pro jazyk český Československé akademie věd from their own microfilm copies.

(b) Printed

Bartoš, F. M. (ed.) *Orationes, quibus Nicolaus de Pelhřimov, taboritarum episcopus, et Ulricus de Znojmo, orphanorum sacerdos, articulos de peccatis publicis puniendis et libertate verbi dei in concilio Basiliensi anno 1433 ineunte defenderunt*, Tábor, 1935.

Bidlo, Jaroslav (ed.). *Akty Jednoty bratrské*, Brno, vol. I, 1915; vol. II, 1923.

Blahoslav, Jan. *O původu Jednoty bratrské a řádu v ní* (ed. N. V. Yastrebov), St. Petersburg, 1902.

Camerarius, Joachimus. *Historica narratio de Fratrum orthodoxorum ecclesiis in Bohemia, Moravia et Polonia* (ed. Ludovicus Camerarius), Heidelberg, [1605].

Chelčický, Petr. *Menší spisy* (ed. Josef Karásek), Prague, vol. I, 1891; vol. II, 1892.

——. *O boji duchovním* (ed. Kamil Krofta), Prague, 1911.

——. *O trojím lidu* and *O církvi svaté* (ed. Rudolf Holinka), Prague, 1940.

——. *Postilla* (ed. Emil Smetánka), Prague, vol. I, 1900; vol. II, 1903.

——. *Replika proti Mikuláši Biskupci Táborskému* (ed. Y. S. Annenkov and I. V. Jagič), St. Petersburg, 1893.

——. 'Replika proti Rokycanovi' (ed. Karel Černý), *Listy filologické*, Prague, vol. XXV, 1898.

——. *Sít' víry* (ed. Smetánka), Prague, 1912.

Dobiáš, Josef (ed.). 'Psaní jakéhos kněze Jana Appolinařského učiněné a poslaně paní Krescencii Zmezlíkové na Vorlík,' *Časopis historický*, Pardubice, 1882, no. 2.

Fontes rerum bohemicarum. 'Vavřince z Březové kronika hustiská' (ed. Jaroslav Goll), Prague, vol. V, 1893.

——. 'Kronika pražská Bartoše Pisaře' and 'Paměti o bouři pražskě roku 1524' (ed. Josef V. Šimek), Prague, vol. VI, 1907.

Gindely, Anton (ed.). *Dekrety Jednoty bratrské*, Prague, 1865.

Goll, Jaroslav (ed.). 'Několiké prameny k náboženským dějinám v 15. století,' *Věstník královské české společnosti náuk*, Prague, 1895.

Jireček, Josef (ed.). 'B. Jana Jafeta krátká zpráva o biskupích a starších Jednoty bratrské,' *Č. Č. M.*, Prague, vol. XXXV, 1861.

Kabátník, Martin. *Cesta z Čech do Jerusalema a Kaira r. 1491–92* (ed. Justin V. Prášek), Prague, 1894.

Komenský, Jan Amos. *The History of the Bohemian Persecution from the Beginning of their Conversion to Christianity in the year 894 to the year 1632*, London, 1650.

——. *Primitive Church Government in the Practice of the Reformed in Bohemia*, London, 1703.

——. *A Short History of the Slavonian Church*, London, 1661.

Koranda, Václav. *Manualník* (ed. Josef Truchlář), Prague, 1888.

Łasicki, Jan. *Johannis Lasitii, nobilis Poloni, historiae de origine et rebus gestis Fratrum Bohemorum liber octavus ... Adduntur tamen reliquorum VII librorum argumenta et particularia quaedam excerpta*, [Leszno], 1649.

Brother Lukáš. *Odpis proti odtržencom genž se malau stránku nazywagí na spis wydaný pod gmenem Kalencowym proti spisu o mocy zřizene swěta wydanemu od Bratřij*, Mladá Boleslav, 1524. [Knihovna Narodního Musea, Knihopis 5025]

——. *Odpowěd na spis Kalencuo kteryž přiliss hanliwě a nekřestiansky swymi neprawymi smyssleenkami bez bazně božie naplnil: W němž wssecky napořad y odsuzuge na zatracenij smělе A to naywiecz Bratřie a Lukasse zegmeena Na něgž slussny odpis gemu zase čynij*, Litomyšl, 1523. [Knihovna Narodního Musea, Knihopis 5028]

——. *Spis tento genž gest počtu wydanij Nayprw o mocy swěta, o puowodu y o příčinách zřizenie gegieho y o prawdě gegie w nowém swědectwí, pokud a w čem zamezena ku poživaníj gest neb nenie Potom pak podobně též y o přísaze etc.*, Mladá Boleslav, 1523. [Knihovna Narodního Musea, Knihopis 5051]

Macek, Josef. *Ktož jsú boží bojovníci*: *Čtení o Táboře v husitském revolučním hnutí*, Prague, 1951.

Mansi, Johannes Dominicus (ed.) *Sacrorum conciliorum nova et amplissima collectio*, Venice, vol. XXIX, 1788; vol. XXX, 1792.

Orlík, Vavřinec. *Todtenbuch der Geistlichkeit der Böhmischen Brüder* (ed. J. Fiedler), Vienna, 1863.

Přeloučský, Tůma. *Spis o původu Jednoty bratrské a o chudých lidech* (ed. Vojtěch Sokol), Prague, 1947.

Regenvolscius, Adrianus. *Systema historico-chronologicum ecclesiarum slavonicarum per provincias varias*, Utrecht, 1652.

Rokycana, Jan. *Postilla* (ed. F. Šimek), Prague, vol. I, 1928; vol. II, 1929.

Wyclif, John. *De Christo et suo adversario Antichristo* (ed. Rudolf Buddensieg), Gotha, 1880.

——. *Dialogus sive speculum ecclesie militantis* (ed. Alfred W. Pollard), London, 1886.

——. *Sermones* (ed. Johann Loserth), London, vol. III, 1889.

——. *Tractatus de civili dominio*. London, vol. I, 1885 (ed. Reginald Lane Poole); vol. II, 1900 (ed. Johann Loserth).

——. *Trialogus cum supplemento Trialogi* (ed. Gotthard Lechler), Oxford, 1869.

(II) SECONDARY WORKS

(a) Articles

Adeney, Walter F. 'Waldenses,' *Encyclopaedia of Religion and Ethics* (ed. James Hastings), Edinburgh, vol. XII, 1921.

*Annenkov, Y. S. and Patera, Adolf. 'O nově nalezeném rukopise spisů Petra Chelčického,' *Č. Č. M.*, Prague, vol. LVI, 1882.

Bartoš, F. M. 'Chelčický a Rokycana,' *Listy filologické*, Prague, vol. XLVIII, 1922.

——. 'Chelčický a Valdenští,' *Jihočeský sborník historický*, Tábor, vol. XVI, 1947.

——. 'Kdo byl Petr Chelčický,' *J. S. H.*, Tábor, vol. XV, 1946.

——. 'Kněz Martin zv. z Krčína,' *Č. Č. M.*, Prague, vol. XCI, 1917.

——. 'K počátkům Petra Chelčického,' *Č.Č.M.*, Prague, vol. LXXXVIII, 1914.

——. 'Neznámá díla Jana Rokycany v musejních rukopisech,' *Č.Č.M.*, Prague, vol. XCIII, 1919.

——. 'Památce Petra Chelčického,' *J. S. H.*, Tábor, vol. XVI, 1947.

——. 'Valdenský biskup Štěpán z Basileje a jeho účast při vstavení Jednoty bratrské,' *Č.Č.M.*, Prague, vol. XC, 1916.

——. 'Z počátku Jednoty bratrské,' *Č.Č.M.*, Prague, vol. XCV, 1921.

Betts, R. R. 'Social and Constitutional Development in Bohemia in the Hussite Period,' *Past and Present*, Cambridge, no. 7, 1955.

——. 'Some Political Ideas of the Early Czech Reformers,' *The Slavonic and East European Review*, London, vol. XXXI, 1952.

Böhmer, H. 'Waldenser,' *Realencyklopädie für protestantische Theologie und Kirche* (ed. Albert Hauck – J. J. Herzog), Leipzig, vol. XX, 1908.

Cedlová, Marie. 'Náboženské názory Petra Chelčického a brata Řehoře i jejich vzájemný poměr,' *Č.Č.M.*, Prague, vol. CVI, 1932.

Chaloupecký, Václav. 'K dějinám Valdenských v Čechách před hnutím husitským,' *Č.Č.H.*, Prague, vol. XXI, 1925.

——. 'Štitný a Chelčický', *Č.M.M.*, Brno, 1914.

Dobiáš, F. M. 'Hodnocení lukášových zpráv kněžských,' *Křesťanská revue*, Prague, vol. XX, 1953.

Goll, Jaroslav. 'Petr Chelčický a jeho spisy,' *Vybrané spisy drobné*, Prague, vol. II, 1929.

Goll, Jaroslav. 'Rokycanova postilla,' *Č.Č.M.*, Prague, vol. LIII, 1879.

Hanák, Jan. 'Bratři a starší z Hory lilecké,' *Č.M.M.*, Brno, vol. LII, 1928; vol. LIII, 1929.

Harrison Thomson, S. 'Pre-Hussite Heresy in Bohemia,' *English Historical Review*, London, vol. XLVIII, 1933.

Herben, Jan. 'Klenovský-Paleček,' *Sborník historický*, Prague, vol. I, 1883.

Hoch, Karel. 'Husité a válka,' *Česká mysl*, Prague, vol. VIII, 1907.

Hrejsa, Ferdinand. 'Sborové Jednoty bratrské,' *Reformační sborník*, Prague, vol. V, 1935.

Jacob, E. F. 'The Bohemians at the Council of Basel, 1433,' *Prague Essays* (ed. R. W. Seton-Watson), Oxford, 1949.

Jireček, Josef. 'Mikulášenci,' *Č.Č.M.*, Prague, vol. L, 1876.

——. 'P. J. Šafaříka studie o Petru Chelčickém,' *Č.Č.M.*, Prague, vol. XLVIII, 1874.

Keller, Ludwig. 'Die Böhmischen Brüder und ihre Vorläufer,' *Monatshefte der Comenius-Gesellschaft*, Leipzig, vol. III, 1894.

Krofta, Kamil. 'Bohemia in the Fifteenth Century,' *Cambridge Medieval History*, Cambridge, vol. VIII, 1936.

——. 'Kněz Jan Protiva z Nové Vsi a Chelčického 'Mistr Protiva',' *Č.Č.M.*, Prague, vol. LXXIV, 1900.

——. 'N. V. Jastrebova Studie o Petru Chelčickém a jehe době,' *Č.Č.H.*, Prague, vol. XV, 1909.

——. 'O spisech Václava Korandy mladšího z Nové Plzně,' *Listy filologické*, Prague, vol. XXXIX, 1912.

Kulbakin, S. 'Petr. Khelchitsky: Cheshskyy Tolstoy XV-go stoletiya,' *Vestnik Evropy*, St. Petersburg, vol. VI, 1909.

Lenz Antonín. 'Soustava učení Petra Chelčického na základě pramenů,' *Sborník historického kroužku*, Prague, vol. I, 1900; vol. II, 1901.

Mágr, A. S. 'Piotr Chelczycki i Szymon Budny,' *Przegląd zachodni*, Poznań, vol. VII (I), 1951.

Měrka, Vojtěch. 'Tomáš Přeloučský,' *Časopis pro moderní filologii a literatury*, Prague, vol. III, 1913.

Molnár, Amadeo. 'Lukáš Pražský před svým vstupem do Jednoty bratrské,' *Theologia evangelica*, Prague, vol. I, 1948.

Müller, J. Th. 'Der Waldenserbischof Stephan und die Weihe der ersten Brüderpriester,' *Zeitschrift für Brüdergeschichte*, Herrnhut, 1916.

——. 'Die Gemeinde-Verfassung der Böhmischen Brüder in ihren Grundzügen,' *Monatshefte der Comenius-Gesellschaft*, Berlin-Münster, vol. V, 1896.

——. 'Magister Nikolaus von Dresden,' *Z. f. B.*, Herrnhut, 1915.

*——. 'Starý rukopis dvou spisů Petra Chelčického,' *Č.Č.H.*, Prague, vol. XIII, 1907.

Odložilík, Otakar. 'Bratra Jana Blahoslava Přerovského spis O původu Jednoty bratrské a řádu v ní,' *Věstník královské české společnosti nauk*, Prague, 1928.

——. 'Jednota bratří habrovanských,' *Č.Č.H.*, Prague, vol. XXIX, 1923.

Palacký, František. 'O stycích a poměru sekty Waldenské k někdejším sektám v Čechách,' *Č.Č.M.*, Prague, vol. XLII, 1868.

Pawlow, A. 'L. N. Tolstoj und T. G. Masaryk,' *Wiener Slavistisches Jahrbuch*, Graz-Köln, vol. IV, 1955.

Previté-Orton, C. W. 'Marsilius of Padua,' *Proceedings of the British Academy*, London, vol. XXI, 1935.

*Šafařík, Pavel Josef. 'Br. Jana Blahoslava historie bratří českých,' *Č.Č.M.*, Prague, vol. XXXVI, 1862.

Šimek, František. 'O životě a díle Petra Chelčického,' Modern Czech edition of *Sít' víry*, Prague, 1950.

............, 1933.

Smolík, Josef. 'Sociální působení Jednoty bratrské,' *Theologia evangelica*, Prague, vol. I, 1948.

Tolstoy, Leo. 'Petr Khelchitsky,' *Krug Chteniya*, New York, vol. III, [1925].

Yastrebov, N. V. 'Br. Jana Blahoslava spis O původu Jednoty bratrské a řádu v ní', *Č.Č.H.*, Prague, vol. VIII, 1902.

————. 'Khelchitsky i Gus,' *Novyy sbornik izd. uchenikami V. I. Lamanskago*, St. Petersburg, 1905.

(b) Books

Ball, Hermann. *Das Schulwesen der Böhmischen Brüder*, Berlin, 1898.

Bartoš, F. M. *Husitství a cizina*, Prague, 1931.

————. *Světci a kacíři*, Prague, 1949.

Chaloupecký, Václav. *Selská otázka v husitství*, Bratislava, 1926.

Denis, Ernest. *Fin de l'Indépendance Bohême*, Paris, vol. I, 1890.

Foustka, Radim N. *Politické názory Petra Chelčického*, Prague, 1948.

Gindely, Anton. *Geschichte der Böhmischen Brüder*, Prague, vols. I, II, 1857.

*Goll, Jaroslav. *Chelčický a Jednota v XV. století* (ed. Kamil Krofta), Prague, 1916.

*————. *Quellen und Untersuchungen zur Geschichte der Böhmischen Brüder*, Prague, vol. I, 1878; vol. II, 1882.

Holinka, Rudolf. *Sektářství v Čechách před revolucí husitskou*, Bratislava, 1929.

Hrejsa, Ferdinand. *Dějiny křesťanství v Československu*, Prague, vol. I, 1947; vols. II – V, 1948.

Hrubý, Hynek. *České postilly*, Prague, 1901.

Hutton, J. E. *A History of the Moravian Church*, London, 1909.

Jakubec, Jan. *Dějiny literatury české*, Prague, vol. I, 1929.

Jireček, Josef. *Rukověť k dějinám literatury české do konce XVIII věku*, Prague, vol. I, 1875; vol. II, 1876.

Jones, Rufus M. *Studies in Mystical Religion*, London, 1936.

Jung, Andreas and Schmidt, Walther E. *Friedrich Reiser: Eine Ketzergeschichte aus dem fünfzehnten Jahrhundert*, Herrnhut, [no date].

Kautsky, Karl. *Communism in Central Europe in the Time of the Reformation* (transl. by J. L. and E. G. Mulliken), London, 1897.

Kot, Stanisław. *Ideologja polityczna i społeczna Braci Polskich zwanych Arjanami*, Warsaw, 1932.

Krofta, Kamil. *Dějiny selského stavu*, Prague, 1949.

————. *Listy z náboženských dějin českých*, Prague, 1936.

————. *O bratrském dějepisectví*, Prague, 1946.

————. *Petr Chelčický*, Vodňany, [1913].

Macek, Josef. *Husitské revoluční hnutí*, Prague, 1952.

————. *Tábor v husitském revolutčním hnutí*, Prague, vol. II, 1955.

Martinů, Johann. *Die Waldesier und die husitische Reformation in Böhmen*, Vienna-Leipzig, 1910.

Molnár, Amadeo. *Boleslavští bratří*, Prague, 1952.

Müller, J. Th. *Dějiny Jednoty bratrské* (ed. F. M. Bartoš), Prague, vol. I, 1923.

————. *Geschichte der Böhmischen Brüder*, Herrnhut, vol. I, 1922; vols. II, III, 1931.

Nejedlý, Zdeněk. *Dějiny husitského zpěvu*, Prague, vol. II, 1913.

Neumann, Augustin. *České sekty ve století XIV. a XV.*, Velehrad, 1920.

Odložilík, Otakar. *Wyclif and Bohemia*, Prague, 1937.

Palacký, František. *Dějiny náro̶... ...eno v Cec̶... ...̶...̶ ...̶... (̶...̶. Bôhu̶... ...̶...̶)̶,* Prague, vols. IV, V, [no date].

*Palmov, Ivan. *Cheshkie bratya v svoikh konfessiyakh do nachala sblizheniya ikh s protestantomi v kontse pervoy chetverti XVI. stoletiya,* Prague, vols. I, II, 1904.

Pekař, Josef. *Žižka a jeho doba,* Prague, vol. I, 1927.

Pitter, Přemysl. *Chelčický, Tolstoi, Masaryk,* Prague, 1931.

Preger, Wilhelm. *Über das Verhältnis der Taboriten zu den Waldesiern des 14. Jahrhunderts,* Munich, 1887.

*Peschke, Erhard. *Die Theologie der Böhmischen Brüder in ihrer Frühzeit,* Stuttgart, vol. I, 1935; vol. II, 1940.

de Schweinitz, Edmund. *The History of the Unitas Fratrum,* Bethlehem (Pennsylvania), 1885.

Smith, C. Henry. *The Story of the Mennonites,* Newton (Kansas), 1950.

Svoboda, Milan (ed.). *Mistra Jakoubka ze Stříbra překlad viklefova dialogu,* Prague, 1909.

Tapié, Victor-L. *Une église tchèque au XVe siècle: L'Unité des Frères,* Paris, 1934.

Tobolka, Zdeněk V. *Tisk Chelčického Síti víry z roku 1521,* Prague, 1926.

Tolstoy, Leo. *The Kingdom of God and Peace Essays* (trans. by Aylmer Maude). London, 1936.

Troeltsch, Ernst. *The Social Teaching of the Christian Churches* (trans. by Olive Wyon), London, vol. I, 1931.

Urbánek, Rudolf. *Věk poděbradský,* vol. III (*České dějiny,* vol. III), Prague, 1930.

——. *Jednota bratrská a vyšší vzdělání až do doby blahoslavovy,* Brno, 1923.

Vlček, Jaroslav. *Dějiny české literatury,* vol. I, Prague, 1897.

Vogl, Carl. *Peter Cheltschizki, ein Prophet an der Wende der Zeiten,* Zürich-Leipzig, 1926.

Winter, Zikmund. *Dějiny řemesel a obchodu v Čechách v XIV. and XV. století,* Prague, 1906.

——. *Kulturní obraz českých měst: Život veřejný v XV. a XVI. věky,* Prague, vol. I, 1890; vol. II, 1892.

——. *Život a učení na partikularních školách v Čechách v XV. a XVI. století,* Prague, 1901.

——. *Život církevní v Čechách: Kulturně-historický obraz z XV. and XVI. století,* Prague, vol. I, 1895.

Yastrebov, N. V. *Etyudy o Petre Khelchitskom i ego vremeny,* St. Petersburg, vol. I, 1908.

INDEX

[Br. = Brother, i.e. a member of the Unity of Brethren.]